Computability

Computability

Turing, Gödel, Church, and Beyond

edited by B. Jack Copeland, Carl J. Posy, and Oron Shagrir

The MIT Press
Cambridge, Massachusetts
London, England

MIT Press books may be purchased at special quantity discounts for business or sales promotional use. For information, please email special_sales@mitpress.mit.edu or write to Special Sales Department, The MIT Press, 55 Hayward Street, Cambridge, MA 02142.

This book was set in Sabon by Toppan Best-set Premedia Limited, Hong Kong. Printed and bound in the United States of America.

Library of Congress Cataloging-in-Publication Data

Computability : Turing, Gödel, Church, and beyond / edited by B. Jack Copeland, Carl J. Posy, and Oron Shagrir.
   pages   cm
Includes bibliographical references and index.
ISBN 978-0-262-01899-9 (hardcover : alk. paper)
1. Computational complexity. 2. Mathematics—Philosophy. I. Copeland, B. Jack, editor of compilation. II. Posy, Carl J., editor of compilation. III. Shagrir, Oron, 1961– editor of compilation.
QA267.7.C677   2013
511.3'52—dc23
2012039321

10 9 8 7 6 5 4 3 2 1

Contents

Introduction: The 1930s Revolution

The theory of computability was launched in the 1930s by a group of young mathematicians and logicians who proposed new, exact, characterizations of the idea of algorithmic computability. The most prominent of these young iconoclasts were Kurt Gödel, Alonzo Church, and Alan Turing. Others also contributed to the new field, most notably Jacques Herbrand, Emil Post, Stephen Kleene, and J. Barkley Rosser. This seminal research not only established the theoretical basis for computability: these key thinkers revolutionized and reshaped the mathematical world—a revolution that culminated in the Information Age.

Their motive, however, was not to pioneer the discipline that we now know as theoretical computer science, although with hindsight this is indeed what they did. Nor was their motive to design electronic digital computers, although Turing did go on to do so (in fact producing the first complete paper design that the world had seen for an electronic stored-program universal computer). Their work was rather the continuation of decades of intensive investigation into that most abstract of subjects, the foundations of mathematics—investigations carried out by such great thinkers as Leopold Kronecker, Richard Dedekind, Gottlob Frege, Bertrand Russell, David Hilbert, L. E. J. Brouwer, Paul Bernays, and John von Neumann. The concept of an algorithm, or an effective or computable procedure, was central during these decades of foundational study, although for a long time no attempt was made to characterize the intuitive concept formally. This changed when Hilbert's foundationalist program, and especially the issue of decidability, made it imperative to provide an exact characterization of the idea of a computable function—or algorithmically calculable function, or effectively calculable function, or decidable predicate. Different authors used different terminology for this central intuitive concept, which, they realized, stood in need of precise analysis.

Computability: Turing, Gödel, Church, and Beyond examines not only the historic breakthroughs made in the 1930s by these three great thinkers, but also the legacy of their work in the modern world. The 1930s began with Gödel's publication of his completeness theorem for first-order logic, and a year later, in

1931, he published his famous incompleteness results. The latter concerned formal systems of arithmetic involving (what we now call) primitive recursive axioms and inference rules. A first major step had been taken in the development of modern computability theory. In 1934, in a series of lectures at the Princeton Institute for Advanced Study, Gödel went on to present the concept of a *general* recursive function (which he created by refining a suggestion that Herbrand had communicated to him in 1931). Notes of these landmark lectures, taken at the time by Church's students Kleene and Rosser, were published in Martin Davis's classic volume *The Undecidable*, under the title "On undecidable propositions of formal mathematical systems." In 1936, Kleene published his own formulation of the theory of general recursive functions—the version standardly used today—and in 1938 Kleene extended his analysis to cover partial recursive functions as well.

Church began his work on what he called the lambda calculus early in the 1930s, and was soon joined by his Princeton students Kleene and Rosser. When Gödel visited Princeton in 1934, Church suggested to him that the new concept of "lambda-definability" be taken as a precise, formal definition of the intuitive idea of effective calculability, but Gödel famously rejected Church's suggestion, calling it "thoroughly unsatisfactory." Nevertheless, Church did go on to propose this identification publicly, in a 1935 presentation and then the following year in a journal article. He also made the alternative suggestion that the intuitive idea of an effectively calculable function could be identified with the concept of a recursive function. These two suggestions are mathematically equivalent and are now known collectively as "Church's thesis." The name "Church-Turing thesis" is also used, in recognition of Turing's slightly later work, also published in 1936.

In his strikingly original paper of 1936, Turing characterized the intuitive idea of computability in terms of the activity of an abstract automatic computing machine. This machine, now called simply the "Turing machine," figures in modern theoretical computer science as the most fundamental model of computation. (Post, in 1947, recast the Turing machine into the mathematical formulation usually used today, a finite collection of 4-tuples.) In 1936, Turing also described one of the most important scientific ideas of the twentieth century, his "universal computing machine"—a single Turing machine that, by making use of what we now call "programs" stored in its memory, can compute *everything* that is computable in the intuitive sense (or so Turing persuasively argued). Turing's thesis, that the universal Turing machine can compute anything and everything computable in the intuitive sense, is equivalent to each of Church's formulations of Church's thesis. Now, numerous equivalent formulations of the Church-Turing thesis are known. Arguably, Turing's formulation is the most fundamental, since it links the intuitive idea of computability with the concept of a computing *machine*.

Within a dozen or so years, Turing's universal machine had been realized electronically—the world's first stored-program electronic digital computers had arrived. The transformation from abstract conception to physical machine was brought about by Tom Flowers, Max Newman, Freddie Williams, Tom Kilburn, Maurice Wilkes, John von Neumann, Presper Eckert, John Mauchly, Harry Huskey, and others—and certainly not forgetting Turing himself, in his postwar guise as computer designer. Turing's electronic computer, the Automatic Computing Engine, or ACE, was in the event not the first of the new machines to operate, but it was by a wide margin the fastest.

The early work by Turing, Gödel, Church, and the other founding fathers of computability has blossomed into what is today a vast bouquet of fields of study, as diverse as recursive function theory, computer engineering and computer programming, numerical analysis, computational linguistics, virtual reality, artificial intelligence, artificial life, computational theories of mind, complexity theory, machine learning, quantum computing, and modern cryptography—and much more besides. This multidisciplinary book is about what all these fields rest upon: the foundations of computability.

Several chapters of the book are historical in perspective, focusing closely on the work of the founding fathers of computability. Soare and Sieg review the emergence of the various characterizations of computability in the 1930s, detailing Gödel's role in these developments. Kripke clarifies and develops an important argument put forward by Turing in support of his 1936 analysis of computability. Copeland and Shagrir examine the theoretical underpinnings of the historic analyses of computability, and also elucidate what Gödel and Turing wrote about computability and the mind. More recent work in the foundations of computability is discussed by Davis, whose topic is the solution of Hilbert's tenth problem; and by Putnam, who discusses the impact of Gödel's work on modern mathematical logic and recursion theory; and Soare, who describes the legacy of Turing and Post in modern interactive and online computing. Aharonov, Vazirani, and Aaronson focus on recent issues in complexity theory and quantum computing, and Feferman and Posy discuss developments in the theory of computability over the real numbers.

A number of chapters address the relationship between computability and the mind. Copeland and Shagrir, Putnam, and Sieg discuss the issue of whether Turing-computability places an upper bound on the powers of the human mind, while Aaronson raises the question whether the mind is limited to solving problems whose solutions are obtainable in polynomial time. Other chapters target issues in the philosophy of mathematics and the philosophy of science. Posy discusses the relationship between computability and constructivity in mathematics, and Aaronson the relationship between computational complexity and mathematical proof. Kripke, Soare, and Shapiro investigate issues concerning the Church-Turing thesis itself, and

Kripke explains the significance that Gödel's 1931 theorem IX holds for Hilbert's *Entscheidungsproblem*. Aharonov and Vazirani ask how the natural world can be studied at all, given that quantum mechanics exhibits exponential complexity, and they describe a foundation for experimental science that is based on the mathematical concept of interactive proof.

The computational revolution of the 1930s can fairly be said to have fuelled the rocketing expansion of the horizons of knowledge that characterizes our modern scientific era. Turing, Gödel, and Church, although relatively unsung heroes, are pivotal figures in the story of modern science.

1 Turing versus Gödel on Computability and the Mind

B. Jack Copeland and Oron Shagrir

Nowadays the work of Alan Turing and Kurt Gödel rightly takes center stage in discussions of the relationships between computability and the mind. After decades of comparative neglect, Turing's 1936 paper "On Computable Numbers" is now regarded as the foundation stone of computability theory, and it is the *fons et origo* of the concept of computability employed in modern theoretical computer science. Moreover, Turing's 1950 essay, "Computing Machinery and Intelligence," sparked a rich literature on the mind-machine issue. Gödel's 1931 incompleteness results triggered, on the one hand, precise definitions of effective computability and its allied notions, and on the other, some much-criticized arguments for the conclusion that the mathematical power of the mind exceeds the limitations of Turing machines. Gödel himself is widely believed to have held that minds are more powerful than machines, whereas Turing is usually said to have taken the opposite position. In fact, neither of these characterizations is much more than a caricature. The actual picture is subtle and complex. To complicate matters still further, Gödel repeatedly praised Turing's analysis of computability, and yet in later life he accused Turing of fallaciously assuming, in the course of this analysis, that mental procedures cannot go beyond effective procedures. How can Turing's analysis be "unquestionably adequate" (Gödel 1964, 71) and yet involve a fallacy?

We will present fresh interpretations of the positions of Turing and Gödel on computability and the mind. We argue that, contrary to first impressions, their views about computability are closer than might appear to be the case; and we will also argue that their views about the mind-machine issue are closer than Gödel—and others—have believed.[1] In section 1.1, we show that Gödel's attribution of philosophical error to Turing is baseless; and we present a revisionary account of Turing's position regarding (what Gödel called) Hilbert's "rationalistic attitude." In section 1.2, we distinguish between two approaches to the analysis of computability, the cognitive and the noncognitive. We argue that Gödel pursued the noncognitive approach. As we will explain, we believe that Gödel mistook some cognitivist-style rhetoric in Turing's 1936 paper for an endorsement of the claim that the mind is computable. In section 1.3, we suggest that Turing held what we call the *Multi-Machine theory of mind*, according to which mental processes, when taken diachronically, form a finite procedure that need not be *mechanical*, in the technical sense of that term (in which it means the same as "effective").

1.1   Gödel on Turing's "Philosophical Error"

In about 1970, Gödel wrote a brief note entitled "A Philosophical Error in Turing's Work" (1972).[2] The note was, he said, to be regarded as a footnote to the postscript, which he had composed in 1964, to his 1934 undecidability paper. The main purpose of the 1964 postscript was to state generalized versions of incompleteness, applicable to algorithms and formal systems. It was in this postscript that Gödel officially adopted Turing's "analysis of the concept of 'mechanical procedure' ... (alias 'algorithm' or 'computation procedure')" (1964, 72); and he there emphasized that it was "due to A. M. Turing's work, [that] a precise and unquestionably adequate definition of the general concept of formal system can now be given ... [A] formal system can simply be defined to be any mechanical procedure for producing formulas, called provable formulas" (71–72). In the postscript, Gödel also raised the intriguing "question of whether there exist finite *non-mechanical* procedures" (72); and he observed that the generalized incompleteness results "do not establish any bounds for the powers of human reason, but rather for the potentialities of pure formalism in mathematics" (73).

Gödel's retrospective footnote to his 1964 postscript attributed the view that "mental procedures cannot go beyond mechanical procedures" to Turing in "On Computable Numbers." Gödel criticized an argument for this view that he claimed to find there:

A philosophical error in Turing's work.   Turing in [section 9 of "On Computable Numbers" (1936, 75–76)] gives an argument which is supposed to show that mental procedures cannot go beyond mechanical procedures. However ... [w]hat Turing disregards completely is the fact that *mind, in its use, is not static, but constantly developing* ... [A]lthough at each stage the number and precision of the abstract terms at our disposal may be *finite*, both (and, therefore, also Turing's number of *distinguishable states of mind*) may *converge toward infinity* in the course of the application of the procedure. (Gödel 1972, 306)

Gödel later gave Hao Wang a different version of the same note, in which Gödel says explicitly that Turing's argument involves "the supposition that a finite mind is capable of only a finite number of distinguishable states." The later version runs:

Turing ... [in "On Computable Numbers"] gives an argument which is supposed to show that mental procedures cannot carry any farther than mechanical procedures. However, this argument is inconclusive, because it depends on the supposition that a finite mind is capable of only a finite number of distinguishable states. What Turing disregards completely is the fact that *mind, in its use, is not static, but constantly developing*. This is seen, e. g., from the infinite series of ever stronger axioms of infinity in set theory, each of which expresses a new idea or insight. ... Therefore, although at each stage of the mind's development the number of its possible states is finite, there is no reason why this number should not converge to infinity in the course of its development. (Gödel in Wang 1974, 325)

However, Turing can readily be defended against Gödel's charge of philosophical error. In what follows we will show that it is far from the case that "Turing disregards completely ... the fact that *mind, in its use, is not static, but constantly developing*." Gödel's blunt criticism of Turing is entirely misdirected. In fact, we will argue in part 3 that the dynamic aspect of mind emphasized here by Gödel lies at the very center of Turing's account.

Gödel was too hasty in his claim that, in "On Computable Numbers," Turing put forward an argument supposed to show that mental procedures cannot go beyond mechanical procedures. There is no such argument to be found in Turing's paper; nor is there even any trace of a statement endorsing the conclusion of the supposed argument. Turing, on the page discussed by Gödel, was not talking about the general scope of mental procedures; he was addressing a different question, namely, "What are the possible processes which can be carried out in computing a number?"[3] Furthermore, there is a passage in "On Computable Numbers" that seemingly runs counter to the view attributed to Turing by Gödel. Having defined a certain infinite binary sequence δ, which he shows to be uncomputable, Turing says: "It is (so far as we know at present) possible that any assigned number of figures of δ can be calculated, but not by a uniform process. When sufficiently many figures of δ have been calculated, an essentially new method is necessary in order to obtain more figures" (1936, 79). This is an interesting passage. Turing is envisaging the possibility that the human mathematician can calculate any desired number of digits of an uncomputable sequence by virtue of creating new methods when necessary. Gödel, on the other hand, considered Turing to have offered an "alleged proof that every mental procedure for producing an infinite series of integers is equivalent to a mechanical procedure."[4]

Even without focusing on the detail of Turing's views on mind (which emerged in his post-1936 work), attention to what Turing actually said in his 1936 paper is sufficient to show that Gödel's criticism of Turing bears at best a tenuous relation to the text Gödel was supposedly discussing. Turing did not say that "a finite mind is capable of only a finite number of distinguishable states." He said: "We will ... suppose that the number of states of mind which need be taken into account [for the purpose of analyzing computability] is finite" (75). He immediately acknowledges that beyond these there may be "more complicated states of mind," but points out that, again for the purpose of analyzing computability, reference to these more complicated states "can be avoided by writing more symbols on the tape" (76). Turing is in effect distinguishing between elementary states of mind and complex states of mind, and is noting that symbols on the tape can serve as a surrogate for complex states of mind. Turing nowhere suggests that the "more complicated states of mind" are finite in number (and nor does he suggest that they fail to be distinguishable unless finite in number).

1.1.1 Turing on Mathematical Intuition

In short, Turing's 1936 text does not support Gödel's interpretation. The situation becomes bleaker still for Gödel's interpretation when Turing's 1939 publication "Systems of Logic Based on Ordinals" is taken into account. There Turing emphasized the aspect of mathematical reasoning that he referred to as "intuition." He said:

> In pre-Gödel times it was thought by some that … all the intuitive judgments of mathematics could be replaced by a finite number of … [formal] rules. … In consequence of the impossibility of finding a formal logic which wholly eliminates the necessity of using intuition, we naturally turn to "non-constructive" systems of logic with which not all the steps in a proof are mechanical, some being intuitive. (Turing 1939, 192–193)

In Turing's view, the activity of what he called the *faculty* of intuition brings it about that mathematical *judgments*—again, his word—exceed what can be expressed by means of a single formal system (192). "The activity of the intuition," he said, "consists in making spontaneous judgments which are not the result of conscious trains of reasoning" (192). Turing's cheerful use of mentalistic vocabulary in this connection makes it very unlikely that Gödel was correct in finding an argument in the 1936 paper supposedly showing that mental procedures cannot go beyond mechanical procedures.

During the early part of the war, probably in 1940, Turing wrote a number of letters to Max Newman explaining his thinking about intuition. The following passage is illuminating:

> I think you take a much more radically Hilbertian attitude about mathematics than I do. You say "If all this whole formal outfit is not about finding proofs which can be checked on a machine it's difficult to know what it is about." When you say "on a machine" do you have in mind that there is (or should be or could be, but has not been actually described anywhere) some fixed machine on which proofs are to be checked, and that the formal outfit is, as it were about this machine. If you take this attitude (and it is this one that seems to me so extreme Hilbertian [*sic*]) there is little more to be said: we simply have to get used to the technique of this machine and resign ourselves to the fact that there are some problems to which we can never get the answer. On these lines my ordinal logics would make no sense. However I don't think you really hold quite this attitude because you admit that in the case of the Gödel example one can decide that the formula is true i. e. you admit that there is a

fairly definite idea of a true formula which is quite different from the idea of a provable one. Throughout my paper on ordinal logics I have been assuming this too. ... If you think of various machines I don't see your difficulty. One imagines different machines allowing different sets of proofs, and by choosing a suitable machine one can approximate "truth" by "provability" better than with a less suitable machine, and can in a sense approximate it as well as you please. The choice of a ... machine involves intuition ... (Turing to Newman, ca. 1940b, 215)

The picture described in this letter will be called Turing's Multi-Machine picture of mathematics. In this picture, the role of intuition is localized very precisely. Intuition is responsible for the selection of the appropriate theorem-proving machine (the appropriate Turing machine), and the rest is mechanical. The intuition involved in selecting the appropriate theorem-proving machine is, Turing said, "interchangeable" with the intuition involved in finding a proof of the theorem.

1.1.2   Gödel and Turing on Rationalistic Optimism

"Rationalistic optimism" is the view that there are no mathematical questions that the human mind is incapable of settling, in principle at any rate, even if this is not so in practice (due, say, to the occurrence of the heat-death of the universe).[5] In a striking observation about the implications of his incompleteness result, Gödel said:

My incompleteness theorem makes it likely that mind is not mechanical, or else mind cannot understand its own mechanism. If my result is taken together with the rationalistic attitude which Hilbert had and which was not refuted by my results, then [we can infer] the sharp result that mind is not mechanical. This is so, because, if the mind were a machine, there would, contrary to this rationalistic attitude, exist number-theoretic questions undecidable for the human mind. (Gödel in Wang 1996, 186–187)

What Gödel calls Hilbert's "rationalistic attitude" was summed up in Hilbert's celebrated remark that "in mathematics there is no *ignorabimus*" — no mathematical question that in principle the mind is incapable of settling (Hilbert 1902, 445). Gödel gave no clear indication whether, or to what extent, he himself agreed with what he called Hilbert's "rationalistic attitude" (a point to which we shall return in section 1.3). On the other hand, Turing's criticism (in his letter to Newman) of the "extreme Hilbertian" view is accompanied by what seems to be a cautious endorsement of the rationalistic attitude. The "sharp result" stated by Gödel seems in effect to be that there is no *single* machine equivalent to the mind (at any rate, no more is justified by the reasoning that Gödel presented) — and with this Turing was in agreement, as his letter makes clear. Incompleteness, if taken together with a Hilbertian optimism, excludes the extreme Hilbertian position that the "whole formal outfit" corresponds to some one fixed machine.

Turing's view, as he expressed it to Newman and in "Systems of Logic Based on Ordinals," appears to have been that mathematicians achieve progressive approximations to truth via a non-mechanical process involving intuition. This picture, in which minds devise and adopt successive, increasingly powerful mechanical formalisms in their quest for truth, is consonant with Gödel's view that "mind, in its use, is not static, but constantly developing." Gödel's own illustration of his claim that mind is constantly developing is certainly related to Turing's concerns. Gödel said: "This [that mind is not static but constantly developing] is seen, e. g., from the infinite series of ever stronger axioms of infinity in set theory, each of which expresses a new idea or insight" (Gödel in Wang 1974, 325).

So the two great founders of the study of computability were perhaps not quite as philosophically distant on the mind-machine issue as Gödel supposed. We shall have more to say about their views on this issue in section 1.3. But first, let us look at what these founding fathers thought about the concept of computability itself. Gödel repeatedly praised Turing's analysis of computability, saying it produces a "correct and unique" definition of "the concept of mechanical" in terms of "the sharp concept of 'performable by a Turing machine'" (Gödel in Wang 1974, 84).[6] Yet Turing's analysis appears in the very same passages of his 1936 paper in which Gödel thought he found "an argument which is supposed to show that mental procedures cannot go beyond mechanical procedures" (Gödel ca. 1972, 306). How could Gödel praise Turing's analysis while at the same time rejecting what seems to be a key element in it, namely the constraint of a fixed bound on the number of internal states that a computer can be in? Our answer to this question will illuminate Gödel's reasons for thinking that in the course of his analysis of computability Turing proposed an argument about minds and machines.

1.2   Two Approaches to the Analysis of Computability

We will start with a brief summary of Turing's analysis of computability and will then describe Gödel's reaction to it in more detail. Against that background, we will distinguish between two approaches to the analysis of computability, which we call the *cognitive* and *noncognitive* approaches, respectively. We will then explain where Gödel, Turing, and Kleene stand vis-à-vis this distinction, especially with respect to the boundedness constraint on the number of states of mind. We argue that the distinction sheds light on the puzzle of how Gödel took the very same passages in Turing to provide both an erroneous philosophical argument about the limits of the mind *and* a unique and correct definition of computability.

1.2.1   Preamble: Turing's Analysis of Computability

Turing's 1936 analysis of computability has been explicated by Kleene (1952, 376–81)—who unfortunately misdated the analysis to 1937—and by Gandy (1988).

Gandy's explication has been further developed by Sieg (1994, 2002). A key point, often misunderstood, is that Turing's "computability" concerns calculations by an ideal *human*, a human computer. Turing, as Gandy said, "makes no reference whatsoever to calculating machines" (1988, 77).[7]

In section 9 of his paper, Turing presents three arguments that his analysis catches everything that, as he put it, "would naturally be regarded as computable" (1936, 74). The first argument can be set out like this (Shagrir 2002):

Premise 1 ("the central thesis")   A human computer operates under the restrictive conditions 1–5 (below).

Premise 2 ("Turing's theorem")   Any function that can be computed by a computer operating under conditions 1–5 is Turing-machine computable.

Conclusion ("Turing's thesis")   Any function that can be computed by a human computer is Turing-machine computable.

Turing calls this his "Type (a)" argument (1936, 74–77). He enumerates the five restrictive conditions somewhat informally. The first concerns the deterministic relationship between the computation steps:

1. "The behavior of the computer at any moment is determined by the symbols which he is observing, and his 'state of mind' at that moment" (75).

Turing then formulates boundedness conditions on each of the two determining factors, namely, the observed symbols and states of mind:

2. "[T]here is a bound B to the number of symbols or squares which the computer can observe at one moment" (75).

3. "[T]he number of states of mind which need be taken into account is finite" (75).

There are three "simple operations" (behaviors) that the computer may perform at each moment: a change in the symbols written on the tape, a change of the observed squares, and a change of state of mind. Turing gives additional boundedness conditions on the first and second types of operation (the third having already been dealt with):

4. "We may suppose that in a simple operation not more than one symbol is altered" (76).

5. "[E]ach of the new observed squares is within L squares of an immediately previously observed square" (76).

The second premise of the argument is a *reduction theorem* stating that *any* system operating under conditions 1–5 is bounded by Turing machine computability. Turing provides an outline of the proof (77); a more detailed demonstration is given by Kleene (1952). Gandy (1980) proves the theorem with respect to "Gandy machines," which operate under more relaxed restrictions.[8]

1.2.2 Gödel on Computability

Gödel's rather sparse statements on computability are now well documented.[9] We provide an overview of his thoughts on the subject. Gödel's interest in a precise definition of computability stemmed from the incompleteness results. A precise definition is required for understanding not only the *philosophical implications* of the incompleteness results but also, first and foremost, for establishing the *generality* of the results. As the title of Gödel's 1931 paper noted, the incompleteness results apply in their original forms to "Principia Mathematica and related systems." More precisely, they apply to the formal system P, which is "essentially the system obtained when the logic of *PM* is superposed upon the Peano axioms" (1931, 151), and to the extensions of P that are the "ω-consistent systems that result from P when [primitive] recursively definable classes of axioms are added" (185, note 53). But it was still an open question whether there exist extensions of P whose class of theorems is effectively but not recursively enumerable. The precise definitions of computability that emerged later secured the generality of Gödel's incompleteness results. As Gödel put it in the 1964 *Postscriptum*, the precise definitions of computability imply the general definition of a formal system; hence "the existence of undecidable arithmetical propositions and the non-demonstrability of the consistency of a system in the same system can now be proved rigorously for *every* consistent formal system containing a certain amount of finitary number theory" (1964, 71).

As Gödel explained it, a formal system is governed by what we now call an effective procedure. Gödel did not use the term "effective" himself; he characterized the governing procedure as a *mechanical and finite* one. The property of *being mechanical* is spelled out in Gödel's 1933 address to the Mathematical Association of America (entitled "The Present Situation in the Foundations of Mathematics"). He opened with a rough characterization of formal systems, pointing out that the "outstanding feature of the rules of inference [is] that they are purely formal, i. e., refer only to the outward structure of the formulas, not to their meaning, so that they could be applied by someone who knew nothing about mathematics, or by a machine" (45). Gödel's reference to machines signals his fascination with calculating machines,[10] but also implies that Gödel was primarily thinking of humans—even "someone who knew nothing about mathematics"—as the ones who proceed mechanically. He discussed the property of *finiteness* in his 1934 Princeton address, where he characterized a "formal mathematical system" (346) as follows:

We require that the rules of inference, and the definitions of meaningful formulas and axioms, be constructive; that is, for each rule of inference there shall be a finite procedure for determining whether a given formula B is an immediate consequence (by that rule) of given formulas $A_1, ..., A_n$, and there shall be a finite procedure for determining whether a given formula A is a meaningful formula or an axiom. $(346)^{11}$

At this point Gödel did not have a precise definition of what can be computed by a finite and mechanical procedure. A statement that seems to be much like the Church-Turing thesis appears in the printed version of Gödel's 1934 Princeton lectures, where he formulates what is generally taken to be the "easy" part of the Church-Turing thesis, namely, that "[primitive] [r]ecursive functions have the important property that, for each given set of values of the arguments, the value of the function can be computed by a finite procedure" (348). In a footnote to this statement, Gödel remarks that "[t]he converse seems to be true if, besides [primitive] recursions ... recursions of other forms (e. g., with respect to two variables simultaneously) are admitted [i. e., general recursions]. This cannot be proved, since the notion of finite computation is not defined, but it serves as a heuristic principle" (348, note 3). However, in a letter to Martin Davis (on February 15, 1965) Gödel denied that his 1934 paper anticipated the Church–Turing thesis:

It is not true that footnote 3 is a statement of Church's Thesis. The conjecture stated there only refers to the equivalence of "finite (computation) procedure" and "recursive procedure." However, I was, at the time of these lectures, not at all convinced that my concept of recursion comprises all possible recursions; and in fact the equivalence between my definition and Kleene [1936] is not quite trivial. (Gödel in Davis 1982, 8)

Church, who first met Gödel early in 1934, gave some additional information in a letter to Kleene dated November 29, 1935:

In regard to Gödel and the notions of recursiveness and effective calculability, the history is the following. In discussion with him the notion of lambda-definability [*sic*], it developed that there was no good definition of effective calculability. My proposal that lambda-definability be taken as a definition of it he regarded as thoroughly unsatisfactory. (Church in Davis 1982, 8)

Gödel's attitude changed not long after. In an unpublished paper dating from about 1938, he wrote:

When I first published my paper about undecidable propositions the result could not be pronounced in this generality, because for the notions of mechanical procedure and of formal system no mathematically satisfactory definition had been given at that time. This gap has since been filled by Herbrand, Church and Turing. $(Gödel\ 193?,\ 166)^{12}$

So, just a few years after having rejected Church's proposal, Gödel embraced it, attributing the "mathematically satisfactory definition" of computability to

Herbrand, Church, and Turing. Why did Gödel change his mind? Turing's work was clearly a significant factor. Initially, Gödel mentions Turing together with Herbrand and Church, but a few pages later he refers to Turing's work alone as having demonstrated the correctness of the various equivalent mathematical definitions: "[t]hat this really is the correct definition of mechanical computability was established beyond any doubt by Turing," he wrote (193?, 168). More specifically:

[Turing] has shown that the computable functions defined in this way are exactly those for which you can construct a machine with a finite number of parts which will do the following thing. If you write down any number $n_1, \ldots, n_r$ on a slip of paper and put the slip into the machine and turn the crank, then after a finite number of turns the machine will stop and the value of the function for the argument $n_1, \ldots, n_r$ will be printed on the paper. (193?, 168).

It is hard to tell, though, precisely why Gödel found Turing's definition correct "beyond any doubt." Possibly he regarded the concept of a mechanical and finite procedure as somehow captured by the notion of "a machine with a finite number of parts." Gödel is presumably referring to the reduction of human computability to Turing-machine computability. He does not mention that Turing characterized mechanical and finite procedures in terms of the finiteness conditions 1–5 on *human computation*.

In his 1946 Princeton lecture, Gödel returned to the issue of computability. Referring to Tarski's lecture at the same conference, he said:

Tarski has stressed in his lecture (and I think justly) the great importance of the concept of general recursiveness (or Turing's computability). It seems to me that this importance is largely due to the fact that with this concept one has for the first time succeeded in giving an absolute definition of an interesting epistemological notion, i. e., one not depending on the formalism chosen. (150)

In referring to computability as an *epistemological* concept Gödel was quite likely thinking of the major epistemological role played by computability in Hilbert's finitistic program, and probably also of the normative role played by computability in logic and mathematics generally from the end of the nineteenth century.[13] The epistemological dimension highlights the tight relationship between formal systems and *human* calculators—it is an (ideal) human who decides, by means of a finite and mechanical procedure, whether a sequence of symbolic configurations is a formal proof or not.[14]

In his Gibbs lecture, Gödel was very explicit in his support for Turing's general approach to computability:

The greatest improvement was made possible through the precise definition of the concept of finite procedure, which plays a decisive role in these [incompleteness] results. There are several different ways of arriving at such a definition, which, however, all lead to exactly the same concept. The most satisfactory way, in my opinion, is that of reducing the concept of finite procedure to that of a machine with a finite number of parts, as has been done by the British mathematician Turing. (1951, 304–305)

Again, Turing's way of arriving at a definition of the "concept of finite procedure" is "most satisfactory." Its satisfactoriness has something to do with the reduction of the concept of finite procedure to that of "a machine with a finite number of parts." Yet, as before, Gödel said nothing about the reduction itself, nor did he say why he thought it so successful.

In his 1964 postscript, Gödel emphasized the contribution of Turing's definition to the generality of the incompleteness results:

In consequence of later advances, in particular of the fact that, due to A. M. Turing's work, a precise and unquestionably adequate definition of the general concept of a formal system can now be given, the existence of undecidable arithmetical propositions and the non-demonstrability of the consistency of a system in the same system can now be proved rigorously for *every* consistent formal system containing a certain amount of finitary number theory. Turing's work gives an analysis of the concept of "mechanical procedure" (alias "algorithm" or "computation procedure" or "finite combinatorial procedure"). This concept is shown to be equivalent with that of a "Turing machine." (71–72)

According to Gödel, then, Turing provided a precise and unquestionably adequate definition of the general concept of a formal system. Turing does so, Gödel says, by providing a *conceptual analysis*, an analysis of the concept of a finite and mechanical procedure.

During the last decade of Gödel's life, he continued to praise Turing's analysis in conversations with Wang, saying that it provides a "correct and unique" definition of "the concept of mechanical" in terms of "the sharp concept of 'performable by a Turing machine.'" He said that computability is "an excellent example … of a concept which did not appear sharp to us but has become so as a result of careful reflection," and that it is "absolutely impossible that anybody who understands the question and knows Turing's definition should decide for a different concept" (Gödel in Wang 1974, 84).

Gödel's remarks on Turing's analysis are not to be taken lightly. Gödel made them at a time when others were failing to ascribe any special merit to Turing's analysis.[15] Logic and computer science textbooks from the decades following the pioneering work of the 1930s by and large ignored Turing's analysis altogether, and that trend continues to this day.[16] The full significance of Turing's analysis has been appreciated only relatively recently.[17]

It is thus somewhat surprising that Gödel complained to Wang that Turing's analysis contains a philosophical error. The puzzle is twofold. First, how could Gödel embrace Turing's analysis despite the error of its ways? Second, how could

Gödel go so wrong in attributing to Turing an argument about minds and machines that Turing did not advance? What is it in Turing's analysis of computability that prompted Gödel to think the analysis involves an argument that is supposed to show mental procedures cannot go beyond mechanical procedures? Answering these questions is no easy task. Given the sparse and sometimes obscure textual evidence, any interpretation is bound to include a grain of speculation. Our interpretation invokes a distinction between two ways of understanding computability. We believe that this distinction is important for reasons transcending its ability to make sense of Gödel's remarks on Turing. The distinction accounts for differing perspectives that exist concerning the concept of an effective procedure (alias algorithm), and concerning the Church-Turing thesis and issues about computability in general.

1.2.3 Distinguishing the Two Approaches

The cognitive and the noncognitive approaches differ with respect to the status of the restrictive conditions 1–5. The cognitive approach offers conditions 1–5 as reflections of (or abstractions from) limitations on human cognitive capacities. These limitations *give warrant to* or *justify* the correctness of the restrictive conditions. According to the cognitive approach, computability is constrained by conditions 1–5 *because* these constraints reflect the limitations of human cognitive capacities as these capacities are involved in calculation—or, as we shall say for short, because these constraints reflect limitations of the *faculty of calculation*.[18] A cognitivist need not claim that these limitations apply to human mental processes *in general*. As we saw, Gödel accused Turing of being a cognitivist in this more general sense, which he was not. As is explained below, Turing was most likely not even a cognitivist in the narrower sense of relating conditions 1–5 to the limitations of the faculty of calculation.

The noncognitivist, on the other hand, does not think that the restrictive conditions 1–5 necessarily reflect limitations on human cognitive capacities. The noncognitivist need not deny the existence of a faculty of calculation; the claim is that its limitations do not warrant the restrictive conditions. According to the noncognitivist, conditions 1–5 merely explicate the concept of effective computation as it is properly used and as it functions in the discourse of logic and mathematics. The noncognitivist offers no other justification for the five conditions. In fact, a call for further justification might not have a place at all in the analysis of computability, according to the noncognitivist.

The difference between the two approaches can be made crystal clear by considering what the consequences for the extension of the concept of computability would be should the human faculty of calculation be found to violate one or more of conditions 1–5. As we have seen, Gödel himself challenged the assumption that the number of states of mind is bounded. Let's imagine scientists discover that human memory can involve an unbounded number of states and, further, that this results in hypercomputational mental powers—i. e., results in humans being able to calculate the values of functions that are not Turing-machine computable.[19] Would these discoveries threaten Turing's analysis of computability?[20] The cognitivist and the noncognitivist give different answers.

The cognitivist answers "Yes." If it turns out that humans could, as a matter of cognitive fact, encode an infinite procedure, perform supertasks, or even observe, at any given step, an unbounded number of symbols when calculating a value of a function, cognitivists would regard this as undermining the analysis. If some of the restrictive conditions among 1–5 do not reflect actual upper limits on the faculty of calculation, then on the cognitive approach these conditions have no place in the analysis. In the circumstances we are imagining, the cognitivist would discard, weaken, or otherwise modify some of the conditions in order to produce a set of restrictive conditions that do reflect our true cognitive capacities. The cognitivist who finds herself or himself in the situation we are describing will jettison Turing's analysis of computability and will replace it with a nonequivalent analysis that deems some non–Turing-machine computable functions to be computable.

According to the noncognitivist, on the other hand, the answer is "No." Discoveries about the human mind have no bearing on the analysis of computability. The noncognitivist does not exclude the empirical possibility of the discovery that human memory is unbounded; nor is noncognitivism inconsistent with other ways in which the human mind might violate conditions 1–5. Rather, the analysis of computability invokes a finite number of states of mind because the analyzed concept is that of computation *by means of a finite procedure.* The focus is on what can be achieved by "finite means"—not on whether, as a matter of fact, human beings are limited to calculation by finite means.

The differences between cognitivism and noncognitivism have far-reaching implications in discussion of foundational issues in logic and mathematics. What, for example, should one say about a mathematician who is able to calculate any assigned number of digits of Turing's δ? The cognitivist would say that the mathematician is in the role of human computer and that the Church-Turing thesis is false, since the thesis identifies computability with Turing-machine computability. According to the noncognitivist, however, these spectacular claims are unwarranted. If Turing's analysis of computability is correct, then the mathematician who calculates arbitrary numbers of digits of δ is doing something that a human computer cannot do, *qua* human computer.

Let us now consider some ways in which cognitivism and noncognitivism do *not* differ. First, the distinction is not between human computation and other-than-human computation. Both approaches tie computability in the first instance to the activity of human computers, idealized humans who calculate with (perhaps) pencil and paper; and both approaches assume (absent the discoveries imagined above) that the human computer operates under the restrictive conditions 1–5. The difference has to do with what is meant by a human *computer*. According to the cognitivist, whatever calculations can be carried out by means of the human faculty of calculation count as computations. The human computer operates under the restrictive conditions 1–5 simply because these restrictions reflect the cognitive limitations of the faculty of calculation. According to the noncognitivist, however, the human computer is characterized by the restrictive conditions 1–5 simply because this is part and parcel of what it is to be a human computer.

Second, the distinction is not about empirical versus nonempirical analysis. Both approaches assume that Turing's analysis involves some form of *conceptual* analysis. The cognitive approach might be "empirical" only in the sense that the cognitivist's restrictive conditions reflect empirical facts about human cognition. But it is not the task of the analysis itself to discover these facts through empirical research; arguably, the fact that the human operates under these restrictive conditions is self-evident. Third, the distinction is not between the epistemic and the nonepistemic. According to both approaches, effective procedures play an important epistemic role, namely that of generating trustworthy results whose validity is beyond doubt. The approaches differ, rather, about the source of this epistemic role. According to the cognitive approach, the epistemic role is grounded in our calculative abilities. What counts as an effective procedure depends upon the upper limits of the faculty of calculation; thus discovering hypercomputational powers of the mind would immediately enlarge the class of trustworthy results. According to the noncognitive approach, the epistemic status of the effective procedures is rooted in their finite nature. An effective procedure generates trustworthy results *because* it is limited by finiteness constraints. (This is not to say, however, that effective procedures are the only way to generate trustworthy results. The discovery of hypercalculative abilities might indicate that there are other, noneffective, methods that generate trustworthy results. The noncognitivist's claim, rather, is that this discovery does not enlarge the class of effective, finite, computations.)[21]

There is not necessarily a sharp line between the cognitive and noncognitive approaches. One might hold, for example, that some of the restrictive conditions are arrived at by abstracting from cognitive capacities, while others arise from the nature of anything properly describable as "finite means." Emil Post has one foot, or possibly even both feet, in the cognitive camp, saying that the purpose of his analysis "is not only to present a system of a certain logical potency but also, in its restricted field, of psychological fidelity" (1936, 105). Post likens Church's identification of effective calculability with recursiveness "not so much to a definition or to an axiom but to a *natural law*" (105), adding that "to mask this identification under a definition hides the fact that a fundamental discovery in the limitations of the mathematicizing power of Homo Sapiens has been made" (105, note 8).[22]

We will argue that Gödel's own allegiances lie with noncognitivism; but first we discuss Turing's and Kleene's positions.

1.2.4 Turing, a Pragmatic Noncognitivist

"The 'computable' numbers," Turing said in the opening sentence of his 1936 paper, are the numbers whose decimals "are calculable by finite means" (58). Although there is certainly some cognitivist rhetoric to be found in Turing's paper, this opening statement, and other textual evidence, makes it difficult to view him as a cognitivist. His remarks about the sequence δ are pertinent here. How could a cognitivist who accepts Turing's statement that "It is (so far as we know at present) possible that any assigned number of figures of δ can be calculated" (1936, 79) think that δ is known to be uncomputable? If it is in fact true that the faculty of calculation is such as to enable any assigned number of figures of δ to be calculated, then what reasons could a cognitivist have for thinking that δ is uncomputable? Turing, on the other hand, does say that δ is *not* computable; he says that it "is an immediate consequence of the theorem of [section] 8 that δ is not computable" (79). For Turing, δ is an example of a definable but uncomputable number that may nevertheless be calculable, although not by a uniform process.

Turing offers "the definitions" in his paper as a conceptual analysis of *calculable by finite means*.[23] Nevertheless, he is perfectly happy to appeal to cognitivist-style arguments from time to time, and his writing is a subtle blend of the two approaches. For example, he says that "the justification [of the definitions] lies in the fact that the human memory is necessarily limited" (59), a statement that will warm the cockles of any cognitivist's heart. He also appeals to the fact that "arbitrarily close" states of mind or symbols "will be confused" as a justification for disallowing the possibility of an infinity of (noncomplex) states of mind or of noncompound symbols (75–76). Turing is casting around for any viable "appeals to intuition" or "propaganda" that will help to win acceptance for his thesis "that the 'computable' numbers include all numbers which would naturally be regarded as computable" (74)."Propaganda is more appropriate to it than proof," he said elsewhere of a related thesis (1954, 588).[24]

A few pages after delivering a bouquet of cognitivist-style propaganda for his thesis, Turing eschews cognitive talk. He elides all reference to states of mind in favor of "a more physical and definite counterpart," the instruction-note (79).

1.2.5   Kleene and Fixed-in-Advance Public Processes

Gödel's assertion that the number of mental states could converge to infinity—
which Kleene described as "pie in the sky"—has no "bearing on what number-
theoretic functions are effectively calculable," Kleene argued (1987, 493–94). He
continued:

> For, in the idea of "effective calculability" or of an "algorithm" as I understand it, it is essential
> that all of the infinitely many calculations, depending on what values of the independent
> variable(s) are used, are performable—determined in their whole potentially infinite totality
> of steps—by following a set of instructions fixed in advance of all calculations. (Kleene 1987,
> 493)

However, this statement is in good accord with what Gödel thought. In his 1934
Princeton address (as we saw above), Gödel said that the computation procedure
is finite, and he identifies it with primitive recursive operations. The interesting
question for the cognitivist is whether or not this fixed-in-advanced-ness is a feature
of our faculty of calculation; and if not, what is the justification of this restriction.
Turing clearly thought that this is not a limitation on (what we are calling) the faculty
of calculation, as Gödel did not.

Kleene suggested the requirement that a computation be *finite* is rooted in the
necessity that *communication* be finite:

> The notion of an "effective calculation procedure" or "algorithm" (for which I believe
> Church's thesis) involves its being possible to convey a complete description of the effective
> procedure or algorithm by a finite communication, in advance of performing computations
> in accordance with it. My version of the Church-Turing thesis is thus the "*Public-Processes
> Version*" (Kleene 1987, 493–94).[25]

Yet why assume that communication must be carried out by a finite procedure?[26]
For example, an accelerating Turing machine, which executes infinitely many steps
in a finite period of time, is able to communicate an infinite amount of information
in a temporally finite transmission.[27] One response, in accord with the cognitive
approach, is that the necessity that communication be finite in all respects is rooted
in the finiteness of our cognitive capacities. But this reply hardly addresses Gödel's
arguments, since Gödel thought that the number of mental states could converge to
infinity.

A noncognitivist, on the other hand, can cut across this issue of whether communication must be finite: whether or not knowledge can be conveyed by means of
infinite procedures, we *begin* with the concept of a finite, fixed-in-advance mechanical procedure, and we analyze it in terms of a transition through a finite number of
states (whether physical or mental).[28]

1.2.6   Gödel's Position, a Reconstruction

So how could Gödel embrace Turing's analysis of computability despite finding it
to involve a fallacy, namely the imposition of a boundedness restriction on the
number of states of mind? Unfortunately, Gödel says very little about his reasons
for endorsing Turing's analysis, and any answer to this question is necessarily speculative. Gödel, it seems to us, was a thoroughgoing noncognitivist. As early as 1934
he was thinking of a computation procedure as a finite procedure, and at no point
did he imply that this reflects, or is justified in terms of, limitations in human cognition. In fact, Gödel made no explicit mention of human computability at all. He
suggested (in 1934) that sharpening the intuitive notion involves the formulation of
a "set of axioms which would embody the generally accepted properties of this
notion" (Gödel in Davis 1982, 9) and it is fair to assume that Gödel's reading of
Turing's analysis was not along cognitivist lines.

In our view, Gödel probably regarded Turing's statements about human cognition as entirely superfluous.[29] The fact that he disagreed with these statements was
therefore no obstacle to his accepting the analysis. From a noncognitive perspective, the restrictive condition on the number of states of mind—that there is a fixed
bound on the number of states that have to be "taken into account"—is correct,
but not because "the human memory is necessarily limited," nor because "if we
admitted an infinity of states of mind, some of them will be 'arbitrarily close' and
will be confused" (Turing 1936, 59, 79). It is exactly the other way around: the procedure can be implemented via a finite and fixed number of states (of mind, or
more generally) *because* computability is analyzed in terms of a fixed finite
procedure.

Thus Gödel embraced the analysis not because he thought that the finiteness of
the procedure could be justified by other limitations (on the sensory apparatus, say).
For Gödel the finiteness of the procedure is not grounded in the human condition
at all—the restrictive condition on the number of states of mind (that "need be
taken into account") is adequate simply because this condition correctly explicates
the finite, fixed-in-advance nature of the computation procedure. It might well be
the case, as Gödel thought, that the number of distinguishable states of mind can
converge to infinity, and that this convergence process is not effective, but all this is
simply irrelevant to the analysis of the concept of computability.

Although Gödel was able to disregard Turing's cognitivist rhetoric while the focus
was the analysis of computability, he nevertheless took Turing to task for philosophical error once the focus shifted to the mathematical powers of the human mind
more generally. Yet in fact Gödel misunderstood Turing, and their views about the
mind were not as different as Gödel supposed.

1.3   Gödel and Turing on the Mind

1.3.1   The Mind-Machine Issue

Famously, the incompleteness and undecidability results of Gödel and Turing have been used to argue that there must be more to human mathematical thinking than can possibly be achieved by a computing machine.[30] In the Wang period (1967–1976[31]), Gödel's discussions of the implications of these results were notably open-minded and cautious. For example, he said (in conversation with Wang): "The incompleteness results do not rule out the possibility that there is a theorem-proving computer which is in fact equivalent to mathematical intuition" (Wang 1996, 186). On "the basis of what has been proved so far," Gödel said, "it remains possible that there may exist (and even be empirically discoverable) a theorem-proving machine which in fact *is* equivalent to mathematical intuition, but cannot be *proved* to be so, nor even be proved to yield only *correct* theorems of finitary number theory" (184–85).

However, the textual evidence indicates that Gödel's position changed dramatically over time. In 1939 his answer to the question "Is the human mind a machine?" is a bold "No." By 1951, his discussion of the relevant issues is nuanced and cautious. His position in his Gibbs lecture of that year seems to be that the answer to the question is not known. By 1956, however, he entertains—somewhat guardedly and with qualifications—the view that the "thinking of a mathematician in the case of yes-or-no questions could be completely replaced by machines" (1956, 375). In later life, his position appears to have moved once again in the direction of his earlier views (although the evidence from this period is less clear). We believe that a diachronic approach to the analysis of Gödel's thinking about the mind-machine issue is illuminating. It has in the past been assumed that Gödel's basic position on the issue remained essentially unchanged, although was refined over time, and thus that his earlier remarks (e. g., in 1939) could be used to guide exegesis of his later work.[32] However, such an approach risks conflating his earlier and later views.

1.3.2   The Younger Gödel

The early Gödel argued (on the basis of the limitative results) that the mind is not a machine:

[I]t would actually be possible to construct a machine which would do the following thing: the supposed machine is to have a crank and whenever you turn the crank once around the machine would write down a tautology of the calculus of predicates. ... So this machine would really replace thinking completely as far as deriving formulas of the calculus of predicates is concerned. It would be a thinking machine in the literal sense of the word.

For the calculus of propositions, you could do even more. You could construct a machine in [the] form of a typewriter, such that if you type down a formula of the calculus of propositions then the machine would ring a bell [if it is a tautology] and if it is not it would not. You could do the same thing for the calculus of monadic predicates. But one can prove that it is impossible to construct a machine which would do the same thing for the whole calculus of predicates. So here already one can prove that [the] Leibnitzian program of the "calculemus" cannot be carried through i. e. one knows that the human mind will never be able to be replaced by a machine already for this comparatively simple question to decide whether a formula is a tautology or not. (Gödel in his 1939 introductory logic lectures in Cassou-Nogues 2009, 85)[33]

In his paper "Undecidable Diophantine Propositions" (193?), Gödel said—as he much later emphasized again in discussion with Wang—that Hilbert's rationalistic optimism "remains entirely untouched" by the incompleteness results (193?, 164). However, on neither occasion did Gödel himself endorse rational optimism, notwithstanding claims by Wang and Sieg to the contrary. Wang claimed that in the second version of the "philosophical error" note (quoted above) Gödel was "arguing for a 'rationalistic optimism'" (Wang 1996, 185), but there is no evidence whatsoever of this in the text. Sieg attributes to Gödel, in our view mistakenly, a "background assumption" of a "deeply rationalistic and optimistic perspective" (Sieg 2007, 193).[34]

1.3.3 The Gibbs Lecture

By the time of the Gibbs lecture (1951), Gödel had drawn back from his firm conclusion of 1939 and offered a much more nuanced and guarded discussion. He introduced a sophisticated distinction between *subjective* and *objective* mathematics (1951, 309). Objective mathematics is "the system of all true mathematical propositions." Subjective mathematics is "the system of all [humanly] demonstrable propositions." Gödel pointed out that "no well-defined system of correct axioms can comprise all objective mathematics, since the proposition which states the consistency of the system is true, but not demonstrable in the system" (309). In the case of subjective mathematics, on the other hand, "it is not precluded that there should exist a finite rule" (309). Gödel appears to be leaving the question of whether there is such a rule open (in contradistinction to his 1939 remark).

Once the objective/subjective distinction has been framed, Gödel's 1939 remarks should probably be amended in something like the following way:

But one can prove that it is impossible to construct a machine which would do the same thing [ring a bell if the typed formula is a tautology] for the whole calculus of predicates. So here already one can prove that *objective mathematics* will never be able to be replaced by a machine already for this comparatively simple question to decide whether a formula is a tautology or not. But it is not settled whether *subjective* mathematics will ever be able to be replaced by a machine; that is, one does not know whether the human mind will ever be able to be replaced by a machine.

The conclusion that Gödel draws in his Gibbs lecture is—unlike his bold statement of 1939—a cautious disjunction. He says:

[I]f the human mind were equivalent to a finite machine, then objective mathematics not only would be incompletable in the sense of not being contained in any well-defined axiomatic system, but moreover there would exist *absolutely* unsolvable diophantine problems ... where the epithet "absolutely" means that they would be undecidable, not just within some particular axiomatic system, but by *any* mathematical proof the human mind can conceive. So the following disjunctive conclusion is inevitable: *Either ... the human mind ... infinitely surpasses the powers of any finite machine* [*], *or else there exist absolutely unsolvable diophantine problems* [**]. (Gödel 1951, 310; emphasis in original)

Concerning alternative [*], Gödel says only that "It is not known whether the first alternative holds" (312). He also says, "It is conceivable (although far outside the limits of present-day science) that brain physiology would advance so far that it would be known with empirical certainty ... that the brain suffices for the explanation of all mental phenomena and is a machine in the sense of Turing" (309, note 13). Gödel takes alternative [**], asserted under the hypothesis that the human mind is equivalent to a finite machine, very seriously and uses it as the basis of an extended argument for mathematical Platonism.

1.3.4   The 1956 Letter to von Neumann

In a letter written to von Neumann five years after the Gibbs lecture, Gödel offers a new argument that it is "quite within the realm of possibility" that "the thinking of a mathematician in the case of yes-or-no questions could be completely replaced by machines, in spite of the unsolvability of the *Entscheidungsproblem*."[35]

Obviously, it is easy to construct a Turing machine that allows us to decide, for each formula F of the restricted functional calculus and every natural number n, whether F has a proof of length n [length=number of symbols]. Let $\psi(F, n)$ be the number of steps required for the machine to do that, and let $\varphi(n) = \max_F \psi(F, n)$. The question is, how rapidly does $\varphi(n)$ grow for an optimal machine? It is possible to show that $\varphi(n) \geq Kn$. If there really were a machine with $\varphi(n) \sim Kn$ (or even just $\sim Kn^2$) then this would have consequences of the greatest significance. Namely, this would clearly mean that the thinking of a mathematician in the case of yes-or-no questions could be completely replaced by machines, in spite of the unsolvability of the Entscheidungsproblem. n would merely have to be chosen so large that, when the machine does not provide a result, it also does not make any sense to think about the problem. Now it seems to me to be quite within the realm of possibility that $\varphi(n)$ grows that slowly. (Gödel to von Neumann 1956, 375)

1.3.5 The Wang Period

Gödel's note on Turing's "philosophical error" perhaps indicates that, by this stage, Gödel was once again setting aside the mechanical view of subjective mathematics. However, it is also perfectly possible that Gödel was merely objecting to what he took to be Turing's *argument* for a positive answer to the question, "Is the human mind a machine?" Everything that Gödel says in both versions of the note is consistent with the view that this question is open.

However, Wang reported that in 1972, in comments at a meeting to honor von Neumann, Gödel said: "The brain is a computing machine connected with a spirit" (Wang 1996, 189). In discussion with Wang at about that time, Gödel amplified this remark:

Even if the finite brain cannot store an infinite amount of information, the spirit may be able to. The brain is a computing machine connected with a spirit. If the brain is taken to be physical and as a digital computer, from quantum mechanics there are then only a finite number of states. Only by connecting it to a spirit might it work in some other way. (Gödel in Wang 1996, 193)

Some caution is required in interpreting the remarks recorded by Wang, since the context is not always clear. Nevertheless Wang's reports create the impression that, by the time of his note about Turing, Gödel was again tending toward a negative answer to the question, "Is the human mind replaceable by a machine?"

1.3.6 Turing and the "Mathematical Objection"

Gödel's way—immaterialism—was certainly not Turing's way. Turing's subtle and interesting treatment of what he called the *Mathematical Objection* has a lot to teach us about his view of mind—which, like Gödel's view in the Wang period, had at its center the fact that mind is not static but constantly developing.

The mathematician Jack Good, formerly Turing's colleague at Bletchley Park, Britain's wartime code-breaking headquarters, gave a succinct statement of the Mathematical Objection in a 1948 letter to Turing:

Can you pin-point the fallacy in the following argument? "No machine can exist for which there are no problems that we can solve and it can't. But we are machines: a contradiction." (Good 1948)

At the time of Good's letter Turing was already deeply interested in the Mathematical Objection. More than eighteen months previously he had given a lecture, in London, in which he expounded and criticized an argument flowing from his negative result concerning the *Entscheidungsproblem* and concluding that "there is a fundamental contradiction in the idea of a machine with intelligence" (1947, 393).

Refined forms of essentially the same argument have been advocated by Lucas, Penrose, and others (despite Turing's definitive critique, of which few writers seem aware).[36] The earliest formulation that we have encountered of the argument was by Emil Post: "We see that a *machine* would never give a complete logic; for once the machine is made *we* could prove a theorem it does not prove," Post wrote in 1941 (417). He concluded that mathematicians are "much more than a kind of clever being who can do quickly what a *machine* could do ultimately."

Turing believed that the Mathematical Objection has no force at all as an objection to machine intelligence—but not because the objection is necessarily mistaken in its claim that what the mind does is not always computable. He gave this pithy statement of the Mathematical Objection in his 1947 lecture:

[W]ith certain logical systems there can be no machine which will distinguish provable formulae of the system from unprovable ... On the other hand if a mathematician is confronted with such a problem he would search around and find new methods of proof, so that he ought eventually to be able to reach a decision about any given formula. (393–394)

As we showed in section 1.1, this idea—that the devising of new methods is a nonmechanical aspect of mathematics—is found in Turing's logical work from an early stage. He also mentions the idea in another of his wartime letters to Newman:

The straightforward unsolvability or incompleteness results about systems of logic amount to this

α) One cannot expect to be able to solve the *Entscheidungsproblem* for a system

β) One cannot expect that a system will cover all possible methods of proof. (Turing to Newman, ca. 1940a, 212)

Here Turing is putting an interesting spin on the incompleteness results, which are usually stated in terms of there being true mathematical statements that are not provable. On Turing's way of looking at matters, the incompleteness results show that no single system of logic can include all methods of proof; and he advocates a progression of logical systems—his ordinal logics—each more inclusive than its predecessors. He continued in the letter:

[W]e... make proofs ... by hitting on one and then checking up to see that it is right. ... When one takes β) into account one has to admit that not one but many methods of checking up are needed. In writing about ordinal logics I had this kind of idea in mind. (212–213)

1.3.7 Turing and Rationalistic Optimism

We suggested in section 1.1.2 that Turing gave cautious expression to a form of rationalistic optimism when he said in 1936, "It is (so far as we know at present) possible that any assigned number of figures of δ can be calculated, but not by a uniform process" (79). Scattered throughout his later writings are passages indicating that Turing was in some sense a rationalistic optimist. He said in a lecture given circa 1951: "By Gödel's famous theorem, or some similar argument, one can show that however the [theorem-proving] machine is constructed there are bound to be cases where the machine fails to give an answer, *but a mathematician would be able to*" (italics added; ca. 1951, 472). We have already noted that in his pithy 1947 statement of the Mathematical Objection he said: "On the other hand if a mathematician is confronted with such a problem he would search around and find new methods of proof, so that he ought eventually to be able to reach a decision about any given formula." And in 1948, again discussing the Mathematical Objection, he said: "On the other hand the human intelligence seems to be able to find methods of ever-increasing power for dealing with such problems, 'transcending' the methods available to machines" (411).

In 1950 Turing considered the obvious countermove against the Mathematical Objection, namely the move of denying rationalistic optimism—but he did not endorse it. He said:

The short answer to [the Mathematical Objection] ... is that although it is established that there are limitations to the powers of any particular machine, it has only been stated, without any sort of proof, that no such limitations apply to the human intellect. (Turing 1950, 451)

Rather than letting matters rest there, however, he continued: "But I do not think [the Mathematical Objection] ... can be dismissed quite so lightly."

1.3.8   What Would Turing Have Said about Gödel's "Sharp Result"?

Gödel might appear to have hit the nail right on the head with what he called his "sharp result" ("If my result is taken together with the rationalistic attitude ... then [we can infer] the sharp result that mind is not mechanical. This is so, because, if the mind were a machine, there would, contrary to this rationalistic attitude, exist number-theoretic questions undecidable for the human mind." [Gödel in Wang 1996, 186–87]). The incompleteness results by themselves certainly do not show that the mind is not a computer. An essential extra ingredient that must be added to the incompleteness results is, as Gödel said, the premise of rationalistic optimism. But even if this premise is added, is the inference that the mind is not mechanical validly drawn?

If our interpretation of Turing is correct, Turing would have answered this question negatively. He would have emphasized the point made in his letter, quoted earlier:

If you think of various machines I don't see your difficulty. One imagines different machines allowing different sets of proofs ...

What is the significance of Turing's statement? The Gödel argument is usually thought of as being a *reductio*. Assume that the mind is equivalent to some Turing machine, say T. Then the usual moves show that the mind cannot be equivalent to T; from which it is concluded that the mind is not mechanical. However, as we pointed out earlier, Gödel's sharp result tells us only that there is no *single* machine that is equivalent to mathematical intuition. If one allows that, from time to time, the mind is identical to *different* Turing machines, allowing *different* sets of proofs, then there is no inconsistency between the sharp result and the claim that every stage of a dynamically changing mind (or of a dynamically changing collection of a number of minds) is a Turing machine. Turing employed the image of a sequence of increasingly powerful proof-producing machines in his 1950 discussion of the Mathematical Objection:

In short, then, there might be men cleverer than any given machine, but then again there might be other machines cleverer again, and so on. (Turing 1950, 451)

If we are correct, Turing's answer to the Mathematical Objection is as follows: Pick any Turing machine T, then there may be a (developmental stage of) some mind M that is cleverer than T, but this has no tendency to show that (this stage of) M is not itself a Turing machine. — *It is perfectly consistent with the sharp result that this stage of M is a proof-producing Turing machine.*

Underlying this answer to the Mathematical Objection is what we call the *Multi-Machine theory of mind*: human minds are Turing machines, in the sense that each developmental stage of a mind M is equivalent to some Turing machine, while different stages of M are equivalent to *different* Turing machines. This interpretation appears in Copeland (2004b); and sections 1. 3. 6–1. 3. 10 of the present chapter are based on Copeland 2006.[37] (Wilfried Sieg puts forward a similar interpretation of Turing in his chapter in this volume.)

1.3.9   The Post-War Turing on Learning

Turing did not attempt to explain what he called the "activity of the intuition," either in his 1939 paper nor the wartime letters to Newman. A human mathematician working according to the rules of a fixed logical system is in effect a proof-producing machine; and when intuition supplies the mathematician with some new means of proof, he or she becomes a different proof-producing machine, capable of a larger set of proofs. How does the mathematician achieve this transformation from one proof-finding machine to another? The pre-war Turing was content to leave this question to one side, but the post-war Turing had a lot to say that is relevant to this question. In his post-war writing on mind, the term "intuition" drops from view and what comes to the fore is the idea of *learning*—in the sense of devising or discovering—new methods of proof.[38]

Turing's discussions of learning repeatedly emphasized:

• The importance of search: he hypothesized boldly that "intellectual activity consists mainly of various kinds of search." (1948, 431)

• The importance of the learner making and correcting mistakes: "[T]his danger of the mathematician making mistakes is an unavoidable corollary of his power of sometimes hitting upon an entirely new method." (ca. 1951, 472)

• The importance of involving a random element: "[O]ne feature that ... should be incorporated ... is a "random element." ... This would result in the behavior of the machine not being by any means completely determined by the experiences to which it was subjected." (ca. 1951, 475)

• The importance of instruction modification: "What we want is a machine that can learn from experience. The possibility of letting the machine alter its own instructions provides the mechanism for this. ... One can imagine that after the machine had been operating for some time, the instructions would have altered out of all recognition." (1947, 393)

Instruction-modification leads from one Turing machine to another; and underpins the central feature of the Multi-Machine theory of mind, the transformation of one Turing machine into another. Different instruction table, different Turing machine. In a lecture given circa 1951, Turing made it clear that his—then radical— idea that machines can learn is the crux of his reply to the Mathematical Objection; and he stressed the importance of the idea of learning new methods of proof in his 1947 discussion of the objection, describing the mathematician as searching around and finding new methods of proof.

Modifying the table of instructions in effect transforms the learning machine into a different Turing machine. So a machine with the ability to learn is able to traverse the space of proof-finding Turing machines. The learning machine successively mutates from one proof-finding Turing machine into another, becoming capable of wider sets of proofs as it searches for and acquires new, more powerful methods of proof.

How is this learning of new methods of proof actually to be accomplished? Of course, Turing did not say in any detail. He posed a question about the human mind whose answer is still fundamentally unknown.

1.3.10   Computability and the Multi-Machine Theory of Mind

Figure 1.1 shows a diagrammatic representation of the Multi-Machine theory of mind. The Turing machines are enumerated as points on the y-axis, beginning with the first (relative to some unspecified underlying ordering of the Turing machines). Along the x-axis are the successive stages of development of learning

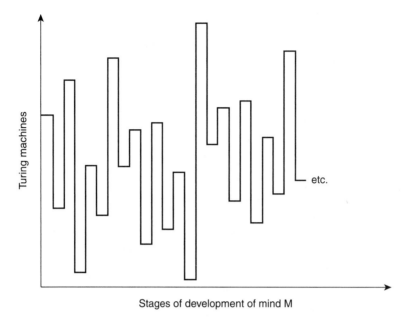

Figure 1.1
The Multi-Machine theory of mind.

mind *M*. *M* successively mutates (in discrete jumps) from one theorem-proving Turing machine into another. Idealizing away death and other contingent resource-constraints, we can imagine the trajectory continuing indefinitely to the right.

Is the function from mind-stages to Turing machines computable? Not if rationalistic optimism is true. If it is an open question whether some appropriate version of rationalistic optimism is true, then it is an open question whether this function is computable.

How could this function *fail* to be computable? Where could the uncomputability come from? Had Gödel commented specifically on the Multi-Machine theory of the human mind, he might have said the following (he was actually commenting on the idea of a "race" of theorem-proving machines, analogous to the mind stages of the Multi-Machine theory):

Such a state of affairs would show that there is something nonmechanical in the sense that the overall plan for the historical development of machines is not mechanical. If the general plan is mechanical, then the whole race can be summarized in one machine. (Gödel in Wang 1996, 207)[39]

However, Gödel did not cash out this notion of an "overall plan," and although his remark gets the issues into sharp focus, it does not really help very much with the specific question of *where* the uncomputability might come from.

We can only guess how Turing would have answered if questioned on this point. But given the emphasis that he placed on the inclusion of a random element in the learning process, he *might* have said: The answer to your question is simple—the source of the uncomputability is randomness. For, as Church had pointed out in 1940, "If a sequence of integers $a_1, a_2, \ldots a_n, \ldots$ is random, then there is no function $f(n) = a_n$ that is calculable by Turing machine" (134–35).

The core idea is that the partially random learning machine emulates the "activity of the intuition" in its walk through the space of proof-finding Turing machines. Heuristic and other forms of search, together with learning algorithms and instruction modification, coupled with the activity from time to time of a random element, produce the evolving sequence of proof-finding Turing machines described by the Multi-Machine theory. Turing spoke in several places about the idea of including "a random element in a learning machine," saying, "A random element is rather useful when we are searching." He emphasized that the same process of search involving a random element "is used in the analogous process of evolution" (1950, 463).

In the situation envisaged by the Multi-Machine theory, the trajectory through the space of proof-finding Turing machines could indeed be uncomputable, in the precise sense that the function on the non-negative integers whose value at i is the ith Turing machine on the trajectory might be uncomputable. If this trajectory is uncomputable, then although the mind is at every stage identical to some Turing machine, it is not the case that the mind as a whole "can be summarized in one machine."

1.4   Conclusion

Gödel's critical note on Turing is of interest not because Turing committed a philosophical error about the mind-machine issue, for he did not, but because of the light that the critical note helps to shed on the similarities, and the differences, in the views of these two great founders of the study of computability. Gödel praised Turing's analysis of computability but objected to the thought that Turing's restrictive conditions are grounded in facts about human cognition, and he misinterpreted some of Turing's statements about the analysis of computability as claims about the mind in general. In fact, Turing agreed with Gödel that the mind is more powerful than any given Turing machine. Unlike Gödel, however, Turing did not think that the mind is something different from machinery.

Acknowledgments

Copeland's research was supported in part by the Royal Society of New Zealand Marsden Fund, grant UOC905, and Shagrir's research was supported by the Israel Science Foundation, grant 1509/11.

Notes

1. See also Copeland (2011), "Epilogue: The Computer and the Mind."

2. Wang reports that Gödel wrote the note "around 1970" (1996, 195). The note is included in the *Collected Works* (Gödel 1990, 305–306), with an introduction by Judson Webb. In 1972, Gödel gave Wang a revised version of the note, which Wang published in his *From Mathematics to Philosophy* (1974, 325–326).

3. The quotation is from the preceding page of "On Computable Numbers" (Turing 1936, 74).

4. Quoted by Wang in *A Logical Journey* (1996, 197).

5. The term "rationalistic optimism" seems to be Wang's (see Wang 1974, 325).

6. Gödel quoted by Wang.

7. See also Copeland (1997a, 1998a, 2000).

8. See also Sieg and Byrnes (1999), Sieg (2002), Copeland and Shagrir (2007).

9. See, for example, Copeland's "Computable Numbers: A Guide," in *The Essential Turing* (Copeland, 2004a); Shagrir (2006); Sieg (2006); and Soare (this volume).

10. See the discussion in Sieg (2007).

11. Gödel often vacillates between the terms "mechanical procedure" and "finite procedure" when referring to formal systems (see the discussion in Shagrir 2006). But from his 1972 note it is clear that he does not take the two to be synonymous; he talks there about *finite but non-mechanical* procedures.

12. Davis dates the article to 1938 (see his introduction to Gödel 193? in the *Collected Works*, [Gödel 1995, 156–163]).

13. For a discussion see Sieg (2009).

14. In a footnote to this lecture, added in 1964, Gödel defines computability in terms of representability; a function is computable just in case (to simplify a bit) the corresponding representing formal expression is a theorem in the relevant formal system. Similar characterizations are advanced by Church (1936), Turing (1936, section 9, part 2); see the discussion by Kripke (this volume), and Hilbert and Bernays (1939).

15. Church describes Turing's identification of effectiveness with Turing-machine computability as "evident immediately" (1937a, 43), "an adequate representation of the ordinary notion" (1937b, 43), and as having "more immediate intuitive appeal" (1941, 41), but he does not say it is more convincing than other arguments; see also Kleene (1952).

16. Turing's argument is mentioned in the early days of automata theory, e. g., by McCulloch and Pitts (1943); Shannon and McCarthy (1956), in their introduction to *Automata Studies*; and Minsky (1967, 108–11), who cites it almost in full in his *Finite and Infinite Machines*. Yet even Minsky asserts that the "strongest argument in favor of Turing's thesis is the fact that ... satisfactory definitions of 'effective procedure' have turned out to be equivalent" (111). As far as we know there is no mention of Turing's argument in current logic and computer science textbooks. The two arguments always given for the Church-Turing thesis are the confluence (equivalence) of definitions, and the lack of counterexamples; see, e. g., Boolos and Jeffrey (1989, 20) and Lewis and Papadimitriou (1981, 223–224).

17. See Gandy (1988), Sieg (1994), Copeland (1997a, 2000). The relatively recent rediscovery of Turing's analysis is underscored by Martin Davis's comment (1982, 14, note 15) that "this [Turing's] analysis is still very much worth reading. I regard my having failed to mention this analysis in my introduction to Turing's paper in Davis (1965) as an embarrassing omission."

18. The term "faculty of calculation" does not necessarily refer to a designated functional or neural module but to the cognitive capacities as they are involved in calculating numbers or the values of functions.

19. For discussion of hypercomputation, see Copeland (1997b, 1998b, 2002b), Copeland and Proudfoot (1999), Copeland and Sylvan (1999). On the relationships between acceleration and hypercomputation, see Copeland and Shagrir (2011).

20. One could question the possibility of such discoveries. Following Kripke and Putnam, one could argue that *if* it is true that the restrictions 1–5 reflect the upper limits of the faculty of calculation, then it is necessarily true (analogously to the claim that if it is true that water is H_2O, then it is necessarily true). This is also in accord with the wisdom that if the Church-Turing thesis is true then it is necessarily true. Thus if it is true that the restrictions 1–5 reflect the upper limits on the faculty of calculation, it is not possible to discover that the faculty of calculation violates one of these restrictions (for discussion see Yaari 2005, who concludes that the thesis is of the *necessary a posteriori* kind). Our suggestion is that these scenarios are conceivable even if metaphysically impossible (for the distinction between conceivability and possibility see, e.g., Chalmers 2004). Our question is whether, in this scenario, the first premise in Turing's argument is true or false.

21. It should be mentioned in this context that Gödel himself proposed in the 1930s finite and nonmechanistic ("constructive") methods, partly as an attempt to rescue Hilbert's program. The hope of Gödel and others was to devise trustworthy "initary" methods that transcend the limitation of the incompleteness results. Yet he never claimed (as emphasized below) that these methods enlarge the class of effective computations.

22. Contemporary researchers who take this approach are Yaari (2005) and Bringsjord (see Bringsjord and Arkoudas [2006] and Bringsjord and Sundar [2011]).

23. See, for example, Turing (1936, 59).

24. See also Copeland (2004a, 577–578).

25. See also Kleene (1988, 50).

26. See also Kripke (this volume), who challenges this requirement altogether.

27. On accelerating Turing machines see Copeland (1998b, 1998c, 2002a), Shagrir (2004), and Copeland and Shagrir (2011).

28. Following Kleene, Sieg also grounds the finiteness of the procedure in the "normative requirement on the fully explicit presentation of mathematical proofs in order to insure inter-subjectivity" (2009, 532; see also 2008); see also Seligman (2002, section 4). On the other hand, Sieg (2006) contends that two "central restrictive conditions" on our sensory apparatus suffice to secure the conclusion of the analysis. One restrictive condition is that "[t]here is a fixed finite bound on the number of configurations a computer can immediately recognize" (boundedness). The other is that "[a] computer can change only immediately recognizable (sub-) configurations" (locality; 203). It thus seems to us that Sieg holds a dual position that is a mixture of cognitive and noncognitive elements.

29. See also Shagrir (2006).

30. For example, Lucas (1961, 1996), Penrose (1994; see, e.g., 65).

31. See Wang (1996, xi, 7).

32. See, for example, Sieg (2006).

33. Extract from Gödel's notes for his 1939 introductory logic course at the University of Notre Dame.

34. See also the first paragraph of Sieg's section 2 (2007, 191).

35. This letter is discussed in Wigderson (2011).

36. A full history of the argument will be presented in Copeland and Piccinini (in preparation). Modern scholarship on Turing's mathematical objection began with Piccinini (2003).

37. See also: Copeland (2008); Copeland's "Turing's Answer to the Mathematical Objection" in *The Essential Turing* (Copeland 2004a, 469–70); and Copeland and Proudfoot (2007).

38. See also Copeland (2006, 168).

39. Gödel quoted by Wang.

References

Baaz, M., C. H. Papadimitriou, H. W. Putnam, D. S. Scott, and C. L. Harper, Jr., eds. 2011. *Kurt Gödel and the Foundations of Mathematics*. New York: Cambridge University Press.

Boolos, G. S., and R. C. Jeffrey. 1989. *Computability and Logic*. 3rd ed. Cambridge: Cambridge University Press.

Bringsjord, S., and K. Arkoudas. 2006. On the provability, veracity, and AI-relevance of the Church-Turing thesis. In *Church's Thesis after 70 Years*, ed. A. Olszewski, J. Wolenski, and R. Janusz, 66–118. Frankfurt: Ontos-Verlag.

Bringsjord, S., and G. N. Sundar. 2011. In defense of the unprovability of the Church-Turing thesis. *Journal of Unconventional Computing* 6:353–373.

Cassou-Nogues, P. 2009. Gödel's introduction to logic in 1939. *History and Philosophy of Logic* 30:69–90.

Chalmers, D. 2004. Epistemic two-dimensional semantics. *Philosophical Studies* 18:153–226.

Church, A. 1936. An unsolvable problem of elementary number theory. *American Journal of Mathematics* 58:345–63. Reprinted in Davis, *The Undecidable*, 88–107.

Church, A. 1937a. Review of Turing (1936). *Journal of Symbolic Logic* 2:42–43.

Church, A. 1937b. Review of Post (1936). *Journal of Symbolic Logic* 2:43.

Church, A. 1940. On the concept of a random sequence. *Bulletin of the American Mathematical Society* 46:130–135.

Church, A. 1941. *The Calculi of Lambda-Conversion*. Princeton: Princeton University Press.

Copeland, B. J. 1997a. The Church-Turing thesis. *The Stanford Encyclopedia of Philosophy*, ed. E. Zalta. http://plato. stanford. edu/entries/church-turing/.

Copeland, B. J. 1997b. The broad conception of computation. *American Behavioral Scientist* 40:690–716.

Copeland, B. J. 1998a. Turing's O-machines, Penrose, Searle, and the brain. *Analysis* 58:128–138.

Copeland, B. J. 1998b. Even Turing machines can compute uncomputable functions. In *Unconventional Models of Computation*, ed. C. Calude, J. Casti, and M. Dinneen, 150–164. London: Springer-Verlag.

Copeland, B. J. 1998c. Super Turing-machines. *Complexity* 4:30–32.

Copeland, B. J. 2000. Narrow versus wide mechanism. *Journal of Philosophy* 97:5–32. Reprinted in *Computationalism: New Directions*, ed. M. Scheutz, 59–86. Cambridge: MIT Press, 2002.

Copeland, B. J. 2002a. Accelerating Turing machines. *Minds and Machines* 12:281–301.

Copeland, B. J. 2002b. Hypercomputation. In *Hypercomputation*, special issue, *Minds and Machines* 12:461–502.

Copeland, B. J., ed. 2002–2003. *Hypercomputation*. Special issue, *Minds and Machines* 12, 13.

Copeland, B. J. 2004a. *The Essential Turing*. Oxford: Oxford University Press.

Copeland, B. J. 2004b. Hypercomputation: Philosophical issues. *Theoretical Computer Science* 317:251–267.

Copeland, B. J. 2006. The Mathematical Objection: Turing, Penrose, and creativity. A lecture at the MIT Computer Science and Artificial Intelligence Laboratory, December 2, 2006.

Copeland, B. J. 2008. The Mathematical Objection: Turing, Gödel, and Penrose on the mind. http://people .ds.cam.ac.uk/mds26/cogsci/program.html.

Copeland, B. J. 2011. From the *Entscheidungsproblem* to the personal computer—and beyond. In Baaz, Papadimitriou, Putnam, Scott, and Harper, eds., *Kurt Gödel and the Foundations of Mathematics*, 151–184.

Copeland, B. J., and G. Piccinini. On Turing on uncomputability and the mind. Manuscript in preparation.

Copeland, B. J., and D. Proudfoot. 1999. Alan Turing's forgotten ideas in computer science. *Scientific American* 280:76–81.

Copeland, B. J., and D. Proudfoot. 2007. Artificial intelligence: History, foundations, and philosophical issues. In *Handbook of the Philosophy of Psychology and Cognitive Science*, ed. P. Thagard, 429–82. Amsterdam: Elsevier Science.

Copeland, B. J., and O. Shagrir. 2007. Physical computation: How general are Gandy's principles for mechanisms? *Minds and Machines* 17:217–231.

Copeland, B. J., and O. Shagrir. 2011. Do accelerating Turing machines compute the uncomputable? *Minds and Machines* 21:221–239.

Copeland, B. J., and R. Sylvan. 1999. Beyond the universal Turing machine. *Australasian Journal of Philosophy* 77:46–66.

Davis, M., ed. 1965. *The Undecidable: Basic Papers on Undecidable Propositions, Unsolvable Problems and Computable Functions*. New York: Raven Press.

Davis, M. 1982. Why Gödel didn't have Church's thesis. *Information and Control* 54:3–24.

Gandy, R. 1980. Church's thesis and principles of mechanisms. In *The Kleene Symposium*, ed. J. Barwise, H. J. Keisler, and K. Kunen, 123–148. Amsterdam: North-Holland.

Gandy, R. 1988. The confluence of ideas in 1936. In Herken, *The Universal Turing Machine*, 51–102.

Gödel, K. 1931. Über formal unentscheidbare Sätze der Principia Mathematica und verwandter Systeme, I. *Monatshefte für Mathematik und Physik* 38:173–178. Reprinted with English translation as "On formally undecidable propositions of *Principia Mathematica* and related systems I" in Gödel, *Collected Works I*, 144–195.

Gödel, K. 1933. The present situation in the foundations of mathematics. In Gödel, *Collected Works III*, 45–53.

Gödel, K. 1934. On undecidable propositions of formal mathematical systems. In Gödel, *Collected Works I*, 346–369.

Gödel, K. 193?. Undecidable Diophantine propositions. In Gödel, *Collected Works III*, 164–175.

Gödel, K. 1946. Remarks before the Princeton bicentennial conference on problems in mathematics. In Davis, *The Undecidable*, 84–88, and in Gödel, *Collected Works II*, 150–153. Page references are to *Collected Works*.

Gödel, K. 1951. Some basic theorems on the foundations of mathematics and their implications. In Gödel, *Collected Works III*, 304–323.

Gödel, K. 1956. Letter to John von Neumann, March 20, 1956. In Gödel, *Collected Works V*, 372–377.

Gödel, K. 1964. Postscriptum to Gödel 1934. In Gödel, *Collected Works I*, 369–371, and in Davis, *The Undecidable*, 71–73. Page references are to Davis 1965.

Gödel, K. 1972. Some remarks on the undecidability results. In Gödel, *Collected Works II*, 305–306.

Gödel, K. 1986. *Collected Works, Vol. I: Publications 1929–1936*. ed. S. Feferman, J. W. Dawson Jr., S. C. Kleene, G. H. Moore, R. M. Solovay, and J. van Heijenoort. Oxford: Oxford University Press.

Gödel, K. 1990. *Collected Works, Vol. II: Publications 1938–1974*, ed. S. Feferman, J. W. Dawson Jr., S. C. Kleene, G. H. Moore, R. M. Solovay, and J. van Heijenoort. Oxford: Oxford University Press.

Gödel, K. 1995. *Collected Works, Vol. III: Unpublished Essays and Lectures*, ed. S. Feferman, J. W. Dawson Jr., W. Goldfarb, C. Parsons, and R. M. Solovay. Oxford: Oxford University Press.

Gödel, K. 2003. *Collected Works, Vol. V: Correspondence, H–Z*, ed. S. Feferman, J. W. Dawson Jr., W. Goldfarb, C. Parsons, and W. Sieg. Oxford: Clarendon Press.

Good, I. J. 1948. Early notes on electronic computers. Unpublished. University of Manchester National Archive for the History of Computing, MUC/Series 2/a4.

Herken, R., ed. 1988. *The Universal Turing Machine: A Half-Century Survey*. Oxford: Oxford University Press.

Hilbert, D. 1902. Mathematical problems: Lecture delivered before the International Congress of Mathematicians at Paris in 1900. *Bulletin of the American Mathematical Society* 8:437–479.

Hilbert, D., and P. Bernays. 1939. *Grundlagen der Mathematik II*. Berlin: Springer-Verlag.

Kleene, S. C. 1936. General recursive functions of natural numbers. *Mathematische Annalen* 112:727–742. Reprinted in Davis, *The Undecidable*, 236–253.

Kleene, S. C. 1952. *Introduction to Metamathematics*. Amsterdam: North-Holland.

Kleene, S. C. 1987. Reflections on Church's thesis. *Notre Dame Journal of Formal Logic* 28:490–498.

Kleene, S. C. 1988. Turing's analysis of computability, and major applications of it. In Herken, *The Universal Turing Machine*, 17–54.

Lewis, H. R., and C. H. Papadimitriou. 1981. *Elements of the Theory of Computation*. Englewood Cliffs, NJ: Prentice-Hall.

Lucas, J. R. 1961. Minds, machines and Gödel. *Philosophy* 36:112–127.

Lucas, J. R. 1996. Minds, machines and Gödel: A retrospect. In *Machines and Thought: The Legacy of Alan Turing, Vol. 1*, ed. P. Millican and A. Clark, 103–124. Oxford: Clarendon Press.

McCulloch, W. S., and W. Pitts. 1943. A logical calculus of the ideas immanent in nervous activity. *Bulletin of Mathematical Biophysics* 5:115–133.

Minsky, M. L. 1967. *Computation: Finite and Infinite Machines*. Englewood Cliffs, NJ: Prentice-Hall.

Penrose, R. 1994. *Shadows of the Mind: A Search for the Missing Science of Consciousness*. Oxford: Oxford University Press.

Piccinini, G. 2003. Alan Turing and the Mathematical Objection. *Minds and Machines* 13:23–48.

Post, E. L. 1936. Finite combinatory processes—Formulation I. *Journal of Symbolic Logic* 1:103–105. Reprinted in Davis, *The Undecidable*, 288–291.

Post, E. L. 1941. Absolutely unsolvable problems and relatively undecidable propositions: Account of an anticipation. In Davis, *The Undecidable*, 338–443.

Seligman, J. 2002. The scope of Turing's analysis of effective procedures. *Minds and Machines* 12:203–220.

Shagrir, O. 2002. Effective computation by humans and machines. *Minds and Machines* 12:221–240.

Shagrir, O. 2004. Super-tasks, accelerating Turing machines and uncomputability. *Theoretical Computer Science* 317:105–114.

Shagrir, O. 2006. Gödel on Turing on computability. In *Church's Thesis after 70 years*, ed. A. Olszewski, J. Wolenski, and R. Janusz, 393–419. Frankfurt: Ontos-Verlag.

Shannon, C. E., and J. McCarthy, eds. 1956. *Automata Studies*. Princeton: Princeton University Press.

Sieg, W. 1994. Mechanical procedures and mathematical experience. In *Mathematics and Mind*, ed. A. George, 71–117. Oxford: Oxford University Press.

Sieg, W. 2002. Calculations by man and machine: Conceptual analysis. In *Reflections on the Foundations of Mathematics*, ed. W. Sieg, R. Sommer, and C. Talcott. Lecture Notes in Logic, Vol. 15, 396–415. Natick, MA: Association for Symbolic Logic.

Sieg, W. 2006. Gödel on computability. *Philosophia Mathematica* 14:189–207.

Sieg, W. 2007. On mind and Turing's machines. *Natural Computing* 6:187–205.

Sieg, W. 2008. Church without dogma: Axioms for computability. In *New Computational Paradigms*, ed. B. Lowe, A. Sorbi, and S. New York; B. Cooper, 139–152. New York: Springer-Verlag.

Sieg, W. 2009. On computability. In *Handbook of the Philosophy of Mathematics*, ed. A. Irvine, 535–630. Amsterdam: Elsevier.

Sieg, W., and J. Byrnes. 1999. An abstract model for parallel computations: Gandy's thesis. *Monist* 82:150–164.

Turing, A. M. 1936. On computable numbers, with an application to the *Entscheidungsproblem*. In Copeland, *The Essential Turing*, 58–90.

Turing, A. M. 1939. Systems of logic based on ordinals. In Copeland, *The Essential Turing*, 146–204.

Turing, A. M. ca. 1940a. Letter to Max Newman. In Copeland, *The Essential Turing,* 211–213.

Turing, A. M. ca. 1940b. Letter to Max Newman. In Copeland, *The Essential Turing,* 214–216.

Turing, A. M. 1947. Lecture to the London Mathematical Society on February 20, 1947. In Copeland, *The Essential Turing*, 378–394.

Turing, A. M. 1948. Intelligent machinery. In Copeland, *The Essential Turing,* 410–32.

Turing, A. M. 1950. Computing machinery and intelligence. In Copeland, *The Essential Turing,* 441–464.

Turing, A. M. ca. 1951. Intelligent machinery, a heretical theory. In Copeland, *The Essential Turing,* 472–475.

Turing, A. M. 1954. Solvable and unsolvable problems. In Copeland, *The Essential Turing,* 582–595.

Wang, H. 1974. *From Mathematics to Philosophy*. London: Routledge & Kegan Paul.

Wang, H. 1996. *A Logical Journey: From Gödel to Philosophy*. Cambridge: MIT Press.

Webb, J. C. 1990. Introductory note to Remark 3 of Gödel 1972. In Gödel, *Collected Works II*, 292–304.

Wigderson, A. 2011. The Gödel phenomenon in mathematics: A modern view. In Baaz, Papadimitriou, Putnam, Scott, and Harper, eds., *Kurt Gödel and the Foundations of Mathematics*, 475–508.

Yaari, J. 2005. *On the status and justification of the Church–Turing thesis*. M. Phil Thesis, University of London.

2 Computability and Arithmetic

Martin Davis

It is remarkable that arbitrary computable operations on the natural numbers can be expressed in terms of the basic operations of addition and multiplication. The main obstacle to this accomplishment has been the need to deal with iterative processes. In this article, we will survey some of the work that has led to this achievement. Finally, we will carry out in detail an exercise showing how these results can be used to provide a direct proof that computable relations are representable in first-order arithmetic with minimal need for formalized proofs of substantive mathematics.

2.1 The Chinese Remainder Theorem

We'll be dealing with the natural numbers $N = \{0, 1, 2, \dots\}$. We recall the notion of division with a remainder: given a natural number n and a non-zero number d, we can find a "quotient" q and remainder r, where

$$\frac{n}{d} = q + \frac{r}{d}, \quad r < d.$$

(For example, $17/7 = 2 + 3/7$.) This relation can equivalently be written as

$$n = qd + r, \quad r < d.$$

This expression involves an equation and an inequality, but from the point of view of arithmetic representation, one should note that $r < d$ is equivalent to

$$(\exists z)(r + z + 1 = d).$$

The Chinese remainder theorem first appeared in the work of the Chinese mathematician Sun Tzu in ancient times. A pair of numbers d, d' is said to be *co-prime* if no number other than 1 is a divisor of both of them. (So, for example, 6 and 35 are co-prime since the divisors of 6 are 1, 2, 3, 6 and those of 35 are 1, 5, 7, 35. On the other hand, 6 and 15 are not co-prime because they share the divisor 3.) The theorem may be stated as follows:

Let the numbers $a_1, a_2, \dots, a_m$ be given, and let the numbers $d_1, d_2, \dots, d_m$ be such that each pair of them are co-prime. Then there is a number s such that each a_i is the remainder when s is divided by d_i, *for* i=1, 2, ... , *m*. That is,

$$s = q_i d_i + a_i, a_i < d_i, i = 1, 2, \dots, m.$$

To use the Chinese remainder theorem to code sequences, one needs a supply of mutually co-prime numbers. Gödel used the following device to provide such a supply:

Lemma 2.1 *If g is divisible by the numbers 1, 2, ... , m, then the numbers*

{1 + (i + 1)g | i = 0, 1, 2, ... , m}

are pairwise co-prime.

Proof Any divisor of $1 + (i + 1)g$ other than 1 must be $> m$, because the numbers $\leq m$ are divisors of g. Suppose that d is a divisor of both

$$1 + (i + 1)g$$

and

$$1 + (j + 1)g,$$

where $i > j$. Then d would be a divisor of

$$(i + 1)(1 + (j + 1)g) - (j + 1)(1 + (i + 1)g) = i - j.$$

But this is impossible, because $i - j < m$. $\square$

Gödel defined his "beta function" by

$\beta(x, y, z) = $ the remainder when x is divided by $1 + (z + 1)y$.

Using this we get the following useful form of the Chinese remainder theorem:

Let the numbers $a_0, a_1, a_2, \dots, a_m$ be given. Then there are numbers g, s such that

$$\beta(s, g, i) = a_i, i = 0, 1, 2, \dots, m.$$

The beta function is used to provide arithmetic definitions of certain relations among natural numbers. An arithmetic definition of such a relation is a logical formula equivalent to the relation in question written in terms of the symbols

$\neg \ \vee \ \wedge \ \forall \ \exists \ = \ + \ 0 \ 1.$

As an illustration, we show how the Chinese remainder theorem can be used to provide an arithmetic definition of the set of pairs $< m, n >$ such that $m = 2^n$: the relation $m = 2^n$ is equivalent to the existence of a sequence of $n + 1$ numbers whose first term is 1, and whose subsequent terms are each obtained by doubling its predecessor. That is,

$$(\exists g, s)\{(\beta(s, g, 0) = 1) \& (\forall i < n)[\beta(s, g, i + 1) = 2\beta(s, g, i)] \& \beta(s, g, n) = m\}.$$

In his 1931 paper, Gödel used this technique to show, in a similar manner, that—given that the relations $x = f(t_1, \ldots, t_n)$ and $y = g(s, u, t_1, \ldots, t_n)$ are arithmetically definable—then so is the relation $z = h(s, t_1, \ldots, t_n)$, where

$$h(0, t_1, \ldots, t_n) = f(t_1, \ldots, t_n)$$

$$h(s + 1, t_1, \ldots, t_n) = g(s, h(s, t_1, \ldots, t_n), t_1, \ldots, t_n).$$

A universal quantifier $\forall$ will enter the arithmetic definition as in the simple example. Because this "recursion" operation was to be applied over and over again, more and more of these universal quantifiers accumulate. Moreover (although Gödel didn't call attention to this), just as in the example, each of the universal quantifiers in the arithmetic definitions are bounded. These universal quantifiers were seen as arising out of the inherent need for iteration in computable operations. This story is about a quest to eliminate these universal quantifiers.

2.2 Julia Robinson and Existential Definability

Julia Robinson defined a relation to be *existentially definable* if it possesses an arithmetic definition in which the symbols $\neg\forall$ do not occur. In such a case, the symbols $\vee \wedge$ are eliminable as well, because

$$p = q \vee r = s \Leftrightarrow (p - q)(r - s) = 0 \Leftrightarrow pr + qs = ps + rq$$

$$p = q \wedge r = s \Leftrightarrow (p - q)^2 + (r - s)^2 = 0 \Leftrightarrow p^2 + q^2 + r^2 + s^2 = 2pq + 2rs$$

.

Thus, an existentially definable relation is one that has a definition of the form

$$(\exists x_1, \ldots, x_n)[p(t_1, \ldots, t_m, x_1, \ldots, x_n) = 0],$$

where p is a polynomial with integer (positive or negative) coefficients.

Following a suggestion of Tarski, Julia attempted to prove that exponentiation is not existentially definable. Not succeeding, she reversed course and tried to prove that it is. The so-called Pell equation $x^2 - dy^2 = 1$, where d is not a perfect square, has been well studied. The equation has infinitely many solutions in natural numbers $\{x_n, y_n \mid n \in N\}$ given by

$$x_n + y_n \sqrt{d} = (x_1 + y_1 \sqrt{d})^n.$$

Julia saw this exponential behavior as possibly providing what was needed for the existential definition she sought. She focused on the special case $d = a^2 - 1, a > 1$, where $x_1 = a; y_1 = 1$. Using the properties of this equation, she obtained a result that turned out to be critical for later developments. She introduced what later was called the Julia Robinson Hypothesis, abbreviated JR, which stated:

There exists an existentially definable set R of pairs of natural numbers such that

1. $<u,v> \in R \Rightarrow v \leq u^u$,

2. For every positive integer k, there exists $<u,v> \in R$ such that $v \geq u^k$.

She proved that, assuming JR is true, the relation $w = u^v$ is existentially definable.

2.3   My Own Early Work

In my graduate school days, I also studied existentially definable relations. I was unaware of Robinson's work on this topic, and I used the name *Diophantine* rather than "existentially definable." It was this name that was later generally adopted. I noted the following simple fact:

If $R, S \subseteq N^k$ are Diophantine sets, then so are $R \cup S$ and $R \cap S$.

This follows from the technique shown above for combining a pair of equations under the operation $\vee$ or $\wedge$. Now, Diophantine sets have the property of being *listable,* which means that for each such set, there is an algorithm for making a list of its members; namely, to make a list of

$$\{<t_1, \ldots ,t_m> \in N^m \mid (\exists x_1, \ldots ,x_n)[p(t_1, \ldots ,t_m,x_1, \ldots ,x_n) = 0],$$

one can order all $m + n$-tuples of natural numbers in some convenient manner, successively compute the value of p for each such tuple, and whenever the value computed is 0, place the initial m-tuple of that $m + n$-tuple on the list. (Listable sets are also called *recursively enumerable* or *computably enumerable.*) I made the naive conjecture that the converse is true:

Conjecture   *Every listable set is Diophantine.*

At first glance, it seems implausible that every set of natural numbers that can be algorithmically listed must be Diophantine. However, I noted that the class of listable sets not only shared with the class of Diophantine sets the property of being closed under $\cup$ and $\cap$, but also shared the property of *not* being closed under taking complements. Specifically, I could easily (though not constructively) prove that there is a Diophantine set $S \subseteq N^k$ such that $N^k - S$ is not Diophantine, a well-known property of listable sets. The proof is that because $\neg \exists \neg = \forall$, if this assertion were false, then every arithmetically definable set would be Diophantine. But this is impossible, because every Diophantine set is listable and it is known that not every arithmetically definable set is listable. (It is not hard to see that one can then get this same result with $k = 1$.)

This coincidence of the properties of these two classes made me think that my conjecture wasn't completely crazy, and I knew that if it were true it would have important consequences. In particular, because there are listable sets of natural numbers that are not computable, it would follow from this conjecture that there can be no algorithm for testing polynomial equations with integer coefficients for possessing a solution in natural numbers. This would constitute a negative solution of the tenth problem in the famous list from Hilbert's 1900 address.

In any case, I tried to prove the conjecture. I didn't succeed, but I did prove something that, at least formally, looked close. Namely, I proved that, for any listable $S \subseteq N^m$, there is a polynomial p with integer coefficients such that

$$< t_1, \ \ldots \ , t_m > \in S \Leftrightarrow (\exists y)(\forall k)_{k \leq y}(\exists x_1, \ \ldots \ , x_n)[p(t_1, \ \ldots \ , t_m, k, y, x_1, \ \ldots \ , x_n) = 0].$$

The proof uses Gödel's beta function. It can be carried out by beginning with what Gödel had established and then showing how to eliminate all but one of the universal quantifiers, or, as I did it, by beginning with one of the simple combinatorial structures that were known to generate the listable sets of natural numbers and using the beta function to code derivations in these structures. Raphael Robinson called my result *Davis normal form* and proved that the index n could be taken to be 4. Much later this was reduced to 2 by Yuri Matiyasevich.

I met Julia and Raphael at the 1950 International Congress of Mathematicians at Harvard University. Listening to her contribution, I realized that we had been working on the same problem, but from opposite directions. I was excited to tell her about my normal form; I had spoken about it at a meeting several months earlier.

2.4   Enter Hilary Putnam

Hilary and I began working together while we were at a five-week "Institute for Logic" at Cornell University during the summer of 1957. We continued working together during summers for several years. Hilary had the fruitful idea of applying the Gödel beta function to Davis normal form as follows:

$$(\forall k)_{k \leq y}(\exists x_1, \ \ldots \ , x_n)[p(t_1, \ \ldots \ , t_m, k, y, x_1, \ \ldots \ , x_n) = 0]$$

$$\Leftrightarrow (\exists s_1, g_1, \ \ldots \ , s_n, g_n)(\forall k)_{k \leq y}[p(t_1, \ \ldots \ , t_m, k, y, \beta(s_1, g_1, k), \ \ldots \ , \beta(s_n, g_n, k)) = 0]$$

Using the equivalence

$$(\forall k)_{k \le y}[p(t_1, \ldots, t_m, k, y, \beta(s_1, g_1, k), \ldots, \beta(s_n, g_n, k)) = 0]$$

$$\Leftrightarrow \sum_{k=0}^{y} p^2(t_1, \ldots, t_m, k, y, \beta(s_1, g_1, k), \ldots, \beta(s_n, g_n, k)) = 0$$

we were able to find two relations about which we could prove that if both of them are Diophantine, then all listable sets are Diophantine.

It was in the summer of 1959 that we achieved something of a breakthrough. Following the lead of Julia's earlier work, we considered what could be done if, instead of polynomials, we permitted exponential polynomials in our defining relationships. By exponential polynomials we simply meant polynomial expressions in which some of the variables were allowed to occur as exponents. In such a case we spoke of *exponential Diophantine* relations. Continuing to use the beta function as in our 1957 work, we found a proof that every listable set is exponential Diophantine. But given what was known in 1959, our proof had a serious gap. We needed to assume that there are arbitrarily long sequences of prime numbers in arithmetic progression, and this fact was only proved 45 years later! We wrote up our work as it stood and sent a copy to Julia. She wrote soon after as follows:

I am very pleased, surprised, and impressed with your results on Hilbert's tenth problem. Quite frankly, I did not think your methods could be pushed further ...

She continued:

I believe I have succeeded in eliminating the need for [the assumption about primes in arithmetic progression] by extending and modifying your proof. (personal communication)

Ultimately, she not only did that, but also greatly simplified the proof, and the three of us agreed to publish a joint paper in which our main result was:

DPR Theorem   *If $S \subseteq N^k$ is listable, then there is an exponential polynomial with integer coefficients $p(t_1, t_2, \ldots, t_k, x_1, x_2, \ldots, x_n)$ such that*

$$< t_1, t_2, \ldots, t_k > \in S \Leftrightarrow (\exists x_1, \ldots, x_n)[p(t_1, t_2, \ldots, t_k, x_1, x_2, \ldots, x_n) = 0].$$

In the paper we also pointed out that because Julia had previously proved that her hypothesis JR implies that the exponential function itself is Diophantine, we had shown that JR implies that every listable set is Diophantine, and therefore that JR implies that Hilbert's tenth problem has no algorithmic solution. Nevertheless, Georg Kreisel, reviewing our paper for *Mathematical Reviews*, did not mention this fact, but did write:

... it is likely the present result is not closely connected with Hilbert's tenth problem.[1]

2.5 Yuri Matiyasevich's Triumph

In January 1970, I received a phone call from a friend informing me that JR had apparently been proved by a Russian mathematician. This was Yuri Matiyasevich, then twenty-two years old. He had provided a Diophantine definition for the set $\{< u, v > \mid v = F_{2u}\}$, where F_n is the nth Fibonacci number, defined as follows:

$$F_0 = 0, F_1 = 1, F_{n+2} = F_{n+1} + F_n.$$

Since F_{2n} is asymptotic to $((3 + \sqrt{5})/2)^n$ (meaning, as usual, that their ratio approaches 1 as $n \to \infty$), it is readily seen that the conditions laid down by Julia Robinson were fulfilled. Julia wrote Yuri telling him that since he was evidently a baby when she began working on the problem, to get the solution she needed only to wait for him to grow up. Yuri's proof is quite short, but it is a wonderful tapestry, delicate and beautiful. Putting the pieces together, we now had:

DPRM Theorem[2]   *If $S \subseteq N^k$ is listable, then there is a polynomial with integer coefficients $p(t_1, t_2, \ldots, t_k, x_1, x_2, \ldots, x_n)$ such that*

$$< t_1, t_2, \ldots, t_k > \in S \Leftrightarrow (\exists x_1, \ldots, x_n)[p(t_1, t_2, \ldots, t_k, x_1, x_2, \ldots, x_n) = 0].$$

Because there are listable sets that are not computable, it follows that there is a polynomial p such that

$$\{r \in N \mid (\exists x_1, x_2, \ldots, x_n) p(r, x_1, x_2, \ldots, x_n) = 0\}$$

is not computable. So there can be no algorithm for testing an arbitrary polynomial equation for natural number solutions. Hence,

Corollary   *Hilbert's tenth problem is unsolvable.*

2.6 Computable Sets in Formal Arithmetic

One of the key steps in proving Gödel undecidability in arithmetic is showing how to represent computable sets in appropriate formal systems. There is a trade-off between the effort involved in tailoring a formulation of computability to the task at hand and the corresponding effort in formalizing enough number theory to provide what is needed in carrying out the proof. The DPRM theorem makes available an equivalent of computability that is particularly attractive for this purpose, requiring only very simple and straightforward formalization. As an application of the DPRM theorem, this exercise will be carried out in detail.

Familiarity with first-order logic will be assumed. To emphasize the distinction between using logical symbolism as abbreviations in ordinary discourse and their occurrence in formal languages, in the latter case boldface is used, as in

$$\neg \supset \wedge \vee \forall \exists =$$

For Γ a set of sentences and σ a sentence, we write $\Gamma \vdash \sigma$ to mean that σ follows from the premises Γ by the rules of first-order logic. Parentheses will be freely omitted when no ambiguity results. In writing sentences, initial universal quantifiers are usually omitted.

The additional symbols

0 S + × and ≤

constitute the *language of arithmetic*.[3] In what follows the words "formula" and "sentence" will be understood to be used with respect to the language of arithmetic. The *standard model* of this language takes the natural numbers

$$N = \{0, 1, 2, \dots \}$$

as its domain, and interprets **0** as the number 0, **S** as the successor operator that associates with each natural number, the immediately following number, **+** as addition, **×** as multiplication, and ≤ as less than or equal to.

A *theory* T is a set of sentences such that $T \vdash \sigma$ implies $\sigma \in T$. Theory T_2 is called an extension of theory T_1 if $T_1 \subseteq T_2$. For a theory T, we write $\vdash_T \sigma$ to mean that $\sigma \in T$, and $\Gamma \vdash_T \sigma$ to mean that $\Gamma \cup T \vdash \sigma$. T is *consistent* if there is no sentence σ such that $\vdash_T \sigma$ and $\vdash_T \neg\sigma$. T is *complete* if for every sentence σ either $\vdash_T \sigma$ or $\vdash_T \neg\sigma$.

A set of sentences Γ constitute *axioms* for a theory T if $\Gamma \vdash \sigma$ if and only if $\sigma \in T$. T is *axiomatizable* if it has an axiom set that is computable, and *finitely axiomatizable* if it has a finite axiom set. Any set of sentences Γ is an axiom set for the theory consisting of all the consequences of Γ in first-order logic.

We shall work with the theory Q, which has the finite axiom set:[4]

2.1. $\neg(Sx = 0)$

2.2. $(Sx = Sy) \supset (x = y)$

2.3. $(x + 0) = x$

2.4. $(x + Sy) = S(x + y)$

2.5. $(x \times 0) = 0$

2.6. $(x \times Sy) = ((x \times y) + x)$

2.7. $(x \leq 0) \supset (x = 0)$

2.8. $(x \le Sy) \supset [(x \le y) \lor (x = Sy)]$

2.9. $(x \le y) \lor (y \le x)$

The theory *PA*, also known as *Peano Arithmetic*, may be defined as having the infinite axiom set consisting of 2.1–2.9 above, and in addition, all sentences of the form:[5]

2.10. $[\gamma(0) \land (\forall x)(\gamma(x) \supset \gamma(Sx))] \supset (\forall x)\gamma(x)$

An expression like 2.10, which represents infinitely many sentences intended to be axioms, is called an *axiom scheme*. Since the axiom set we have just given is clearly computable, it follows that *PA* is an axiomatizable theory. *Q* is of course finitely axiomatizable. As it turns out, *PA*, an extension of *Q*, is not finitely axiomatizable, although this is not at all obvious. It is routine to check that the standard model is a model of *PA*, from which we can conclude that *PA* is consistent, although any skeptic who seriously doubted the consistency of *PA* would hardly be convinced.

Terms are built from the constant symbol **0**, and variables by iterating the operations that proceed from terms μ, v to $S\mu$, to $\mu + v$, and to $\mu \times v$. Terms μ with no variables are called *constant terms*. In particular, with each natural number n is associated a constant term n^* (called a *numeral*) defined by the recursion:

$0^* = 0$; $(n + 1)^* = Sn^*$.

For a set $P \subseteq N^k$ of k-tuples of natural numbers, we write $\bar{P}$ for its complement $N^k - P$. P is *numerated* in a theory T by a formula α with k free variables if

$< m_1, m_2, \ldots, m_k > \in P$ *if and only if* $\vdash_T \alpha(m_1^*, m_2^*, \ldots, m_k^*)$.

P is *numerable* in T if there is a formula that numerates it in T. A formula α *binumerates* P in T if α numerates P and $\neg\alpha$ numerates $\bar{P}$ in T. P is *binumerable* in T if there is a formula that binumerates it in T. For a consistent theory T, this condition can be weakened:

Lemma 2.2 *Binumerability: if T is consistent, then the pair of conditions*

$< m_1, m_2, \ldots, m_k > \in P$ *implies* $\vdash_T \alpha(m_1^*, m_2^*, \ldots, m_k^*)$,

$< m_1, m_2, \ldots, m_k > \notin P$ *implies* $\vdash_T \neg\alpha(m_1^*, m_2^*, \ldots, m_k^*)$,

suffice for concluding that α binumerates P in T.

Proof The two "implies" need to be replaced by "if and only if." Now, if $\vdash_T \alpha(m_1^*, m_2^*, \ldots, m_k^*)$ while $< m_1, m_2, \ldots, m_k > \notin P$, then also

$\vdash_T \neg\alpha(m_1^*, m_2^*, \ldots, m_k^*)$

contradicting the consistency of T, and similarly for the other converse implication. $\square$

T is called ω-*inconsistent* if there is a sentence $(\exists x)\ \gamma$ such that $\vdash_T \neg\ \gamma(n^*)$ for each natural number n, but also $\vdash_T (\exists x)\ \gamma$. Note that at least one of these sentences must be false in the standard model of arithmetic. T is ω-*consistent* if it is not ω-*inconsistent*, while ω-consistent theories are obviously consistent.

We are going to prove two well-known theorems below:

Theorem A   *All listable sets are numerable in every ω-consistent extension of Q.*

Corollary   *All computable sets are binumerable in every ω-consistent extension of Q.*

Proof of Corollary   If S is computable, S and $\bar{S}$ are both listable. $\square$

Theorem B   *All computable sets are binumerable in every consistent extension of Q.*

Although the corollary to theorem A is a consequence of theorem B, the proof of theorem A is simpler than that of theorem B.

Theorem B is used in the proof (not presented here) that no consistent axiomatizable extension of Q is complete, from which it follows that, in particular, PA is incomplete. Early proofs of the incompleteness of PA made use of Gödel's beta function and therefore proceeded via a proof *in PA* of the Chinese remainder theorem. This is not only rather tedious when carefully carried out, but also is not of any use for Q, which is much too weak for the purpose. The DPRM theorem makes it all very easy.

2.7   Arithmetic in Q

With each constant term μ, we associate a value $|\mu|$ computed as follows:

$|0| = 0$

$|S\mu| = |\mu|+1$

$|\mu+v| = |\mu|+|v|$

$|\mu \times v| = |\mu|\cdot|v|$

In the propositions below, we show how to prove the simplest facts about the arithmetic of natural numbers in Q. We will write $\vdash$ to mean $\vdash_Q$.

Proposition 2.1   *If $m \neq n$, then $\vdash \neg(m^* = n^*)$.*

Proof Without loss of generality, assume $m > n$. The proof is by induction on n. If $n = 0$, then $n^* = 0$. Since $m > 0$, we can write $m^* = S\mu$ for some term μ. Using axiom 2.1 of Q, we have the result for $n = 0$. Assume the result known for $n = k$, and let $n = k + 1$. Since $m > k + 1 > 0$, we have

$$m^* = S(m - 1)^*; n^* = Sk^*.$$

Using axiom 2.2, we have

$$\vdash (m^* = n^*) \supset ((m-1)^* = k^*).$$

By induction hypothesis:

$$\vdash \neg ((m-1)^* = k^*),$$

which gives the result. $\square$

Proposition 2.2 $\vdash (m^* + n^*) = (m + n)^*.$

Proof For $n = 0$, this follows from axiom 2.3. Assuming the result for $n = k$, we get the result for $n = k + 1$ using axiom 2.4. $\square$

Proposition 2.3 $\vdash (m^* \times n^*) = (mn)^*.$

Proof Use induction on n, axioms 2.5 and 2.6, and proposition 2.2. $\square$

Proposition 2.4 *For any constant term* μ, $\vdash (\mu = |\mu|^*).$

Proof By induction on the length of μ. If this length is 1, then $\mu = 0$ and $|\mu|^* = 0$. Proceeding by induction, we need to consider the three cases,

$$\mu = S\nu \,; \mu = \nu + \eta \,; \mu = \nu \times \eta,$$

where the result can be assumed to hold for ν and η.

Case 1: $\mu = S\nu$: then, by induction hypothesis, $\vdash \nu = |\nu|^*$, from which the result follows, since $|\mu| = |\nu| + 1$.

Case 2: $\mu = (\nu + \eta)$: the result follows from proposition 2.2.

Case 3: $\mu = (\nu \times \eta)$: the result follows from proposition 2.3. $\square$

Proposition 2.5 $\vdash (\forall x)(x \le x).$

Proof By axiom 2.9,

$$\vdash (\forall x)(x \le x \vee x \le x). \quad \square$$

Proposition 2.6 $\vdash (\forall x)(0 \leq x)$.

Proof It follows from axioms 2.7 and 2.9 and proposition 2.5. □

Proposition 2.7 *The formula $x \leq y$ binumerates in Q the set*

$\{(m,n) \mid m \leq n\}$.

Proof Since Q is consistent, by binumerability lemma 2.2, it will suffice to prove:

$m \leq n$ *implies* $\vdash (m^* \leq n^*)$

and

$m > n$ *implies* $\vdash \neg (m^* \leq n^*)$.

If $m = n$, the result follows from proposition 2.5. To complete the proof, we will use induction on m to show that if $m < n$, then

1. $\vdash (m^* \leq n^*)$,

and

2. $\vdash \neg (n^* \leq m^*)$.

For $m = 0$, proposition 2.6 implies (1). Since $n > 0$, using proposition 2.1, $\vdash \neg (n^* = 0)$. Using axiom 2.7 $\vdash \neg (n^* \leq 0)$, so (2) also holds.

Now assume the result known for $m = k$ and all n, and consider $m = k + 1 < n$. By induction hypothesis,

$\vdash \neg (n^* \leq k^*)$.

Using axiom 2.8,

$\vdash [(n^* \leq (k+1)^*) \supset [(n^* \leq k^*) \vee (n^* = (k+1)^*)]]$.

Using proposition 2.1,

$\vdash \neg (n^* \leq (k+1)^*)$,

which proves (2). Using axiom 2.9,

$\vdash [(n^* \leq (k+1)^*) \vee ((k+1)^* \leq n^*)]$,

which yields (1). □

Proposition 2.8 *For each $m \in N$, we have*

$\vdash (\forall x)[(x \leq m^*) \supset [(x = 0^*) \vee (x = 1^*) \vee \ldots \vee (x = m^*)]]$.

Proof For $m = 0$, this is just axiom 2.7. Assume the result known for $m = k$. By the induction hypothesis,

$$\vdash (\forall x)[(x \le k^*) \supset [(x = 0^*) \vee (x = 1^*) \vee \ ... \ \vee \ (x = k^*)]].$$

By axiom 2.8,

$$\vdash (\forall x)[(x \le (k+1)^*) \supset [(x \le k^*) \vee (x = (k+1)^*)]].$$

This gives the result. $\square$

Proposition 2.9 *Let α contain the single free variable x, and suppose that $\vdash \alpha(i^*)$, for $i = 0, 1, \ldots , m$. Then,*

$$\vdash (\forall x)[(x \le m^*) \supset \alpha].$$

Proof By proposition 2.8,

$$\vdash (\forall x)[(x \le m^*) \supset [(x = 0^*) \vee (x = 1^*) \vee \ ... \ \vee \ (x = m^*)]].$$

For $i = 0, 1, \ldots , m$, using the substitutivity of equality, we obtain

$$\vdash (\forall x)[(x = i^*) \supset [\alpha(i^*) \supset \alpha]].$$

The result follows. $\square$

Proposition 2.10 *Let α contain the single free variable x, and suppose that $\vdash \neg\alpha(i^*)$, for $i = 0, 1, \ldots , m$. Then,*

$$\vdash \neg(\exists x)[(x \le m^*) \wedge \alpha].$$

Proof By proposition 2.9,

$$\vdash (\forall x)[(x \le m^*) \supset \neg\alpha],$$

which is equivalent to the claimed result. $\square$

If μ is any term in the language of arithmetic, and $n \in N$, we define μ^n, itself a term, as follows:

$$\mu^0 = S0,$$

$$\mu^{n+1} = (\mu^n \times \mu).$$

Thus, if μ contains no variables, $|\mu^m| = |\mu|^m$.

Next let

$$w(u_1, u_2, \ \ldots \ , u_k) = cu_1^{m_1} u_2^{m_2} \ \ldots \ u_k^{m_k}$$

be a monomial with positive coefficient c. Then, we define a term μ_w, which "represents" w in the language of arithmetic:

$$\mu_w = c^* \times x_1^{m_1} \times x_2^{m_2} \times \ldots \times x_k^{m_k}.$$

Thus, for $r_1, r_2, \ldots, r_k \in N$, we have:

$$\mu_w(r_1, r_2, \ldots, r_k) = c^* \times (r_1^*)^{m_1} \times (r_2^*)^{m_2} \times \ldots \times (r_k^*)^{m_k}.$$

Now, let

$$A(u_1, u_2, \ldots, u_k) = w_1 + w_2 + \ldots + w_s$$

be a polynomial that is the sum of the monomials w_i with positive coefficients. Then, we define the term:

$$\mu_A = \mu_{w_1} + \mu_{w_2} + \ldots + \mu_{w_s}.$$

Then,

$$|\mu_A(r_1^*, r_2^*, \ldots, r_k^*)| = A(r_1, r_2, \ldots, r_k).$$

Given a polynomial equation with integer coefficients

$$p(u_1, u_2, \ldots, u_k) = 0,$$

it can be rewritten as

$$A(u_1, u_2, \ldots, u_k) = B(u_1, u_2, \ldots, u_k),$$

where A and B are each the sum of monomials with positive coefficients. Then we will see that the set

$$\{< r_1, r_2, \ldots, r_k > \in N \mid A(r_1, r_2, \ldots, r_k) = B(r_1, r_2, \ldots, r_k)\}$$

is binumerated in Q by the formula $\mu_A = \mu_B$.

To see this, first suppose that $r_1, r_2, \ldots, r_k \in N$ are such that

$$A(r_1, r_2, \ldots, r_k) = B(r_1, r_2, \ldots, r_k).$$

Then,

$$|\mu_A(r_1^*, r_2^*, \ldots, r_k^*)| = A(r_1, r_2, \ldots, r_k)$$

$$= A(r_1, r_2, \ldots, r_k)$$

$$= B(r_1, r_2, \ldots, r_k)$$

$$= |\mu_B(r_1^*, r_2^*, \ldots, r_k^*)|$$

Using proposition 2.4 above, we have:

$$\vdash \mu_A(r_1^*, r_2^*, \ \dots \ , r_k^*) = \mu_B(r_1^*, r_2^*, \ \dots \ , r_k^*).$$

Now, suppose that

$$A(r_1, r_2, \dots , r_k) \neq B(r_1, r_2, \dots , r_k).$$

Then,

$$| \mu_A(r_1^*, r_2^*, \ \dots \ , r_k^*) | \neq | \mu_B(r_1^*, r_2^*, \ \dots \ , r_k^*) |.$$

Using propositions 2.1 and 2.4 above, we have

$$\vdash \neg \ [\mu_A(r_1^*, r_2^*, \ \dots \ , r_k^*) = \mu_B(r_1^*, r_2^*, \ \dots \ , r_k^*)].$$

Thus, we have proved:

Proposition 2.11   *The set of solutions of a polynomial equation*

$$p(u_1, u_2, \dots , u_n) = 0$$

with integer coefficients is binumerable in Q.

  Continuing, we have:

Proposition 2.12   *Let*

$$M = \{< a_1, a_2, \ \dots \ , a_k, q > \in N^{k+1} \mid (\exists z)_{\leq q} \ (a_1, a_2, \ \dots \ , a_k, q, z) \in P\},$$

where P is binumerable in Q. Then M is binumerable in Q.

Proof   Let P be binumerated in Q by

$$\alpha(x_1, x_2, \ \dots \ , x_k, x_{k+1}, x_{k+2}),$$

where the notation exhibits the variables free in α, and similarly, let

$$\beta(x_1, x_2, \ \dots \ , x_k, x_{k+1}) = (\exists x_{k+2})[(x_{k+2} \leq x_{k+1}) \wedge \alpha(x_1, x_2, \ \dots \ , x_k, x_{k+1}, x_{k+2})].$$

We claim that β binumerates M in Q.

  First suppose that $(a_1, a_2, \dots , a_k, q) \in M$. Then, there is a number $r \leq q$ such that $(a_1^*, a_2^*, \ \dots \ , a_k^*, q^*, r^*) \in P$. By proposition 2.7 above, $\vdash (r^* \leq q^*)$. Also,

$$\vdash \alpha(a_1^*, a_2^*, \ \dots \ , a_k^*, q^*, r^*).$$

Hence,

$$\vdash \beta(a_1^*, a_2^*, \ \dots \ , a_k^*, q^*).$$

Next suppose that $(a_1, a_2, \ldots, a_k, q) \notin M$. Then, for $i = 0, 1, \ldots r$, we have

$(a_1, a_2, \ldots, a_k, q, i) \notin P$,

and therefore

$\vdash \neg \alpha(a_1^*, a_2^*, \ldots, a_k^*, q^*, i^*)$.

Using proposition 2.10, we get

$\vdash \neg \beta(a_1^*, a_2^*, \ldots, a_k^*, q^*)$. □

It will be useful to employ the DPRM theorem in the following form:

If $S \subseteq N^k$ is listable, then there is a polynomial with integer coefficients $p(a_1, a_2, \ldots, a_k, u_1, u_2, \ldots, u_n)$ such that

$< r_1, r_2, \ldots, r_k > \in S \Leftrightarrow (\exists z)(\exists u_1, \ldots, u_n)_{\leq z}[p(r_1, r_2, \ldots, r_k, u_1, u_2, \ldots, u_n) = 0]$.

This form of the DPRM theorem is obtained by simply taking z to be the maximum of the numbers $u_1, u_2, \ldots, u_n$ corresponding to a given $< r_1, r_2, \ldots, r_k > \in S$. Using it together with propositions 2.11 and 2.12, we obtain:

Proposition 2.13   *If $S \subseteq N^k$ is listable, then there is a set $P \subseteq N^{k+1}$ that is binumerable in Q such that*

$S = \{< r_1, r_2, \ldots, r_k > \in N^k \mid (\exists z)[< r_1, r_2, \ldots, r_k, z > \in P]\}$.

Using proposition 2.13, it is easy to provide our:

Proof of Theorem A   Let T be an ω-consistent extension of Q, let $S \subseteq N^k$ be listable, and let P be as in proposition 2.13. So P is binumerated in Q by a formula $\alpha(x_1, x_2, \ldots, x_k, x_{k+1})$. By binumerability lemma 2.2, the same formula also binumerates P in T. Let

$\beta(x_1, x_2, \ldots, x_k) = (\exists x_{k+1})\alpha(x_1, x_2, \ldots, x_k, x_{k+1})$

We will prove that β numerates S in T.
First suppose that $(r_1, r_2, \ldots, r_k) \in S$. So there is a number q such that $(r_1, r_2, \ldots, r_k, q) \in P$. Therefore,

$\vdash_T \alpha(r_1^*, r_2^*, \ldots, r_k^*, q^*)$.

Hence,

$\vdash_T \beta(r_1^*, r_2^*, \ldots, r_k^*)$.

Conversely, let

$$\vdash_T \beta(r_1^*, r_2^*, \ldots, r_k^*)$$

for some $(r^1, r^2, \ldots, r^k) \in N^k$. Then, because T is ω-consistent, there is a number q such that the sentence $\neg \alpha(r_1^*, r_2^*, \ldots, r_k^*, q^*)$ is not provable in T. Therefore $(r_1, r_2, \ldots, r_k, q) \in P$, and finally $(r_1, r_2, \ldots, r_k) \in S$. $\square$

2.8 The Rosser–Smullyan Theorem

Our proof of theorem B will make use of an application by Raymond Smullyan of a famous device due to J. B. Rosser. We continue to write $\vdash$ with no subscript for $\vdash_Q$.

Rosser–Smullyan Theorem   *Let $U, V \subseteq N^k$ be listable and such that $U \cap V = \emptyset$. Then there is a formula $\gamma(x_1, x_2, \ldots, x_k)$, such that for all $< r_1, r_2, \ldots, r_k > \in N^k$:*

$$< r_1, r_2, \ldots, r_k > \in U \Rightarrow \vdash \gamma(r_1^*, r_2^*, \ldots, r_k^*)$$

$$< r_1, r_2, \ldots, r_k > \in V \Rightarrow \vdash \neg \gamma(r_1^*, r_2^*, \ldots, r_k^*).$$

Proof   Using proposition 2.13, there are sets $A, B \subseteq N^{k+1}$ that are binumerable in Q such that:

$$< r_1, r_2, \ldots, r_k > \in U \Rightarrow < r_1, r_2, \ldots, r_k, a > \in A \quad \text{for some } a \in N$$

$$< r_1, r_2, \ldots, r_k > \in V \Rightarrow < r_1, r_2, \ldots, r_k, b > \in B \quad \text{for some } b \in$$

Let A, B be binumerated in Q by $\alpha(x_1, \ldots, x_k, x_{k+1})$, $\beta(x_1, \ldots, x_k, x_{k+1})$, respectively. Write $\delta(x_1, \ldots, x_k, x_{k+1})$ for the formula:

$$\alpha(x_1, \ldots, x_k, x_{k+1}) \wedge \neg (\exists x_{k+2})[x_{k+2} \leq x_{k+1} \wedge \beta(x_1, \ldots, x_k, x_{k+2})]$$

and $\gamma(x_1, \ldots, x_k)$ for the formula $(\exists x_{k+1})\delta(x_1, \ldots, x_k, x_{k+1})$.
  Below we use the abbreviations

$\vec{r}$ for $r_1, r_2, \ldots, r_k$

$\vec{r}^*$ for $r_1^*, r_2^*, \ldots, r_k^*$.

Now suppose that $< \vec{r} > \in U$. Then, $< \vec{r}, a > \in A$ for some $a \in N$, and (since U and V are disjoint), $< \vec{r}, q > \notin B$ for all $q \in N$. So $\vdash \alpha(\vec{r}^*, a)$ and for all $q \in N, \vdash \neg \beta(\vec{r}^*, q)$. By proposition 2.10,

$$\vdash \neg (\exists x_{k+1})[(x_{k+1} \leq a^*) \wedge \beta(\vec{r}^*, x_{k+1})].$$

Therefore $\vdash \delta(\vec{r}^*, a^*)$, and then $\vdash \gamma(\vec{r}^*)$.

Next suppose that $<\vec{r}> \in V$. Then $<\vec{r},b> \in B$ for some $b \in N$, and (since U and V are disjoint), $(\vec{r},q) \notin A$ for all $q \in N$. Thus,

$$\vdash \beta(\vec{r}^{*},b^{*}), \tag{2.1}$$

and using proposition 2.10,

$$\vdash \;\; \neg\,(\exists x_{k+1})[(x_{k+1} \leq b^{*}) \wedge \alpha(\vec{r}^{*},x_{k+1})]. \tag{2.2}$$

To obtain $\vdash \neg\, \gamma(\vec{r}^{*})$ we take $\gamma(\vec{r}^{*})$ as a premise and, using first-order logic, show that it leads to a contradiction. This premise is $(\exists x_{k+1})\delta(\vec{r}^{*},x_{k+1})$. Letting c be a "witness" we get $\delta(\vec{r}^{*},c)$. By the properties of $\wedge$, we have

$$\alpha(\vec{r}^{*},c) \tag{2.3}$$

and

$$\neg\,(\exists x_{k+2})[(x_{k+2} \leq c) \wedge \beta(\vec{r}^{*},x_{k+2})].$$

This last yields $\neg\,[(b^{*} \leq c) \wedge \beta(\vec{r}^{*},b^{*})]$. Using (2.1) we have $\neg\,(b^{*} \leq c)$. Now, by axiom 2.9 of Q,

$$\vdash (b^{*} \leq c) \vee (c \leq b^{*})$$

So we have $c \leq b*$. Combining this with (2.3) yields $(c \leq b^{*}) \wedge \alpha(\vec{r}^{*},c)$ and therefore $(\exists x_{k+1})[(x_{k+1} \leq b^{*}) \wedge \alpha(\vec{r}^{*},x_{k+1})]$. This contradicts (2.2); therefore, the proof is complete. $\square$

We conclude with:

Proof of Theorem B   Let $S \subseteq N^{k}$ be computable, and let T be a consistent extension of Q. Since S and $\bar{S}$ are both listable, the Rosser-Smullyan theorem furnishes a formula γ such that

$$<r_1,r_2, \ldots ,r_k> \in S \Rightarrow \vdash_{Q} \gamma(r_1^{*},r_2^{*}, \ldots ,r_k^{*})$$

$$<r_1,r_2, \ldots ,r_k> \notin S \Rightarrow \vdash_{Q} \neg\, \gamma(r_1^{*},r_2^{*}, \ldots ,r_k^{*}).$$

Since T is an extension of Q, we have

$$<r_1,r_2, \ldots ,r_k> \in S \Rightarrow \vdash_{T} \gamma(r_1^{*},r_2^{*}, \ldots ,r_k^{*})$$

$$<r_1,r_2, \ldots ,r_k> \notin S \Rightarrow \vdash_{T} \neg\, \gamma(r_1^{*},r_2^{*}, \ldots ,r_k^{*}).$$

Since T is consistent, by the binumerability lemma 2.2 this suffices. $\square$

Notes

1. Kreisel, Georg. 1962. Review of "Davis, Martin, Putnam, Hilary and Robinson, Julia. The decision problem for exponential Diophantine equations." *Mathematical Reviews* 24A:573.

2. Also known as Matiyasevich's theorem, or the MRDP theorem. It was Yuri Matiyasevich himself who proposed the name "DPRM," which acknowledges the contributions of the four of us.

3. The symbol ≤, which we have included in the language of arithmetic for convenience, is often introduced instead by defining $x \leq y$ as $(\exists z)[x + z = y]$.

4. When ≤ is introduced by definition as explained above, the final three axioms can be replaced by the single axiom $\neg(0 = Sx)$.

5. The notation is meant to indicate that a free variable in γ is successively replaced by: $0, x, Sx, x$.

3 About and around Computing over the Reals

Solomon Feferman

3.1 One Theory or Many?

In 2004 a very interesting and readable article by Lenore Blum, entitled "Computing over the Reals: Where Turing meets Newton," appeared in the *Notices of the American Mathematical Society*. It explained a basic model of computation over the reals developed by Blum, Shub, and Smale (1989)—referred to herein as the BSS model—and subsequently exposited at length in their influential book, *Complexity and Real Computation* (1997), coauthored with Felipe Cucker. The "Turing" in the title of Blum's article refers of course to Alan Turing, famous for his explication of the notion of mechanical computation on discrete data such as the integers. The "Newton" there has to do to with the well-known numerical method of Isaac Newton's for approximating the zeros of continuous functions under suitable conditions that is taken to be a paradigm of scientific computing. Finally, the meaning of "Turing meets Newton" in the title of Blum's article has another, more particular aspect: in connection with the problem of controlling errors in the numerical solution of linear equations and inversion of matrices, Turing in 1948 defined a notion of *condition* for the relation of changes in the output of a computation due to small changes in the input that is analogous to Newton's definition of the derivative.

The thrust of Blum's 2004 article was that the BSS model of computation on the reals is the appropriate foundation for scientific computing in general. By way of response, two years later another very interesting and equally readable article appeared in the *Notices*, this time by Mark Braverman and Stephen Cook (2006) entitled "Computing over the Reals: Foundations for Scientific Computing," in which the authors argued that the requisite foundation is provided by a quite different "bit computation" model, that is in fact *prima facie* incompatible with the BSS model. The bit computation model goes back to ideas from Stefan Banach and Stanislaw Mazur in the latter part of the 1930s, but the first publication was not made until Mazur (1963). In the meantime, the model was refined and improved by Andrzej Grzegorczyk (1955) and independently by Daniel Lacombe (1955a, b, c) in terms of a theory of recursively computable functionals of the sort familiar to logicians. Terminologically, something like "effective approximation computability" is preferable to "bit computability" as a name for this approach in its applications to analysis.[1]

There are functions that are computable in each of these two models of computation over the reals that are not computable in the other. For example, the exponential function is computable in the effective approximation model, but not in the BSS model. And in the latter—but not in the former—given a nontrivial polynomial p over the rationals, one can compute the function of x that is 1 just in case $p(x) = 0$ and is 0 otherwise. *Despite their incompatibility, is there any way that these can both be considered to be reasonable candidates for computation on the real numbers?* As we shall see, an obvious answer is provided very quickly by the observation that the BSS model may be considered to be given in terms of computation over the reals as an *algebraic structure*, while that of the effective approximation model can be given in terms of computation over the reals as a *topological structure* of a particular kind, or alternatively as a *second-order structure* over the rationals. But all such explanations presume a general theory of *computation over an arbitrary structure*.

After explaining the BSS and effective computation models, respectively, in sections 2 and 3 below, my main purpose here is to describe three theories of computation over (more or less) arbitrary structures in sections 4 and 5, the first due to Harvey Friedman, the second due to John Tucker and Jeffery Zucker, and the third due to the author, adapting earlier work of Richard Platek and Yiannis Moschovakis. Finally, and in part as an aside, I shall relate the effective approximation approach to the foundations of constructive analysis in its groundbreaking form due to Errett Bishop.

Before engaging in all that, let us return to the issue of computation over the reals as a foundation for *scientific computation*, aka *computational science* or *numerical analysis*. That subject is problem-oriented toward the development of techniques for such diverse tasks as solving systems of one or more linear and polynomial equations, interpolation from data, numerical integration and differentiation, determination of maxima and minima, optimization, and solutions of differential and integral equations. Though nowadays these techniques are formulated as programs to be carried out on actual computers—large and small—many of them predate the use of computers by hundreds of years (viz., Newton's method, Lagrange interpolation, Gaussian elimination, Euler's method, etc., etc.). The justification for particular techniques varies with the areas of application, but there are common themes that have to do with identifying the source and control of errors and with efficiency of computation. However, there is no concern in the literature on scientific computation with the underlying nature of computing over the reals as exact objects. For, in practice, those computations are made in "floating point arithmetic" using finite decimals with relatively few significant digits, for which computation per se simply reduces to computation with rational numbers.

Besides offering a theory of computation on the real numbers, the main emphasis in the articles of Blum (2004) and Braverman and Cook (2006) and the book by Blum et al. (1997) is on the relevance of their approaches to the subject of scientific computation in terms of measures of complexity. These sources use, among other things, analogs to the well-known P and NP classifications from the theory of discrete computation.[2] In addition to examples of complexity questions in numerical analysis, they are illustrated with more recent popular examples, such as those having to do with the degree of difficulty of deciding membership in the Mandlebrot set or various Julia sets. While complexity issues must certainly be taken into account in choosing between the various theories of computation over the reals on offer as a foundation for scientific computation, I take no position as to which of these is most appropriate for that purpose. Rather, my main aim here is to compare them on purely conceptual grounds.

3.2 The BSS Model

A brief but informative description is given in Blum (2004, 1028), while a detailed exposition is to be found in Blum et al. (1997), chapters 2 and 3, with the first of these chapters devoted to what is called the finite-dimensional case and the second to its extension to the infinite-dimensional case. As stated in these sources, the BSS definition makes sense for any ring or field A, not only the reals $\mathbb{R}$ and the complex numbers $\mathbb{C}$, and so on the face of it, it is an *algebraic* conception of computability. This is reflected in the fact that inputs to a machine for computing a given algorithm are unanalyzed entities in the algebra A, and that a basic admitted step in a computation procedure is to test whether two machine contents x and y are equal or not, and then to branch to further instructions accordingly. (In case A is ordered, one can also test similarly whether $x < y$ or not.) In the BSS description, an algorithmic procedure is given by a directed graph whose top node represents the input stage, and passage from a given node to a successor node is made either by a direct computation, which in the case of a ring is effected by a polynomial function (and in the case of a field by a rational function), or by a decision step whose branches may proceed to a new node or return to an earlier node. In the finite-dimensional case, the inputs are finite sequences of any fixed length, while in the infinite-dimensional case they are sequences of arbitrary length from A. The finite-dimensional case is illustrated by the Newton algorithm for $\mathbb{R}$ or $\mathbb{C}$ as follows: given a rational function f, to find a zero of f within a prescribed degree of accuracy $\varepsilon > 0$, one starts with an input x, and successively updates that by replacing x by

$x - f(x)/f'(x),$

until one reaches a value of x (if at all) for which $|f(x)| < \varepsilon$. The infinite-dimensional case is illustrated by a BSS algorithm to decide whether or not m given polynomials $f_1, \ldots, f_m$ in n variables over $\mathbb{C}$ have a common zero, where the procedure is to be described for n, m arbitrary; this is related in an essential way to the Hilbert Nullstellensatz of 1893.[3]

It is pointed out in Blum et al. (1997) that a BSS algorithm for the finite-dimensional case may be thought of more concretely in terms of register machines as a direct generalization of the notion due to Shepherdson and Sturgis (1963).[4] Actually, such a generalization to arbitrary fields was already made by Herman and Isard (1970). For the infinite-dimensional case, the BSS machine picture is treated instead as a form of a Turing machine with a two-way infinite tape whose squares may be occupied by elements of the ring or field A; the infinite tape allows for inputs consisting of sequences of arbitrary length. Alternatively, it could be treated as a register machine with so-called stack registers. Indeed, this falls under a very general adaptation of the register machine approach to arbitrary structures that was made by Friedman (1971); this will be described in section 3.4 below.

It may be seen that in the case of rings, respectively fields, only piecewise polynomial functions, respectively rational functions, are BSS computable. In particular, the Newton algorithm can only be applied to such. But one could add any continuous function f to the basic field structure and relativize the notion of BSS computable function to that. Of course, doing so affects the complexity questions that are of major concern in Blum et al. (1997). In the opposite direction, one may ask what BSS algorithms can actually be carried out on a computer. Tarski's decision procedure (1951) for the algebra of real numbers may be considered as a special case of such. Its centerpiece method reduces the question of whether or not a system of polynomial equations and inequalities in one variable with coefficients in $\mathbb{R}$ has a common solution, to a quantifier-free condition on the coefficients of the polynomials. On the face of it, Tarski's procedure runs in time complexity as a tower of exponentials. That was cut down considerably to doubly exponential upper bounds by George Collins in 1973 using a new method that he called cylindrical algebraic decomposition (CAD); Collins' original work and many relevant articles are to be found in the valuable source Caviness and Johnson (1998). The CAD algorithm has actually been implemented for computers by one of Collins' students, and in a modified form in the system *Mathematica*; that works in reasonable time for polynomials of relatively low degree. But in principle, Fischer and Rabin (1974; reprinted in Caviness and Johnson) give an EXPTIME lower bound of the form 2^{cn} for deciding for sentences of length n whether or not they are true in $\mathbb{R}$, no matter what algorithm is used; the same applies even with non-deterministic algorithms, such as via proof systems. They also showed that the "cut-point" by which EXPTIME sets in—that is, the least n_0 such that for all inputs of length $n \geq n_0$, at least 2^{cn} steps are needed—is not larger than the length of the given algorithm or axiom system for proofs. Thus real algebra is definitely infeasible on sufficiently large, though not exceptionally large inputs.

3.3   The Theory of Computability over $\mathbb{R}$ by Effective Approximation

In contrast to the BSS model, the effective approximation, or "bit computation," model of computation over the reals is an analytic theory, specific to $\mathbb{R}$, though the same idea can be generalized to complete separable metric spaces relative to an enumerated dense subset. There are actually two approaches to this model of computation: one that works with sequences approximating arguments and values, referred to here as S-effective approximation; and one that works by approximation of functions by polynomials, referred to as P-effective approximation. It turns out that these are equivalent.

To show that a real valued function $f: I \to \mathbb{R}$, where I is a finite or infinite interval, is computable by S-effective approximation, given any x in I as argument to f, one must work *not* with x but rather with an arbitrary *sequential representation of x*— that is, with a Cauchy sequence of rationals $\langle q_n \rangle_{n \in \mathbb{N}}$ which approaches x as its limit— in order to effectively determine another such sequence $\langle r_m \rangle_{m \in \mathbb{N}}$ that approaches $f(x)$ as limit.[5] The sequences in question are functions from $\mathbb{N}$ to $\mathbb{Q}$, and so the passage from $\langle q_n \rangle_{n \in \mathbb{N}}$ to $\langle r_m \rangle_{m \in \mathbb{N}}$ is given by a computable type-2 functional F. One can standardize the requirements here by restriction, for example, to dyadic rationals $q_n = \varphi(n)/2^n$, where

$\varphi: \mathbb{N} \to \mathbb{Z}$ is such that

$$|x - \varphi(n)/2^n| \leq 1/2^n \text{ for all } n. \tag{3.1}$$

In these terms, the requirement for S-effective approximation computability of f reduces to obtaining a computable functional $F: \mathbb{Z}^{\mathbb{N}} \to \mathbb{Z}^{\mathbb{N}}$, such that for any $\varphi: \mathbb{N} \to \mathbb{Z}$ satisfying (3.1) and for $F(\varphi) = \psi$, we have

$$(\forall n) |x - \varphi(n)/2^n| \leq 1/2^n \Rightarrow (\forall m) |f(x) - \psi(m)/2^m| \leq 1/2^m. \tag{3.2}$$

When this holds for all x in the domain of f, we say that F effectively represents f. This notion of computability of real functions is due independently to Grzegorczyk (1955) and Lacombe (1955a, b, c). It is illustrated in Braverman and Cook (2006) by proof of the bit-computability of $f(x) = e^x$ using its usual power series expansion, thus showing that for many such functions, one goes well beyond BSS computability over the reals in this model.

Using the effective correspondence of $\mathbb{Z}$ with $\mathbb{N}$, the preceding explanation of S-effective approximation computability of real functions reduces to the explanation from classical recursion theory of the notion of effectively computable functional $F\colon \mathbb{N}^{\mathbb{N}} \to \mathbb{N}^{\mathbb{N}}$. Write **T** for the class $\mathbb{N}^{\mathbb{N}}$ of all *total* functions from $\mathbb{N}$ to $\mathbb{N}$, and **P** for the class of all *partial* functions from $\mathbb{N}$ to $\mathbb{N}$. The original explanation of what is an effectively computable functional (of type 2 over N) was that given by Kleene (1952, 326) for $F\colon \boldsymbol{P} \to \boldsymbol{P}$, in terms of Herbrand-Gödel calculability from a suitable system of equations E, with a symbol for an arbitrary partial function φ and a symbol ψ for a function defined by E from φ. The idea is that for any φ in **P**, the values $\psi(m)$ can be calculated by the equational rules from E together with the diagram (i.e., formal graph) of φ. It follows immediately that any partial recursive F is monotonic in its arguments; that is, if φ and φ' are partial functions with φ' an extension of φ, then $F(\varphi')$ is an extension of $F(\varphi)$. Moreover, we have the continuity property that if $F(\varphi) = \psi$, then each value $\psi(n)$ depends only on a finite number of values of φ; that is, there is a finite subfunction φ_0 of φ such that if φ' is any extension of φ_0 and $\psi' = F(\varphi')$, then $\psi'(m) = \psi(m)$. Combining these facts, one has that $F(\varphi)$ is the union of $F(\varphi_0)$ for all finite $\varphi_0 \subseteq \varphi$. Kleene's main result for the partial recursive functionals is his ("first") recursion theorem, according to which each such F has a least fixed point, obtained by taking the union of all finite iterations of F starting with the empty function. An alternative approach to partial recursive functionals (that yields the same class as Kleene's) is via recursive operators, as exposited for example in Cutland (1980, chapter 10); it only presumes the notion of partial recursive function, independently of how that is defined.

Now the computable functionals $F\colon \boldsymbol{T} \to \boldsymbol{T}$ may be defined to be those partial recursive functionals F whose value for each total function φ is a total function $F(\varphi)$. (It is not enough to restrict a partial recursive functional to **T**, since its value on a total argument f may still be partial.) But there are several other ways of defining which are the computable functionals $F\colon \boldsymbol{T} \to \boldsymbol{T}$ without appealing to the notion of partial recursive functional. One is from Grzegorczyk (1955) by means of a direct generalization of Kleene's schemata for the general recursive functions using both primitive recursion and the least number operator μ. Grzegorczyk deals with $F(\varphi)$ $(\underline{x})$, where $\underline{\varphi} = \varphi_1, \dots, \varphi_j$ is a sequence (possibly empty) of total functions, and $\underline{x}$ is a sequence $x_1, \dots, x_k$ of numerical arguments with $k \geq 1$. For simplicity, we shall write $F(\underline{\varphi}, \underline{x})$ for Grzegorczyk's $F(\underline{\varphi})(\underline{x})$. These functionals reduce to functions of natural numbers $F(\underline{x})$ when $j = 0$. A basic computable functional F taken in the schemata is that for application; that is, $F(\varphi, x) = \varphi(x)$. Then, in addition to the primitive recursive schemata[6] relativized uniformly to function arguments $\underline{\varphi}$, one has a scheme for the μ (minimum) operator formulated as follows.

Suppose given computable $F(\underline{\varphi}, \underline{x}, y)$ such that $\forall \underline{\varphi}, \underline{x} \, \exists y \, [F(\underline{\varphi}, \underline{x}, y) = 0]$; then the functional G defined by

$$G(\varphi, \underline{x}) = \mu y \, [F(\varphi, \underline{x}, y) = 0]$$

is computable.

An equivalent definition of computable functionals from total functions to total functions has been given by Weirauch (2000) via uniform oracle Turing machines, called by him the type 2 theory of effectivity (TTE). In my view, Kleene's notion of partial recursive functional is the fundamental one, in that it specializes to Grzegor-czyk's (or Weirauch's) in the following sense: if F is a partial recursive functional F: $P \to P$, and $F|T$—the restriction of F to T—maps T to T, then $F|T$ is definable by the Grzegorczyk schemata, as may easily be shown.[7]

It is a consequence of the continuity of partial recursive functionals that if F effectively represents a real-valued function f on its domain I, then f is continuous at each point of I. In particular, take I to contain 0 and consider the function f on I that is 0 on x just in case $x < 0$ or $x > 0$ and otherwise is 1; since f is not continuous on I, it is not computable in the S-approximation sense. Thus, unlike the BSS model, the order relation on $\mathbb{R}$ is not computable. In general, in the case that I is a finite closed interval, if f is computable on I in the S-effective approximation sense, one has that it is effectively uniformly continuous relative to the sequential limit representations of its arguments (Grzegorczyk 1955, 192). As we shall see, this connects with the Bishop constructive approach to continuous functions, to be discussed in the final section.

Let us turn now to the notion of P-effective approximation computability due to Marian B. Pour-El (1974). That is suggested by the Weierstrass approximation theorem, according to which every continuous function on a closed interval I is uniformly approximable by a sequence of polynomials over $\mathbb{Q}$. There is an effective enumeration of all possible polynomials $p_n(x)$ over $\mathbb{Q}$ with non-zero rational coefficients. Then, Pour-El defines f with domain I to be computable by P-effective approximation if there are recursive functions φ and ψ such that for all $M > 0$, all $n \geq \psi(M)$, and all x in I,

$$|f(x) - p_{\varphi(n)}(x)| \leq 1/2^M . \tag{3.3}$$

She extends this to f defined on $\mathbb{R}$, by asking for a recursive function φ of two variables such that for all k, and all M, n as above and all x in $[-k, k]$,

$$|f(\mathrm{x}) - p_{\varphi(k,n)}(x)| \leq 1/2^M . \tag{3.4}$$

It is proved in Pour-El and Caldwell (1975) that P-effective computability is equivalent to S-effective computability of functions on any closed interval I and on the full real line $\mathbb{R}$. Slightly more general results with an alternative proof are given in Shepherdson (1976). Though the notions of P-effective computability are simpler than those of S-effective computability, Shepherdson remarks that insofar as actual computation is concerned, the values are still inescapably given via approximating sequences of rationals to reals.

3.4 The View from Generalized Recursion Theory; Two Theories of Computability on Arbitrary Structures

Beginning in the 1960s, and continuing through the 1970s and beyond, there was much work on generalizations of recursion theory to arbitrary structures. One of these generalizations was made by Harvey Friedman (1971) by adaptation of the register machine approach, as explained below.[8] As will be seen, this approach to computability over arbitrary structures considerably antedates and comprehends the BSS notions.

By a (first-order) structure, or algebra $\mathfrak{A}$, is meant one of the form

$$\mathfrak{A} = (A, c_1, \dots, c_j, f_1, \dots, f_k, R_1, \dots, R_m), \tag{3.5}$$

where A is a non-empty set, each c_i is a member of A, each f_i is a partial function of one or more arguments from A to A, and each R_i is a relation of one or more arguments on A.[9] For nontriviality, both k and m are not zero. The signature of $\mathfrak{A}$ is given by the triple (j, k, m) and the arity of each f_i and each R_i. Of special note is that the test for equality of elements of A is *not* assumed as one of the basic operations; rather, if equality is to be a basic test, that is to be included as one of the relations R_i. A *finite algorithmic procedure* (fap) π on $\mathfrak{A}$ is given by a finite list of instructions $I_1, I_2, \dots, I_t$ for some t, with I_1 being the initial instruction and I_t the terminal one. The machine has register names $r_0, r_1, r_2, \dots$, though only a finite number are needed for any given computation, namely those mentioned in π; the register r_0 is reserved for the output. The r_i may also be thought of as variables. The fap π may be used to calculate a partial n-ary function f on A^n to A for any n. Given an input $(x_1, \dots, x_n)$, one enters x_i into register r_i, and proceeds to I_1. Each instruction other than I_t has one of the following four forms:

$r_a := r_b \,; r_a := c_i \,; r_a := f_i(r_{b1}, \dots, r_{bj})$, for j-ary f_i; if $R_i(r_{b1}, \dots, r_{bj})$ then go to I_u, else I_v,
     for j-ary R_i. $\tag{3.6}$

In the first three cases, one goes to the next instruction after executing it. The computation terminates only if the third instruction is defined at each stage where it is called and if one eventually lands in I_t, at which point the content of register r_0 is the value of $f(x_1, \dots, x_n)$. An n-ary relation R is decidable by a fap π if its characteristic function is computable by π. The class of fap computable partial functions on $\mathfrak{A}$ is denoted by **FAP**$(\mathfrak{A})$.

For the structure $\mathfrak{N} = (\mathbb{N}, 0, Sc, Pd, =)$, where $\mathbb{N}$ is the set of natural numbers and *Sc* and *Pd* are, respectively, the successor and predecessor operations (taking $Pd(0) = 0$), **FAP**($\mathfrak{N}$) is equal to the class of partial recursive functions. For general structures $\mathfrak{A}$, Friedman (1971) also introduced the notion of *finite algorithmic procedure with counting*, in which certain registers are reserved for natural numbers and one can perform the operations and tests on the contents of those registers that go with the structure $\mathfrak{N}$. Then **FAPC**($\mathfrak{A}$) is used to denote the partial functions on A computable by means of such procedures.

The notion of finite algorithmic procedure is directly generalized to many-sorted structures

$$\mathfrak{A} = (A_1, \ldots, A_n, c_1, \ldots, c_j, f_1, \ldots, f_k, R_1, \ldots, R_m), \tag{3.7}$$

with the arity modified accordingly, while each register comes with a sort index limiting which elements can be admitted as its contents. In particular, **FAPC**($\mathfrak{A}$) can be identified with **FAP**($\mathfrak{A}, \mathfrak{N}$), where ($\mathfrak{A}, \mathfrak{N}$) denotes the structure $\mathfrak{A}$ augmented by that for $\mathfrak{N}$. A further extension of Friedman's notions was made by Moldestad, Stoltenberg-Hansen, and Tucker (1980a, 1980b), with *stack registers* that may contain finite sequences of elements of any one of the basic domains A_i, including the empty sequence. The basic operations for such a register are *pop* (remove the top element of a stack) and *push* (add the contents of one of the registers of type A_i). This leads to the notion of what is computable by *finite algorithmic procedures with stacks*, **FAPS**($\mathfrak{A}$), where we take the structure $\mathfrak{A}$ to contain with each domain A_i the domain $A_i{}^*$ of all finite sequences of elements of A_i, and with operations corresponding to *pop* and *push*. If we want to be able to calculate the length n of a stack and the qth element of a stack, we need also to have the structure $\mathfrak{N}$ included. This leads to the notion of *finite algorithmic procedure with stacks and counting,* whose computable partial functions are denoted by **FAPCS**($\mathfrak{A}$). In the case of the structure $\mathfrak{N}$, by any one of the usual primitive recursive codings of finite sequences of natural numbers, we have

$$\textbf{FAP}(\mathfrak{N}) = \textbf{FAPC}(\mathfrak{N}) = \textbf{FAPS}(\mathfrak{N}) = \textbf{FAPCS}(\mathfrak{N}). \tag{3.8}$$

Trivially, in general for any structure $\mathfrak{A}$ we have the inclusions,

$$\textbf{FAP}(\mathfrak{A}) \subseteq \textbf{FAPC}(\mathfrak{A}) \subseteq \textbf{FAPCS}(\mathfrak{A}), \text{ and} \tag{3.9}$$
$$\textbf{FAP}(\mathfrak{A}) \subseteq \textbf{FAPS}(\mathfrak{A}) \subseteq \textbf{FAPCS}(\mathfrak{A}).$$

It is proved in Moldestad, Stoltenberg-Hansen, and Tucker (1980b) that for each of these inclusions there is a structure $\mathfrak{A}$ which makes that inclusion strict.

Consider the structure of real numbers as an ordered field,

$$\mathfrak{R} = (\mathbb{R}, 0, 1, +, -, \times, {}^{-1}, =, <).$$

It is stated in Friedman and Mansfield (1992, 298) that "with a little programming" the **FAP**($\Re$) functions are exactly the same as the BSS functions computable in the finite-dimensional case, and the **FAPS**($\Re$) functions are exactly the same as the BSS functions computable in the infinite-dimensional case. It also follows from Friedman and Mansfield (1992, 300) that **FAPS**($\Re$) = **FAPCS**($\Re$), because $\mathfrak{N}$ can be embedded in $\Re$. Appropriate generalizations of these results hold for arbitrary rings and fields $\mathfrak{A}$, ordered or unordered.

An alternative approach to computability over arbitrary structures developed by John Tucker and Jeffery Zucker over a number of years, is provided in their very usefully detailed expository piece, Tucker and Zucker (2000); this uses definition by schemata or procedural statements rather than machines. Their approach works over many-sorted algebras

$$\mathfrak{A} = (A_1, \dots, A_n, c_1, \dots, c_j, f_1, \dots, f_k), \tag{3.10}$$

where the f_i may be partial. A *standard structure* $\mathfrak{A}$ is one that includes the structure $\mathfrak{B}$ with domain $\{t, f\}$ and basic Boolean functions as its operations. Then relations are treated as (possibly partial) functions into $\{t, f\}$, and branching on a relation is executed via the *if … then … else* command. The basic notion of computability for standard algebras is given by *"while" schemata* generated by the following rules (Tucker and Zucker 2000, 362) for procedure statements S:

$$S:: = \text{skip} \mid x: = t \mid S_1; S_2 \mid \text{if } b \text{ then } S_1 \text{ else } S_2 \mid \text{while } b \text{ do } S, \tag{3.11}$$

where "b" is a Boolean term. The set of partial functions computable on $\mathfrak{A}$ by means of these rules or schemata is denoted by **While**($\mathfrak{A}$). Then, to deal with computability with counting, Tucker and Zucker simply expand the algebra $\mathfrak{A}$ to the algebra ($\mathfrak{A}$, $\mathfrak{N}$). To incorporate finite sequences for each domain A_i, they make a *further* expansion of that to $\mathfrak{A}^*$. This leads to the following notions of computability over $\mathfrak{A}$: **While**$^{\mathfrak{N}}$($\mathfrak{A}$) and **While***($\mathfrak{A}$), given simply by **While**($\mathfrak{A}$, $\mathfrak{N}$) and **While**($\mathfrak{A}^*$), respectively. The following result is stated in Tucker and Zucker (2000, 487) for any standard algebra $\mathfrak{A}$:

$$\textbf{While}(\mathfrak{A}) = \textbf{FAP}(\mathfrak{A}), \textbf{While}^{\mathfrak{N}}(\mathfrak{A}) = \textbf{FAPC}(\mathfrak{A}), \text{ and} \tag{3.12}$$
$$\textbf{While}^*(\mathfrak{A}) = \textbf{FAPCS}(\mathfrak{A}).$$

In other words, we have a certain robustness of computability in the **While*** sense. Tucker and Zucker (1988) present a number of arguments in favor of a generalized Church-Turing thesis for computability, according to which the functions that are effectively computable on a many-sorted algebra $\mathfrak{A}$ in the informal sense are precisely the functions that are **While*** computable on $\mathfrak{A}$; see also Tucker and Zucker (2000, 493ff.) for a briefer sketch of these arguments.

So far, we are still dealing with essentially algebraic notions of computability. To extend the **While** approaches to notions of computability on the reals, it would seem that topological considerations must be brought to bear. This is done in a more general setting in section 7 of Tucker and Zucker (2000, 451–78). It is more difficult to describe informally the several ways this is carried out, so I shall simply give the names of the notions introduced there, with the hope that they at least indicate what is involved. First of all, the structures $\mathfrak{A} = (A, \dots)$ dealt with are *topological partial algebras*, where the partiality essentially has to do with the Boolean-valued functions of equality and—in the case of $\mathbb{R}$—order; as total functions these are discontinuous, so one must replace them by partial functions that are undefined at (x, y) in A when $x = y$ and—in the case of $\mathbb{R}$—when neither $x < y$ nor $y < x$. If the other basic functions on A are taken to be continuous, then so also are all the **While*** computable functions. That is then specialized to *metric partial algebras*, which are used to explain *effectively uniform While, resp. While*,* and then *approximable computability* on $\mathfrak{A}$ and *effective Weierstrass approximable computability* on $\mathfrak{A}$; these three notions are shown to be equivalent for suitable $\mathfrak{A}$ (Tucker and Zucker 2000, 473). The Weierstrass notion is a generalization of Pour-El's P-computability described above. When further specialized to functions on I to $\mathbb{R}$, where I is a closed interval, they are further shown (474) to be equivalent to Grzegorczyk-Lacombe computability; that is, S-effective computability as described above.[10] Thus the notions of **While** and **While*** computability serve to subsume under a single framework the notions of computability in the BSS sense with those computable in the effective approximation sense.

Another framework from generalized recursion theory that does not require direct appeal to topological notions for the two notions of computability on the real numbers is provided in the next section.

3.5 The Higher Type Approach to Computation on Arbitrary Structures

From the schematic point of view, computable functions are generated from given functions by explicit definition and by recursion; that is, definition of a function in terms of itself. Abstractly, recursion is given by a functional equation, $f = F(f)$, which determines a unique function f as the least fixed point (LFP) of F only if F is monotonic; moreover, the LFP of F is in general a partial function. (For reasons that will be seen below, we now use "f," "g," ... for partial function arguments of functionals in place of "φ," "ψ," ... as was done in section 3.3 above.) But then one has to ask where F comes from if it is not itself explicitly generated; that would require determining it as the LFP of a higher type operator G, and so on. This idea formed the underpinning of Richard Platek's definition of computability over fairly arbitrary structures $\mathfrak{A}$ in his famous (but regrettably never published) Stanford PhD dissertation (Platek 1966), in terms of a hierarchy of monotonic partial functionals of arbitrary finite type over the domains of $\mathfrak{A}$. That allows one to start not only with given functions over $\mathfrak{A}$ but also given functionals in that hierarchy. For the applications that concern us here, it would be sufficient to start with functionals of type level $\leq$ 2 over the domains of $\mathfrak{A}$. Platek showed that in that case, everything of type level ≤ 2 that can be generated via recursion in higher types from such initial data can already be generated via explicit definition and LFP definition with F of type level equal to 2.

Yiannis Moschovakis also took the LFP approach restricted to functionals of type level ≤ 2 in his explanation of the notion of algorithm over arbitrary structures in his papers (Moschovakis 1984, 1989), featuring simultaneous LFP definitions, though those can be eliminated in favor of single LFP definitions of the above form. Both the Platek and Moschovakis approaches are *extensional* in a sense to be described below. In order to tie that up both with computation over abstract data types and with Bishop's approach to constructive mathematics, in a pair of papers (Feferman 1992a, 1992b), I extended the use of LFP schemata to cover *intensional* situations, by requiring each basic domain A_i of $\mathfrak{A}$ to be equipped with an equivalence relation $=_i$ that the functions and functionals must preserve.[11] But unlike the approach to computation over $\mathbb{R}$ taken in these papers, in which real numbers are dealt with as one of the basic domains, I here treat them as genuinely type 1 objects, via functions on $\mathbb{N}$ representing Cauchy sequences of rational numbers. For simplicity, I will reserve description of the intensional approach to the case of computation over $\mathbb{N}$, so that, in effect, each $=_i$ is taken to be the identity relation; but intensionality has to be revisited for type 1 objects, as will be explained below.

In more detail, this is how the development proceeds for what I call *abstract computation procedures* (ACPs) over an algebra

$$\mathfrak{A} = (A_0, A_1, \ldots, A_k, F_0, \ldots, F_m), \qquad\qquad (3.13)$$

where each A_i is non-empty and the F_js are individuals, functions, or functionals of type level 2 over the A_i satisfying a monotonicity condition to be explained below; and A_0 is fixed to be the booleans $\{t, f\}$. We use letters $f, g, h, \ldots$ to range over partial functions of arbitrary many-sorted arities given by arguments ranging over some finite product, possibly empty, of the A_is with values in some A_j; in case the product is empty, such f is simply identified with an element of A_j. The arity of f is determined by a pair $\sigma = (\underline{i}, j)$, where $\underline{i} = (i_1, \ldots, i_v)$ lists the sorts of the product domain. Given f of arity σ, $\underline{x} = (x_1, \ldots, x_v)$ of arity $\underline{i}$, and y of sort j, we write $f(\underline{x}) \simeq y$ when $f(\underline{x}) \downarrow$ (i.e., $f(\underline{x})$ is defined) and the value of $f(\underline{x})$ is y. Given f, g of arity $(\underline{i}, j)$ we write $f \subseteq g$ if whenever $f(\underline{x}) \simeq y$ then $g(\underline{x}) \simeq y$.

We can now turn to the functionals (which may reduce to functions or individuals), for which we use the letters $F, G, H, \dots$. These have both a sequence $\underline{f} = (f_1, \dots, f_\mu)$ of partial function arguments of arities $\underline{\sigma} = (\sigma_1, \dots, \sigma_\mu)$, and individual arguments $\underline{x} = (x_1, \dots, x_\nu)$ of arity $\underline{i}$, and have values $F(\underline{f}, \underline{x})$ in a specified domain A_j when defined; the arity of such F is given by the triple $(\underline{\sigma}, \underline{i}, j)$. We allow $\mu = 0$, in which case F reduces to a partial function of arity $(\underline{i}, j)$; we further allow $\nu = 0$ as above, in which case it reduces to an element of A_j when defined. Given $\underline{f}, \underline{g}$ of arity $\underline{\sigma}$, write $\underline{f} \subseteq \underline{g}$, if each $f_\xi \subseteq g_\xi$; then F is said to be *monotonic* if whenever $\underline{f} \subseteq \underline{g}$ and $F(\underline{f}, \underline{x}) \simeq y$ then $F(\underline{g}, \underline{x}) \simeq y$. This is automatically the case when there are no function arguments. The basic assumption on the structure $\mathfrak{A}$ above is that each F_k is monotonic for $k = 0, \dots, m$. We further assume that the basic Boolean functions corresponding to conjunction and negation are among these.

Suppose given monotonic $G(g, \underline{w})$ with a single function argument g of arity $\sigma = (\underline{i}, j)$ where $\underline{w}$ is of arity $\underline{i}$. Then for any g, the function $\lambda\underline{w}.G(g, \underline{w})$ is again of arity σ. Let $\Gamma_G(g) = \lambda\underline{w}.G(g, \underline{w})$; in other words, $\Gamma_G = \lambda g \lambda\underline{w}.G(g, \underline{w})$. Then $\mathrm{LFP}(\Gamma_G)$ is defined to be the unique function h such that

$$\Gamma_G(h) = h, \text{ and if } \Gamma_G(g) = g \text{ then } h \subseteq g. \tag{3.14}$$

We can now list the schemata for ACPs $F, G, H, \dots$ over $\mathfrak{A}$ as follows:

I. (Initial functionals) $F(\underline{f}, \underline{x}) \simeq F_l(\underline{f}, \underline{x})$ for $l = 0, \dots, m$
II. (Identity functions) $F(x) = x$
III. (Application functionals) $F(f, \underline{x}) \simeq f(\underline{x})$
IV. (Conditional definition) $F(\underline{f}, \underline{x}, b) \simeq [\text{if } b = t \text{ then } G(\underline{f}, \underline{x}) \text{ else } H(\underline{f}, \underline{x})]$
V. (Structural) $F(\underline{f}, \underline{x}) \simeq G(\underline{f}_\rho, \underline{x}_\tau)$
VI. (Individual substitution) $F(\underline{f}, \underline{x}) \simeq G(\underline{f}, \underline{x}, H(\underline{f}, \underline{x}))$
VII. (Function substitution) $F(\underline{f}, \underline{x}) \simeq G(\underline{f}, \lambda\underline{u}.H(\underline{f}, \underline{x}, \underline{u}), \underline{x})$
VIII. (Least fixed point) $F(\underline{f}, \underline{x}, \underline{u}) \simeq \mathrm{LFP}[\lambda g \lambda\underline{w}.G(\underline{f}, g, \underline{x}, \underline{w})](\underline{u})$.

In IV of this list, "b" is of Boolean sort. In V, $\rho: \{1, \dots, \mu'\} \to \{1, \dots, \mu\}$ for some μ' and $\underline{f}_\rho = (f_{\rho(1)}, \dots, f_{\rho(\mu)})$; similarly for τ and $\underline{x}_\tau$. In all the other cases the arities are taken to be the appropriate ones. We denote by $\mathbf{ACP}(\mathfrak{A})$ the set of all F of type levels 0, 1, and 2 generated from the initial $F_0, \dots, F_m$ specified by $\mathfrak{A}$, and by $\mathbf{ACP}^1(\mathfrak{A})$ $(\mathbf{ACP}^2(\mathfrak{A}))$ the subset consisting of the functions of type level 1 (functionals of type level 2) among these.

As is easily seen, the reason the ACPs deserve to be called *abstract procedures* is that they are preserved under isomorphism. That they also deserve to be called *computation procedures*, at least in the case of $\mathfrak{N}$-standard structures $\mathfrak{A}$ with arrays, is due to the result of Xu and Zucker (2005) below. A structure $\mathfrak{A}$ is $\mathfrak{N}$-standard if it is an expansion of the structure $\mathfrak{N} = (\mathbb{N}, 0, Sc, Pd)$. An $\mathfrak{N}$-standard structure has arrays if with each basic domain A_i is associated the domain of all finite sequences from A_i, with the appropriate operations of length, term, expansion, and restriction. Let $\mathbf{ACP}^1(\mathfrak{A})$ denote the set of functions generated by the schemata I–VIII above. Xu and Zucker (2005) proved:

If $\mathfrak{A}$ is an $\mathfrak{N}$-standard structure with arrays, then   (3.15)

$\mathbf{While}^*(\mathfrak{A}) = \mathbf{ACP}^1(\mathfrak{A})$.

We also have a matchup with the Moschovakis (1984) theory of algorithms by the result of Feferman (1992b, section 9) that the ACPs are closed under simultaneous LFP recursion.[12]

Since it was seen in the preceding section that the BSS machine model of computation on the real numbers (and on algebraic structures more generally) is subsumed under $\mathbf{While}^*$ computability, to show that we have a generalization of both that and the effective approximation approach to computation on the reals, we specialize to the case of ACPs over the structure $\mathfrak{N}$, which, by the usual coding, includes the associated structure with arrays. And for this, one simply comes down to showing that

$\mathbf{ACP}^2(\mathfrak{N})$ = the partial recursive functionals over the natural numbers.   (3.16)

For, it is easy to show that every partial recursive function is generated by the ACPs over $\mathfrak{N}$, from which one obtains all the partial recursive functionals in the guise of recursive operators, as mentioned above. To prove the converse, one shows inductively that every F in $\mathbf{ACP}(\mathfrak{N})$ is a partial recursive function if of type level 1, and a partial recursive functional if of type level 2. The crucial step is to show that if G is a partial recursive functional, then the function $\mathrm{LFP}(\Gamma_G)$ is a partial recursive function; for details, see Feferman (1992b, sections 10.2 and 11). So, now, the S-approximation theory of effective computability of functions of real numbers is explained essentially as in section 3.3 above in terms of total recursive functionals in $\mathbf{ACP}^2(\mathfrak{N})$. That is, Cauchy sequences of rational numbers with effective moduli of convergence are represented in one way or another by a class $\pmb{Rep}$ of total functions on $\mathbb{N}$. For any two such functions, $f \equiv g$ is defined to hold if the corresponding Cauchy sequences have the same limit, and a function F of real numbers is represented by a functional $\pmb{F}$ if for each real number x and each f representing x we have that $\pmb{F}(f)$ is a function representing $F(x)$. Finally, a functional $\pmb{F}$ serves to do this if it maps $\pmb{Rep}$ to $\pmb{Rep}$ and if $f \equiv g$ implies $\pmb{F}(f) \equiv \pmb{F}(g)$.

Thus, abstract computation procedures provide another way of subsuming the two approaches to computation over the real numbers at a basic conceptual level. Of course, this in no way adjudicates the dispute over the proper way to found scientific computation on the real numbers or to deal with the relevant questions of complexity.

Coming back to basics, the foregoing illustrates another fundamental issue, namely the difference between extensional and intensional aspects of computation. On the face of it, the BSS approach is extensional, while that of S-effective approximation theory is intensional in its essential use of *Rep* and $\equiv$ on *Rep*. But there is an even more basic difference that has been glossed over in the above explanation of ACPs. Namely, functions $f, g, h, \ldots$ there are tacitly understood in the usual set-theoretic sense, for which the extensionality principle—that extensional equality implies identity—holds; that is, if $f(n) = g(n)$ for all n in $\mathbb{N}$, then $f = g$. By the *intensional recursion-theoretic interpretation* of $\mathbf{ACP}(\mathfrak{N})$, I mean what one gets by taking the function variables $f, g, h, \ldots$ to range instead over *indices* of partial recursive functions (of the appropriate arities), rather than the functions themselves. To connect this with the ordinary recursion theoretic interpretation, let us write $\{f\}(\underline{x})$ for $f(\underline{x})$ in the above when f is such an index. Then $f \subseteq g$ and monotonicity of functionals is defined as above; write $f \equiv g$ for $f \subseteq g$ and $g \subseteq f$; that is, if f and g are extensionally equal. Now one proves inductively for this interpretation that each F in $\mathbf{ACP}^2(\mathfrak{N})$ preserves extensional equality and hence is an effective operator in the sense of Myhill and Shepherdson (1955); that is, if $f \equiv g$, then $F(f) \equiv F(g)$. That is also used to show we have closure in this interpretation under the LFP scheme, since by the Myhill-Shepherdson theorem, every effective operator is the restriction to the partial recursive functions of a partial recursive functional; for more details, see Feferman (1992b, sections 10.4 and 11). In the end, when speaking about actual computation, we have intensionality throughout, since computers only work with finite symbolic representations of the objects being manipulated.

3.6   Explicit Mathematics and the Bishop Approach to Constructive Analysis

In 1967, Errett Bishop published his ground-breaking book, *Foundations of Constructive Analysis*. Bishop had for many years been a practicing analyst in the classical tradition, to which he contributed important work on Banach spaces, operator algebras, function algebras, and the theory of functions of several complex variables. In the mid-60s, while spending a year at the Miller Institute at UC Berkeley, Bishop had a radical change of mind about how mathematics ought to be developed. Namely, he became convinced that it should be carried out constructively so that each theorem has "numerical meaning;" that is, can in principle have a computational interpretation. But he found that the most sustained previous effort to redevelop mathematics constructively—in the work of L. E. J. Brouwer and his school of intuitionism—was very unsatisfactory, "partly by extraneous peculiarities of Brouwer's system which made it vague and even ridiculous to practicing mathematicians, but chiefly by the failure of Brouwer and his followers to convince the mathematical public that abandonment of the idealistic [i.e., classical] viewpoint would not sterilize or cripple the development of mathematics" (Bishop 1967, 2). In its place, Bishop explained a way of developing analysis constructively that could be readily understood by classical mathematicians and yet would be constructively meaningful at the same time. Where Brouwer depended in part on the rejection of classical logical reasoning, as exemplified by use of the law of excluded middle to lead to existential conclusions for which one may not have a witness, Bishop depends in part on the systematic replacement of classical notions by related ones in which all witnessing information is explicitly stated and carried along in proofs. Furthermore, Brouwer depended in his redevelopment of analysis on the use of the intuitive notion of "choice sequence," which has no direct classical interpretation, and on principles concerning that notion which allowed him to prove such classically false statements as that every function on a closed interval of the real numbers is uniformly continuous. Bishop, by contrast, when dealing with functions on a closed interval $[a, b]$, simply restricts himself to those f that are not only uniformly continuous, but carry with them a uniform modulus of convergence function; that is, an effective function $m: \mathbb{Q} \to \mathbb{Q}$ such that for each rational $\varepsilon > 0$ we have $m(\varepsilon) > 0$, and for all x, y in $[a, b]$, if $|x - y| < m(\varepsilon)$, then $|f(x) - f(y)| < \varepsilon$. For Bishop, in effect, the objects with which one works are pairs (f, m) of functions satisfying this condition on a given closed interval $[a, b]$. Every theorem in Bishop is also classically true; in practice, he gives a constructive substitute for a classical theorem which is equivalent to the latter under the assumption of the law of excluded middle.[13]

With such modifications, Bishop (1967) showed how substantial tracts of modern analysis could be developed in an informal style meeting everyday standards of rigor. Subsequently—in work with one of his students, Henry Cheng—Bishop and Cheng (1972) published an improved version of his theory of measure; a couple of years later, work on constructive probability theory was carried out by another student, Y.-K. Chan (1974). But despite the evidence of its success in carrying out a great deal of mathematics constructively without using strange notions or assumptions, Bishop's approach did not have any major impact, though it did take hold in a small but steadily widening group. One of the first mathematicians outside of his immediate circle to take it up was Douglas S. Bridges, who made several contributions to constructive functional analysis in the mid-1970s, leading up to a monograph, Bridges (1979). Bishop then began a collaboration with Bridges to make substantial additions and improvements in his book, resulting in the volume *Constructive Analysis* (Bishop and Bridges 1985); the volume appeared after Bishop's life and career were brought to a premature close by his death from cancer. There have been a number of further developments in his school, not only in analysis but also in algebra and topology.[14] But since my main concern here is to relate the essentials of Bishop's approach to constructive mathematics (abbreviated in the following as BCM) to the questions of computation of functions of real numbers, there is no need to refer to anything beyond Bishop and Bridges (1985), abbreviated "BB" in the following.

Chapter 1 of BB is devoted to Bishop's "constructivist manifesto"; the mathematical work begins in chapter 2, on the real numbers and calculus. That begins with some general notions about sets and functions. Membership of an element x in a set A, $x \in A$, is determined by x's meeting certain construction requirements specified by A; these vary from set to set. In addition, each set A carries with it an equivalence relation on A, written $=_A$, which is called the notion of equality for A. If one changes that notion for given construction requirements, one changes the set. In the case of the set $\mathbb{Z}$ of integers (or $\mathbb{Z}^+$ of positive integers), $=_{\mathbb{Z}}$ is taken to be the identity. The set $\mathbb{Q}$ of rational numbers is taken in BB to consist of all pairs (m, n) of integers for which $n \in \mathbf{Z}^+$ and m, n are relatively prime; for this, too, the equality $=_{\mathbb{Q}}$ is the identity. Alternatively, one could take it to consist of all pairs (m, n) of integers for which $n \neq 0$, endowing that set as usual with the equality relation $(m, n) =_{\mathbb{Q}} (m', n')$ iff $m \times n' = m' \times n$.

By an *operation* from a set A into a set B is meant "a finite routine f which assigns an element $f(a)$ of B to each given element a of A. This routine must afford an explicit, finite, mechanical reduction of the procedure for constructing $f(a)$ to the procedure for constructing a" (Bishop and Bridges, 15). By a *function* or *mapping* of a set A into a set B is meant an operation f from A into B such that we have $f(a) =_B f(a')$ whenever $a =_A a'$. The equality of functions f, g from A to B is defined by the condition that for all $a \in A$, $f(a) =_B g(a)$. Note well that this is not the identity relation, since f, g may be given by distinct procedures for computing the same value up to equality in B. By a *sequence* x of elements of a set A is meant a function from $\mathbb{Z}^+$ (or sometimes from $\mathbb{N}$) into A; the nth term of x is given by $x_n = x(n)$; x is also denoted (x_n). Moving on to the real numbers (Bishop and Bridges, 18), a sequence $x = (x_n)$ of rational numbers is called *regular* if for all $m, n \in \mathbb{Z}^+$, $|x_m - x_n| \leq 1/m + 1/n$. Thus regular sequences are Cauchy (or fundamental) in the usual sense of the word. The set $\mathbb{R}$ of all real numbers is defined to consist of all regular sequences, with the equality $x =_{\mathbf{R}} y$ defined by $|x_n - y_n| \leq 2/n$ for all n in $\mathbb{Z}^+$. This is evidently a variant of the explanation of the explicit presentation of real numbers by Cauchy sequences described in section 3 above, though with much slower rates of convergence.

The operations of addition, subtraction, multiplication, and absolute value are defined in a simple way from regular sequences so as to yield the expected functions on $\mathbb{R}$. For example, $x + y$ is defined to be the sequence z with $z_n = x_{2n} + y_{2n}$ for all n. It is only when we come to inverse for nonzero real numbers that we need to introduce some new witnessing information. Classically, if a Cauchy sequence x converges to a positive real number, there will exist positive integers j and m such that for all $n \geq j$ we have $x_n \geq 1/m$. But, constructively, there is in general no way to compute effectively such j and m from the given computation procedure used to exhibit x. Bishop's definition for regular sequences x is simply that x *is positive* if for some k, $x_k > 1/k$; given such k, we may choose $m^{-1} \leq (x_k - k^{-1})/2$ and $j = m$ to satisfy the preceding conditions. Thus to exhibit x as a positive real number, we must adjoin the number k as part of its presentation. On the other hand, x is defined to be *non-negative* if $x_n \geq -1/n$ for all positive integers n. It is not constructively true that if x is non-negative then either $x =_R 0$ or x is positive, since we don't have enough information to decide which disjunct holds or to produce a suitable k witnessing the positivity of x if x is not zero. Now, given these notions, we may define $y < x$ to hold if $x - y$ is positive, and $y \leq x$ if $x - y$ is non-negative. And with that, we may proceed to define what is meant by a continuous function f on a closed interval, witnessed by a uniform modulus of continuity function $m(\varepsilon)$ as defined above. Functions f on other intervals are described via the modulus information $m_{a,b}$ associated with each closed subinterval $[a, b]$.

The foregoing should give an idea of how Bishop and his followers proceed to produce constructive substitutes for various classical notions in order to provide a thoroughgoing constructive redevelopment of analysis. What is not clear from Bishop's 1967 presentation or that of Bishop and Bridges (1985) is how the computational content of the results obtained is to be accounted for in recursion-theoretic terms, in the sense of ordinary or generalized recursion theory as discussed in sections 3.3–3.5 above. From the logical point of view, that may be accomplished by formalizing the work of BB (and BCM more generally) in a formal system T that has recursive interpretations. A variety of such systems were proposed in the 1970s, first by Bishop himself and then by Nicholas Goodman, Per Martin-Löf, John Myhill, Harvey Friedman, and me and surveyed in Feferman (1979, 173, 192–197; cf. also Beeson 1985). Roughly speaking, those account for the computational content of BCM in two different ways: the first treats witnessing information implicitly and depends for its extraction on the fact that the systems are formalized in intuitionistic logic, while the second kind treats witnessing information explicitly as part of the package explaining each notion and does not require the logic to be intuitionistic. For the first kind of system, the method of extraction is by one form or another of the method of recursive realizability introduced by Kleene or by the use of (recursive) functional interpretations originated by Gödel. Only the system T_0 of explicit mathematics introduced in Feferman (1975) and applied to BCM in Feferman (1979) is of the second kind, and it is only that whose direct interpretation relates it to the theories of computation discussed above. Namely, T_0 has variables of two kinds: individuals $a, b, c, \ldots, x, y, z$ and classes (or "classifications") $A, B, C, \ldots, X, Y, Z$; the ontological axiom tells us that every class is an individual; the informal meaning is that classes are considered intensionally via their explicit defining properties.[15] The basic relation between individuals, besides that of identity, is a three-placed relation $\text{App}(x, y, z)$, also written $xy \simeq z$, satisfying, with suitable constant symbols $\mathbf{k}$, $\mathbf{s}$, $\mathbf{p}$, $\mathbf{p}_0$, and $\mathbf{p}_1$, the conditions for a partial combinatory algebra with pairing and projection operations. The informal meaning of $xy \simeq z$ is that x represents (or codes) a partial operation whose value at y equals z. Thus operations may apply to operations, but also to classes via the ontological axiom. T_0 has a straightforward model in which the individual variables range over the natural numbers and the relation $\text{App}(x, y, z)$ holds just in case $\{x\}(y) \simeq z$, in the notation of ordinary recursion theory. On the other hand, within T_0, Bishop's constructive analysis is formalized directly following the kinds of explanations sketched above for operations f and sets A (considered as classes with equality relations), functions, $\mathbb{Z}$, $\mathbb{Q}$, regular sequences, $\mathbb{R}$, $=_\mathbb{R}$, $<$ and $\leq$ for $\mathbb{R}$, and functions of real variables on closed intervals. Then one can see that the recursion theoretic model of T_0 just described fits the computational content of Bishop's constructive mathematics with the intensional recursion theoretic interpretation of $\mathbf{ACP}(\mathfrak{N})$ described at the end of section 3.5.

As it turns out, and as explained in Feferman (1979), case studies of typical arguments in Bishop's constructive analysis show that it can be formalized in a subsystem of T_0 of the same strength as the system PA of Peano arithmetic. Further work of Feng Ye (2000) on the constructive theory of unbounded linear operators suggests that, in fact, a subsystem of the same strength as the system PRA of primitive recursive arithmetic already suffices for that purpose. It is possible that one can push this further by formalization in systems of feasible analysis such as that in Ferreira (1994); that will take much more work.[16] But the practice of Bishop-style constructive analysis needs to be examined directly for turning its results that predict computability in principle to ones that demonstrate computability in practice.[17] Presumably, all of the specific methods of scientific computation are subsumed under Bishop-style constructive mathematics. Assuming that is the case, here is where a genuine connection might be made between constructive mathematics, the theory of computation, and scientific computation, which puts questions of complexity up front.[18]

Notes

1. These two are not the only theories of computation over the real numbers. See Weirauch (2000) for a useful survey of various such notions.

2. It should be mentioned that pioneering work on a notion of polynomial time complexity in analysis using the effective approximation approach had been made by Ko and Friedman (1982) and Ko (1991); cf. the survey Ko (1998). For further work in this direction, see Stoltenberg-Hansen and Tucker (1999) and Bauer (2002).

3. As stated by Blum (2004, 1027), Hilbert's Nullstellensatz (theorem on the zeros) asserts in the case of the complex numbers $\mathbb{C}$ that if $f_1, \ldots, f_m$ are polynomials in $\mathbb{C}[\underline{x}]$ for indeterminates $\underline{x} = (x_1, \ldots, x_n)$, then

$f_1, \ldots, f_m$ have *no* common zero in $\mathbb{C}^n$ iff there are polynomials $g_1, \ldots, g_m$ in $\mathbb{C}[\underline{x}]$ such that $\Sigma\, g_i f_i = 1$. This gives a semidecision procedure by searching for such g_i. That is turned into a BSS algorithm to decide whether or not the f_i have a common zero by use of effective bounds on the degrees of possible such g_i, found by Grete Hermann in 1926.

4. See Cutland (1980) for a nice exposition and development of recursion theory on the basis of register machines. This is also referred to by some as the random access model (RAM).

5. There is no way to work effectively with real numbers given as Dedekind sections in the rational numbers.

6. Actually, Grzegorczyk only assumes special consequences of primitive recursion from which the general primitive recursive schemata are inferred.

7. One proof is as follows. Let E be a system of equations used to define F, and consider $\psi = F(\varphi)$ for any total φ; by assumption, for each i there is a unique j and a derivation of $\psi(i) = j$ from E together with the diagram of φ. Any such derivation makes use only of a finite subfunction $\varphi|k$ of φ. Now let $D(\varphi, i, j, k, d) = 0$ hold when d is a code of a derivation from $\varphi|k$ of $\psi(i) = j$, otherwise $= 1$. D is primitive recursive uniformly in φ, and for each φ and i there are j, k, d such that $D(\varphi, i, j, k, d) = 0$. Finally, $F(\varphi, i)$ is the first term of the least triple $\langle j, k, d \rangle$ such that $D(\varphi, i, j, k, d) = 0$.

8. Friedman also considered a variant approach using infinite tapes as in Turing machines and as in Blum (2004).

9. Friedman allowed partial relations in a suitable sense.

10. For continuations of this work on computation on metric partial algebras, see Tucker and Zucker (2004, 2005).

11. See also Feferman (1996) where I treated streams in the extensional interpretation.

12. See also Feferman (1996), Appendix A. Note also that Appendix C of that paper contains several corrections to Feferman (1992b).

13. According to Bishop, only the particular consequences of the law of excluded middle, according to which for a function $f: \mathbb{N} \to \mathbb{N}$ either $(\forall n \in \mathbb{N})\, f(n) = 0$ or $(\exists n \in \mathbb{N})\, f(n) \neq 0$ (which he calls the limited principle of omniscience), are needed for these equivalences. Actually, one also needs to invoke certain instances of the Axiom of Choice to infer the classical version from the constructive one.

14. See, for example, Mines, Richman and Ruitenberg (1988) for algebra and Spitters (2003) and Bridges and Vita (2006) for analysis.

15. Later reformulations of systems of explicit mathematics use a relation $\Re(x, X)$ to express that the individual x represents (or codes) the class X.

16. In a personal communication, Stephen Cook has commented on Ferreira (1994) that "it has a first-order part based on polynomial time functions over a discrete space, but this is supplemented by powerful axioms such as the weak pigeonhole principle which allow existence proofs with no feasible algorithmic content." But Ferreira has responded that his theory there is conservative over a feasible (PTime) system.

17. See the suggestions that I made in that direction at the conclusion of Feferman (1984).

18. I would like to thank Michael Beeson, Lenore Blum, Douglas Bridges, Stephen Cook, Jeffery Zucker, and especially the referee for their helpful comments on a draft of this article.

References

Bauer, A. 2002. A relation between equilogical spaces and type two effectivity. *Mathematical Logic Quarterly* 48:1–15.

Beeson, M. J. 1985. *Foundations of Constructive Mathematics*. New York: Springer.

Bishop, E. 1967. *Foundations of Constructive Analysis*. New York: Springer.

Bishop, E., and D. Bridges. 1985. *Constructive Analysis*. New York: Springer.

Bishop, E., and H. Cheng. 1972. *Constructive Measure Theory*. Memoirs of the American Mathematical Society, No. 116. Providence, RI: AMS.

Blum, L. 2004. Computability over the reals: Where Turing meets Newton. *Notices of the American Mathematical Society* 51:1024–1034.

Blum, L., F. Cucker, M. Shub, and S. Smale. 1997. *Complexity and Real Computation*. New York: Springer.

Blum, L., M. Shub, and S. Smale. 1989. On a theory of computation and complexity over the real numbers: NP-completeness, recursive functions and universal machines. *Bulletin of the American Mathematical Society* 21:1–46.

Braverman, M., and S. Cook. 2006. Computing over the reals: Foundations for scientific computing. *Notices of the American Mathematical Society* 53:318–329.

Bridges, D. S. 1979. *Constructive Functional Analysis*. London: Pitman.

Bridges, D. S., and L. S. Vita. 2006. *Techniques of Constructive Analysis*. Universitext. Heidelberg: Springer-Verlag.

Caviness, B. F., and J. R. Johnson, eds. 1998. *Quantifier Elimination and Cylindrical Algebraic Decomposition*. New York: Springer.

Chan, Y.-K. 1974. Notes on constructive probability theory. *Annals of Probability* 2:51–75.

Cutland, N. J. 1980. *Computability: An Introduction to Recursive Function Theory*. Cambridge: Cambridge University Press.

Feferman, S. 1975. A language and axioms for explicit mathematics. In *Algebra and Logic*, ed. J. N. Crossley, 87–139. Berlin: Springer-Verlag.

Feferman, S. 1979. Constructive theories of functions and classes. In *Logic Colloquium '78*, ed. M. Boffa, D. van Dalen, and K. McAloon, 159–224. Amsterdam: North-Holland.

Feferman, S. 1984. Between constructive and classical mathematics. In *Computation and Proof Theory*. Lecture notes in computer science, Vol. 1104, 143–162, ed. M. M. Richter, E. Börger, W. Oberschelp, B. Schinzel, and W. Thomas. Berlin: Springer-Verlag.

Feferman, S. 1992a. A new approach to abstract data types, I: Informal development. *Mathematical Structures in Computer Science* 2:193–229.

Feferman, S. 1992b. A new approach to abstract data types, II: Computability on ADTs as ordinary computation. In *Computer Science Logic*, ed. E. Börger, G. Jäger, H. Kleine Büning, and M. M. Richter. Lecture notes in computer science, No. 626, 79–95. Berlin: Springer-Verlag.

Feferman, S. 1996. Computation on abstract data types: The extensional approach, with an application to streams. *Annals of Pure and Applied Logic* 81:75–113.

Ferreira, F. 1994. A feasible theory for analysis. *Journal of Symbolic Logic* 59:1001–1011.

Fischer, M., and M. Rabin. 1974. Super-exponential complexity of Presburger arithmetic. In *Complexity of Computation*. AMS-SIAM Proceedings, Vol. 7, 27–41. Providence, RI: AMS. Reprinted in B. F. Caviness and J. R. Johnson, *Quantifier Elimination and Cylindrical Algebraic Decomposition*, 122–135.

Friedman, H. 1971. Algorithmic procedures, generalized Turing algorithms, and elementary recursion theory. In *Logic Colloquium '69*, ed. R. O. Gandy and C. M. E. Yates, 361–389. Amsterdam: North-Holland.

Friedman, H., and R. Mansfield. 1992. Algorithmic procedure. *Transactions of the American Mathematical Society* 332:297–312.

Grzegorczyk, A. 1955. Computable functionals. *Fundamenta Mathematicae* 42:168–202.

Herman, G. T., and S. D. Isard. 1970. Computability over arbitrary fields. *Journal of the London Mathematical Society* 2:73–79.

Kleene, S. C. 1952. *Introduction to Metamathematics*. Amsterdam: North-Holland.

Ko, K. 1991. *Complexity Theory of Real Functions*. Boston: Birkhäuser.

Ko, K. 1998. Polynomial-time computability in analysis. In *Handbook of Recursive Mathematics, Vol. 2: Recursive Algebra, Analysis and Combinatorics*, ed. Y. L. Ershov, S. S. Goncharov, A. Nerode, and J. B. Remmel, 1271–1317. Amsterdam: Elsevier.

Ko, K., and H. Friedman. 1982. Computational complexity of real functions. *Theoretical Computer Science* 20:323–352.

Lacombe, D. 1955a. Extension de la notion de fonction récursive aux fonctions d'une ou plusieurs variables réelles, I. *Comptes Rendus de l'Académie des Sciences Paris* 240:2470–2480.

Lacombe, D. 1955b. Extension de la notion de fonction récursive aux fonctions d'une ou plusieurs variables réelles, II. *Comptes Rendus de l'Académie des Sciences Paris* 241:13–14.

Lacombe, D. 1955c. Extension de la notion de fonction récursive aux fonctions d'une ou plusieurs variables réelles, III. *Comptes Rendus de l'Académie des Sciences Paris* 241:151–55.

Mazur, S. 1963. Computable analysis, ed. A. Grzegorczyk, H. Rasiowa. *Rozprawy Matematyczne 33.*

Mines, R., F. Richman, and W. Ruitenberg. 1988. *A Course in Constructive Algebra.* New York: Springer.

Moldestad, J., V. Stoltenberg-Hansen, and J. V. Tucker. 1980a. Finite algorithmic procedures and inductive definability. *Mathematica Scandinavica* 46:62–76.

Moldestad, J., V. Stoltenberg-Hansen, and J. V. Tucker. 1980b. Finite algorithmic procedures and inductive definability. *Mathematica Scandinavica* 46:77–94.

Moschovakis, Y. N. 1984. Abstract recursion as a foundation for the theory of recursive algorithms. In *Computation and Proof Theory.* Lecture notes in computer science, Vol. 1104, 289–364, ed. M. M. Richter, E. Börger, W. Oberschelp, B. Schinzel, and W. Thomas. Berlin: Springer-Verlag.

Moschovakis, Y. N. 1989. The formal language of recursion. *Journal of Symbolic Logic* 54:1216–1252.

Myhill, J., and J. C. Shepherdson. 1955. Effective operations on partial recursive functions. *Zeitschr. für Mathematische Logik und Grundlagen der Mathematik* 1:310–317.

Platek, R. A. 1966. *Foundations of recursion theory,* PhD dissertation, Stanford University.

Pour-El, M. B. 1974. Abstract computability and its relation to the general purpose analog computer. *Transactions of the American Mathematical Society* 199:1–28.

Pour-El, M. B., and J. C. Caldwell. 1975. On a simple definition of computable function of a real variable with applications to functions of a complex variable. *Zeitschr. f ür Mathematische Logik und Grundlagen der Mathematik* 21:1–19.

Shepherdson, J. C. 1976. On the definition of computable function of a real variable. *Zeitschr. für Mathematische Logik und Grundlagen der Mathematik* 22:391–402.

Shepherdson, J. C., and H. E. Sturgis. 1963. Computability of recursive functions. *Journal of the Association for Computing Machinery* 10:217–255.

Spitters, B. 2003. *Constructive and intuitionistic integration theory and functional analysis,* PhD Dissertation, University of Nijmegen.

Stoltenberg-Hansen, V., and J. V. Tucker. 1999. Concrete models of computation for topological spaces. *Theoretical Computer Science* 219:347–378.

Tarski, A. 1951. *A Decision Method for Elementary Algebra and Geometry.* Berkeley: University of California Press. Reprinted in Caviness and Johnson, *Quantifier Elimination and Cylindrical Algebraic Decomposition,* 24–84.

Tucker, J. V., and J. I. Zucker. 1988. *Program Correctness over Abstract Data Types, with Error-State Semantics.* CWI monographs, Vol. 6. Amsterdam: North-Holland.

Tucker, J. V., and J. I. Zucker. 2000. Computable functions and semicomputable sets on many-sorted algebras. In *Handbook of Logic in Computer Science: Logic and Algebraic Methods,* Vol. 5, ed. S. Abramsky, D. M. Gabbay, T. S. E. Maibaum, 317–523. Oxford: Oxford University Press.

Tucker, J. V., and J. I. Zucker. 2004. Abstract versus concrete computation on metric partial algebras. *ACM Transactions on Computational Logic* 5:611–668.

Tucker, J. V., and J. I. Zucker. 2005. Computable total functions, algebraic specifications and dynamical systems. *Journal of Logic and Algebraic Programming* 62:71–108.

Weirauch, K. 2000. *Computable Analysis.* Berlin: Springer.

Xu, J., and J. I. Zucker. 2005. First and second order recursion on abstract data types. *Fundamenta Informaticae* 67:377–419.

Ye, F. 2000. Toward a constructive theory of unbounded linear operators. *Journal of Symbolic Logic* 65:357–370.

4 The Church-Turing "Thesis" as a Special Corollary of Gödel's Completeness Theorem[1]

Saul A. Kripke

Traditionally, many writers, following Kleene (1952), thought of the Church-Turing thesis as unprovable by its nature but having various strong arguments in its favor, including Turing's analysis of human computation. More recently, the beauty, power, and obvious fundamental importance of this analysis—what Turing (1936) calls "argument I"— has led some writers to give an almost exclusive emphasis on this argument as *the* unique justification for the Church-Turing thesis. In this chapter I advocate an alternative justification, essentially presupposed by Turing himself in what he calls "argument II." The idea is that computation is a special form of mathematical deduction. Assuming the steps of the deduction can be stated in a first-order language, the Church-Turing thesis follows as a special case of Gödel's completeness theorem (first-order algorithm theorem). I propose this idea as an alternative foundation for the Church-Turing thesis, both for human and machine computation. Clearly the relevant assumptions are justified for computations presently known. Other issues, such as the significance of Gödel's 1931 Theorem IX for the *Entscheidungsproblem*, are discussed along the way.

4.1 The Previously Received View and More Recent Challenges

It was long a commonplace in most writings on computability theory that the Church-Turing thesis, identifying the several mathematical definitions of recursiveness or computability with intuitive computability, was something that could be given very considerable intuitive evidence, but was not a precise enough issue to be itself susceptible to mathematical treatment (see, for example, Kleene's classic treatise [1952, section 62, 317–323]).[2] Some reservations to this view are already expressed, albeit relatively weakly, in Shoenfield (1967), section 6.5 (see 119–120), though the rest of the section follows Kleene (I owe this observation to Stewart Shapiro). Later in 1993, Shoenfield expressed himself more explicitly (see Shoenfield 1993, 26). What we would need, according to him, would be some self-evident axioms for, or a characterization of, intuitive computability, implying that all intuitively computable functions were Church-Turing recursive (computable). Harvey Friedman, in conversation with me (confirmed by Shapiro), had always taken a similar view.[3]

I too had always felt that the issue of Church's thesis wasn't one that was obviously not a mathematical one, susceptible of proof or disproof, but could be a genuine technical problem, though I thought it may be very difficult.[4] I do think the axiomatic approach may well be viable, and indeed have said so; but I'm going to give a different approach to the issue of Church's thesis here.

Two things had always led me to doubt what I have called the "conventional view" (but see note 3, this paper), as quoted from Kleene. First, one half of the Church-Turing thesis, that the recursive or Turing-computable functions are all in fact effectively calculable, can I think easily be established simply on the basis of an intuitive notion of calculability. No axiomatization is required, just a direct argument. And the argument should be regarded as a rigorous intuitive *proof* of its result.[5]

Second, it always seemed to me, as against those who held that there isn't any actual mathematical question here but just an explication, that there is after all another thesis that might have seemed to have a lot of evidence for it in the old days. That is, that the effectively calculable functions simply should be identified with the primitive recursive functions.[6] Ackermann (1928) actually *disproved* this thesis, by exhibiting a function that was obviously effectively calculable, but not primitive recursive. Now, clearly the Church-Turing thesis could in principle be disproved in the same way.[7,8] Given that this is so, how can we say that a mathematical question is not involved, since there can be a disproof?

I resumed thinking about the subject of mathematical arguments for the Church-Turing thesis as a reaction to Soare (1996). In his admirable survey of the history and philosophy of the subject, he proposed that the subject traditionally called "recursion theory" should be renamed "computability theory," and that correspondingly such terms as "recursively enumerable" should be renamed "computably enumerable." This reform has been generally adopted by writers on the subject.[9] However, I am probably too old and set in my ways, and do not propose here to stick to the reform. Also, in agreement with Slaman, a leading figure in the subject whom I gather does not propose to adopt the reform, I feel that the subject is as much in the area of definability as of computability.[10]

Soare also rightly emphasizes that Turing (1936–37) gives an analysis of *human* computation, and states that only the later work of Gandy (1980) shows that machine-computable functions (which may involve parallel processing) are Turing computable.

In spite of the salutary and correct emphasis by Gandy (1980, 1988), Sieg (1994, 1997), and Soare (1996) that Turing's original paper was an analysis of *human* computation, and that for Turing, following his contemporary usage, "computer" means *a person who computes*,[11, 12] not the later idea of a computing machine, nevertheless the influence of the "Turing machine" (and perhaps the subtle influence of his later philosophical paper Turing 1950) has led in many writings to a computer-science orientation to the problem. The contemporary situation, where high-speed computing machines are an essential part of our culture, is clearly also an influence.[13] I am, however, a logician and wish to explore the issue from a logical orientation. And here I have some genuine issues with what some other people appear to write.

The commonly used phrase "Turing's argument" suggests that Turing's 1936–37 paper gave a single argument for his analysis of human computability. In fact, as Shagrir has already mentioned at a conference in 2006,[14] Turing gave three in the original paper, one of which is the one generally remembered (the first; see section 1, 117, and argument I, 135–38). In many ways, the conventional emphasis on this argument is indeed appropriate, since it directly attempts to show, by a penetrating analysis of human computation and its limits, that anything humanly computable must be computable on his machine. (See also the exposition in Kleene 1952, 356–363, 376–381.) Nevertheless, I myself will primarily be concerned with his second argument (argument II, Turing 1936–37, 138) in the main body of this paper. But that will come later.

Soare, following Sieg (1994, 1997) and Gandy (1988), gives a careful mathematical and philosophical analysis of Turing's first argument. He proposes to break it into two different steps. One equates the informal notion of effective computability with what he calls "computorability," namely computability by an idealized human computer. Presumably this is a philosophical analysis. But then, Soare states (following Gandy 1988, 82; see also Gandy 1980, 124) that "Turing then proved *Turing's theorem: Any computorable function is Turing computable*. Although not proved in a formal system, Turing's proof is as rigorous as many in mathematics" (293).

As Gandy (1980, 124) stated Turing's theorem—"*what can be calculated by an abstract human being working in a routine way is computable*"[15]—it seemed to me to be too vague a statement to be regarded as a theorem without some further explanation. However, Soare's more detailed statement comes much closer, since he carefully divides the argument into a philosophical part, equating intuitive calculability with an analysis of what might be required of an idealized human computer ("computor"), and then a technical or mathematical part, showing that anything computable by such an idealized person is, in fact, Turing computable (i.e., computable on a Turing machine). Nevertheless, aside from the fact that, as Davis remarks, "this is a brilliant paper, but the reader should be warned that many of the technical details are incorrect as given" (Davis 1965, 115) the analysis contains at least one definite piece of handwaving. Turing (1936–37, 135) remarks that "in elementary arithmetic the two-dimensional character of the paper is sometimes used [...] and I think that it will be agreed that the two-dimensional character of the paper is no essential of computation. I assume then that the computation is carried out on one-dimensional paper, i.e. on a tape divided into squares." Maybe it would be agreed, but nothing has been argued, much less proved. Others have commented on this gap, and how it can be filled. Nevertheless, such considerations make it plainly desirable that the philosophical analysis of idealized human computability be built into an axiomatization, so that the argument can be properly evaluated. Soare's remarks already go in that direction, but an actual axiomatization has been given by Sieg (2008).[16]

Soare (1996, 296) proposes that "Turing's Thesis be used as a *definition* of a computable function as Turing and Gödel suggested." *Prima facie* this seems incompatible with his own assertion that Turing gave an elaborate proof of a *theorem* stating that his analysis of human computability gives the right notion. In the interesting section 3.4 (296–298), Soare argues that historically "other *theses* became definitions" [my italics], and quotes the arguments of other unnamed senior logicians who do not agree with his view.[17]

Did Turing regard his first argument, as Gandy, Soare, and perhaps Gödel before them, and many after them, have thought, as proving a theorem? If he did, why did he give two other arguments? In fact, he says: "All arguments which can be given [for the identification of the Turing-computable numbers with those that would intuitively be regarded as computable] are bound to be, fundamentally, appeals to intuition, and for this reason rather unsatisfactory mathematically." His first argument he calls "a direct appeal to intuition" (Turing 1936–37, 135).[18] It is certainly more than just that, since it gives an elaborate philosophical analysis of what an ideal computation might be. Nevertheless, Turing would be a very unusual case of a mathematician who proved a theorem without realizing that his own argument was such a proof.[19] My own alternative analysis will be very close to his second argument, which has mostly been ignored in discussions of Turing's 1936–37 paper. It will also be rather close to the argument given by Church (1936a).[20]

4.2 Computation as a Special Form of Mathematical Argument

My main point is this: a computation is a special form of mathematical argument. One is given a set of instructions, and the steps in the computation are supposed to follow—follow deductively—from the instructions as given. *So a computation is just another mathematical deduction, albeit one of a very specialized form.* In particular, the conclusion of the argument follows from the instructions as given and perhaps some well-known and not explicitly stated mathematical premises. I will assume that the computation is a deductive argument from a finite number of instructions, in analogy to Turing's emphasis on our finite capacity. It is in this sense, namely that I am regarding computation as a special form of deduction, that I am saying I am advocating a logical orientation to the problem.

Now I shall state another thesis, which I shall call "Hilbert's thesis,"[21] namely, that the steps of any mathematical argument can be given in a language based on first-order logic (with identity).[22] The present argument can be regarded as either reducing Church's thesis to Hilbert's thesis, or alternatively as simply pointing out a theorem on all computations whose steps can be formalized in a first-order language.

Suppose one has any valid argument whose steps can be stated in a first-order language. It is an immediate consequence of the Gödel completeness theorem for first-order logic with identity that the premises of the argument can be formalized in any conventional formal system of first-order logic. Granted that the proof relation of such a system is recursive (computable), it immediately follows in the special case where one is computing a function (say, in the language of arithmetic) that the function must be recursive (Turing computable).

For example, if one has a valid argument from finitely many premises, and the natural number n is represented by $0^{(n)}$ (0 with n-strokes, i.e., successor symbols; a single function letter f might be the natural representation of successor), and the premises allow one to conclude for each particular n either $P(0^{(n)})$ or its negation,[23] it follows that the set defined by the predicate P is recursive (Turing computable). The same sort of argument will show that any function whose graph is computable in this sense by an argument whose steps are in a first-order language must also be recursive.

Particular examples are easily found from elementary primitive recursion. For example, which numbers are even can be decided from axioms stating that 0 is even, and that a successor of an even number is not even, while the successor of a number that is not even is even. One could similarly analyze the usual recursive definitions of addition, etc.

Although I do not find his argument II to be entirely clearly presented,[24] I take Turing to be arguing that precisely those sets which are computable in the sense of deducibility in first-order logic ("the Hilbert functional calculus" in his own terminology) are the Turing-computable sets (Turing 1936–37, 138–139). Church also, though not committed at that time, or at least in his initial paper, to any special primacy of conventional first-order logic, also argues that anything formalizable in a symbolic logic that is recursive (λ-definable), in its axioms and rules, must also compute only recursive functions. (See Church 1936a and the exposition in Sieg 1997.)[25] It is because of these considerations that I take myself to be reviving somewhat neglected arguments already given by Church, and especially Turing.

One should therefore notice the following: at the time the classical definitions of Church, Herbrand-Gödel-Kleene, and Turing were given, and in fact even rather earlier, another definition of computability was at hand. One could have defined a set (relation, function) as decidable (computable) if instance-wise membership and non-membership in the set can be decided by a proof from a finite set of instructions (axioms) statable in a first-order language.[26] The point, as I have stressed, is that a computation is a deduction of a special sort. Given the Gödel completeness theorem, it follows immediately that this definition is equivalent to the classical definitions just mentioned, because intuitive provability can be identified with provability in a standard formal system. And these, of course, are systems with a recursive proof predicate in the classical senses just mentioned.

Taking the approach just mentioned as basic has advantages that I will go into shortly. The main advantage of any mathematical definition of computability, with an accompanying thesis identifying it with the intuitive notion, is that it allows one to prove negative results, that various sets are not decidable, etc. The present approach has that advantage in common with the others, but it is especially suited to the *Entscheidungsproblem*, as may already be clear, and will be spelled out below. There are also other advantages, some of a historical sort, also to be spelled out below.

Another relatively minor advantage of the approach of deducibility in a first-order language, but one which has bothered the present writer, is simply pedagogical. Ever since Post's famous paper (1944), the advantages of an intuitive presentation of computability arguments has been evident, rather than the rival approach using a formal definition of computability in the proofs. Although the experienced computability theorist will know how to convert such arguments into proofs using a formal definition, and cannot be said to be relying on an unproved thesis, this is hardly true for a beginner.[27] However, such a beginner, if he has already studied elementary logic, will readily accept that the steps of an argument can be stated in a first-order language, even if they are given verbally. The Gödel completeness theorem guarantees that if the steps really do follow (using any implicit axioms in addition to the actually stated steps), the argument can be formalized in one of the usual systems. Granted that the proof predicate of such a system is recursive/computable by one of the usual definitions, that one really has a technically valid proof will be readily accepted.

Soare remarks (see Soare 1996, 299) that Kleene's equation calculus and μ-recursive formalism, contrary to what some have claimed, is no better than the Turing machine or other formalisms in providing proofs that are readily comprehensible to the reader or student. He applauds the change to intuitive proofs (with reference to a machine formalism), as in Rogers (1967) and subsequent textbooks. Using the present approach, this change is easily justified by the definitions. (However, I cannot quite assert that all formalisms are impossibly difficult for the beginner, at least at an elementary level. In my own lectures [Kripke 1996], I had some success using a formalism roughly equivalent to using Σ_1 definability for recursive enumerability. Students were supposed to give and understand proofs in the formalism, not invoking Church's thesis.[28] There may be other possibilities.)

For the reasons just given, I have thus proposed that derivability from a finite set of instructions statable in a first-order mathematical language be taken to be the basic technical concept of computability. However, if this is not done, one can use the Gödel completeness theorem for any conventional formalism to show the equivalence of this characterization to any standard characterization, by showing that the proofs in this conventional formalism are all decidable in the sense of the standard characterization. I take it to be the point of Turing's second argument for his own characterization in terms of Turing machines, that the equivalence of the characterization of computability in terms of formal first-order logic as just described and his own characterization in terms of Turing machines can be shown to be equivalent. His third argument appears to be a synthesis of the first two. As to the relation of the first two arguments, one can be thought as emphasizing human beings as operating mechanically on paper, the other as thinking beings, deducing the results of their computations from the instructions given.

The reference to Turing's second argument might be used to bring out two things. First, it would not matter if Turing had allowed two-dimensional or indeed n-dimensional computations, provided he had given conventional instructions for the operation of his n-dimensional machine at each stage. The argument would still follow as long as the operation of the machine was deterministically stated in conventional mathematical language, formalizable in first-order logic. The same holds if we view Sheperdson-Sturgis "register machines" as linear computations. The state of the machine at any stage is still a finite configuration that can be coded into a natural number.[29] One can then define a two-place predicate whose graph is a single valued function (or alternatively allow function letters; see below), $R(n, m)$, meaning that the nth stage of the computation is the state coded by m. Single valuedness can be an axiom, and the transition from a given stage to its successor can be given by stable axioms describing the operation of the machine. The value of the function being computed or predicate being decided can then be determined by appropriate axioms describing how it is to be retrieved from the final state. This approach is possible whenever we have a deterministic linear computation. So my second point is this characterization of arbitrary deterministic linear computations. Of course, one need not be so explicit, numbering the linear steps. One can simply present a particular computation, step by step, as linear.

However, one need not restrict oneself to linear computations. Kleene's formalism (Kleene 1952) with an equation calculus is an example of a nonlinear formalism. Generalizing this, one needs only a finite set of instructions for the computation, and the equations (or predicate assertions and their negations; see below) are whatever can be deduced from these instructions by allowable rules. In such a case, the basic postulates may allow inconsistencies to be deduced (conflicting values for functions, or proofs of a formula and its negation). No real computation will allow such inconsistencies, but there will not in general be a syntactic criterion to rule them out. However, to obtain an enumeration theorem for all such computations, one will have to have a priority ordering for different deductions, with "least" deductions being preferred. This is, in effect, what Kleene does.

Some side remarks: Kleene pointed out that the formalism of recursion theory and the avoidability of a diagonal argument is best handled by making the theory a theory of "partial recursive" functions. If the formalism of first-order logic allows function letters and terms, it would thus be best to allow them to be partial. Given this, we might use free logic rather than traditional first-order logic, so that universal instantiation is allowed only in the presence of an existential premise. That is, the axiom scheme of universal instantiation becomes $((x) (Fx \wedge (\exists y)(y = t)) \supset Ft)$ (or in a natural deduction system the rule of universal instantiation is correspondingly modified; we assume the usual restrictions on substitution). In spite of its obvious connection with the theory of partial recursion, for some reason free logic has been of much more interest to philosophical logicians than to mathematical logicians.

Alternatively, one could not allow function letters and terms in the language, only relation symbols. Any function can be replaced by its graph. One can then use conventional first-order logic and not worry about the question of empty terms. Essentially, this was one of Russell's main ideas in his theory of descriptions (see Russell 1905 and Whitehead and Russell 1910).

Second, for the special type of mathematical argument I am considering (namely, computation), conventional first-order logic is clearly more than sufficient. Who would use in such an argument steps with premises involving many changes of quantifiers over an infinite domain? So, I think a really much more restricted language has to suffice here. (It would resemble Skolem arithmetic in allowing only bounded existential quantifiers.)[30] However, we do not need to worry about such restrictions. No argument needed here seems to be affected if we allow all first-order logic.

Also, when I refer to first-order logic, it is convenient in practice to allow many sorted systems, though one could reduce them to a conventional system with only one domain, and in my theoretical discussions immediately below, I will assume that this has been done.

Finally, though I believe, given the limitations of the human mind, that any actual computation is a derivation from a finite number of instructions, nothing is lost in terms of the actual power of the definition if infinitely many premises are allowed, provided these are already known to form a computable set (for example, a primitive recursive set of axioms).[31]

4.3 Von Neumann's Problem of Characterizing and Proving Unsolvability and Gödel's Theorem IX

Suppose we had taken derivability by a computation expressible in a first-order language as one's basic definition of computability. Then given the Gödel completeness theorem, any conventional formalism for first-order logic will be sufficient to formalize such derivability. In fact, in addition, one can give a universal characterization, also formalized in a first-order system, of derivability in arbitrary first-order systems. This will be the analog of the "universal Turing machine." It will be a short and direct step to conclude the undecidability in this sense of the *Entscheidungsproblem*.

Gandy (1988) gives a fascinating history of the development of notions of effective calculability.[32] He shows that the Hilbert school hoped and expected that the *Entscheidungsproblem* would prove to be solvable. It also hoped that such usual systems as Peano arithmetic would prove to be complete. The first expression of pessimism Gandy quotes within the Hilbert school[33] is from von Neumann (1927), who worries that a decision procedure for the *Entscheidungsproblem* would in effect abolish mathematics in place of a mechanical procedure, and therefore conjectures that such a procedure does not exist. He states, "We cannot at the moment prove this. We have no clue as to how such a proof of undecidability would go" (quoted in Gandy 1988, 62).

Gandy also has a somewhat similar quotation from G. H. Hardy:

Suppose, for example, that we could have a finite system of rules which enabled us to say whether any given formula was demonstrable or not [...]. There is of course no such theorem and this is very fortunate, since if there were we should have a mechanical set of rules for the solution of all mathematical problems, and our activities as mathematicians would come to an end. (Hardy 1929, 16; quoted in Gandy 1988, 62)

The context of this quotation is explicitly a discussion of Hilbert's metamathematics, and what would be desirable (a consistency proof) and undesirable (what we have quoted). However, he neither identifies this question with the *Entscheidungsproblem* for first-order logic, nor speculates (as von Neumann does) on the need for a proof of the impossibility of such a solution (or of such a finite set of rules).[34]

Gandy's next section discusses Gödel's Theorem IX in his famous paper (Gödel 1931; references are to the 1986 reprint). I think this theorem, and its anticipation of "Church's theorem," was for a long time neglected, but is now well known. The theorem states:

In any of the formal systems mentioned in Theorem VI, there are undecidable problems of the restricted functional calculus (that is, formulas of the restricted functional calculus for which neither validity nor the existence of a counterexample is provable). (Gödel 1931, 187, quoted in Gandy 1988, 63; italics in text, citations omitted)

Gödel goes on to say,

This is a consequence of Theorem X. *Every problem of the form (x) F(x) (with* [primitive] *recursive F) can be reduced to the question whether a certain formula of the restricted functional calculus is satisfiable* (that is, for every [primitive] recursive *F*, we can find a formula of the restricted functional calculus that is satisfiable if and only if (*x*) *F(x)* is true). (Gödel 1931, 187)

Gandy goes on to comment as follows:

Since the systems considered are ω-consistent extensions of a formulation *P* of the simple theory of types, they are powerful enough to define and prove simple facts about the satisfaction relation for the predicate calculus. For any such system Σ [primitive recursive ω-consistent extensions of simple type theory] Gödel constructs a formula φ_Σ which is satisfiable, but for which this fact cannot be proved in Σ. As a consequence, given any proposed algorithm α for the Entscheidungsproblem and any system Σ, either it cannot be proved in Σ that α always gives an answer, or it cannot be proved in Σ that its answer is always correct. (Gandy 1988, 63)

He concludes: "Thus Gödel's result meant that it was almost inconceivable that the *Entscheidungsproblem* should be decidable: a solution could, so to speak, only work by magic" (63).

Gandy's conclusion here strikes me as much too weak. It seems to me that Gödel's result *proves* that the algorithm α simply *cannot* be correct. First, we can simply suppose that in our extended system Σ we include axioms describing the alleged algorithm α. It describes a computation, which according to my familiar viewpoint, if it is to be an appropriate algorithm, its steps should follow from each other, and therefore be provable given the Gödel completeness theorem.[35] Let $A(x)$ be the statement that α terminates with the conclusion that x satisfies the algorithm. Then for each *n*, either $A(0^{(n)})$ or its negation is provable.[36] If the algorithm α is supposed to coincide with validity, simply add an axiom saying so, $(x)(A(x) \equiv \text{Val } (x))$. The resulting system is not ω-consistent, and therefore its axioms cannot be true. Hence (assuming the fault does not lie in the underlying system), the additional axioms cannot be true: α is supposed to be a genuine algorithm whose steps really follow from each other, so the fault can only lie in the failure of the last axiom $(x)(A(x) \equiv \text{Val } (x))$ to be true.

Note that though Gödel stated his result for extensions of simple type theory, he knew and claimed that it held for a variety of primitive recursively axiomatizable extensions of various systems, ranging from ZF set theory to weaker systems, such as first-order number theory.[37]

Another way of looking at the matter of Gödel's Theorem IX is as follows. In the same paper, Gödel introduces the notion of an *Entscheidungsdefinit* predicate[38] (in modern terminology, one that is strongly representable, binumerable, or numeralwise decidable), and states that his basic undecidability result (Theorem VI) still holds for any *Entscheidungsdefinit* ω-consistent extension of the basic system, since this is the only property of primitive recursiveness that has actually been used. He then states that the predicate of the universal statement that is undecidable would have to be *Entscheidungsdefinit*, not necessarily primitive recursive. A decision procedure for the predicate calculus would lead to an *Entscheidungsdefinit* predicate for validity or provability in some basic extension of the axiom system.

Nowadays, we would know that the form of the undecidable statement would not really change, and could go on to Gödel's Theorem IX as before. However, Gödel does not seem to have known this in 1931. In fact, he does not realize until 1936[39] (about the same time that the work of Church and Turing appeared) that for all reasonably strong systems, the class of sets definable by an *Entscheidungsdefinit* predicate is the same (the recursive sets).

Gandy goes on to state that Gödel's work did lead to skepticism about the solvability of the *Entscheidungsproblem* (63, section 6.1), and specifically mentions Herbrand and Schütte. In section 6.2, he asks, "A natural question to ask is why neither Gödel nor von Neumann *proved* the undecidability of the Entscheidungsproblem" (63). Gödel did not seem to have *regarded* himself as proving the undecidability. In his later paper (Gödel 1933), he gives a decidable class ("the Gödel case") and then shows that what may be natural to regard as the next largest case is a reduction class; that is, a decision procedure for it would lead to the decidability for the whole predicate calculus.[40] He does not say that such a decision procedure has been shown to be impossible. And we all know that he felt the question to be decided only by Turing's work.

From conversation I have the impression that some logicians feel that Gödel came very close to a negative solution to the *Entscheidungsproblem*, or even that all that was lacking was a version of Church's thesis. In any event, I feel that this is so. A decision procedure for the *Entscheidungsproblem* would have to be a procedure statable in the ordinary language of mathematics, whether the procedure operates by a machine program or instructions for a human computation. (Notice that in Gandy's exposition, ending with a weaker claim, it is still assumed that the algorithm α is statable in some extension of *P*, or whatever basic system is involved.) It could presumably be written in the language of *P*, perhaps with additional predicates and an additional finite number of instructions. Gödel's Theorem IX clearly directly implies Turing's result that the *Entscheidungsproblem* is not decidable on one of his machines, since we can simply add an axiomatization of the operation of the machine to his basic system.[41] As I said, the result would still obtain if Turing had allowed many dimensions. Similarly for a large class of mechanical procedures.

Thus I regard Gödel's Theorem IX as already answering von Neumann's 1927 problem, "we have no clue as to how such a proof of undecidability would go" (quoted by Gandy 1988, 62). In this respect, I disagree with the presupposition of Gandy's question quoted before: "A natural question to ask is why neither Gödel nor von Neumann *proved* the undecidability of the Entscheidungsproblem" (63). But Gandy's question is appropriate in the following form: why didn't Gödel and von Neumann regard Theorem IX as such a proof? One problem in the argument I have given that Theorem IX is such a proof is its free use of the notion of truth, and locating the trouble in one extra axiom that must be false. However, it seems very unlikely that Gödel, at least, would have regarded that as a questionable part of the argument.[42] What seems most likely lacking is an appropriate analog of Church's thesis.

4.4   Some Clarificatory Remarks on the Present Characterization

Let me state a few issues that I exclude from the domain of the present characterization of computability. In Gödel (1972), Gödel finds what he regards as "a philosophical error in Turing's work" (306). It is not utterly clear to me what Turing's error is supposed to be, but it is characterized as "an argument which is supposed to show that mental procedures cannot go beyond mechanical procedures" (306).[43] The error appears to be in Turing's assumption that only a finite number of states of mind need to be admitted. He says:

What Turing disregards completely is the fact that *mind, in its use, is not static, but constantly developing* […]. Therefore, although at each stage the number and precision of the abstract terms at our disposal may be *finite*, both (and, therefore, also Turing's number of *distinguishable states of mind*) may *converge toward infinity* in the course of the application of the procedure. Note that something like this indeed seems to happen in the process of forming stronger and stronger axioms of infinity in set theory. This process, however, today is far from being sufficiently understood to form a well-defined procedure. It must be admitted that the construction of a well-defined procedure which could actually be carried out (and would yield a non-recursive number-theoretic function) would require a substantial advance in our understanding of the basic concepts of mathematics.[44] (306)

Arguments by Gödel cannot be taken lightly, but it is difficult for me to see how Gödel has found any philosophical error in Turing's work, if that work is supposed to show what number theoretic functions can be regarded as effectively computable, even though we do not identify mental calculation with mechanical or routine calculation. Gödel directs his argument against Turing's argument I, but the objection, if valid, would apply to my own approach also, similar to Turing's argument II. It is difficult for the present writer to see why Kleene is not obviously correct when he says,

Thus algorithms have been procedures that mathematicians can describe completely to one another *in advance* of their application for various choices of the arguments. How could someone describe completely to me *in a finite interview* a process for finding the values of a number-theoretic function, the execution of which process for various arguments would be keyed to more than the *finite* subset of our mental states that would have developed by the end of the interview, though the total number of our mental states might converge to infinity if we were immortal (Kleene 1988, 50).

Thus I have regarded a function as computable when its values can be obtained for all arguments from some fixed finite set of instructions.[45]

It does not seem to me particularly relevant that the directions be public, that more than one person is involved.[46] It suffices that someone gives a finite set of directions to herself. Also it does not matter that the calculation be "mechanical," if this is a genuine limitation.[47] Any intelligible set of directions suffices, as long as they can be understood in classical first-order logic.

I also exclude from my discussion any consideration of computability based on intuitionism or intuitionistic ideas, in particular on the "intended interpretation" of intuitionistic logic. Kreisel has emphasized the following: if one has a proof of a statement of the existence of a natural number in an intuitionistic formal system, then, if intuitionism is really constructive, one must be able to calculate from the Gödel number of the proof of the existential statement to the numerical instance of that statement *given* by the proof (Kreisel 1970). And notice that though we may have various technical proofs that a particular intuitionistic system has "the numerical instantiation property" and some such technical proof may determine an appropriate recursive or Turing-computable function, who knows whether that is the "right" number in Kreisel's sense?[48] Certainly, Turing's analysis of computation (his argument I) does look irrelevant here, as does that of the present paper, based on classical first-order logic. I simply wish to exclude this problem; intuitionism plays no role in the sense of computability developed here. I think this sense includes anything called a "calculation" in the ordinary sense. (This sense is also developed in Turing's argument I.)

I also wish to exclude questions of empirically or physically based computation (which has already been alluded to in Martin Davis's talk at a 2006 conference). Below I will give an example of what I wish to exclude. Here we are talking about *mathematical* computation, whether done by a human being, or a machine,[49] or anything else.

Robin Gandy wrote a well-known and mathematically ingenious paper trying to generalize Turing's first argument to computing machines (Gandy 1980). He reports that many with whom he discussed the matter doubt that there is any problem to be solved, but others agree with him that Turing's analysis might fail for modern computing systems that use parallel processing. In his paper, Gandy gives a formal model (in hereditary finite sets from a set of atoms) for such computation. He then imposes a locality condition, which is supposed to mean that although parallel processing is allowed, one branch cannot influence another that is too far apart.

My main point in this part of the discussion will be to propose the basic approach of the present paper as an alternative to Gandy's, not only for human computation but for machine computation, including the types of cellular automata that worried Gandy. But no claim will be made about what machines are empirically realizable.

If Gandy had stipulatively defined his class of machines, there would be no issue of an empirical basis.[50] However, in fact Gandy appeals to special relativity to justify his new locality condition. (The idea is that no influence can travel faster than light.) He even wonders whether a machine whose operation is compatible with Newtonian physics might compute a nonrecursive function, even an arbitrary function (in his colorful terminology, exercise "free will").[51]

Some important writers have held that Gandy was indeed the first to prove that actual digital computers do compute only the recursive (Turing-computable) functions.[52] However, an appeal to special relativity makes the adequacy of Gandy's analysis an empirical issue, depending on the actual state of physics. Because of this a wealth of literature gives putative counterexamples, in both hypothetical[53] and possibly true physics (see Copeland and Shagrir 2007 for a survey). There appears to be a particular interest in what I have been inclined to call "Zenonian calculation," where one can perform an infinite number of operations in a finite time, analogously to Zeno's paradox. Then one could plainly go beyond the recursive or Turing-computable functions, as Copeland and Shagrir explain.[54] In particular, many authors are discussed who speculate on models of general relativity in which what appears to be a computation of the infinite (and thus maybe Zenonian) type in one part of the model is only finite in time from another, later point of view. This literature is only slightly known to me, and much is beyond my competence to evaluate, would I have studied it. However, it does seem clear that if one bases Gandy's thesis on empirical questions of physics, one is on dangerous ground, even if there is no known violation by the computing machines of today.

Copeland and Shagrir also do discuss (2007, section 3) "non-discrete machines" that make use of continuously valued quantities. As they say, in Gandy's published paper he explicitly excludes "devices which are *essentially* analogue machines" (Gandy 1980, 125), though he mentions some possibilities. In unpublished work,

Gandy does consider such devices, and conjectures a strategy to succeed in showing that no feasible such device goes beyond Turing computability (see the discussion of Gandy's unpublished manuscript in Copeland and Shagrir 2007, section 3).

One very simple example of that kind that has always troubled me is as follows. Consider such dimensionless physical constants as the electron-proton mass ratio, or the fine structure constant.[55] As far as I have heard, at the present time physical theory has nothing much to say about the mathematical properties of these numbers, whether they are algebraic or transcendental, or even rational or irrational. In particular, it might well be the case that the decimal expansions of these numbers are not Turing computable. Assume this is so, and also assume that time is infinite in extent and that there are no limitations in energy that prevent computations of these decimals to any number of places. As far as I can see, nothing in principle rules this out. Then an empirically possible machine would exist that calculates a decimal not computable in Turing's sense.[56, 57]

This example could have philosophical implications for the physical applicability of other theories. Hermann Weyl, in his famous monograph (Weyl 1918), showed how a great deal of analysis can be done allowing only arithmetically definable reals. Extensive and mathematically impressive work, which I much admire, has been done by Solomon Feferman, extending Weyl's ideas to richer systems with higher types. Feferman emphasizes that everything can be done in a conservative extension of Peano arithmetic (first-order arithmetic). Here we are concerned only with the question of whether this work is adequate for physics, which Feferman has explicitly claimed to be the case (see Feferman 1992).[58]

Not only is there no reason to suppose that the electron-proton mass ratio, described as a decimal, is Turing computable, there is no reason to suppose that it is arithmetical, hyperarithmetical, or, for that matter, definable in set theory. For all we know, the physical theory of the future may somehow imply that the truth set for Peano arithmetic is definable in terms of the electron-proton mass ratio, and even use it to show that physical theory is not a conservative extension of that system.

Let me propose an alternative to Gandy's approach, divorcing the question of machine computability from all empirical assumptions. As I said, computation is simply a form of mathematical argument. Let us consider only those devices that are describable in a first-order language, and whose program is such that the successive states logically follow from each other, one by one, together with the program and perhaps some basic mathematical assumptions. Any particular computation by the machine is assumed to be finite in length, and the machine states describable finitely, and following each other discretely. This I wish to assume whether or not parallel processing is involved. Certainly, this class of machines includes Conway's Game of Life (see Gardner 1970), which Gandy specifically cites as much of the inspiration for his paper.[59, 60, 61]

Let me now return to our basic topic. Church's thesis, in its weakest form, is simply that the decidable sets are recursive, or correspondingly for functions and partial functions. Thus if we know that a set of natural numbers is finite, say by knowing an upper bound to the set, we know that the set is recursive, even though we may have in fact no knowledge which numbers are in the set and which are not.[62]

Thus there is some interest in what might be called an "intensional," or alternatively, "effective," form of Church's thesis. The term "Church's superthesis" has also been used (I think it is due to Kreisel). The idea is that any intuitive set of instructions for a computation can effectively be transformed into a computation given in one of the conventional formalisms (Post's "routine chore"). Philosophically, this strikes me as interesting for the following reason. The usual formalisms for Church-Turing computability transform any argument using the intuitive notion of computability on the natural numbers into one using a chosen formal notion. The intuitive argument can disappear as part of the motivation but not of the argument itself, which can be formalized in set theory, or indeed in number theory. However, this is no longer so for the present case. A significant effectiveness claim is being made, but it is hard to see how it can be replaced by a formal claim, statable in set theory. Nor is it an intuitionistic claim; it is supposed to be directly intelligible to the classical mathematician, and may apply to intuitive effectiveness arguments that require further work to be valid intuitionistically (perhaps it cannot even be made intuitionistically valid). Kleene's S_n^m theorem could be considered a partial formalization of this claim, but not completely so.[63]

If we are given a linear computation, in terms of the present formalism, the problem is simply writing out the steps explicitly in the formalism of first-order logic. The completeness theorem, given that the steps follow from each other, will guarantee that the steps follow in a usual formalism for first-order logic.[64] As I already mentioned from the pedagogical point of view, this is easier than translating into one of the other standard formalisms.

The translation is of course more natural if it is done in a natural deduction system rather than in a Hilbert-type system. Nevertheless, there remains a further problem, also to be stated in terms of the effective form of Church's thesis. For so far, we have shown only that each step of a (discrete) linear computation will follow from its predecessor and the appropriate instructions. However, we have not shown that a formalized deduction will not need irrelevant steps in between the formalized intuitive steps, steps that would not have been used in the intuitive argument. Here Prawitz (1965) is a monograph that would seem to be specifically relevant, since it shows how to eliminate unnecessary steps in a natural deduction argument.[65] (Fine 1985 may also be relevant.)

Although I am trying as much as possible to appeal to actual theorems, in this case to show that the computation can be formalized without unnecessary steps not to be found in the intuitive argument, I certainly cannot claim to have thought this aspect of the matter through. The work of Prawitz (1965) may not always be the right thing to cite because the intuitive computation being formalized may itself contain unnecessary steps that would have been eliminated by a clever researcher. Or, perhaps, one is dealing with a procedure that perversely goes about things in a roundabout way. As in other cases of translating recursion theoretic arguments into a formalism, but here more basically as a special case of the formalization of mathematical arguments, it may be that we should best appeal to practical experience, antedating Gödel's completeness theorem, let alone the more sophisticated work just mentioned. That in practice such arguments can be so formalized already goes back to the early work of Frege, Russell, et al., in formalizing mathematical arguments. Today this would be most naturally done in a natural deduction system. But the steps in the formalization would by definition mirror those in the informal argument. Nevertheless, it would be the Gödel completeness theorem that guarantees that there is not some intuitively valid argument not formalizable in the usual formalisms.

4.5   Conclusion

How far does this paper go toward satisfying the expressed desire of some people (including my earlier self) for a proof of Church's thesis? The basic idea, assuming a set of intuitively evident axioms for computability, is most explicitly given in two contemporary papers, several by Sieg (see Sieg 2008, and other writings), and Dershowitz and Gurevich (2008).

Arguably, the present argument, which does not give a particular axiomatization,[66] but does simply propose a new characterization of computability, only reduces one unproved hypothesis to another one, namely, that the statements in mathematical arguments can be described in first-order systems. It then points out that the formal characterization of computability can be derived from the Gödel completeness theorem (in fact, that the formal characterization might well be given directly in terms of first-order formalizability).

However, surely something is achieved here. Even the form in which I have just stated it, reducing one thesis to another one, is a fact worth noting. And various consequences of this fact have been noted above. But also, we can state a theorem restricted to algorithms whose steps can be stated in first-order logic, and the special case of the Gödel completeness theorem can be called the "first-order algorithm theorem." I took this term to be fundamental in earlier versions of this paper. First-order algorithms happen to include all known algorithms, whether done by human or machine.

Some of the authors I have discussed also let their results depend on the primacy of computations whose steps are statable in first-order logic. Although in its discussion of his machines, Gandy (1980) makes the development entirely independent of any reference to first-order logic, in its discussion of Gödel's Theorem IX (as quoted above), Gandy (1988) does not question that the algorithm α in question should be formalizable (statable) in some suitable axiomatizable extension of the basic system *P* (or whatever), perhaps with new predicates. On this basis, I have argued that his conclusion about Theorem IX ought to have been stronger. More basically, the highly ambitious paper by Dershowitz and Gurevich, giving an axiomatization leading to a proof of Church's thesis that they think is more basic and general than earlier ones (such as are explicit in Sieg and implicit in Gandy et al.), makes a fundamental appeal to the notion of an arbitrary first-order structure. They write: "The justification for postulating that structures or algebras are appropriate for capturing algorithmic states is the enormous experience of mathematicians who have faithfully and transparently presented every kind of static mathematical reality as a first-order structure" (Dershowitz and Gurevich 2008, 317). They rightly state (and see my corresponding discussion above) that their notion of structure is more general than Gandy's idea of a machine as represented as a hereditary finite set, and mention numerous other computing languages, etc. So they appeal to the same mathematical experience that I do.[67]

So, to restate my central thesis: computation is a special form of deduction. If we restrict ourselves to algorithms whose instructions and steps can be stated in a first-order language (first-order algorithms), and these include all algorithms currently known, the Church-Turing characterization of the class of computable functions can be represented as a special corollary of the Gödel completeness theorem.[68,69]

Notes

1. The present paper is an edited transcript of a talk delivered at the 21st International Workshop on the History and Philosophy of Science, "The Origins and Nature of Computation," held in Tel Aviv and Jerusalem, Israel, on June 12–15, 2006. The fact that this is a transcript of a paper delivered orally, rather than written, accounts for a certain amount of conversational tone. A version of this lecture was first given in August 1998 at the Association for Symbolic Logic in conjunction with the International Congress of Mathematicians, Humboldt University, Berlin, Germany.

2. See the explicit statement on 318: "While we cannot prove Church's thesis, since its role is to delimit precisely an hitherto vaguely conceived totality, we require evidence that it cannot conflict with the intuitive notion which it is supposed to complete." Kleene's section 62 is a summary of the evidence. Much of it is presented in detail in other sections. For another statement of the conventional view, see, for example, Cutland (1980). He says: "Note immediately that this thesis [Church's thesis] is not a *theorem* which is susceptible to mathematical proof; it has the status of a *claim* or *belief* which must be substantiated by evidence" (67). Cutland follows this statement with a brief survey of the evidence.

3. Dershowitz and Gurevich (2008, 305), who quote Shoenfield's later statement, also refer to a letter from Church to Kleene, quoted by Davis (1982, 9). This letter, dated November 29, 1935, does quote

Gödel as suggesting "that it might be possible, in terms of effective calculability as an undefined notion, to state a set of axioms which would embody the generally accepted properties of this notion, and to do something on that basis" (Davis 1982, 9). This would indeed be a striking anticipation at a very early date, by the greatest logician of all time, of the later writers I have referred to. However, the full context quoted makes this anticipation a bit weaker. He was fending off a challenge from Church to give a mathematically defined class of effectively computable functions that he (Church) could not prove to be λ-definable. Certainly, he didn't publish this remark.

Nevertheless, by the time my lecture was given in Israel perhaps the number of authors who agree with my view was great enough that I shouldn't have referred to the opposite idea (that no mathematical proof of Church's thesis could possibly be given) as the "conventional view." I should add that both Soare (1996) and Gandy (1980, 1988) think that Turing (1936–37) already gave a mathematical proof that any function calculable by a human being in a routine way was Turing computable, as opposed to simply a convincing argument for this thesis. That Turing himself seems to have held the second and more modest view is argued in my main text. (All future page references to Turing 1936–37 are to the 1965 reprint.)

4. In my (1996) manuscript *Elementary Recursion Theory and Its Applications to Formal Systems*, I express my agreement with the view of Shoenfield (1993) and Harvey Friedman that the equation of mathematical recursiveness and intuitive computability is a meaningful mathematical problem. I even give a proof in one direction that the mathematical concept implies the intuitive one (see next note). However, I state that "while this [a rigorous proof that the intuitive and the mathematical concept are the same] is in principle possible, it has not yet been done (and it seems to be a very difficult task)" (14). See also the references in Dershowitz and Gurevich (2008, 339), quoting me to that effect and Richard Shore in agreement with me. However, Friedman is quoted as more hopeful that reasonably soon Church's thesis will be proved in the appropriate sense (using weak and intuitive axioms for computation).

5. I give my own proof of this (easy) half in my manuscript Kripke (1996, 14–15). Actually, what I proved is that every recursively enumerable relation (or set) is semi-computable (i.e., has a proof procedure). I then characterized a relation as computable when it and its complement are semi-computable. Note my further comments that this is a mathematical proof that cannot be formalized in ZF set theory, so that if the statement that "all mathematics can be formalized in set theory" is taken too strongly, it is not so. The view is sometimes taken that the problem ought to be regarded as one in intuitionistic mathematics. This is not the point of view taken in this version of the argument. Indeed, intuitionistically the characterization of a decidable relation as one such that it and its complement are semi-computable is not obvious, and requires supplementary argument. See also my stipulative exclusion of using intuitionistic ideas in the notion of computation in the text below.

6. In his famous paper, Gödel (1931), Gödel actually calls them "the recursive functions." The term "primitive recursive" stems from Kleene (1936). See also Kleene (1981, 53).

7. I find that Barendregt (1997, 187) also gives the same argument I have just given about the Ackermann function. In fairness to Barendregt, and contrary to what I argue immediately above, his position is that, like the thesis on primitive recursiveness, Church's thesis could be disproved, but it cannot be proved. Our failure to find a similar disproof is thought to be empirical evidence that the thesis is true. On the other hand, Dershowitz and Gurevich (2008, 304) quote Barendregt's argument in the context of a paper whose very title, "A Natural Axiomatization of Computability and Proof of Church's Thesis," indicates their belief that Church's thesis can be proved.

In further fairness to historical accuracy, I should add that giving a counterexample to an identification of the primitive recursive functions with the effectively calculable functions does not appear to have been Ackermann's main goal in the paper.

Today, independently of Ackermann's work, it would be obvious to us that primitive recursion could not exhaust intuitive effective calculability. We can effectively enumerate all directions for computing primitive recursive functions, and then use a diagonal argument to define a calculable function that cannot be primitive recursive. On the basis of Kleene's discussion of the matter I credit this argument as originally given by Péter (1935). Kleene also states that Péter in the same paper (and also Robinson 1948) simplify Ackermann's original example (see Kleene 1952, 271–272).

I might make one remark about the argument I have given. Certainly the existence of a measurable cardinal could be disproved in ZF set theory, and in fact this has been attempted. However, the existence of a measurable (and other large cardinals) cannot be proved in ZF set theory, and I do not detect any particular interest in finding evident seeming extra axioms that might favor their existence. Advocates of large cardinals seem rather to favor them because of their fecundity in proving allegedly plausible consequences. Note that it is still true that, if one believes in conventional ZF set theory, the existence of a measurable cardinal is of course a definite mathematical question.

8. I should mention that Soare (1996) distinguishes between Church's thesis or argument, which he regards as defective, and Turing's thesis or argument as intensionally different, and only the latter as really convincing. Following conventional terminology, I am not worrying about this distinction here, since the "theses" have been proved equivalent.

9. Soare also quotes Davis as telling him that Gödel reacted sharply to the term "recursion theory" for the subject, and that the term should be "used by reference to the kind of work Rózsa Péter did" (307–308). Nevertheless, there are places in print in the Gödel papers themselves where Gödel uses such terms as "general recursiveness (or Turing's computability)" (Gödel 1990, 150) and "a non-recursive number theoretic function" (Gödel 1990, 306). I don't know if this shows very much.

Soare's proposal has been generally adopted, so that terms such as "recursively enumerable" have given way to "computably enumerable." Agreement with Soare has not been unanimous among writers in the subject. I have been told that Martin Davis sees little reason for the change. Slaman, quoted in the text, also dissents from the view.

10. I heard Slaman advocate the view that the subject should be a theory of definability as much as computability in his Gödel lecture at the 2001 meeting of the Association for Symbolic Logic. The title of the lecture is "Recursion Theory."

In my own manuscript Kripke (1996), I independently had taken a definability approach to the subject myself. In fairness to Soare, he states "other concepts [as opposed to computability] (recursion, definability) are very important but not at the center" (Soare 1996, 314), thus explicitly rejecting the view of the subject taken by Slaman and myself.

Looking at this matter again now, I find that Soare may well be correct as to what has become the most important concept. However, like Slaman, I find definability a very important concept (as Soare acknowledges) and important for a good development of the subject and for its applicability to formal systems.

11. Even in much more recent (late-twentieth-century) dictionaries I happen to possess, the definition of a "computer" as such a person is still recognized as one possible meaning. It is actually hard to imagine that it could be otherwise.

12. In these papers the authors propose to adopt the spelling "computor" for Turing's notion of a human being making a computation, so as to avoid confusion with the contemporary notion of a "computer" as a machine. It is even proposed to take Turing's paper as giving a characterization of the "computorable" numbers (functions), again to avoid confusion.

Sieg (1994, 71) quotes Wittgenstein: "Turing's 'Machines'. These machines are *humans* who calculate" (Wittgenstein 1980, § 1096). The quotation, though insightful, is somewhat confusingly put. Better would have been: These machines are Turing's mechanical model of *humans* who calculate.

13. See Shagrir (2002), who argues that whatever the historical situation about Turing's original analysis may be, "Today computer scientists view effective computability in terms of finite machine computation" (221, abstract). I myself recall the lecture notes from one logician who stated the evidence for Turing's thesis in terms of contemporary computing machines. He emphasized that every high-speed computer (idealized appropriately in infinite capacity and in terms of its programming language) is in effect a universal Turing machine. Shagrir gives various other examples from contemporary writings. All or most seem to be written independently of Gandy's worries about the distinction between Turing's original analysis and goals and the machine formulation of the problem.

Yet another influence is Turing's own historical role in the development of high-speed computing devices.

14. Shagrir (2006) refers to both argument I and argument III.

15. To understand Gandy, it ought to be explained that "working in a routine way" is meant to exclude Gödel's objection to Turing's (first) argument, based on the notion that the mind might provide creative insights enabling it to go beyond Turing's analysis. He refers to Wang (1974, 325–26); I will discuss this objection in the main text below.

16. Although Soare is right to state that a rigorous mathematical argument need not be presented in a formal system, once one sees the desirability of an informal axiomatization, in the spirit of other con-

temporary axiomatizations, the rest would only be a routine matter of formalization, though it is not necessary.

17. This discussion raises a fascinating issue in the history and philosophy of mathematics and deserves considerable discussion that cannot be made here.

But to one part of the discussion I would like to make one correction (as I see it). Everyone relies on Kline: "Up to about 1650 no one believed that the length of a curve could equal exactly the length of a line. In fact, in the second book of *La Geometrie*, Descartes says the relation between curved lines and straight lines is not nor ever can be known" (Kline 1972, 354; quoted by Soare 1996, 297). But all this strikes me as very unclear. Descartes does say this. But to say that the relation between curved and straight lines can never be known is not clearly to be construed as claiming that the length of a curve and that of a line must be different, only that they are forever undecided. One might as well take a statement that the relation between the power of the continuum and $\aleph_1$ will never be known as asserting categorically that they are different. (Greater study of Descartes than I have made is needed, but I would presume that Descartes was uncertain whether the geometric straight line is complete. Otherwise, one would have to assume that he was unaware that the circumference of a circle can be arbitrarily approximated by inscribed polygons, and of the way π is calculated.) In addition, Kline presents no evidence that until 1650 everyone assumed that Descartes was right. So here I think Kline has gone considerably beyond his stated evidence.

As again Soare's proposal that Turing computability be taken as a definition of computability: "One senior logician objected to this proposed definition because he said we should view the Church-Turing Thesis as certainly correct, but as 'a one of a kind, without any true analogue in mathematics. I think we recursion theorists [*sic*; note the terminology] should be proud of this, and not (as you seem to suggest) replace it by a change of our definitions.' There is no reason why we cannot use Turing's Thesis as a definition of computability and still maintain awe and pride at a fundamental discovery" (Soare 1996, 296). But Soare regards Turing's argument I as the proof of a *theorem*. Does he give any example where a *theorem* (as opposed to a thesis or analysis *simpliciter*) became a definition? (He proposes other "theses" that, according to him, became definitions.)

18. That Turing says this is pointed out by Sieg (1994, 97). Paradoxically, this is the very same author who has done more than anyone else to justify the later claims that in his first argument Turing proved a theorem, by giving an axiomatic development of his work (see Sieg 2008).

19. Nevertheless, it is of course possible that Turing was excessively modest in his claims, and that he had, in effect, proved a theorem.

Moreover, I myself argue below that Gödel could have regarded his Theorem IX (Gödel 1931) as a proof of the undecidability of the *Entscheidungsproblem*, but did not do so. For this case, see the discussion below.

20. To put the matter more precisely, Turing's second argument presupposes some viewpoint such as the one taken in the present paper. All references to Turing's paper are to the 1965 reprint. See also the exposition, history, and analysis by Sieg (1997).

In addition to crediting Turing and Church themselves, I should add that I have heard reports to the effect that Martin Davis gave some consideration to a justification of Church's thesis in terms of first-order logic some time ago. At the Berlin conference (see note 1, this paper) Ronald Jensen told me that in lectures he had always emphasized formalizability in first-order logic, but had not at that time believed there was a theorem to be proved.

21. Martin Davis originated the term "Hilbert's thesis"; see Barwise (1977, 41). Davis's formulation of Hilbert's thesis, as stated by Barwise, is that "the informal notion of *provable* used in mathematics is made precise by the formal notion *provable in first-order logic*" (Barwise 1977, 41). The version stated here, however, is weaker. Rather than referring to provability, it is simply that any mathematical *statement* can be formulated in a first-order language. Thus, it is about statability, rather than provability. For the purposes of the present paper, it could be restricted to steps of a computation.

Very possibly the weaker thesis about statability might have originally been intended. Certainly Hilbert and Ackermann's famous textbook (Hilbert and Ackermann 1928) still regards the completeness of conventional predicate logic as an open problem, unaware of the significance of the work already done in that direction. Had Gödel not solved the problem in the affirmative a stronger formalism would have been necessary, or conceivably no complete system would have been possible. It is true, however, that Hilbert's program for interpreting proofs with ε-symbols presupposed a predicate calculus of the usual form. There was of course "heuristic" evidence that such a system was adequate, given the experience since Frege, Whitehead and Russell, and others.

Note also that Hilbert and Ackermann do present the "restricted calculus," as they call it, as a fragment of the second-order calculus, and ultimately of the logic of order ω. However, they seem to identify even the second-order calculus with set theory, and mention the paradoxes. Little depends on these exact historical points.

22. Throughout this paper I will mean first-order logic with identity when I refer to first-order logic. Other qualifications and explanations will be given below in the text.

23. But of course not both. A proper computation does not give inconsistent instructions.

24. But the fault may be mine in concentration rather than Turing's in exposition. However, see also the correction to the treatment of the unsolvability of the *Entscheidungsproblem* in Turing (1936–37, 152–153), which Turing attributes to Bernays.

25. According to the account in Sieg (1997)—and, of course, see also Church (1936a)—Church originally thought (in what has been called his "step by step" argument) that if a formal system did not have recursive rules, they would have to be unrecognizably complicated, and it would be doubtful that they could be effective. He also emphasized that his requirements were satisfied by all existing systems of symbolic logic.

All charges of circularity against Church would disappear if one supplemented his argument with a recognition of the primacy of first-order logic (or at least in the metatheory of the formal system described), and Gödel's completeness theorem for an appropriate set of rules for first-order logic. Church's famous paper (1936b) can be regarded as an implicit recognition of this primacy. And his argument is certainly that computation is a form of deduction within a system, very much in the spirit of the present paper.

26. And for sets, similarly for relations and functions. Also, one can regard a set as admitting a proof procedure (or semi-computable) if such a procedure allows us to prove membership in the set if and only if it holds, but says nothing about nonmembership (the analog of what is classically called recursive enumerability). It is of course a classical result of recursion theory (computability theory) that this is a weaker notion than decidability.

27. See Cutland (1980). He says: "For the practiced student there is the additional evidence of his own experience in translating informal algorithms into formal counterparts. For the beginner, our use of Church's thesis in subsequent chapters may call on his willingness to place confidence in the ability of others until self confidence is developed" (70). The trouble is that someone who learns computability theory from a text such as Cutland's probably will never have developed such confidence by himself and will forever rely on others. One who learns the basics from a book such as Kleene (1952) may get lost in the formalism.

28. Some basic theorems, in particular the enumeration theorem for recursively enumerable sets, may be simpler using such a formalism, or one of the traditional formalisms, than the proposed formalism based on logic. However, the logical formalism will have its own version of the universal Turing machine in a formulation in first-order logic of all first-order formalisms. See the text below.

29. Such coding is not really necessary. The states could be directly represented in the first-order language. No doubt the natural numbers, or n-tuples of them, would be natural for representing the individual cells of the machine.

30. The Herbrand-Gödel-Kleene equation–calculus formalism somewhat resembles such a narrow system, but is differently motivated, as stated.

31. Of course, many or most of the conventional systems of mathematical logic have infinitely many axioms above those of logic itself; for example, the usual first-order arithmetic, or the usual formalization of ZF set theory. The philosophical difficulties involved in our ability to understand these systems are interestingly discussed in Martin's paper "Sets versus Classes" (1974), which has circulated but is unpublished.

32. Another interesting and later history and analysis is given by Sieg (1994), and has been used above.

33. For the full quotation from von Neumann, which is very interesting, see Gandy (1988, 61–62). Outside the Hilbert school, Gandy discusses Brouwer's skepticism as to the decidability of all mathematical problems and Post's claim to have early shown the existence of a recursively enumerable set that is not recursive (61). Gandy mentions (62) that in fact mechanizability in principle would not necessarily put mathematics at an end. For example, some problems in elementary geometry that in principle might be

solved by Tarski's decision procedure still are unsolved and require conventional mathematical methods in practice.

34. Gandy writes: "Hardy might have read von Neumann's paper, or have heard of it from F. P. Ramsey; in his lecture he discusses Hilbert's ideas at length, but he does not refer to von Neumann" (Gandy 1988, 63). Actually, Gandy is mistaken on this factual point. Hardy emphasizes a paper by von Neumann, who is explicitly named as "a pupil of Hilbert," whose statement he finds "sharper and more sympathetic than Hilbert's own" (Hardy 1929, 14; see also the postscript, 25). Gandy rightly says, "because he [Hardy] wrote the text for a lecture he gives no precise references" (62). Although Hardy does not say which paper by von Neumann he has read, it seems to me pretty clear from his statement that it is a presentation of Hilbert's point of view and program, as well as the relevant dates, that it is von Neumann (1927), the very paper quoted by Gandy.

35. It is especially clear if the steps are given deterministically, as described above. But even if they are given nondeterministically, the result follows.

36. We assume some Gödel numbering of the formulae of the predicate calculus.

37. For this system, it would be simplest to replace validity by provability. But it could still be proved that any Π_1^0 sentence is equivalent to the consistency of a formula of first-order logic. Actually, and contrary to any impression given by Gandy's discussion, provability of the equivalence in the underlying system is not really needed. One could add axioms asserting the equivalence in each case. Notice also that it is not really relevant whether one can prove that the procedure always gives an answer. Gandy's other alternative that "it cannot be proved in Σ that its answer is always correct" (63) is answered in my text simply by taking this correctness as an axiom.

38. Gödel 1931, 176ff.

39. Gödel 1936.

40. The decidable case for satisfiability is statement in prenex form with just two consecutive existential quantifiers in the prefix, surrounded on both sides by strings of universal quantifiers. He goes on to show that if three consecutive existential quantifiers are allowed, a decision procedure would allow one for the predicate calculus as a whole (in modern terminology, that this is a reduction class for satisfiability). He does not state that he has shown in 1931 that such a decision procedure is impossible (though he may well have believed that such a procedure is in fact impossible, and even implicitly implied this belief).

41. However, of course Gödel could still quite consistently regard the *Entscheidungsproblem* and other such questions about effective calculability, the definition of formal system, and so on, as only decided by Turing's work. This is so even though after it had been done (after the fact, so to speak) it can be seen that the result follows from his Theorem IX.

42. At least, given Gödel's own account of his philosophical orientation.

Notice that even Gandy's late characterization of the consequences of Gödel's theorem IX is, in my opinion, still too weak.

43. Gödel refers to Turing (1936–37, 136).

44. This is the argument that, as we saw above in note 15, leads Gandy to qualify his statement of what Turing achieved in analyzing human computation. The interested reader ought to look at the entire argument, condensed here. The argument has attracted some amount of commentary, not entirely known to the present writer. See both the commentary in Gödel (1990) and by Sieg in the present volume (not known to me at the time of writing).

45. Gödel's argument seems to me to differ little in spirit from Kalmar's argument against Church's thesis. Kalmar argues (1959) in effect that every purely existential predicate (defining a recursively enumerable predicate) ought to be decidable as follows: for a positive solution, search systematically for a numerical instance for the existential quantifier. Simultaneously, for a negative solution, look for a proof by "arbitrary correct means" of the impossibility of such an instance. Is this an algorithm or a procedure? If it were, we should have used it to decide Fermat's last theorem, and should still try it on the Riemann hypothesis and the Goldbach conjecture. In fact, no doubt some people are trying this strategy, but they hardly think of it as an algorithmic procedure. Much less should one try such an "algorithm" on the halting problem or the *Entscheidungsproblem*.

46. Kleene's remarks give the impression that it is important that directions be communicated or communicable from one mathematician to another. But this seems to me to be inessential.

47. Davis writes: "We are not concerned here with attempts to distinguish 'mechanical procedures' (to which Church's thesis is held to apply) from a possible broader class of 'effective procedures'" (Davis 1982, 22). Davis gives two authors as examples of what he has in mind, and, as he indicates, there are others. See also Gandy's claim, quoted above, that Turing's analysis applies to "a human being working in a routine way."

48. Moreover, Kreisel did not believe that it was a necessary condition for the acceptability of an intuitionistic system that it have the numerical instantiation property (even though standard such systems do in fact have it). For all that is required for the intuitionistic acceptability of a proof of an existential statement, even formalized in a system, is that from this proof one could obtain an intuitionistic proof of an instance, not that the proof could be formalized in the same system.

In conversation with me when he was wondering about this issue, he told me he convinced himself that for relevant intuitionistic systems, a cut elimination argument gives the "right" instance.

I have hardly exhausted the many discussions of Church's thesis, considered as a problem for the intuitionistic notion of number theoretic function, both in Kreisel's writings and in many others. The issue is simply excluded in this paper, and the discussion in the text gives one significant example.

49. What do I mean by "mathematical calculation by a machine"? I am not talking about "whether a machine can think." What I mean is that I am considering only machine programs whose successive steps follow from each other mathematically.

50. Shagrir (2002, 235) suggests two such interpretations, and attributes one of them to Sieg.

51. In fact, he gives several conditions to define his class of machines, and argues that dropping any one of them will allow the machine to exercise "free will."

52. For example, Soare (1996) and Sieg (2008).

53. I mean, for example, Newtonian physics.

54. For a quotation from Russell about this possibility see Copeland and Shagrir (2007), at the beginning of section 6. They then go on to explain how one can use what I call "Zenonian machines" to solve the halting problem.

I confess that at times past I have been sympathetic to an assumption that Zenonian calculation could be regarded as a far-fetched possibility, and that if time is finite in extent, the question of what functions are empirically computable would be meaningless.

55. When I discussed this issue in Berlin (1998; see note 1), I assumed that these were universal physical constants. I had seen this assumption in my own reading, and had already explicitly discussed the issue with an eminent physicist, including the question whether anything is known about the mathematical properties of these constants, and in particular, whether they were Turing computable. This discussion confirmed what I have to say in the text.

However, I have now heard that some physicists speculate that (say) the electron-proton mass ratio may be subject to change over time. Then what I have to say in the text would need reformulation, though I don't think it would be invalidated. I do not bother with the question further, since the point is that empirical assumptions cannot guarantee that actual machines compute Turing-computable functions, and that in fact the situation is even worse.

56. Brouwer observed, in effect, that even if we can calculate a real number with an arbitrary degree of precision, this does not mean that we can calculate all its decimal places, because a number representable with a finite decimal, not ending in 0, followed by an infinite string of 0s, can also be represented by a finite decimal with the next-lower last place, followed by a string of 9s. But on the assumptions we have just made, this possibility (and problem) is excluded (see Brouwer 1921). Note that Turing, whose original work was on computable *numbers* rather than computable functions, felt obligated in the published correction to the original paper to worry about this problem (ignored in the original paper). He refers explicitly to Brouwer (see Turing 1936–37, 153–154). I could have stated the present observations using Brouwerian approximations rather than decimals.

57. My editors have pointed out to me that similar thoughts were entertained by Kreisel and by Marian Pour-El and Ian Richards, who asked "Can one predict theoretically on the basis of some current physical theory—e.g. classical mechanics or quantum mechanics—the existence of a physical constant which is not a recursive real?" (Pour-El and Richards 1979, 63; Kreisel 1974, 11). Copeland speculated that the "magnitude of some physical quantity might conceivably be exactly τ units", where τ is a real number that is not Turing computable (Copeland 2000, 18); and computer scientist Hava Siegelmann notes that,

if there are uncomputable real constants in nature, then the "fact that the constants are not known to us or cannot even be measured is irrelevant for the true evolution of the system" (Siegelmann 2003, 110).

58. Much more is at issue than I can discuss here. But I should add that I am not myself in sympathy with the trend, prominent in some analytical philosophers, to say that mathematics ought to be justified (and can only by justified) by its applicability to physics. In fact, if we take physics at any one time, including probably today, the mathematics needed to apply to physics would include some "mathematics" that is not valid. In addition, I think that mathematics is an enterprise justified in itself, not in terms of its use in a particular other discipline. This is not the place to elaborate.

59. My attitude may be close to that of Dershowitz and Gurevich (2008).

60. All the papers quoted above that question Gandy's argument attempt to give (highly speculative) examples of empirically possible machines that go beyond Turing computability. Without knowing anything about the subject, except what I could glean from popular accounts, I have wondered whether quantum computing, an ongoing project known to be contained in Turing computing, might be an example of a hypothetical type of machine not covered by Gandy's theorem, but that might be covered by the present approach, or that of Dershowitz and Gurevich (2008). Gandy's theorem assumes a locality condition. Even though the Einstein-Podolsky-Rosen (EPR) paradox is accepted not to contradict special relativity, correlations at arbitrary distances do appear to be an essential part of quantum computing, using EPR. Thus I am not sure that Gandy's invocation of special relativity really does show that his theorem covers quantum computing. But to repeat, I am hardly really familiar with the subject.

61. Gandy worries that machines obeying Newtonian physics may violate his theorem, since he assumes special relativity, as just mentioned. But there would be no problem if each state is finitely describable in conventional first-order logic, and the operation of the machine is deterministic, so that each state follows from the previous state, and the laws governing the operation of the machine.

62. In Church (1956), section 46, Church himself lists several decidable special cases of the *Entscheidungsproblem*, largely due to others. Later, in the errata (377), Church mentions that one of his cases (case X, 257) is in fact finite (or essentially so, except for such things as changes of bound variables). Hence of course it is decidable, but Church says that there is still some interest in giving an actual decision procedure.

63. Given what we know today, there are further problems with this example, but I choose to leave the matter obscure.

64. Or rather, more exactly, that given the set of basic instructions, the conditional from any one step to the following step will follow in first-order logic.

65. However, perhaps there may be a problem in the use of such a result. After all, the original intuitive computation may itself contain unnecessary steps, that could have been, but were not in fact, eliminated. Arguably, a true translation of the argument should preserve this.

66. Though, I think I might have been able to put the matter that way. But I do not wish to obscure the simplicity of the basic point.

67. They write: "An alternative approach to proving Church's Thesis has been suggested by Kripke, based on 'Hilbert's Thesis' that 'any mathematical argument [...] can be formalized in some first-order language,' and—in particular—arguments about the effects of applying the instructions of an algorithm can be so formalized" (Dershowitz and Gurevich 2008, 340). (They mean "alternative" to various approaches, such as Turing's first argument, Kolmorogov, Gandy, and others whom they cite.)

Remember that my argument about formalizability was, as much as possible, based on the statability of the steps of the argument in a first-order system, and relied on the Gödel completeness theorem for the formalizability in the stronger sense of provability in a formal system. I think I am in agreement with Dershowitz and Gurevich (2008) in this respect. But I am emphasizing deductive argument over computer models.

68. For further reading, see Gödel 1930, 1934, 2003; Kleene 1987.

69. I would like to thank the transcriber, whose identity I don't know, the editors of this volume, Jeff Buechner and Gary Ostertag for revising the original transcription, and especially Romina Padró for her help in producing the present version. This paper has been completed with support from the Saul A. Kripke Center at The Graduate Center of the City University of New York.

References

Ackermann, W. 1928. Zum Hilbertschen Aufbau der reellen Zahlen. *Mathematische Annalen* 93:118–133. English translation, with introduction, in *From Frege to Gödel: A Source Book in Mathematical Logic, 1879–1931.*, ed. J. van Heijenoort, 493–507. Cambridge: Harvard University Press

Barendregt, H. 1997. The impact of the lambda calculus in logic and computer science. *Bulletin of Symbolic Logic* 3(2):181–215.

Barwise, J., ed. 1977. *Handbook of Mathematical Logic*. Amsterdam: North-Holland.

Brouwer, L. E. J. 1921. Besitzt jede reelle Zahl eine Dezimalbruchentwickelung? *Mathematische Annalen* 83:201–10. English translation in *From Brouwer to Hilbert: The Debate on the Foundations of Mathematics in the 1920s,* ed. P. Mancosu, 28–35. Oxford: Oxford University Press.

Church, A. 1936a. An unsolvable problem of elementary number theory. *American Journal of Mathematics* 58:345–63. Reprinted in Davis, *The Undecidable,* 88–107.

Church, A. 1936b. A note on the Entscheidungsproblem. *Journal of Symbolic Logic* 1(1):40–41.

Church, A. 1956. *Introduction to Mathematical Logic*. Princeton: Princeton University Press.

Copeland, B. J. 2000. Narrow versus wide mechanism. *Journal of Philosophy* 96:5–32.

Copeland, B. J., and O. Shagrir. 2007. Physical computation: How general are Gandy's principles for mechanisms? *Minds and Machines* 17:217–231.

Cutland, N. J. 1980. *Computability: An Introduction to Recursive Function Theory*. Cambridge: Cambridge University Press.

Davis, M., ed. 1965. *The Undecidable: Basic Papers on Undecidable Propositions, Unsolvable Problems and Computable Functions*. Hewlett, NY: Raven Press.

Davis, M., ed. 1982. Why Gödel didn't have Church's thesis. *Information and Control* 54:3–24.

Dershowitz, N., and Y. Gurevich. 2008. A natural axiomatization of computability and proof of Church's thesis. *Bulletin of Symbolic Logic* 14 (3):299–350.

Feferman, S. 1992. Why a Little Bit Goes a Long Way: Logical Foundations of Scientifically Applicable Mathematics. In *Proceedings of the Biennial Meeting of the Philosophy of Science Association,* Vol. 2, Symposia and Invited Papers, 442–455.

Fine, K. 1985. *Reasoning with Arbitrary Objects*. Oxford: Blackwell.

Gandy, R. 1980. Church's thesis and principles for mechanisms. In *The Kleene Symposium,* ed. J. Barwise, H. J. Keisler, and K. Kunen, 123–48. Amsterdam: North-Holland.

Gandy, R. 1988. The confluence of ideas in 1936. In *The Universal Turing Machine: A Half-Century Survey,* ed. R. Herken, 55–111. Oxford: Oxford University Press.

Gardner, M. 1970. Mathematical games: The fantastic combinations of John Conway's new solitaire game "Life." *Scientific American* 223:120–123.

Gödel, K. 1930. Die Vollständigkeit der Axiome des logischen Funktionenkaluküls. *Monatshefte für Mathematik und Physik* 37:349–60. Reprinted with English translation as "The Completeness of the Axioms of the Functional Calculus of Logic" in Gödel, *Collected Works I,* 102–123.

Gödel, K. 1931. Über formal unentscheidbare Sätze der Principia Mathematica und verwandter Systeme, I. *Monatshefte für Mathematik und Physik* 38:173–178. Reprinted with English translation as "On formally undecidable propositions of *Principia Mathematica* and related systems I" in Gödel, *Collected Works I,* 144–95. Citations refer to the reprint.

Gödel, K. 1933. Zum Entscheidungsproblem des logischen Funktionenkalküls. *Monatshefte für Mathematik und Physik* 40:433–43. Reprinted with English translation as "On the decision problem for the functional calculus of logic" in Gödel, *Collected Works I,* 306–326.

Gödel, K. 1934. On undecidable propositions of formal mathematical systems. In Gödel, *Collected Works I,* 346–372.

Gödel, K. 1936. Über die Länge von Beweisen. *Ergebnisse eines mathematischen Kolloquiums* 7, 23–24. Reprinted with English translation as "On the length of proofs" in Gödel, *Collected Works I,* 396–98.

Gödel, K. 1972. Some remarks on the undecidability results. In Gödel, *Collected Works II,* 305–06.

Gödel, K. 1986. *Collected Works, Vol. I: Publications 1929–1936,* ed. S. Feferman, J. W. Dawson Jr., S. C. Kleene, G. H. Moore, R. M. Solovay, and J. van Heijenoort. Oxford: Oxford University Press.

Gödel, K. 1990. *Collected Works, Vol. II: Publications 1938–1974,* ed. S. Feferman, J. W. Dawson Jr., S. C. Kleene, G. H. Moore, R. M. Solovay, and J. van Heijenoort. Oxford: Oxford University Press.

Gödel, K. 1995. Undecidable Diophantine propositions. In *Collected Works, Vol. III: Unpublished Essays and Lectures,* ed. S. Feferman, J. W. Dawson Jr., W. Goldfarb, C. Parsons, and R. M. Solovay. Oxford: Oxford University Press.

Gödel, K. 2003. *Collected Works, Vol. V: Correspondence, H–Z,* ed. S. Feferman, J. W. Dawson Jr., W. Goldfarb, C. Parsons, and W. Sieg. Oxford: Clarendon Press.

Hardy, G. H. 1929. Mathematical proof. *Mind* 38(149):1–25.

Hilbert, D., and W. Ackermann. 1928. *Grundzüge der theoretischen Logik.* Berlin: Springer-Verlag. English translation, *Principles of Mathematical Logic,* 1950, ed. R. E. Luce. New York: Chelsea Publishing Company.

Kalmar, L. 1959. An argument against the plausibility of Church's thesis. In *Constructivity in Mathematics,* ed. A. Heyting, 72–80. Amsterdam: North-Holland.

Kleene, S. C. 1936. General recursive functions of natural numbers. *Mathematische Annalen* 112:727–742.

Kleene, S. C. 1952. *Introduction to Metamathematics.* Princeton: D. van Nostrand.

Kleene, S. C. 1981. The theory of recursive functions, approaching its centennial. *Bulletin of the American Mathematical Society* 5:43–61.

Kleene, S. C. 1987. Reflections on Church's thesis. *Notre Dame Journal of Formal Logic* 28:490–98.

Kleene, S. C. 1988. Turing's analysis of computability, and major applications of it. In *The Universal Turing Machine: A Half-Century Survey,* ed. R. Herken, 17–54. Oxford: Oxford University Press.

Kline, M. 1972. *Mathematical Thought from Ancient to Modern Times.* Oxford: Oxford University Press.

Kreisel, G. 1970. Church's thesis: A kind of reducibility axiom for constructive mathematics. In *Intuitionism and Proof Theory,* ed. A. Kino, J. Myhill, and R. E. Vesley, 121–50. Amsterdam: North-Holland.

Kreisel, G. 1974. A notion of mechanistic theory. *Synthese* 29:11–26.

Kripke, S. 1996. Elementary recursion theory and its applications to formal systems. Unpublished manuscript.

Martin, D. A., 1974. Sets versus classes. Unpublished manuscript.

Péter, R. 1935. Konstruktion nichtrekursiver Funktionen. *Mathematische Annalen* 111:42–60.

Post, E. L. 1944. Recursively enumerable sets of integers and their decision problems. *Bulletin of the American Mathematical Society* 50:284–316. Reprinted in Davis, *The Undecidable,* 305–337.

Pour-El, M. B., and J. I. Richards. 1979. A computable ordinary differential equation which possesses no computable solution. *Annals of Mathematical Logic* 17:61–90.

Prawitz, D. 1965. *Natural Deduction: A Proof-Theoretical Study.* Stockholm: Alqvist & Wiksell.

Robinson, R. 1948. Recursion and double recursion. *Bulletin of the American Mathematical Society* 54:987–993.

Rogers, H. 1967. *Theory of Recursive Functions and Effective Computability.* New York: McGraw-Hill.

Russell, B. 1905. On denoting. *Mind* 14:479–493.

Shagrir, O. 2002. Effective computation by humans and machines. *Minds and Machines* 12:221–240.

Shagrir, O. 2006. Gödel on Turing on computability. In *Church's Thesis after 70 Years,* ed. Olszewski, A., J. Wolenski, and R. Janusz, 393–419. Frankfurt: Ontos-Verlag.

Shoenfield, J. R. 1967. *Mathematical Logic.* Reading, MA: Addison-Wesley.

Shoenfield, J. R. 1993. *Recursion Theory.* Lecture Notes in Logic, Vol. 1. Berlin: Springer Verlag.

Sieg, W. 1994. Mechanical procedures and mathematical experience. In *Mathematics and Mind,* ed. A. George, 71–117. New York: Oxford University Press.

Sieg, W. 1997. Step by recursive step: Church's analysis of effective calculability. *Bulletin of Symbolic Logic* 3:154–180.

Sieg, W. 2008. Church without dogma: Axioms for computability. In *New Computational Paradigms: Changing Conceptions of What is Computable,* ed. S. B. Cooper, B. Löwe, and A. Sorbi, 139–152. New York: Springer.

Siegelmann, H. T. 2003. Neural and super-Turing computing. *Minds and Machines* 13:103–114.

Soare, R. 1996. Computability and recursion. *Bulletin of Symbolic Logic* 2(3):284–321.

Turing, A. M. 1936–37. On computable numbers, with an application to the *Entscheidungsproblem*. *Proceedings of the London Mathematical Society* 2(42):230–65. Reprinted in M. Davis, *The Undecidable,* 115–153.

Turing, A. M. 1950. Computing machinery and intelligence. *Mind* 59:433–460.

von Neumann, J. 1927. Zur Hilbertschen Beweistheorie. *Mathematische Zeitschrift* 26:1–46.

Wang, H. 1974. *From Mathematics to Philosophy*. London: Routledge and Kegan Paul Ltd.

Weyl, H. 1918. *Das Kontinuum*. Leipzig: Veit. English translation, *The Continuum: A Critical Examination of the Foundation of Analysis*. Trans. S. Pollard, and T. Bole. Kirksville, MO: Thomas Jefferson University Press, 1987.

Whitehead, A., and B. Russell. 1910. *Principia Mathematica*, Vol. 1. Cambridge: Cambridge University Press.

Wittgenstein, L. 1980. *Remarks on the Philosophy of Psychology*, Vol. 1. Oxford: Blackwell.

5 Computability and Constructibility

Carl J. Posy

The thoughts behind this essay began when I read a passage in which Hilary Putnam chides mathematical constructivism because applications of mathematics in physics require non-constructive methods (2002). He cites a paper by Pour-El and Richards displaying a physical wave equation that has nonrecursive solutions for recursive initial data (1981).[1] There are, thus, physical values that are not recursively generable. This seemed to me striking. Mathematical constructivism is an arm of general empiricism in philosophy of science. Empiricism says that reality is constrained by the limits of human knowledge (the technical term is the "limits of intuition"[2]), and constructivism says the same for mathematical reality and mathematical intuition. Yet physical applications should lie at the heart of empiricism. Thinking about it, I saw that Putnam's accusation rests on three assumptions:

(i) Empiricism and mathematical constructivism go hand in hand; constructivism is an extension of empiricism.

(ii) The constructive and the computable coincide.

(iii) The computable and the recursive coincide.

The last assumption is Church's thesis, and I'll not question it. Mainly I'll address the second assumption. I'll ask: do the mathematically constructive and the recursive coincide? Or, to put it philosophically, I'll ask: do the mathematically intuitive and the computable coincide? I won't answer the question, but I hope to unravel the philosophical choices from which answers could emerge and to point to the historical precedents of those choices. In the end I will also show an historical connection between constructivism and the empirical point of view.

In section 5.1 I'll tell you about constructive mathematics, a rich and varied modern field. The literature on constructive foundations for mathematics has several individual projects (e.g., Weyl 1918, Fitch 1959, and Lorenzen 1971); but I will concentrate on the three approaches which have become major research projects: constructive recursive analysis (the Russian school), intuitionism, and Bishop's constructive mathematics. I'll point out their common aspects and the differences among them. This is important in its own right, but constructive mathematics alone doesn't give us the tools to approach our question. Pure mathematics doesn't analyze philosophical assumptions. In particular, the Russian school and intuitionism derive the mathematical consequences of diametrically opposed answers to our question about mathematical intuition, and Bishop shows how far you can get with a studiously neutral attitude to the question.

On the other hand, David Hilbert and L. E. J. Brouwer do provide philosophical analyses of intuition that aim to support one side or the other. This is the point of section 5.2. Brouwer, as is well known, is the father of intuitionism, and I'll point out that Hilbert inspired the recursive approach. I will tell you about how their conflicting views of mathematical intuition led them to rival "foundations" for mathematics. I'll point out, in particular, that their differences about recursion stem from different theories of mathematical intuition. Yet here, too, the analyses will be incomplete. In particular, the rival foundational views, standing alone, seem arbitrary and unmotivated. That impression dissolves, however, when we view these positions in their historical context. They are, in particular, updated adaptations of Kant's constructivism, a constructivism that was indeed fully integrated into an overall empiricism. I'll sketch the Kantian picture in section 5.3, and then in section 5.4 I'll use that to sort out the philosophical positions and the grounds for answering my question.

5.1 Constructive Mathematics

5.1.1 General Constructive Mathematics

Analysis Is the Heart

The Pour-El–Richards example that Putnam cites focuses on a point of discontinuity in the wave function it examines. In fact, mathematical constructivism of all stripes revolves around questions of continuity and the continuum, and for good reason: the continuum and real valued functions are steeped in infinity, and we humans have a problem with infinity.

Infinity pops in at the very beginning of real analysis. Here are the basic notions, on the assumption that the natural numbers (N) and the rationals (Q) are given:

• A real number generator (rng) is a convergent sequence, $\{q_n\}_n$, of rational numbers (a Cauchy sequence). Formally, this means:

$$\forall k \exists n \forall i \forall j |q_{n+j} - q_{n+i}| < 10^{-k}.$$

• Two rng's $\{q_n\}_n$ and $\{s_n\}_n$ co-converge if:

$$\forall k \exists n \forall i \, |q_{n+i} - s_{n+i}| < 10^{-k}.$$

• Co-convergence is an equivalence relation, and a real number is an equivalence class of such sequences under this relation.

• $\Re$ is the set of all real numbers.

• A sequence of real numbers is a total function from N to $\Re$.

• A real valued function is a univalued subset of $(\Re \times \Re)$.

• A functional operator (such as an integral or derivative) is a function of functions, and so on.

So, you see, a real number generator is already two levels deep in infinity; the set of all real numbers is yet another level deep, and the functions and operators go deeper yet.

The trouble is that our human cognitive grasp is finite and cannot comprehend even a single rng in its entirety. So we are speaking here of entities that exceed our grasp, further entities made in ungraspable ways from those first elusive things, and then things further and further removed from our human ability to comprehend. Constructive mathematics plays out against the lurking specter of this ungraspable infinity.

In the nineteenth century Kronecker notoriously wanted to purge mathematics of infinitary notions, and opposed the reduction to set theory. He did not prevail,[3] and the modern mathematical constructivist aims, by contrast, not to banish infinity, but to tame it and make it graspable.

Aristotle, when he moved from completed to potential infinity, took the first step in this direction. According to him, we can consider a process any finite initial piece of which can be continued, but we cannot admit that any such process is carried out in its entirety. On this Aristotelian view we think of those nested infinities as nested processes. The modern constructivists with whom we will deal focus on the way a human can grasp such an infinitely continuable process. And then they banish anything that is not thus graspable.

Common Denominators

All the approaches agree that a graspable infinite process is one that is generated by a rule. As we shall see they differ in what and how much they say about those generating rules. Nevertheless, three common denominators unite all of the constructivist approaches: logic, number, and continuous functions.

Logic

All three of the constructivist schools reject as invalid the logical principle of the excluded third. Syntactically this is the principle that says that $(p \vee \neg p)$ is admissible in any formal proof. Semantically, it is the principle that says that for each proposition p, either p or its negation is true. Intuitionistic logic, which differs from classical logic in many respects, is the logic generated from the constructivist rejection of this principle.[4]

The principle of excluded third bespeaks a semantic determinacy that the constructivist schools all abjure. Semantics, for them, is tied to epistemology, and that in turn brings indeterminacy: there are propositions that are unknown and unrefuted. Bishop and some others equate the principle of excluded third in particular with a sort of omniscience that we humans do not enjoy.[5] But, in fact, intuitionistic logic rests on a systematic epistemic reading of *all* of the logical particles (not just negation and disjunction). Traditionally this reading ties truth with "warranted assertability" at an epistemic situation and characterizes that notion inductively. Here are the clauses:

(A1) (A&B) is assertable in an epistemic situation if and only if A and B are both assertable in that situation.

(A2) (Av B) is assertable in an epistemic situation if and only if the situation contains a guarantee that A will eventually be assertable or that B will eventually be assertable.[6]

(A3) (A→B) is assertable in an epistemic situation if and only if the situation contains a guarantee (i.e., proof) that any proof of A can be converted into a proof of B.

(A4) ¬A is assertable in an epistemic situation if and only if the situation contains sufficient evidence that A will never be assertable.[7]

(A5) (∃x)A is assertable in an epistemic situation if and only if the situation contains a guarantee that some a in the domain A(a) will eventually be assertable in the situation.[8]

(A6) (∀x)A is assertable in an epistemic situation if and only if the situation contains a method of converting a demonstration that *x* is in the domain (for any x) to a demonstration of A(x).

Clauses A2 and A5 present what I call a mild assertabilism, for they allow the assertion of a disjunction or existential claim even without an explicit witness in hand.

The constructivist, then, as I said, equates *assertability* at a situation with *truth* at that situation and defines logical truth as assertability in every situation. This has come to be called the Brouwer-Heyting-Kolmogorov (BKH) interpretation of the logical particles.[9]

The principle of the excluded third now obviously fails to be logically valid because we have propositions, p, for which neither p nor ¬p can be asserted in our current epistemic state. Goldbach's conjecture is a standard current example. The principle expresses omniscience, because if we were to be omniscient (or, given the liberality of clauses A2 and A5, just optimistic about our ability to decide every mathematical question), then in fact excluded third propositions would be true in every situation, and the logic would be classical.[10]

Kripke in 1965 exploited a result of Gödel's to produce a formal semantics for this logic.[11] A Kripke model is an *ordered triple* <G, K, R> together with a *domain function* ψ, and an *evaluation function* ϕ. The domain function associates a particular domain with each node, H, and thus determines the union: $\mathbf{U} = \mathbf{U}_{H \in K}\ \psi(\mathbf{H})$. The evaluation function then gives the referents with respect to U of singular and general terms at each node and defines truth at a node in a way that is inspired by the BKH conditions.[12]

Now, adopting intuitionistic logic limits the ways in which a constructivist can carry out a mathematical proof. A standard example is the classical proof that there are irrational r and s such that r^s is a rational number: either $\sqrt{2}^{\sqrt{2}}$ is rational or it is irrational. If it is rational, then take r=s=$\sqrt{2}$. If it is irrational, then take r= $\sqrt{2}^{\sqrt{2}}$ and s = $\sqrt{2}$. In this case $r^s = (\sqrt{2}^{\sqrt{2}})^{\sqrt{2}} = (\sqrt{2})^2 = 2$. The constructivist cannot make that initial assumption that $\sqrt{2}^{\sqrt{2}}$ is either rational or irrational.

Though this particular theorem is in fact constructively recoverable,[13] there are classical theorems that are not constructively provable. Thus, for instance, the classical theorem that every increasing infinite sequence of rational numbers that is bounded from above converges to a real number is generally not constructively provable. Neither is the related theorem that every infinite sequence $\{r_n\}_n$ of real numbers that is bounded from above will converge to a real number r. In both cases, the limiting real number r need not itself be constructible.[14]

The Primacy of the Natural Numbers

Whatever it may mean for a mathematical object to exist constructively (i.e., to be "intuitable"), every natural number will pass that test. All three schools agree about that. They also all speak of real numbers and indeed of real valued functions as legitimate mathematical objects. But it is important to keep in mind that these are "higher-order" objects. In the end, each of these things comes down to numbers and to processes taking numbers into numbers.

Thus, to use the Aristotelian image, we can then pick a standard enumeration of the rational numbers and view an rng simply as a number theoretic process. Similarly, a sequence of real numbers will be a process taking natural numbers to reals, functions on real numbers will reduce to operations on the elements of their rng's, and so on for operations on real valued functions. For the constructivist, of course, these processes must themselves pass intuitive muster. This indeed is the force of the BKH interpretation: when you say that a process f:A $\rightarrow$ B is fully defined, you are saying that $\forall x_{\in A} \exists y_{\in B}\ (y=f(x))$. The BHK interpretation of this quantifier combination requires a graspable procedure. And when you unpack the nestings, this will reduce to a procedure taking numbers to numbers.[15]

Continuity and the Continuum

Now, constructive approaches will be weaker than classical mathematics in several ways. The constructivist, for example, will not be able to say that for any pair r_1 and r_2 of real numbers,

$(r_1 < r_2) \lor (r_1 = r_2) \lor (r_1 > r_2).$

This is because you might need an infinite amount of information about one or both of the real numbers in order to determine which relation holds. And indeed, in constructive mathematics one cannot always separate real numbers. The principle

$r_1 = r_2 \lor r_1 \neq r_2$

is not logically valid, and once again will not always hold.

But it is in the theory of continuous functions that constructive mathematics deviates most blatantly from its classical counterpart, for the constructivists are led to hold that every real valued function is continuous at every point at which it is defined. That is something that is certainly not true in standard, classical mathematics. The general idea is this:

A function, g, is continuous at argument x if as x' gets closer to x, then g(x') gets closer to g(x). Formally:

$\forall k \exists n \forall x'(|x-x'| < 10^{-n} \rightarrow |g(x) - g(x')| < 10^{-n}).$

In general g is continuous on its domain, D, if it is continuous at each point in D:

$\forall x_{\in D} \forall k \exists n \forall x'(|x-x'| < 10^{-n} \rightarrow |g(x) - g(x')| < 10^{-k}).$

Now if, as I said above, g is to be viewed as a graspable process for producing an rng $\{y_n\}_n$ for y= g(x) given an rng, $\{x_n\}_n$ for x, then in particular for each k, g must be able to produce y_k from information derived from the rng $\{x_n\}_n$. Constructively, of course, this information must be gleaned from a finite initial sequence $x_1, \ldots, x_j$ of $\{x_n\}_n$. And thus for any x' with an rng that coincides with $\{x_n\}_n$ up to x_j, f(x') will coincide with $\{y_n\}_n$ up to y_k. This holds for all k. And that is just what is needed for continuity at x.

This theorem shows that from the point of view of constructive mathematics, the continuum is not "splittable": that is, there is no real number r, such that $\Re= \{x: x \leq r\} \cup \{x: x > r\}$. For if there were, we could define the step-function, f, such that

f(x) = 0 for $x \leq r$

f(x) = 1 for $x > r$,

which would be a totally defined function that is discontinuous at r. Indeed, in general, other than $\{\Re, \varnothing\}$ there is no pair of sets $\{A, B\}$ such that

$A \cup B = \Re$ and $A \cap B = \varnothing$.

As I said, all the schools of constructive mathematics agree on these issues of intuitionistic logic, the primacy of the natural numbers, and the continuity of functions. But, agree as they may about these very general issues, the different programs will differ about what they mean by a constructive process. Those differences in turn yield significant technical differences among the schools. The schools are not inter-reducible.

5.1.2   Varieties of Constructive Analysis

Constructive Recursive Analysis (the Russian School)

Markov (in the 1940s) gave the first thorough development of recursive analysis from a constructive point of view. This was carried forward by his students Shanin, Zaslavakiĭ, and Tseĭtin in the 1940s and '50s, and later by Kushner.[16] Their fundamental credo: a graspable infinite process will be a process describable by an algorithm for generating its outputs.

Markov's own work used Markov algorithms, which are rules for converting strings of symbols built from a basic alphabet. But his method is equivalent to recursion. So here we have a straightforward "yes" answer to our guiding question: the constructive and the recursive do coincide. We consider only recursive enumerations of the rationals and only recursively generated rng's. Since the recursive functions are themselves effectively enumerable, we can then restrict attention to recursive real valued functions, and so on up the line.

We use the word "constructive" in the title of this approach to emphasize that the underlying logic is intuitionistic. For, within the classical framework, there has been a great deal of research on applying recursive functions and their generalizations to analysis.[17] But in classical recursive function theory, one can define the following number theoretic function, h:

h(n) = 1 if Goldbach's conjecture is true

h(n) = 0 if not.

Classically, h is a constant function, and thus indeed primitive recursive. Constructively, h is not defined at all.

Three special characteristics of constructive recursive analysis are worth noting here: Markov's principle, Specker sequences, and Tseĭtin's theorem on nonuniform continuity.

(i) *Markov's principle*   Mathematicians of the Russian school accept the following principle: if $\{n_i\}_i$ is a recursive binary sequence (i.e., for each i, $n_i = 0$ or $n_i = 1$), and if we know that not for all i does $n_i = 0$, then we may say that there is an i such that $n_i = 1$. Formally, in terms of a binary number theoretic function, f:

$$\neg\forall x(f(x)=0) \rightarrow \exists n(f(n) =1).$$

Advocates of intuitionistic logic often find this unpalatable. Existential statements should be harder than this to prove. But in fact this is the principle that allows one to prove in constructive recursive analysis that every real valued function is continuous at each point in which it is defined. This was first proved by Tseĭtin. Markov himself had proved weaker versions, which are classically but not constructively equivalent.

(ii) *Specker sequences*   Generally, as I pointed out, we cannot constructively prove that every infinite increasing sequence of real numbers or of rational numbers that is bounded from above converges to a real number as its limit. However, using techniques from recursive function theory, Specker went further and produced strong refutations of these classical theorems. The technique is recursively to generate an infinite sequence of rationals that is bounded from above whose natural limit is not a computable real number. And so too for sequences of recursive reals. One generates the desired sequence of rationals from the enumeration of a set, S, that is recursively enumerable but not recursive in such a way that the recursiveness of the limit of the sequence would entail the recursiveness S.

(iii) *Nonuniform continuity*   In the definition of continuity that I gave in the section on "Continuity and the Continuum," above, the way that n depends on k may itself be determined by the argument x. And so for a given k and two different arguments x_1 and x_2, the corresponding n_1 and n_2 might be determined differently. This is called pointwise continuity. A function, g, is *uniformly* continuous on a domain D if this determination is independent of the argument, x. Formally this is expressed simply by a quantifier shift: g is uniformly continuous on domain D if

$$\forall k \exists n \forall x_{\in D} \forall x'(|x-x'| < 10^{-n} \rightarrow |g(x) - g(x')| < 10^{-n}).$$

Classically, one can prove that every pointwise continuous function on a closed interval is uniformly continuous on that interval. The standard classical proof of this is an indirect proof that uses the fact that a closed interval is a compact metric space.[18] This is a property of the compact set itself.

However, using Specker sequences, one can construct pointwise continuous functions on a closed interval that are not uniformly continuous, a strong refutation of this property of the continuum.

Intuitionistic Mathematics

Intuitionism, developed by L. E. J. Brouwer, was first set out in his dissertation in 1907,[19] and then developed in a series of his publications spanning over 50 years. It was further developed by Brouwer's student A. Heyting and by a generation of other mathematicians. From the 1960s, various formal systems have been proposed for intuitionistic analysis.[20]

The heart of intuitionistic analysis is Brouwer's unique approach to the graspable infinite processes: this is his notion of "choice sequences," a notion that is patently different from the notion of a recursive function.

To be sure, in intuitionism, as in all constructive mathematics, one grasps an infinite sequence, $\{s_n\}_n$, *via* a rule or principle for generating its elements, a rule which guarantees that the sequence of elements can be continued without stop. But, following Brouwer, the intuitionists loosen the requirement that the generating principle be fully deterministic. The rule can now allow a degree of free choice in determining s_n for some (or all) n. (Hence the title "choice sequence.")

Thus, for example, the elements of the sequence might be rational numbers, and the generating rule might require that for each k, $|s_k - s_{k+1}| < 10^{-k}$, thereby giving us an rng. Now, to be sure, the generating rule could be an algorithm strictly determining each s_{k+1} based on the prior values.[21] But it need not be. Indeed, the rule might say nothing more than "for each k, pick s_{k+1} so that $|s_k - s_{k+1}| < 10^{-k}$ holds." For the intuitionist such a sequence will be still a legitimate mathematical object, generated by an acceptable infinite process. It is in fact a full-fledged rng.

The intuitionists do not even require that the rules for choice themselves be set from the start. It is perfectly possible to allow a rule for determining the available choices itself to evolve as the sequence grows. Indeed, it is possible that at each n you choose s_n and you also choose the rule for choosing s_{n+1}. Both the choice of element and the choice of rule might well depend upon prior choices. Thus for instance, if you want to generate a decimal rng $\{q_n\}_n$ that falls within the interval [0, ½], and your first two choices have so far generated 0.5, you have painted yourself into a corner with only one way out: you will not be free to choose anything but 0 from then on.[22]

I should add, by the way, that the element of free choice is not the only (or even, at some places, the primary) way the intuitionists get indeterminacy into their infinite processes. There are places in which they speak of generating a sequence by throwing a die or some other epistemically nondeterminate empirical process.[23] And Brouwer, himself, starting from the 1940s, concentrated on sequences that were generated by the activity of what he called "the creating subject." The idea was to concentrate on the activity of some idealized mathematician (or the community of all mathematicians) concerned with deciding some as yet undecided mathematical question Q (again, say, Goldbach's conjecture). We then generate a sequence according to the outcome of that research at fixed stages (at fixed dates, for instance). Thus, for instance, we could define the real number r* by the following rng $\{q_n\}_n$:

q_n = ½ if by the nth stage the subject has neither proved nor refuted Q

q_n =(½ – (½)^k) if n≥k and at the kth stage Q was proved

q_n =(½ + (½)^k) if n≥k and at the kth stage Q was refuted.

Brouwer firmly held that we shall always be able to supply undecided propositions in order to generate such indeterminate real numbers. (Indeed, keep in mind that were he to be an epistemic optimist, then he would have to adopt classical logic.)

The intuitionists have their own version of set theory designed to accommodate the freedom built into choice sequences as mathematical objects. As in ordinary set theory, one can form a collection of such objects in virtue of a common property. The intuitionists call this a species, and they have developed their own constructive theory of species.

But for us the important intuitionistic set theoretic concept is the notion of a spread: a collection of choice sequences with some common constraint on their growth principles.[24] Thus, in particular, an interval will be given by a spread of choice sequences, all of which converge in that interval. A *finitary spread* (*fan*) is a spread whose elements are choice sequences $\{s_n\}_n$ that allow only finitely many possible choices for each s_n.

Using this set theory, the intuitionist can prove rather straightforwardly that any real valued function is pointwise continuous on its domain. Indeed, Brouwer himself provided two versions of this theorem: a positive version, which says that every total function on a domain is continuous, and a negative version, which says that a function cannot be both total on its domain and discontinuous at some point on the domain. He proves the negative version indirectly, by assuming we have a fully defined function that is discontinuous at a point r. (Say, for instance,

f(x) = 0 for x ≤ r

f(x) = 1 for x > r.)

He then defines a point r′ in that interval which remains forever indeterminate between r′ ≤ r or r′> r. He does this by a second-order restriction that limits the available rules. And thus f is undefined at r′.[25]

But the intuitionists in fact have a stronger result: any continuous real valued function on a closed interval is uniformly continuous. They get this from something called the "fan theorem," together with the fact that any closed interval is given by a fan of real number generators. (You can take a fan whose elements are decimal expansions.)[26] This is indeed a strongly non-classical result; for, together with point-wise continuity, it says that every total function on a closed interval is uniformly continuous.

As to my initial question: Choice sequences are prima facie not recursive.[27]

Bishop's Constructive Analysis

Let me add a quick word about Bishop's constructive analysis. Erret Bishop was a dues-paying, card-carrying classical mathematician, who, late in his career, came to question the infinitary heart of classical mathematics (analysis in particular). "The pure mathematician," said Bishop

… is isolated from the world, which has little need of his brilliant creations. He suffers from an alienation which is seemingly inevitable: he has followed the gleam and it has led him out of this world. (Bishop 1967, vii)

And so he proposed to build a more "realistic" constructive mathematics. To be sure, he adds,

We are not contending that idealistic mathematics is worthless from the constructive point of view. This would be as silly as contending that unrigorous mathematics is worthless from the classical point of view. Every theorem proved with idealistic methods presents a challenge: to find a constructive version, and to give it a constructive proof. (Bishop 1967, x)

And that is what he set out to do.

His original monograph in 1967 and the subsequent contributions to his project, by Bridges, Richmond, and Beeson[28] are packed with constructively proved theorems that are classically equivalent or close to standard classical theorems (from the intermediate value theorem of elementary calculus to deep theorems about measure theory, Hilbert space, and group theory, and through to Fourier transforms and Banach algebras).

But Bishop and those who develop his ideas are studiously—indeed doctrinally—neutral about the fine structure of constructive processes. Bishop had no truck with the intuitionist's choice sequences. He thought them extraneous and unconvincing. However, he was not prepared to limit the constructive to recursive methods either. In fact, he is not prepared to pin down the content of "constructive" at all beyond speaking of "finite routines."[29]

Yes, Bishop concentrates on continuous functions. But he does not derive continuity—as do the recursivists and intuitionists—from the fine structure of number theoretic and higher-order processes. He has no explicit fine structure. Rather, he gets continuity by fiat. And though he cannot construct the Specker sequences and cannot derive nonuniformity over a closed interval, he cannot positively derive uniform continuity either. So, once again, he assumes it.

The result is a project that, though constructive, is relatively consistent with classical mathematics. Some have complained about this and see it as remaining at an imprecise level of generality. On the one hand, I believe that this level of generality is perfectly mathematically proper. It is the same level of generality that characterizes modern algebra. On the other hand, this does leave our initial question — is the constructive the same as the recursive? — quite intentionally up in the air.

And so, as I said at the outset, looking at the practice alone of contemporary constructive mathematics will do nothing to tell us whether we should equate, as Putnam does, the constructive with the recursive.

5.2   Hilbert and Brouwer: Constructivism in the Foundations of Mathematics

Those who write about constructive mathematics often take pains to minimize the clashes among the constructivist schools and between constructive mathematics in general and its classical counterpart. One often hears that these different approaches simply are talking about different objects.[30] And indeed, even within classical mathematics the non-classical results can hold with the proper relativization of domains. Thus for instance, in classical recursion theory recursive real valued functions that are defined over recursive real numbers are pointwise continuous. And even the intuitionistic fan theorem corresponds to the classical König's lemma. But this attitude masks the truly philosophical issues that divide the recursive and intuitionistic approaches.

This was not the case in the Brouwer-Hilbert foundational debate that came to a head in the 1920s. Brouwer and Hilbert clashed mathematically: they debated about logic, about the solvability of mathematical problems, about the use of formalization, and most of all about mathematical revisionism. But philosophically they disagreed no less. Yes, both Brouwer and Hilbert wanted to "found" mathematics on mathematical intuition, and they both held in general that intuitability is a criterion of existence. But they clashed philosophically about how mathematics is to be "founded" on intuition and about the nature of mathematical intuition itself. And that philosophical clash underwrites the intuitionist and recursive approaches no less than do their mathematical differences.

5.2.1   Brouwer's Revisionism

Brouwer set out his view about how to base mathematics on mathematical intuition in his doctoral dissertation and never deviated from that view: one constructs mathematical objects in intuition, and mathematics goes as far as we can extend our mathematical intuition. For Brouwer that was far indeed: we can build complex and subtle objects by exercising our intuitive powers. But it can go no further.

This "inside mathematics" constructivism had, for Brouwer, two consequences: for one thing, he was intolerant of formalization as a means of advancing mathematics. Formal systems themselves are perfectly constructible objects. But they are mechanical and static; no system will ever represent all that intuition can produce. And secondly, he always had an eye toward what I call tempting spectral notions that are not mathematically intuitable, and thus mathematically inadmissible.

This much, as I said, was constant throughout Brouwer's career. But his view of the nature of that mathematical intuition actually evolved in the course of his career. I trace three stages below, each of which had its own mathematical content and its own corresponding philosophical view about the nature of mathematical intuition.

Stage 1: The dissertation Mathematically, Brouwer stood head on against Cantorian set theory and rejected outright any hierarchy of higher infinities. Instead he admitted only finite numbers, constructively generated infinite sequences, and something he called "denumerably unfinished" collections. These are sets such that, given a denumerable subset, we can straightaway find an element of the set that is not in the given subset. The real numbers are a prime example. This is a strictly negative notion, and there is no positive existence claim about a higher cardinality.

As for the continuum, Brouwer held three principles about the continuum that are inconsistent with Cantor's theory:

a. The continuum is unsplittable. He uses the image of "flowing" to capture this aspect.

b. It has integral unity: properties of the continuum are not derived from the properties of its parts.

c. The continuum is not a set: it is not the sum of individual, independently generable points. Though you can superimpose various points and constructions on the continuum, you cannot build up the continuum out of a set of independently given points. No set of points can exhaust the continuum.

Corresponding to all this, Brouwer held four main philosophical doctrines about mathematical intuition:

i. He held, of course, that we can intuit each natural number.

ii. He held that we can intuitively grasp a constructively generated sequence. In effect, he already espouses here the BKH reading of the ∀∃ combination underlying an infinite sequence. And already in this period he quite vocally denies the sort of epistemic optimism—the solvability of all mathematical problems—that would reduce this semantic reading to a classical logic. Brouwer's view in the dissertation is quite consistent with the claim that all such sequences are given by algorithms.

And so, at this point we can speak of the numbers as intuited and of algorithms as keeping us within the realm of the intuited. This restriction to algorithmic sequences is still sufficient to generate unanswered questions, and non-classical logic.

iii. But that is the only sort of numerically infinite set that we can intuit. To be sure, he admits that we often think and perhaps speak of other large sets. But these are no more than *façons de parler*. The problem with them is that they are not finished or finishable. They will always have parts that are not determined by the initial grasp. And so they are not legitimate objects, and our grasp of them is not an intuition. They are the spectral background.

iv. Finally, he held that there is a separate and self-standing intuition of the continuum itself. This too is an intuitive grasp. It shows directly, without proof, that the continuum is an integral unity and that it is unsplittable.

Stage II: Choice sequences and spreads   On the mathematical side, by 1917 Brouwer had found a way to maintain the continuum's unsplittability and integral unity but nonetheless to have a set theoretic notion of the continuum, a notion according to which the continuum is indeed made up of independently given points. This was the idea of choice sequences and spreads.

If the continuum is built out of choice sequences, that will be enough to prove pointwise continuity. And as we saw, this guarantees unsplittability. The fan theorem, in turn, and most specifically the uniform continuity of all functions—these things provide the counterpart of integral unity, for they display continuity properties of functions that devolve from the domain itself, and not from the specific nature of the function.

But having made this mathematical breakthrough, having admitted choice sequences as legitimate processes (and thus as legitimate mathematical objects), Brouwer needed to adjust his philosophical views accordingly. For one thing, he no longer needed to appeal to an independent intuition of the continuum in order to establish its unity and unsplittability. He could get all he wants just from the grasp of infinite sequences.

But more than that, he now needed to revise his view about the intuitive grasp of infinite processes and, indeed, of existence in general. Having admitted things some of whose properties are not determined (and indeed some of whose properties will remain forever undetermined), Brouwer now had to say that we intuitively grasp such wiggly things and the processes that generate them.[31] He had to espouse a very liberal version of what I called above the mild assertability conditions. If we want to say that $\{q_n\}_n$ is indeed an infinite sequence, that is that $\forall n \exists x (x = q_n)$, then we cannot demand that "there is a method for getting q_n." We can only say that we have a guarantee that for each n, q_n will turn up. No restrictions to algorithms will work here.

Stage III: The creating subject In 1948, Brouwer explicitly introduced creating subject sequences into a published paper,[32] and he continued to appeal to these throughout his subsequent career. This change represents a further stage in Brouwer's notion of intuition. For he now gives up the idea that he can build an infinite degree of indeterminacy and guarantee it by definition, as he did in the negative continuity theorem. Indeed, at this point in his career Brouwer explicitly retreated from using second-order restrictions at all.[33]

As a mathematical technique, the notion of creating subject sequences represents perhaps a small change. But it is an important move in his notion of mathematical intuition in two senses. For one thing, building this technique formally into the definition of a graspable sequence in effect makes the BHK interpretation explicit in the practice of mathematics. This view is of course inextricably tied to his epistemic pessimism, to the view that there will always be a supply of unanswered questions.

Secondly, making the BHK interpretation explicit gives very specific content to what I have been calling the spectral background: this will be the idea of an eternally unsolvable mathematical problem or an eternally undecidable proposition. Of course, we have no choice but to think of such a proposition. (If we knew that there is no such problem, then optimism would be justified.) On the other hand, one can never specify that any given proposition is such a proposition. To do so would yield a contradiction: If P expresses such a proposition, then by BHK, since we know that P will never be proved, we can assert the negation of P. And that means that P has been refuted, contradicting its unsolvability. The idea of knowing that P is such a proposition is tantamount to taking some external point of view, from which we can survey the future of all human knowledge. As I said, we naturally and necessarily think of such things, but we can never assert their existence. That is the spectral background, par excellence.

5.2.2 Hilbert's Program: Constructivism of the Right

The Program

It might seem strange to call Hilbert a constructivist. After all, he himself introduced non-constructive methods into algebra,[34] he was unfriendly toward the Kroneckerian restrictions, and—in opposition to Brouwer—he was a staunch supporter of classical logic. Indeed, Hilbert did not practice or condone "constructive mathematics" in the sense that I have been using that term. Nevertheless, he was a constructivist: he saw infinity as a problem for mathematics (or, more precisely, as the source of mathematics' problems), and as a solution he aimed to found mathematics on a base of intuition, just as do all the constructivists we have considered.

Hilbert in fact was driven by an opposing pair of pulls, and his program for the foundation of mathematics was the result of those pulls.

On the one hand, Hilbert held that there is no infinity in physical reality, and none in mathematical reality either. Only intuitable objects truly exist, and only an intuitively grounded process (he spoke of "finitary thought") can keep us within the realm of the intuitable. This is his constructivism. Mathematical paradox arises, he said, when we exceed those bounds. And indeed, he held that infinite mathematical objects do go beyond the bounds of mathematical intuition. For him finite arithmetic gave the basic objects, and he held that arithmetic reasoning together was the paradigm of finitary thought. Together this comprised the "real" part of mathematics. All the rest—set theory, analysis, and the like—he called the "ideal" part, which had no independent "real content."

On the other hand, Hilbert also believed that this ideal mathematics was sacrosanct. No part of it was to be jettisoned or even truncated. This is why I dub it "constructivism of the right." "No one will expel us," he famously declared, "from the paradise into which Cantor has led us" (Hilbert 1926).

Hilbert's program, which was first announced in 1904 and was further developed in the 1920s, was designed to reconcile these dual pulls.[35] The outline of the program for a branch of mathematics whose consistency is in question is generally familiar: axiomatize that branch of mathematics; formalize the axiomatization in an appropriate formal language; show that the resulting formal system is adequate to the given branch of mathematics (i.e., sound and complete); and then prove the formal system to be consistent.

The important assumptions here are that formal systems are finitely graspable things and that the study of formal systems is a securely finitary study.[36] Thus, he is proposing to use the finitary, trustworthy part of mathematics to establish the consistency of the ideal part.

Today, of course, we know that the program as thus formulated cannot succeed. Gödel's theorems tell us that. But in the late 1920s, Hilbert still had ample encouraging evidence. Russell and Whitehead's *Principia Mathematica* stood as a monument to formalization. He and his students successfully had axiomatized and formalized several branches of mathematics. Moreover, he firmly believed that within each branch of mathematics we can prove or refute any relevant statement. He believed that is, optimistically, in the solvability of all mathematical problems.[37] And so he was confident in our ability to produce provably adequate formal systems. And—assuming in advance the success of his program—he was comfortable in developing the abstract, unanchored realms of ideal mathematics.

Hilbert's Notion of Intuitable Objects and Procedures

Intuition
The foundational notion of intuition is the notion of intuition that is akin to ordinary sensory perception. Hilbert spells this out as follows:

[A]s a condition for the use of logical inference and the performance of logical operations, something must already be given to our faculty of representation, certain extralogical concrete objects that are intuitively present as immediate experience prior to all thought. If logical inference is to be reliable, it must be possible to survey these objects completely in all their parts, and the fact that they occur, that they differ from one another, and that they follow each other, or are concatenated, is immediately given intuitively, together with the object, as something that can neither be reduced to anything else nor requires reduction. This is the basic philosophical position that I consider requisite for mathematics, and in general for all scientific thinking, understanding and communication. (1926)

For Hilbert, an immediate intuitive grasp will give full information about the object grasped; it has the effect of surveying the object completely; it will enable us to distinguish that object from any other; and it will immediately reveal the ordering relations that the object bears to other objects. Ordinary perception does that for physical objects. In mathematics we grasp natural numbers in this way. Formulas are not generally perceivable—we are talking here of formulas as types and not as tokens—but nevertheless our grasp of them meets this criterion.

And, for Hilbert, these things and only these are intuitively graspable. Second and higher-order objects—real numbers, real valued functions, and the like—these belong only to the ideal part of mathematics.[38]

Constructive Procedures

Hilbert had a pair of distinct pictures about the processes by means of which one goes from one intuited thing to another:

(i) Formal deduction. The idea of moving from a given formula in a formal system to another according to preset logical rules: this, Hilbert thought, is a paradigmatic dynamic constructive procedure. It matters not, of course, whether the formulas refer to concrete entities or to the most arcane, ideal objects; the formula is real, and logically manipulating it is constructive.

(ii) Recursion. Hilbert viewed recursive functions as an important part of his meta-mathematical studies.[39] He thought that they provide a good framework to represent the finitary thinking that was necessary in order to study formal systems. And he investigated the question of what would be needed in order to define a basic notion of a finitary function. To be sure, the characterization that he preferred—functions definable only by substitution and recursion—is in the end not strong enough to capture the full modern notion of a recursive function. It is not equivalent to the notion of derivability in a formal system. But, certainly, he persuasively advanced the idea that intuition-preserving processes are the recursive processes.[40]

Finally, Hilbert concentrated the notion of the spectral background and put it in explicit form, the ε-symbol. In particular, εxFx picks out an x such that Fx holds if there is one, and gives nothing if there isn't. Hilbert's ε-Axiom states that

$F(\varepsilon x F x) \leftrightarrow \exists x F x.$

When F represents an infinite sequence, then, of course, it may well not be finitely decidable which alternative is true. The general use of ε is tantamount to omniscience.

5.2.3   Summing Up So Far

We have seen here two rival notions of mathematical intuition, each with its own notion of intuition-preserving operation. Hilbert admits only first-order objects as intuitable, and takes intuition as a complete grasp that determines identity and relations. And for him, the only intuition-preserving processes are the recursively defined ones. Brouwer admits second-order objects as intuitable (real numbers in particular), and in his mature period he allows some wiggle both in intuition (there will be nonrecursive reals) and in the intuition-preserving processes. Indeed, in his third stage, he explicitly connects the wiggle to his epistemic pessimism.

As for the later intuitionists, to be sure, their formalizations are not to Brouwer's taste; but their practice of mathematics is a straightforward homage to Brouwer's notions of intuition and wiggle. And the recursivists have a similar relation to Hilbert. Yes, unlike Hilbert, they apply their constructivism from the "inside." (*Pace* Markov's principle, of course.) And they are second-orderists; they accept processes as objects. But these processes are, as Hilbert insists, recursively defined. They also adopt Hilbert's notion of the ideal: nonrecursive objects are objects which would require an infinite amount of information to determine their properties and identity relations. This is precisely what is at work in the Specker sequences and in similar constructions.

So we could perhaps stop here, with these rival philosophical parameters about intuition underwriting each of the rival answers to the question whether the constructive is the recursive. Nevertheless, this is not a good place to end. To stop here would be to leave both of the rival theories of intuition hanging in the air and unmotivated. We are left to wonder why Hilbert's and Brouwer's shared antipathy to infinite totalities should lead in such opposite directions. What *philosophical* ground is there for adopting the constructivists' inner perspective of the left, and what besides sheer conservatism can justify Hilbert's outer perspective of the right? Moreover, we must still ask what stands behind Hilbert's optimism. And what is the source of his narrow take on intuition? By the same token, we must ask of Brouwer: why are the continuum's unsplittability and integral unity sacrosanct? Moreover, what lies behind his third stage? Why the sudden rejection of second-order restrictions and the explicit use of creating subject sequences? Is it just to make the spectral public?

As I said, historical roots will help here, Kant in particular. Kant was the founder of mathematical constructivism, and he quite explicitly integrated it into an overall empiricism. Understanding how he does this will show the factors at play in both positions and will, as I promised, provide an historical link between general empiricism and constructivism.

5.3 Kant, The Father of Modern Constructivism

5.3.1 Kant's Empiricism

Mathematics wasn't Kant's primary target; empirical science was. In his time it was science that needed a "foundation," and Kant's primary notion of intuition is empirical intuition. Indeed, his theory of scientific knowledge has empirical versions of all the elements that I have discussed: intuition and existence, intuition-preserving processes, epistemology, semantics, and logic, and even a theory of spectral awareness. Mathematics, for Kant, is simply a formal component of this empiricist picture. It is part of the solution, and not of the problem. So I'll first tell you about Kant's empirical theory before turning to his views about mathematics and mathematical intuition.

Empirical Intuition

Kant's empirical intuition is sense perception, which he contrasted with purely conceptual thought;

• Perception is receptive. We are dependent on external sources for the sensory input. Conception is "spontaneous."

• Intuition gives evidence for existence. (We need that external source.) Conception alone never proves existence.

• Kant insists that an intuitive grasp of an object enables the knower to distinguish this object from any other and gives grounds to decide between any pair of opposing predicates that might be relevant to the object. He does this because an intuition gives an individual object, and he holds that a legitimate object (as opposed to a mere aggregate) must be distinguishable from all other objects and must be predicatively complete regarding all relevant predicates. A merely conceptual grasp will always leave some questions about the individual open.

• Indeed, that is why intuition is singular, and conception is always general.

• Finally, the intuition-preserving process is, in empirical science, just causal reasoning. Indeed, because of causal reasoning, we are not fettered by perceptual thresholds.[41] By contrast, purely conceptual processes (for Kant these amount to making analytic judgments) are no more than manipulating well-defined concepts and extracting from them the more general concepts composing them. Kant takes from Leibniz the view that such unalloyed conceptual thought is combinatorial—indeed, computational.[42] Leibniz held that all adequate knowledge is ultimately conceptual, and indeed analytic. But for Kant, conceptual analysis alone gives no empirical information and will never increase our knowledge. It is intuition only—and in empirical knowledge, empirical intuition—that gives contentual information.

Empirical Knowledge

From this notion of empirical intuition and its causal extension, Kant derives an epistemic pessimism (there will always be open empirical questions), an assertability notion of truth, and an intuitionism-like logic. You can see all of these things from Kant's famous argument that the physical universe (the expanse of matter through space) is neither finite nor infinite. Here's an updated version of the argument:

Let's suppose that we have so far found a sequence of **n** inhabited spatial regions, each further from the earth than its predecessor by at least a fixed minimal distance, and that we now want to know whether or not there is a yet farther inhabited region (call it the **n+1st** region). So we commission a task force to report on the first of each month as to whether or not it has found an n+1st region containing some material thing (an asteroid, say). The search will continue so long as no n+1st region is found, and it stops as soon as such a region is found. Naturally, should our commission ever report an **n+1st** materially inhabited region, then we'd extend its mandate to find an **n+2nd** region, and so on. So right now our prospects look like this chart (figure 5.1):

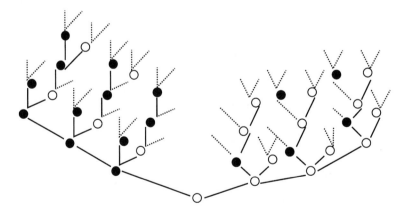

Figure 5.1

Determining the extent of the physical universe. White circles denote a situation in which no further region has been found since the last report. Each solid circle denotes a situation in which we have found a new region and thus embark upon a fresh search.

Kant's argument is simply this: at any solid node, we can never know that this is the last such node in our epistemic path (in which case the universe would be finite), nor can we know that there will be a next solid node and always a next one after that (in which case the universe would be infinite). For we can't escape our skins and "look from outside" or look from the infinite end of time, where the whole history would be known and the branching would be irrelevant. *At any given node* there's always the possibility that we will find no more, and there is always the opposite possibility that we will indeed find more.

The flowchart is all we can contemplate as we consider the future, and it always leaves open the question of whether there will be a next solid node. This is Kant's pessimism. It stems from receptivity.[43]

But Kant goes on to conclude that the physical universe is in fact not finite.[44] That, of course, is an inference warranted only according to assertabilism. Indeed, if we think of this chart as a Kripke model, we can see that it validates the following formulas:

$$\neg(\exists x)(\forall y_{\neq x})Fxy \tag{5.1}$$

$$\neg(\forall y)(\exists x)Fxy \tag{5.2}$$

(where x and y range over populated spatial regions, and Fxy stands for: x is further from us than y). This is a pair of formulas that is co-possible in intuitionistic logic but not in classical logic.

There is, by the way, no anachronism here. I'm simply using our modern notation to model principles that are present, though differently articulated, in Kant's thought.

Let me say, however, that Kant's logic is not quite the standard intuitionistic logic. Because existent objects are completely predicatively determined, we must say that schema (5.3) is also valid:

$$(\exists x)(x=t) \rightarrow (Pt \lor \neg Pt) \tag{5.3}$$

Spectral Awareness

The Universe as a Regulative Idea
We can intuitively grasp any finite chunk of the physical universe, no matter how large. (Perceptual thresholds, recall, are no impediment.) But our grasp of the physical universe as a whole is merely conceptual, for it lacks predicative completeness — there are unanswerable questions. (We might never come to know that there is no next occupied region.) Thinking about the physical universe may well guide our scientific research. (It's regulative; it goads us to keep the commission working.) But we can't intuit the world as an object, and we should not speak of it as if it were an object.

Transcendental Philosophy

Now you might say that we are violating this very stricture when we speak of our "actual path" (a code-word for the world-whole) or when we use the chart above as a Kripke model. Indeed, the union $\mathbf{U} = \mathrm{U}_{H \in K}\ \psi(\mathbf{H})$ is exactly that forbidden world-whole.

But we're not. When we build the model, when we reflect on the conditions of knowledge in general, we are not doing empirical science. Rather we are engaged in what Kant calls "transcendental philosophy," the meta-theoretic study of the underlying assumptions of empirical knowledge. Transcendental philosophy tells us what the elements of knowledge are (the division, for instance, between intuitions and concepts), and it highlights the presuppositions of knowledge (principles like that of causality, for instance).

Now, according to Kant, transcendental philosophy is free of receptivity. The key to answering any question, he says, is within us. There is no wait and see, and thus no ground to plead ignorance, no ground for pessimism.[45]

Freed of receptivity and pessimism, the logic of this transcendental philosophy is going to be classical logic. It has the air of an "external perspective." But, in fact, this metaphor doesn't deliver very much. It leads us to think about the size of the universe; but it tells us nothing at all about that size. It is a different field than cosmology, not a broader or more perspicuous one.

It's a useful field. It reveals necessary presuppositions and goads us on to further explorations. It's the usefulness that gives transcendental philosophy what Kant calls "objective validity." But Kant also insists that the objects it posits—the world whole in particular—are not empirical objects. They have no real ontological status. Not only do these posited things not exist in any real sense, they are not even candidates for existence. Indeed, as we have seen, there is no intuition at all of the world-whole. Our grasp of the world-whole is the paradigmatic spectral awareness.

5.3.2 Mathematics

Mathematics as a Transcendental Science

Mathematics studies the formal conditions of empirical intuition. This makes it an a priori science and a "pure science."

It is an a priori science because it shows the necessary components of experience. Space, for instance, underlies the possibility of differentiating and relating physical objects; and, recall, these are what make them objects altogether.

And it is a "pure" science because it abstracts from the sensory content of perceptions, and studies the pure form of perceived and perceivable objects. To study rectangles I might take a page, abstract from its color and texture and even from its size, and attend only to its shape. So a drawn or even imagined rectangle would do just as well. This gives a "pure intuition." Any consequences I draw from manipulating the abstracted pure intuition will automatically apply to anything of the same shape. This is how it is an arm of empirical knowledge.

But notice that this abstraction, once again, frees mathematics from receptivity, and—just like transcendental philosophy—mathematics enjoys an epistemic optimism. Kant says this quite explicitly:

> It is not so extraordinary as at first seems the case, that a science should be in a position to demand and expect none but assured answers to all the questions within its domain (*quaestiones domesticae*), ... although up to the present they have perhaps not been found. In addition to transcendental philosophy there are two pure rational sciences, namely, *pure mathematics* and *pure ethics*. (Kant 1781/1787, A480/B508)

And so, like transcendental philosophy, mathematics will have a full classical logic, the trappings of an external perspective.

Mathematical Intuition

Now mathematics—unlike strict transcendental philosophy—does have intuitions of its own, and it does have a notion of intuition-preserving process. The intuition of mathematical space exemplifies both.

The Intuition of Space

For Kant this is notoriously Euclidean. Importantly, this means that space is given as an infinite magnitude. For, given any finite spatial region, we know how to extend that region to a larger one: we can start with a line spanning some initial region and then simply extend it by a fixed amount. So mathematical space, unlike physical space, satisfies the formula

$$(\forall y)(\exists x)Fxy \tag{5.4}$$

In addition, space has what I called integral unity: it is given as a whole and not as an amalgam of parts.[46] It is also an intuition of an unsplittable manifold. And indeed it is not reducible to points. Points are only limits.[47] This is simply an Aristotelian view of continuity in general.[48]

Intuition-Preserving Processes

For Kant these are just motions. In mathematics, they can be imagined motions. We can't "think a line," Kant says, "without *drawing* it in thought, or a circle without *describing* [i.e., tracing] it" (Kant 1781/1787, B154). And those limiting points are just the termini of describing motions. That's how we get the infinity of space, and indeed the unsplittability.

Three things need to be said here:

First, in stressing motion Kant is insisting that physical intuition is a source for mathematical intuition. To be sure, Kant will say that mathematics (space included) has no real ontological status. Space, he says, is not an object,[49] and indeed in mathematics there is no question of existence at all.[50] For him, mathematics is no less spectral than transcendental philosophy.[51] And like transcendental philosophy, mathematics gets its legitimacy only from its physical applications, and here Kant is emphasizing that it is built with those applications in mind.

Secondly, the process of extension that gives us infinite space is algorithmic: it involves simply following through a predefined routine. To be sure, the fact that it can be done is encoded in the intuition of space, but the process itself is purely conceptually defined.

But third, in insisting on the primacy of physical intuition, Kant is making a further move. He is expanding the range of intuition-preserving motion beyond predefined movements. Kant is in fact siding with Euler (indeed almost exactly quoting Euler) in a deep dispute that Euler had with d'Alembert. D'Alembert held that a mathematical solution to a physical problem must be expressible by a single equation taken from a restricted class of expressible equations. And, indeed, he believed that the theory of space in mathematics itself is limited to relations among points that are analytically expressible in such equations. Euler, on the other hand, claimed that we must allow ourselves to consider spatial relations that cannot be calculated by such predefined procedures. There are more relations than can be so defined, and thus more ways go from point to point in space. These additional unrepresented processes are given, he says, by "description" in the geometric sense. And he speaks of the various possible free motions of a hand.[52]

In favoring Euler, Kant is viewing d'Alembert as an avatar of the Leibnizian conceptualism that he had abandoned, and Euler as inspiration for his own claim that intuition outruns abstract conception. Kant's larger point—like Euler's—is that conceptual description alone cannot suffice to give us a grasp of reality.

5.3.3 The Antinomy

Kant tells us that the successes, both of mathematics and of transcendental philosophy, tempt us to mistake our spectral awareness—our transcendental grasp of the world-whole, our grasp of mathematical space—for full-fledged empirical intuitions. So we are led to speak of ideal objects as if they were real empirical objects; and that in turn leads to paradox and contradiction.

His antinomy is a flagship example: if we think of physical space (the world-whole) as an empirical object, we automatically apply principle 5.3, the principle of complete determination; and from this we would derive that the physical world is either finite or infinite:

$$[(\exists x)(\forall y_{\neq x})Fxy \vee (\forall y)(\exists x)Fxy]. \tag{5.5}$$

But we are still speaking of physical space, and we still grasp this from the "inside," so to speak. So formulas (5.1) and (5.2) and the arguments behind them still hold. These together give an outright contradiction.

Kant's solution, as always: maintain the inner perspective, and keep the regulative in its place. We are finite, receptive beings and cannot grasp the indeterminate whole. To be sure, we reflect upon our own capacities, and we inevitably think the world-whole. But we must avoid the temptation to treat this idea from transcendental philosophy or from mathematics as if it designated a real thing. It doesn't.

5.4 Closing the Loop

This Kantian picture, by itself, speaks directly to Putnam's two assumptions. We have an integrated empiricism in which mathematical intuition is the formal aspect of physical intuition. Indeed, the intuition of space is so fully integrated that the physical intuition of motion is one of its components. This, I believe, is a paradigm of the empiricism that Putnam presupposed in his first assumption.

Putnam's second assumption was that the intuition-preserving mathematical processes are recursive. We've seen one place in Kant that supports this assumption: the process of extending a line, which shows the infinite extent of space, is indeed a recursive-like process. But we've also seen a place—his siding with Euler—where Kant clearly rejects any restriction to algorithmic procedures. And I believe that we can look at the explicit definability that he rejects as a forerunner of contemporary recursion.

And thus from Kant alone we would get a negative answer to my initial question: mathematical intuition—the basis for constructivism—need not be recursive. And indeed, it is the tie to physical applications—Eulerian motion in particular—that scotches recursiveness.

But jump now a hundred and fifty years, and the pieces of this Kantian picture—put together in different ways—will illuminate Hilbert and Brouwer's rival views as well.

Mathematics changed in two important ways between Kant's time and the twentieth century. For one thing, it grew to be autonomous and less focused on physical applications. Indeed, mathematicians no longer could appeal to an a priori intuition of Euclidean space. Secondly, with the reduction of analysis to set theory, mathematics became inextricably infinitary. Hilbert and Brouwer and those who built on their ideas all worked in this new autonomous and infinitary atmosphere. So they could not adopt Kant's empiricism as it stood.

Nonetheless, Kant's way of thinking does explain their philosophical positions. Because of these autonomous and infinitary turns, mathematics itself demanded a metatheoretic enquiry. It is now a "problem" in its own right. Hilbert and Brouwer, each in his own way, took mathematics as the target, in analogy to empirical science in Kant's system.

Turning first to Hilbert: I asked, what lies behind his epistemic optimism? Well, we can say that he adopts Kant's optimism for mathematics as a whole, and classical logic with it. But then he lets his metamathematical systems behave toward mathematical theories in the way that mathematics itself in Kant's philosophy behaves toward empirical science: these systems name and examine the formal structure of mathematical theories, just as in Kant's philosophy mathematics does this for empirical science.

And Hilbert copies into mathematics itself Kant's distinction between concrete scientific thought and spectral thought. This is for Hilbert the distinction between finitary and ideal mathematical thought. Infinity for Hilbert is an ideal notion, useful when tamed, but a disaster when not. And indeed, as we saw, infinity plays quite a similar role in Kant's antinomy.[53]

I asked, what motivated Hilbert's stringent view of intuition; why did he require an intuition to promise a full survey of the object and determine identity and relations? Well, as we saw, for Kant, that's what intuitions do. And for Kant, only things thus intuitable are legitimate objects. So, in translating this Kantian theme, Hilbert holds that numbers are the only legitimate mathematical objects, and numerical grasp is the only mathematical intuition. This mathematical intuition will have all the trappings of completeness and differentiation.

And as for intuition-preserving processes: unlike Kant—and more in the spirit of d'Alembert—Hilbert says that only conceptual (now recursive) processes can preserve intuitability. Why is that? Well, as I said, Kant's appeal to physical intuition is no longer mathematically proper. And for Hilbert, since second-order processes are not objects, there is no mathematical intuition of these things. There is nothing left but the well-defined conceptual processes. And we can go a step further: I pointed out that Kant, resting on Leibniz, equated the conceptual, the deductive, and the algorithmic. Hilbert, too, as we saw, assumed this affinity. It took the work of Gödel, Turing, Church, and the others formally to establish the truth of this identity that was assumed for so long.

Brouwer, by contrast, makes a different translation of the Kantian program. He and his disciples, along with the Russian school and Bishop, copy the full machinery of the "inner perspective" —its intuitionistic logic, its global indeterminacy—into mathematics as a whole.

But having followed Brouwer this far, the recursivists follow Hilbert in his notion of basic numerical intuition and in the doctrine that the infinite is the spectral. And most of all, they follow him in restricting the intuition-preserving processes to the recursive. And so they find themselves in an intermediate position: the continuum is unsplittable (that's the intuitionistic side), but it is not integrally unified. (Because there is no uniform continuity theorem.)

Let me add, however, that Markov's principle, which seemed rather unmotivated, is in fact an updated version of Kant's principle of complete determination, formula (5.3): the complete determination of all elementary predicates for objects whose existence has been established.

Now Brouwer and the intuitionists deviate from this Kantian idea that intuited objects are fully determined and distinguishable one from the other. Choice sequences simply don't behave that way, and for the intuitionists these sequences are nevertheless intuitively graspable. On the other hand, the intuitionists do adopt Kant's notion of the continuum: unsplittable and integrally unified.

Brouwer himself follows Kant (and ultimately Euler) in his view that purely conceptual methods cannot fully represent the intuitive content of mathematics. This is why he denigrated formalization.

In his first stage, he followed Kant as well regarding the continuum: it is unsplittable, integrally unified, noncompositional, and given by a separate intuition. This, as I mentioned, has Aristotelian roots. Brouwer dropped the latter two aspects in his second stage. It was a brilliant mathematical move—the theory of choice sequences.

This theory, as we saw, invokes a nonrecursive notion of intuition-preserving process. But, now like Hilbert and others of his time, Brouwer could not take the Kantian route: he could not appeal to physical processes in order to generate that nonrecursiveness. In his second period, he used second-order restrictions to ensure the nonrecursive wiggle in his objects. But then he dropped them and turned to the creating subject. I asked why; and the fact is that we can use Kant to explain Brouwer's third stage move as well. Here is how:

Think of the negative continuity theorem, described above. It says that a function f cannot be fully defined on an interval and still have a point of discontinuity in that interval. He used a second-order restriction to guarantee the eternal wiggle of a point r' that is indeterminately close to r. However, as it turns out, there is no way to build such a restriction. Any restriction working in this way will eventually dictate that r'=r. By insisting that you not paint yourself into a corner, you will in fact force yourself into a corner.[54]

Brouwer's creating subject sequences are, I claim, the positive solution to his problem, and a Kantian one at that.[55] Recall that for Brouwer, the spectral notion is the notion of an eternally unsolvable problem. Such a thing is of course conceptually describable, and as we saw, indispensable. But it cannot be intuited. This was exactly Brouwer's mistake in the negative continuity proof. That r' from which he tried to build the counterexample is just such a thing, but he nonetheless spoke of it as if it existed. This is the mistake of the antinomy!

And his solution is Kantian indeed: the creating subject sequences derive their indeterminacy—just as does the Kantian space exploration—from receptivity, from the fact that we have to wait around to find out what will happen.

I asked how it could be that their shared antipathy toward infinite totalities led Hilbert and Brouwer to such divergent paths: Hilbert to his outer perspective and recursiveness, Brouwer to the inner perspective and nonrecursive processes. Well, the answer is that for Brouwer it is not infinity alone that limits our powers. There are infinite things that we intuitively grasp. It is our human receptivity, rather than infinity, that leads him to a nonrecursive notion of constructivity. This is what his appeal to the creating subject makes explicit.

To be sure, my Kantian analysis will not decide between the modern recursive and nonrecursive accounts of constructability. But it does show us the philosophical questions that lie at the base of each side, and it does connect this constructivity with the doctrines of scientific empiricism. That is what I set out to do.[56]

Notes

1. H. Putnam, "Wittgenstein, Realism, and Mathematics" (2002). The paper he cites is Pour-El and Richards (1981).

2. To be sure, some empiricists and constructivists shun talk of reality and replace it with talk of truth. But the point remains the same: the notion of empirical truth should reflect the constraints on empirical intuition, and, in parallel, mathematical truth should reflect the limits of mathematical intuition. This is a rather special philosophical use of the notion of intuition, quite different from the common understanding of that term: it is something like perception. But this is the notion of intuition that is at work in philosophical discussions of empiricism and constructivism.

3. Nowadays there remains a contemporary school of "strict finitism" that would still ban the infinite from mathematics altogether. The main advocate is A. S. Yessenin-Volpin (see Yessenin-Volpin 1970). This approach is fraught with conceptual difficulties, and it has not caught on either. See, for instance, Dummett's "Wang's Paradox" in Dummett (1978), and Magidor (2012).

4. Formal intuitionistic logic was first formulated by Heyting in 1930 to codify the reasoning underlying Brouwer's intuitionistic mathematics (see Heyting 1930a). Kleene (1952) axiomatized this logical system so that it differs from classical logic just on the principle of the excluded third.

5. See, for instance, Bishop (1967, 9).

6. Ordinarily, this guarantee will be a method that will lead to a proof of A or of B. A good example is the claim that $10^{10^{10}} + 1$ is either prime or composite.

7. Ordinarily, this is interpreted as $(A \rightarrow F)$, where F is a contradiction or some known falsehood.

8. Once again, ordinarily this guarantee will be a method for producing the requisite a.

9. These conditions were set out by Heyting in 1930. (See Heyting 1930a, 1930b.) The term "warranted assertability" was actually introduced by John Dewey in Dewey (1938), but it has now come to be used generically to cover this sort of epistemic theory of meaning. Kolmogorov's version in Kolmogorov (1932)

used the notion of mathematical problems. But he pointed out that it was equivalent to Heyting's proof interpretation.

10. My "Kant's Mathematical Realism" (in Posy 1992) works out some subtle considerations here.

11. See Kripke (1965) and Gödel (1932).

12. Here is the formal definition: a *Kripke Model*, *M*, is an *ordered triple* <G,K,R> together with a *domain function* ψ, and an *evaluation function* ϕ. K is the set of nodes (evidential situations), G ($\in$ K)is the actual situation, and *R* is the (transitive and reflexive) accessibility relation.

Conditions on ψ :
For any node H ($\in$ K), ψ(H) $\neq\varnothing$, and for any pair of nodes H, H', HRH' $\rightarrow$ ψ(H) $\subseteq$ ψ(H'). Define **U** = $U_{H\in K}$ ψ**(H).**

Conditions on ϕ:
(i) For each node H and each unary predicate P, ϕ(H,P) $\subseteq$ ψ(H).
In general for n-ary predicate P^n: ϕ(H,P^n) $\subseteq$ [ψ(H)]^n .

(ii) For each atomic proposition p and node H, ϕ(H,p) $\in$ {1,0}, and for any pair of nodes H,H', if HRH' and ϕ(H,p) =1, then ϕ(H',p) =1.

For any pair of wff's, A, B, and node H:

(iii) ϕ(H, A&B) = 1 iff ϕ(H,A)= ϕ(H,B)=1, otherwise ϕ(H, A&B) = 0.

(iv) ϕ(H, A$\vee$B) = 1 iff ϕ(H,A)= 1 or ϕ(H,B)=1, otherwise ϕ(H, A$\vee$B) = 0.

(v) ϕ(H, A$\rightarrow$B) = 1 iff for all H'($\in$ K) such that HRH, ϕ(H',A)= 0 or ϕ(H',B)= 1, otherwise ϕ(H, A$\rightarrow$B) = 1.

(vi) ϕ(H, $\neg$A) = 1 iff for all H'($\in$ K) such that HRH, ϕ(H',A)= 0, otherwise ϕ(H, $\neg$A) = 0.

For the following clauses let elements a_1, ... , a_n of **U** be assigned to x_1, ... , x_n, respectively.

(vii) ϕ(H, P^n(x_1, ... , x_n)) = 1iff <a_1, ... , a_n >$\in$ ϕ(H,P^n); and ϕ(H, P^n(x_1, ... , x_n)) = 0 iff <a_1, ... , a_n >$\notin$ ϕ(H,P^n).
(viii) ϕ(H,$\exists$yA(x1, ... , xn, y)) = 1 iff there is a c $\in$ ψ(H) such that ϕ(H, A(x_1, ... , x_n, y)) =1 when y is assigned to c; otherwise ϕ(H, $\exists$y A(x_1, ... , x_n, y)) =0
(ix) ϕ(H,$\forall$yA(x_1, ... , x_n, y)) = 1 iff for each H'($\in$K) such that HRH, ϕ(H', A(x_1, ... , x_n, y)) =1 and y is assigned any element, c, of ψ(H'); otherwise ϕ(H, $\forall$yA (x_1, ... , x_n, y)) = 0.

A wff, B, is true in *M* if ϕ(G,B) = 1. A wff is *valid* if it is true in all Kripke models, **M**.

13. The main approach uses something called the Gelfond-Schneider theorem, which shows that if a is an algebraic number such that a$\neq$0 and a$\neq$1, and b is an irrational algebraic number, then a^b is irrational. So $\sqrt{2}^{\sqrt{2}}$ is irrational, and one uses the second alternative.

14. Thus, in the second case, each real in the sequence {r_n}$_n$ would be given by an rng {q^n_i}$_i$, and the limit r would have to be given by an rng {s_n}$_n$ such that $\forall n \exists k \forall j_{>k} \exists i \forall m_{>i} |q^j_m - s_m| < 10^{-n}$. In general, even when the sequences {r_n}$_n$ and each {q^n_i}$_i$ are constructively generated, we cannot construct a sequence {s_n}$_n$ for which the existential claims in this inequality can be constructively proved.

15. Thus, Bishop says:

The primary concern of mathematics is number, and this means the positive integers. ... [E]very mathematical statement ultimately expresses the fact that if we perform certain computations within the set of positive integers, we shall obtain certain results. (Bishop 1967, 2–3)

See also Bishop (1970).

16. An excellent summary is Kushner (1984).

17. See Lacombe (1955a b,c), Mazur (1963), Péter (1950), Goodenstein (1961), Grzegorczyk (1955), to name a few. See also Feferman's "About and Around Computing Over the Reals" (Feferman 2012, this volume) for an account of recent work in this direction.

18. The compactness of an infinite set—the fact that every covering of the set by a collection of open sets can be reduced to a finite subcollection of those open sets—approximates some aspects of finiteness for the given set.

19. See Brouwer (1907).

20. Dummett (2000) gives a good survey.

21. Brouwer sometimes calls such a sequence a "sharp arrow."

22. Technically a choice sequence (say, of numbers) is a sequence of pairs $\{s_n, L_n\}_n$, where s_n is the nth numerical element, and L_n is a set from which s_{n+1} is to be chosen. The definition of the sequence may give a finite initial subsequence $<s_1, \ldots, s_k>$, and then set constraints on the allowable L_n's for $n>k$. Thus, if we are generating a decimal rng, L_n is always a subset of $\{0, 1, \ldots, 9\}$. In the case above, the constraint that the real number fall in $[0, \frac{1}{2}]$ and the fact that 0 and 5 were the first two numerical choices mean that $L_n = \{0\}$ from then on. In general, the mathematical properties of a choice sequence are determined solely by the numerical component, and thus we often omit mention of the L_n's.

23. Even though the element of free choice is removed, one standardly still speaks of these as choice sequences.

24. Here are the main technical ideas: A *spread* is a pair of rules for admissible finite sequences. These are called the *spread law* and the *complementary law*.

• The spread law determines for each finite sequence of natural numbers $<n_1, \ldots, n_o>$ whether or not it is an admissible sequence, and is such that each admissible sequence $<n_1, \ldots, n_o>$ has at least one admissible successor $<n_1, \ldots, n_o, n_{k+1}>$.

• An infinite sequence of natural numbers will belong to the spread if each finite subsequence is admissible.

• We get sequences whose components arc more sophisticated objects by assigning such an object to each admissible finite sequence. The complementary law makes these assignments.

• An element of the spread is an infinite sequence of entities generated by the complementary law.

• Thus, for instance, given some enumeration of the rationals, the complementary law might assign the rational number q_n to the admissible sequence $<n_1, \ldots, n_k, n>$ and the spread law might restrict admissible sequences to those $<n_1, \ldots, n_{k-1}, n_o>$ such that $|q_{n_{k-1}} - q_{n_k}| < 10^{-k}$. The elements of this spread will be rng's.

• A *finitary spread* (*fan*) is a spread that has an empty initial admissible sequence, and is such that for each admissible sequence there are only finitely many admissible continuations.

25. This proof is in Brouwer (1927). The second-order restriction requires that what in note 22 I called the L_n's in the rng for r' must always include choices that allow the rng to converge to r, together with those that allow it to converge above r. See Posy (2008) for a discussion of what it means to say that f is undefined at r.

26. This might not be surprising. The fact that an interval is given by a fan of rngs recreates in the intuitionistic setting some of the aspects of compactness. But the fan theorem itself is actually quite difficult to prove. Effectively, it says that if every element of the fan (i.e., every infinite sequence in the fan) has a finite subsequence with a particular property, then the initial (empty) sequence will have that property.

27. Let me mention that Kleene proposed a semantics for a formal system of intuitionism (including intuitionistic analysis) that uses recursive functions to interpret the logical particles. This interpretation is called "recursive realizability." It was developed in a series of papers stemming from 1945 and in the monograph of Kleene and Vesley (1965). In this work, the main properties of the continuum are derived, not directly from the indeterminacy of rng's, but rather from a number of initial continuity principles taken on their own. In this context I should also mention Kripke's schema, the axiom schema: $\exists f(A \leftrightarrow \exists nf(n)=0)$ (where A is a place holder for sentences of the language). Kripke's schema is meant to mimic the effect of creating subject sequences in formal systems. It has been shown that this schema is formally inconsistent with the assumption that every number theoretic function (and hence every rng) is recursive. See Myhill (1967, 1970) and Kreisel (1970). But also see Vesley (1970) and Moschovakis (1971).

28. See Beeson (1985), Bishop and Bridges (1985), Richman (1981), and Bridges and Richman (1987).

29. Section 6 of Feferman's "About and Around Computing Over the Reals" (Feferman 2012, this volume) surveys recursive interpretations of Bishop's work.

30. Heyting said something like this years ago. See Heyting (1966).

31. Indeed, Brouwer held this broader view not only about number theoretic functions but about real valued functions as well. He allows real valued functions that themselves "develop freely." His example is an infinite sum the sign of whose summands is freely chosen:

$$h(x) = \sum \pm \frac{x^n}{n!},$$

where for each n the sign preceding the expression

$$\frac{x^n}{n!}$$

is freely chosen. See Brouwer (1942). So his notions of existence and intuition-preserving process had to be broad enough to accommodate that as well.

32. See Brouwer (1949).

33. In a 1952 footnote he says.

In former publications I have sometimes admitted restrictions of freedom with regard also to future restrictions of freedom. However this admission is not justified by close introspection and moreover would endanger the simplicity and rigour of further developments. (Brouwer 1952, 142; also in Brouwer 1974, 511)

34. This is his 1890 proof that every ideal in the ring of polynomials in several variables over a field has a finite set of generators.

35. It was announced in Hilbert's lecture "Über die Grundlagen der Logik und der Arithmetik" (published as Hilbert 1905). He developed the Program more fully in the 1920s. Hilbert and Bernays' book *Grundlagen der Mathematik* (1934) contains the most mature statement of the program.

36. He called it "proof theory"; it has come to be known as "metamathematics."

37. This doctrine was prominent in Hilbert's (1900) lecture "Mathematische Probleme." It came up again in "Axiomatische Denken" (Hilbert 1918) and again in Hilbert (1926). Sometimes he set the mathematical confirmation of this belief as a problem in its own right.

38. See section 1.1 of Jack Copeland and Oron Shagrir, "Turing versus Gödel on Computability and the Mind" (2012, this volume) for a discussion of Turing's take on this notion of intuition.

39. Hilbert also used his version of recursive functions in his attempts to prove the continuum hypothesis. An interesting study of Hilbert's use of recursiveness is chapter 3 in Adams (2011).

40. There is a certain irony here, for, on the one hand, Gödel perfected the mathematical tools that confirm Hilbert's equation between formal systems and effective calculability. He showed that the class of functions representable in a formal system for number theory is the class of general recursive functions. And, indeed, he confirmed Hilbert's belief that the metatheory of formal systems is a finitary study. Yet this same tool serves to show that Hilbert's program cannot be carried out.

41. "Thus from the perception of the attracted iron filings we know of the existence of a magnetic matter pervading all bodies, although the constitution of our organs cuts us off from all immediate perception of this medium. For in accordance with the laws of sensibility and the context of our perceptions, we should, were our senses more refined, also come in an experience upon the immediate empirical intuition of it. The grossness of our senses does not in any way decide the form of possible experience in general. Our knowledge of the existence of things reaches then, only so far as perception and its advance according to empirical laws can extend." (Kant 1781/1787, A226/B273)

42. This is a central Leibnizian theme, applying to logic, mathematics, and indeed any domain. He was fascinated by computation—he invented a calculating machine—and his career is peppered with attempts to reduce all thought to calculation.

43. "In natural science, on the other hand, there is endless conjecture, and certainty is not to be counted upon. For the natural appearances are objects that are given to us independently of our concepts, and the key to them lies not in us and our pure thinking but outside us; and therefore, in many cases since the key is not to be found, an assured solution is not to be expected." (Kant 1781/1787, A480/B508)

44. "Thus the first and negative answer to the cosmological problem regarding the magnitude of the world is that the world has no ... outermost limit in space." (Kant 1781/1787, A520/B548)

45. "Now I maintain that transcendental philosophy is unique in the whole field of speculative knowledge, in that no question which concerns an object given to pure reason can be insoluble for this same human reason, and that no excuse of an unavoidable ignorance, or of the problem's unfathomable depth, can release us from the obligation to answer it thoroughly and completely. That very concept which puts us in a position to ask the question must also qualify us to answer it, since, as in the case of right and wrong, the object is not to be met with outside the concept." (Kant 1781/1787, A477/B505.)

46. "Space is essentially one; the manifold in it, and therefore the general concept of spaces, depends solely on [the introduction of] limitations." (Kant 1781/1787, A25/B39)

47. "Space therefore consists solely of spaces, time solely of times. Points and instants are only limits, that is, mere positions which limit space and time. But positions always presuppose the intuitions which they limit; and out of mere positions, viewed as constituents capable of being given prior to space or time, neither space nor time can be constructed. Such magnitudes may also be called *flowing*, since the synthesis of productive imagination involved in their production is a progression in time, and the continuity of time is ordinarily designated by the term flowing or flowing away." (Kant 1781/1787, A169–70/B211–12)

48. See, for instance, *Physics* (231a21–37) and *De Generatione et Corruptione* (316a1–317b30).

49. "Space is merely the form of outer intuition (formal intuition). It is not a real object which can be outwardly intuited." (Kant 1781/1787, A428/B457 n.).

50. "But in mathematical problems there is no question of ... existence at all ..." (Kant 1781/1787, A719/B747).

51. At (A239/B298), Kant (1781/1787) says that without "the data for possible experience," a priori principles "have no objective validity, and with respect of their representations are a mere a play of the imagination or of understanding." The context makes it clear that it is mathematics that would be "a mere play of the imagination" without empirical applicability. Transcendental philosophy is what would be the "mere play of the understanding" without such application.

52. The most famous instance of this dispute concerned d'Alembert's solution to the vibrating string problem. D'Alembert says, "...But under this supposition one can only find the solution of the problem for the case where the different forms of the vibrating string can be written in a single equation. In all other cases it seems to me impossible to give a more general form" (d'Alembert 1750, 358). Euler responds: "The various similar parts of the curve are therefore not connected with each other by any law of continuity, and it is only by the description that they are joined together. For this reason it is impossible that all of this curve should be included in any equation" (Euler 1755). But the dispute was quite general.

53. Indeed, Hilbert makes the Kantian allusion explicitly: "The role that remains for the infinite to play is solely that of an idea—if one means by an idea, in Kant's terminology, a concept of reason which transcends all experience and which completes the concrete as a totality—that of an idea which we may unhesitatingly trust within the framework erected by our theory" (Hilbert 1926).

54. See my "Brouwerian Infinity" (Posy 2008) for a fuller account of the problem with Brouwer's proof. The point is that if we view the rng for r' as $\{q_n, L_n\}_n$ in the notation I suggested in note 22 above, then the second-order restriction is that L_n must always have more than one element. The problem is that this second-order restriction is self-contradictory. Using a backward induction, one can show the restriction entails that L_n is always a unit set.

55. Posy (2008).

56. I owe special thanks to Oron Shagrir for very helpful comments on an earlier draft.

References

Adams, R. 2011. *An Early History of Recursive Functions and Computability from Gödel to Turing.* Boston: Docent Press.

Beeson, M. J. 1985. *Foundations of Constructive Mathematics.* Berlin: Springer.

Bishop, E. 1967. *Foundations of Constructive Analysis.* New York: McGraw-Hill.

Bishop, E. 1970. Mathematics as a Numerical Language. In *Intuitionism and Proof Theory,* ed. A. Kino, J. Myhill, and R. E. Vesley, 53–71. Amsterdam: North-Holland.

Bishop, E., and D. Bridges. 1985. *Constructive Analysis.* Berlin: Springer.

Bridges, D., and F. Richman. 1987. *Varieties of Constructive Mathematics.* Cambridge: Cambridge University Press.

Brouwer, L. E. J. 1907. *Over de grondslagen der wiskunde.* Dissertation, University of Amsterdam. Translated as "On the Foundations of Mathematics" in Brouwer, *Collected Works,* Vol. 1, 11–101.

Brouwer, L. E. J. 1927. Über Definitionsbereiche von Funktionen. *Mathematische Annalen* 97:60–75.

Brouwer, L. E. J. 1942. Zum freien Werden von Mengen und Funktionen. *Koninklijke Nederlandse Akademie van Wetenschappen te Amsterdam* 45:322–323. Reprinted in Brouwer, *Collected Works,* Vol. 1, 459–460.

Brouwer, L. E. J. 1949. Consciousness, Philosophy and Mathematics. In *Proceedings of the Tenth International Congress of Philosophy,* 1235–1249. Amsterdam: North-Holland.

Brouwer, L. E. J. 1952. Historical background, principles and methods of intuitionism. *South African Journal of Science* 49:139–146. Reprinted in Brouwer, *Collected Works,* Vol. 1

Brouwer, L. E. J. 1974. *Collected Works,* Vol. 1, ed. A. Heyting. Amsterdam: North-Holland.

d'Alembert, J. L. R. 1750. Addition au mémoire sur la courbe que forme une corde tendüe mise en vibration [Addition to research on the curve formed by a vibrating string]. *Histoire de l'académie royale des sciences et belles lettres de Berlin,* Vol. 6, 355–360.

Dewey, J. 1938. *Logic: The Theory of Inquiry.* New York: Holt.

Dummett, M. A. E. 1978. *Truth and Other Enigmas.* Cambridge: Harvard University Press.

Dummett, M. A. E. 2000. *Elements of Intuitionism,* 2nd ed. Oxford: Clarendon Press.

Euler, L. 1755. Remarques sur les memoires precedens de M. Bernoulli [Remarks on the preceding memoirs of M. Bernoulli]. In *Opera Omnia,* Series 2, Vol. 10, 233–254.

Fitch, F. 1959. Quasi-constructive foundations for mathematics. In *Constructivity in Mathematics,* ed. A. Heyting, 26–36. Amsterdam: North Holland.

Gödel, K. 1932. Zum intuitionistischen Aussagenkalkül. *Anzeiger der Akademie der Wissenschaften in Wien* 69:65–66.

Goodenstein, R. L. 1961. *Recursive Analysis.* Amsterdam: North-Holland.

Grzegorczyk, A. 1955. Computable functionals. *Fundamenta Mathematicae* 42:168–202.

Heyting, A. 1930a. Die formalen Regeln der intuitionistischen Logik. *Sitzungsberichte der preuszischen Akademie von Wissenschaften, physikalisch-mathematische Klasse* 16(1):42–56.

Heyting, A. 1930b. Sur la logique intuitionniste. *Aacadémie Royale de Belgique Bulletin* 16:957–963.

Heyting, A. 1966. *Intuitionism: An Introduction,* 2nd rev. ed. Amsterdam: North-Holland.

Hilbert, D. 1900. Mathematische Probleme. *Nachrichten von der Königlichen Gesellschaft der Wissenschaften zu Göttingen, Mathematisch-physikalische Klasse* 253–97.

Hilbert, D. 1905. Über die Grundlagen der Logik und der Arithmetik. In *Verhandlungen des dritten Internationalen Mathematiker-Kongresses in Heidelberg vom 8 bis 13 August 1904,* ed. A. Krazer, 174–85. Leipzig: Teubner. English translation in *From Frege to Gödel: A Source Book in Mathematical Logic, 1897–1931,* ed. J. van Heijenoort, 129–38. Cambridge: Harvard University Press.

Hilbert, D. 1918. Axiomatisches Denken. *Mathematische Annalen* 78:405–415.

Hilbert, D. 1926. Über das Unendliche. *Mathematische Annalen* 95:161–90. Translated as "On the Infinite." In *From Frege to Gödel: A Source Book in Mathematical Logic, 1897–1931,* ed. J. van Heijenoort, 367–392. Cambridge: Harvard University Press.

Hilbert, D., and P. Bernays. 1934. *Grundlagen der Mathematik, I.* Berlin, New York: Springer-Verlag.

Kant, I. *Kritik der reinen Vernunft* [*Critique of Pure Reason*], ed. A: 1st ed. (1781) Vol. IV and B: 2nd ed. (1787) Vol. III of *Kant's gesammelte Schriften,* ed. B. Erdmann and the Koniglich Preussischen Akademie der Wissenschaften, Berlin 1911. Trans. N. K. Smith, New York: St. Martin's Press, 1931.

Kleene, S. C. 1952. *Introduction to Metamathematics.* New York: D. van Nostrand.

Kleene, S. C., and R. E. Vesley. 1965. *Foundations of Intuitionistic Mathematics.* Amsterdam: North Holland.

Kolmogorov, A. N. 1932. Zur Deutung der intuitionistischen Logik. *Mathematische Zeitschrift* 35 (1):58–65.

Kripke, S. 1965. Semantical analysis of intuitionistic logic, I. In *Formal Systems and Recursive Functions,* ed. J. N. Crossley and M. A. E. Dummett, 92–130. Amsterdam: North Holland.

Kreisel, G. 1970. Church's thesis: A kind of reducibility axiom for constructive mathematics. In *Intuitionism and Proof Theory,* ed. A. Kino, J. Myhill, and R. E. Vesley, 151–162. Amsterdam: North-Holland.

Kushner, B. A. 1984. *Lectures on Constructive Mathematical Analysis.* Trans. E. Mendelson. Providence, RI: American Mathematical Society.

Lacombe, D. 1955a. Extension de la notion de fonction récursive aux fonctions d'une ou plusieurs variables réelles, I. *Comptes Rendus de l'Académie des Science Paris* 240:2470–80.

Lacombe, D. 1955b. Extension de la notion de fonction récursive aux fonctions d'une ou plusieurs variables réelles, II. *Comptes Rendus de l'Académie des Science Paris* 241:13–14.

Lacombe, D. 1955c. Extension de la notion de fonction récursive aux fonctions d'une ou plusieurs variables réelles, III. *Comptes Rendus de l'Académie des Science Paris* 241:151–55.

Lorenzen, P. 1971. *Differential and Integral: A Constructive Introduction to Classical Analysis.* Trans. J. Bacon. Austin: University of Texas Press.

Magidor, O. 2012. Strict finitism and the happy sorites. *Journal of Philosophical Logic* 41 (2):471–491.

Mazur, S. 1963. Computable analysis. In *Rozprawy Matematyczne,* 33, ed. A. Grzegorczyk and H. Rasiowa. Warsaw: Państwowe Wydawnictwo Naukowe.

Moschovakis, J. R. 1971. Can there be no nonrecursive functions? *Journal of Symbolic Logic* 36:309–315.

Myhill, J. 1967. Notes towards an axiomatization of intuitionistic analysis. *Logique et Analyse* 35:280–297.

Myhill, J. 1970. Formal systems of intuitionistic analysis II: The theory of species. In *Intuitionism and Proof Theory,* ed. A. Kino, J. Myhill, and R. E. Vesley, 151–162. Amsterdam: North-Holland.

Péter, R. 1950. Zum Begriffe der rekursiven reellen Zahl. *Acta scientiarum mathematicarum* (Szeged) 12A:239–45.

Posy, C. J., ed. 1992. *Kant's Philosophy of Mathematics: Modern Essays.* Dordrecht: Kluwer Academic.

Posy, C. J. 2008. Brouwerian infinity. In *One Hundred Years of Intuitionism (1907–2007),* ed. M. van Atten, P. Boldini, M. Bourdeau, G. Heinzmann, 21–36. Basel: Birkhäuser.

Pour-El, M. B., and I. Richards. 1981. The wave equation with computable initial data such that its unique solution is not computable. *Advances in Mathematics* 39 (3):215–239.

Putnam, H. 2002. Wittgenstein, le réalisme et les mathematiques. In *Wittgenstein, dernières pensées,* ed. J. Bouveresse, S. Laugier, and J.-J. Rosat, 289–313. Marseilles: Agone.

Translated as "Wittgenstein, realism and mathematics." In H. Putnam, *Philosophy in an Age of Science,* ed. M. De Caro and D. Macarthur. Harvard University Press, 2012.

Richman, F., ed. 1981. *Constructive Mathematics*. Lecture notes in mathematics, Vol. 873. Berlin: Springer.

Vesley, R. E. 1970. A palatable substitute for Kripke's schema. In *Intuitionism and Proof Theory,* ed. A. Kino, J. Myhill, and R. E. Vesley, 197–207. Amsterdam: North-Holland.

Weyl, H. 1918. *Das Kontinuum*. Leipzig: De Gruyter.

Yessenin-Volpin, A. S. 1970. The ultra-intuitionistic criticism and the antitraditional program for foundation of mathematics. In *Intuitionism and Proof Theory,* ed. A. Kino, J. Myhill, and R. E. Vesley, 3–45. Amsterdam: North-Holland.

6 After Gödel

Hilary Putnam

Some years ago, I heard a famous logician say that "Alfred Tarski was the greatest logician after Aristotle." Tarski was indeed a great logician, but for reasons I will explain in a moment, it seems clear to me that the title "greatest logician after Aristotle" belongs to Kurt Gödel and not Alfred Tarski. On another occasion, the famous mathematician David Mumford (who later "went into" computer science) said to me, "As far as I am concerned, Gödel wasn't a mathematician. He was just a philosopher." I don't know if Mumford still thinks this, but if he does, he is wrong too.

Gödel is, of course, known best for the famous incompleteness theorems, but they are only a part of his contribution to logic. If they were the whole, or the only part of such fundamental importance, then the claim that Tarski's formalization of the notion of "satisfaction," and his use of that notion to show us how to define truth of a formula in a formalized language over a model, was at least as great a contribution might be tenable.[1] However, the very field for which Tarski is most famous, model theory, was launched by two theorems, one of which bears Gödel's name: I refer to the Skolem–Löwenheim theorem and the Gödel completeness (or completeness and compactness) theorem. Moreover, Church's theorem was clearly known to Gödel before Church, as a careful reading of the footnotes to the famous paper on undecidable sentences makes clear. And without question, what I may call the "Gödel–Cohen theorems"—that the axiom of choice (AC) and the continuum hypothesis (CH) are both independent of the other axioms of set theory (unless those axioms are inconsistent)—are by far the most stunning results ever obtained in set theory. (Gödel proved that the AC and the CH are consistent with the axiom of Zermelo and Fraenkel in the '30s, and in 1962 Paul Cohen showed that their negations are likewise consistent. These results are extremely robust, in the sense that it is unlikely that any further axioms one could add to set theory will both resolve the continuum problem and be found sufficiently "intuitively evident" to command acceptance by the mathematical community, although Gödel hoped the contrary.)

One could also mention many other contributions by Gödel, including important contributions to recursion theory. For example, in the course of proving the incompleteness theorems, Gödel showed that in any formal system which contains expressions for all the primitive recursive functions, there is a primitive recursive function f such that for any predicate $F(x)$ in that system, there is an integer N, such that the Gödel number of the formula $F(f(N))$ is equal to precisely $f(N)$ (i.e., the formula is true if and only if its own Gödel number has the property F).[2] (I shall refer to this as "Gödel's diagonal lemma," although he did not give it a name.) This means that, for example, there is a formula which is true if and only if its own Gödel number is prime (just take $F(n)$ to be the formula Prime(n)), a formula which is true if and only if its own Gödel number is even, etc. This is not just *similar* to the fixed point theorem of recursion theory; it introduced precisely the technique of proof we need for that fixed point theorem (Kleene's recursion theorem).

What I want to do now is describe some of the ways logicians after Gödel have built upon and extended his results.

6.1 Diophantine Equations

Gödel's own undecidable sentence can easily be put into the form, "There does not exist a natural number n such that $f(n) = 0$," where $f(n)$ is primitive recursive. But primitive recursive functions are not a topic the average mathematician is particularly interested in. (Probably David Mumford was not when he made the remark I quoted earlier.)

The tenth problem in Hilbert's famous list was to give a decision method for determining whether an arbitrary Diophantine equation has a solution. However, in the late 1950s, Martin Davis, Julia Robinson, and myself proved that the decision problem for exponential Diophantine equations[3] is recursively unsolvable. Robinson had already shown that the decision problem for ordinary Diophantine equations is equivalent to the decision problem for exponential Diophantine equations if and only if there exists a single ordinary Diophantine equation whose solutions (considered as functions of any one of the unknowns) have roughly exponential rate of growth, and a few years later Yuri Matiyasevich proved that such an equation exists. This Davis-Matiyasevich-Putnam-Robinson theorem showed that the decision problem for ordinary Diophantine equations is recursively unsolvable, thus providing a negative solution to Hilbert's tenth problem. In fact, we showed that for every recursively enumerable set S, there is a polynomial P with integral coefficients such that $P(n, x_1, x_2, \ldots, x_k) = 0$ has a solution in natural numbers exactly when n belongs to S. Applied to Gödel's original paper on undecidable sentences, this yields the fact that the undecidable sentence can have the mathematically very familiar form, "the Diophantine equation P = 0 has no solution." To quote I don't know whom, "Who woulda thunk it?"

6.2 Model Theory

In 1930, Gödel also showed that the standard axioms and rules of quantification theory (which was known at that time by the name the American philosopher Charles Peirce, the founder of pragmatism, gave it—"first-order logic") are *complete*, in the sense that every valid formula, every formula which is true in all possible models, is a theorem. His proof also establishes that if every finite subset of an infinite set of formulas of quantification theory has a model, then the whole infinite set has a model. This is the compactness theorem, and is still of fundamental importance in model theory.

To illustrate the importance of the compactness theorem, let P be any set of axioms for Peano arithmetic, or, for that matter, for any consistent system which extends Peano arithmetic. Let $\underline{a}$ be a new individual constant, that is, one not used in P. Consider the theory T with the following recursively enumerable set of axioms: the axioms of P *plus* "$\underline{a}$ is a natural number," "$\underline{a} \neq 0$," "$\underline{a} \neq 1$," "$\underline{a} \neq 2$," $\underline{a} \neq 3$," ... and so on *ad infinitum*. Let S be any finite subset of these axioms, and let N be the largest integer such that "$\underline{a} \neq N$" is a member of S. Then S obviously has a model—just take any model for P, and interpret $\underline{a}$ as denoting N + 1. By the compactness theorem, T has a model. In that model, the object denoted by "$\underline{a}$" is an infinite integer—and so is $\underline{a} + 1, \underline{a} + 2, \underline{a} + 3 \dots$. Moreover, $\underline{a}$ has a predecessor $\underline{a} - 1$ in the model (otherwise, by a theorem of Peano arithmetic, and hence a theorem of P, it would be 0, violating the axiom "$\underline{a} \neq 0$"), and that predecessor has a predecessor, etc., and all of these "natural numbers" $\underline{a} - 1, \underline{a} - 2, \underline{a} - 3 \dots$ are likewise infinite integers. Thus we have the existence of nonstandard models for arithmetic! (By a "nonstandard" model I mean a model in which, in addition to the integers 0, 1, 2, ... there are also, viewed from the outside, "infinite integers." I say "viewed from the outside" because within the formal system itself there is no way to single out these nonstandard elements, or even to say they exist: it is only in the metalanguage in which we prove the existence of the nonstandard model that we can say that there are "foreign elements" in the model, elements other than the "real" natural numbers.) Abraham Robinson showed, in fact, that by using such models one can carry out Leibniz's dream of a true calculus of infinitesimals, and the resulting branch of mathematics, which has been called nonstandard analysis, already has significant applications in many areas to the theory of Lie groups, to the study of Brownian motion, to Lebesgue integration, etc. What gives the subject its power is that, because the "infinite numbers" all belong to a model for the theory of the standard (finite) integers and real numbers, a model within which they are not distinguished by any predicate of the language from the standard numbers, we are guaranteed from the start that they will obey all the laws that standard numbers obey.

6.3 Kripke's Proof

In the last twenty-five years or so various workers, the most famous being Paris and Harrington, have begun to use the existence of nonstandard models to give independence proofs in number theory itself (see Paris and Harrington 1977). The very existence of independent (or "undecidable") propositions of elementary number theory was proved by Gödel in 1934 by syntactic, not model theoretic, means. The proposition proved independent by Paris and Harrington is a statement of graph theory (a strengthened version of Ramsey's theorem). What I want to tell you about now, however, is a different model-theoretic proof of the existence of undecidable sentences. This proof is due to Saul Kripke, and was written up by myself in a paper published in 2000.

Because Kripke's theorem does not aim at establishing the independence of a statement which is nearly as complicated as the proposition Paris and Harrington wished to prove independent, the proof is much simpler than theirs. Also, because the independence proof is semantic rather than syntactic, we do not need to arithmetize the relation "x is a proof of y," as Gödel had to do for his proof. We do not need the famous predicate $Bew(x)$ (x is the Gödel number of a theorem), or the famous self-referring sentence which is true if and only if its own Gödel number is not the Gödel number of a theorem. In short, Kripke gave us a different proof of the Gödel theorem, not just a different *version* of Gödel's proof.

While I will not give Kripke's proof in full—you can find it in the paper I mentioned (Putnam 2000)—I do want to give some idea of the remarkable ingenuity it displays, ingenuity that I am sure Gödel himself would have very much appreciated.

First, Kripke introduces what we might call "finite partial models" (the term is my own) of statements in number theory. To be specific: consider a finite monotone-increasing series $\underline{s}$ of natural numbers, say

182, 267, 349, 518, ..., 3987654345

Such a series will be what I am calling a "finite partial model" for a formula A of number theory, say $(\forall x)(\exists y)Rxy$ (with primitive recursive R), if the series fulfills the formula in the sense I will now explain. In our explanation we will identify a sequence with its Kleene "Gödel number" $\underline{s}$, where convenient. Following Kleene's convention, the successive members of the sequence will be denoted $(\underline{s})_0, (\underline{s})_1, \ldots$.

We shall say s̲ fulfills A if the second player (the "defending player") has a winning strategy in the game I shall describe.

6.3.1 The Game G

The game is played as follows. The first player (the "attacking player") picks a number less than the length of the given sequence s̲, say 3. The sequence s̲ is examined to determine the third place in the sequence. The same player (the attacker) now picks a number less than the number in that place (less than 349, in the case of our example.) Let us suppose she picks 17. We assume the number picked by the first player was less than the length of the sequence (otherwise the first player has lost). If so, the second player (the "defending player") gets to look at the next number in the sequence (at $(s̲)_3$ or 518, in the case of the example). She must pick a number less than this number (less than $(s̲)_{n+1}$, if the first player picked the place $(s̲)_n$). Let us suppose she picks 56. We now evaluate the statement R(17, 56) (the statement $R(n, m)$, where n is the number picked by the first player and m is the number picked by the second player). Since R is primitive recursive, this can be done effectively. If the statement is true, the defending player has won; if false, the attacking player has won.

The statement that a sequence s̲ fulfills this statement A (that there is a winning strategy for the defending player) can itself be written out in number theory, as follows:

(I) $(\forall i < \text{length}(s̲) - 1)(\forall n < (s̲)_{i-1})(\exists m \leq (s̲)_i)Rnm$.

Similarly, if we are given a statement A with four, or six, or however many alternating quantifiers in the prefix, we can define s̲ fulfills A to mean that there is a winning strategy for the defending player in a game that is played very much like the game G: a game in which the attacking player gets to choose a new place in the sequence, each time it is her turn to play. The attacking player must also choose a number less than $(s̲)_{i-1}$, where $(s̲)_{i-1}$ is the number in the position she had chosen in the sequence.[4] Each time she plays, the attacking player has to choose a place that is to the right of the place in the sequence she chose before (unless it is her first turn to play) and not the last place in the sequence (unless she has no legal alternative, in which case she loses), and the defending player must then pick a number less than $(s̲)_i$ (less than the number in the next place in the sequence). The game ends when as many numbers have been chosen as there are quantifiers in the prefix of the formula. (We assume all formulas are prenex, and that quantifiers alternate universal, existential, universal, existential ... .) The numbers chosen are then substituted for the variables in the matrix of the formula A in order (first number chosen for x_1, second number chosen for x_2, etc., where x_1 is the variable in the first argument place, x_2 the variable in the second argument place, and so on). The resulting primitive recursive statement is evaluated and, as before, the defending player wins if the statement is true and the first (attacking) player wins if the statement is false. Once again, for any fixed formula A we can easily express the statement that $\underline{s}$ fulfills A arithmetically (primitive recursively in $\underline{s}$). And for any fixed recursively enumerable sequence of formulas $A_1, A_2, \ldots$, the statement that $\underline{s}$ fulfills A_n can be expressed as a primitive recursive relation between $\underline{s}$ and n, say $Fulfills(\underline{s}, A_n)$. Note that we can also speak (by an obvious extension) of an ordinary infinite monotone increasing sequence "fulfilling" a formula. (This means that if one picks any number less than a given number in the sequence to be the value of the first universal quantifier, it is always possible to pick a number less than the next place to the right in the sequence to be a value for the succeeding existential quantifier. Thus, no matter what number less than the number in an arbitrarily selected place still further to the right in the sequence a hypothetical adversary picks for the *next* universal quantifier, it is possible for one to pick a number less than the number in the place just after that arbitrarily selected place for the immediately following existential quantifier [and continue in the same way], so that the statement A comes out true.) And note that a statement that is fulfilled by an infinite monotone increasing sequence is true. (Since the restriction that one must pick numbers as values for the universal quantifiers that are bounded by the numbers in the sequence is, in effect, no restriction on the "attacking player" at all—the numbers in the sequence get arbitrarily large, so she can pick any number she wants by going out far enough in the sequence!)

In Kripke's proof, one confines attention to sequences with the following two properties (call them good sequences):

(1) The first number in the sequence is larger than the length of the sequence.

(2) Each number in the sequence after the first is larger than the square of the number before. (This is to ensure that the sum and product of numbers $\leq (\underline{s})_i$ are $\leq (\underline{s})_{i+1}$)

Finally (this is the last of the preliminaries!) let P1, P2, P3, ... be the axioms of Peano arithmetic.

We will say that a statement is *n*-fulfillable if there is a good sequence of length *n* which fulfills the statement. The following is the statement which Kripke showed to be independent of Peano arithmetic:

(II) For every n and every m, the conjunction of the first m axioms of Peano arithmetic is n-fulfillable.

If we think of good sequences that fulfill a formula A as "finite partial models" for A, then what this says is that the first *m* axioms of Peano arithmetic have finite partial models that are as big as you like. It is easy to see that (II) is true in the standard model of Peano arithmetic.

Kripke's construction of a nonstandard model in which (II) is *false* is actually very short and elegant. Thus we have the remarkable result that post-Gödelian model theory can be used to replace recursion theory in the proof of the Gödel incompleteness theorem!

6.4 Prime Numbers

Here is yet another result which "milks" Gödel's theorem. This is actually an easy corollary of the results about Diophantine equations that I mentioned earlier, but number theorists expressed amazement when I published it in 1960:

If $P(x_1, x_2, \ldots, x_k)$ is a polynomial, let us refer to the positive integers n such that $P(x_1, x_2, \ldots, x_k) = n$ for some integers $x_1, x_2, \ldots, x_k$ as the *positive range* of P. Then the theorem I proved is that there *exists a polynomial whose positive range is exactly the prime numbers* (see Putnam 1960).

The proof is sufficiently simple for me to give it in full.

The primes are a recursively enumerable set. So by the Davis-Matiyasevich-Putnam-Robinson theorem, there is a polynomial P with integral coefficients such that

(1) The equation $P(n, x_1, x_2, \ldots, x_k) = 0$ has a solution in integers when and only when n is a prime number.

It is a theorem of number theory that every positive integer is the sum of four squares. So, I claim that the following equation has an integral solution with positive n when and only when n is a prime number:

(2) $n = (y_1^2 + y_2^2 + y_3^2 + y_4^2) \cdot [1 - P(y_1^2 + y_2^2 + y_3^2 + y_4^2, x_1, x_2, \ldots, x_k)]^2$ where P is the polynomial in (1).

Proof First, suppose n is a prime number. Then there are $x_1, x_2, \ldots, x_k$ such that $P(n, x_1, x_2, \ldots, x_k) = 0$, by (1). Choose such $x_1, x_2, \ldots, x_k$ and let y_1, y_2, y_3, y_4 be such that $n = y_1^2 + y_2^2 + y_3^2 + y_4^2$ (by the four squares theorem, there are such y_1, y_2, y_3, y_4). Then $P(y_1^2 + y_2^2 + y_3^2 + y_4^2, x_1, x_2, \ldots, x_k) = 0$ and the second factor in (2) is equal to 1. So (2) reduces to $n = (y_1^2 + y_2^2 + y_3^2 + y_4^2)$, which is correct, by the choice of y_1, y_2, y_3, y_4.

Second, suppose that (2) is true for natural numbers n, y_1, y_2, y_3, y_4, and $x_1, x_2, \ldots, x_k$. If

$P(n, x_1, x_2, \ldots, x_k) \neq 0$, then

$[P(\,y_1^2 + y_2^2 + y_3^2 + y_4^2, x_1, x_2, \ldots, x_k)]^2 \geq 1$, and

$(1 - [P(\,y_1^2 + y_2^2 + y_3^2 + y_4^2, x_1, x_2, \ldots, x_k)]^2)$ is zero or negative. In either case

$n = (\,y_1^2 + y_2^2 + y_3^2 + y_4^2) \cdot (1 - [P(\,y_1^2 + y_2^2 + y_3^2 + y_4^2, x_1, x_2, \ldots, x_k)]^2)$ is non-positive. And if $P(\,y_1^2 + y_2^2 + y_3^2 + y_4^2, x_1, x_2, \ldots, x_k) = 0$, then by (1), $y_1^2 + y_2^2 + y_3^2 + y_4^2$ is a prime number and since $[1 - P(\,y_1^2 + y_2^2 + y_3^2 + y_4^2, x_1, x_2, \ldots, x_k)]^2 = 1$, (2) reduces to $n = y_1^2 + y_2^2 + y_3^2 + y_4^2$, so n is a prime. Thus the prime numbers are all, and only, the *positive* integers taken on as values by the polynomial

$$(\,y_1^2 + y_2^2 + y_3^2 + y_4^2) \cdot [1 - P(\,y_1^2 + y_2^2 + y_3^2 + y_4^2, x_1, x_2, \ldots, x_k)]^2. \quad \square$$

This last result, generalized to say that *every* recursively enumerable set is the positive range of some polynomial with integral coefficients, yields a very simple "model of computation": in this model a "program" is simply a polynomial with integral coefficients, and one recursively enumerates a set simply by plugging in k-tuples of integers for the variables in the polynomial, calculating the numerical value of the resulting expression, and writing down the result whenever that numerical value is positive. I think the mathematical interest of this model is clear; alas, it is also clear that as a method of computation it is also extremely impractical!

6.5   An Application of Gödel's Method: Can our "scientific competence" be simulated by a Turing Machine? And if yes, can we know that fact?

I shall close by describing some recent research of mine. What provoked this research is actually a conversation I had with Noam Chomsky more than twenty years ago. I asked Chomsky whether he thought our *total* competence—not just the competence of the "language organ" that he postulates, but also the competence of the "scientific faculty" that he also postulates—can be represented by a Turing machine (where the notion of "competence" is supposed to distinguish between our true ability and our "performance errors"). He said "yes." I at once thought that a Gödelian argument could be constructed to show that if that were right, then we could never *know*—not just never prove mathematically, but never know even with the help of empirical investigation—*which* Turing machine it is that simulates our "scientific competence." One such Gödelian argument was given in a paper titled "Reflexive Reflections" that I published in 1985 (see Putnam 1985b), but I have always been dissatisfied with one of the assumptions that I used in that proof (I called it a "criterion of adequacy" for formalizations of the notion of justification), namely the assumption that no empirical evidence can justify believing p if p is *mathematically false.*[5] Finally I am ready to show you a proof whose assumptions seem to me unproblematic.

In order to think about Chomsky's conjecture in a rigorous Gödelian way, let "COMPETENCE" abbreviate the empirical hypothesis that a particular Turing machine T_k perfectly simulates the competence of our "scientific faculty," in Chomsky's sense. To make this concrete, we may take this to assert that, for any scientific proposition **p**, and for any evidence **u** (expressible in the language that T_k uses for expressing scientific propositions and expressing evidence), T_k sooner or later prints out *Justified_u*(**p**) if and only if it is justified to accept **p** when **u** is our total relevant evidence. In addition, COMPETENCE asserts that whatever hypotheses and evidence we can describe in an arbitrary natural language can also be represented in T_k's language—i.e., that language has the full expressive power of the "Mentalese" that Chomskians talk about. In accordance with usual formal treatments of the notions of justification, we assume that justification is closed under logical inference. What I shall show is that if this is true, then COMPETENCE cannot be both true and justified.

My proof will, of course, proceed via *reductio ad absurdum*. So let us assume from now on that 'e' is evidence that justifies accepting "COMPETENCE," and let "$T_k \Rightarrow$ *Justified_e*(**p**)" symbolize, "Machine T_k sooner or later prints out *Justified_e*(**p**)" (the "$\Rightarrow$" can be read simply as "says"). Note that "e" and "k" are constants throughout the following argument.

Applying Gödel's diagonal lemma to the predicate $\neg$(*Justified_e*(**p**)), we can construct a sentence in the language of T_k that "says" that acceptance of itself is not justified on evidence e. That sentence has the following GÖDEL PROPERTY:

Justified_e(GÖDEL) ° Justified_e($\neg$($T_k \Rightarrow$ Justified_e(GÖDEL)).

Where does this property come from? Well, by the diagonal lemma, "(GÖDEL) ° $\neg$($T_k \Rightarrow$ *Justified_e*(GÖDEL))" is provable (that is, the sense in which GÖDEL "says" $\neg$($T_k \Rightarrow$ *Justified_e*(GÖDEL))—here I am just mimicking Gödel's proof. But since we know this equivalence, the left side is justified just in case the right side is justified.

Here are the axioms we shall assume concerning these notions:

Axiom A1   Justified_e(p) iff Justified_e(Justified_e(p)).[6]

Axiom A2   It is never both the case that *Justified_e*(p) and *Justified_e*($\neg$p).

Finally, since COMPETENCE is the statement that T_k perfectly represents our competence, we have: if *Justified_e*(**p**) and COMPETENCE is true, $T_k \Rightarrow$ *Justified_e*(**p**). Since we are assuming we know that this is the case, we have:

Axiom A3   If *Justified_e*(p) and *Justified_e*(COMPETENCE), then *Justified_e*($T_k \Rightarrow$ *Justified_e*(p)).

6.6   An Anti-Chomskian Incompleteness Theorem: "COMPETENCE" can't be both true and justified

To guide the reader, here is an outline of the proof we shall give (in both parts of the proof we will assume that COMPETENCE is both true and justified by the evidence e):

Part I We will prove (by assuming the opposite and deriving a contradiction) that it is not the case that $T_k \Rightarrow$ *Justified*$_e$(GÖDEL) (i.e., the machine T_k, which we assumed to be the one that simulates our epistemic competence, does not tell us that we are justified in accepting the Gödelian sentence, on the evidence which, we assumed, justifies our acceptance of COMPETENCE).

Part II The conclusion of part I can be expressed thus in our notation:

(a) $\neg(T_k \Rightarrow$ *Justified*$_e$(GÖDEL)).

Since this proof can be known to us if we have empirically justified COMPE-TENCE, and a proof is a justification, it follows immediately that:

(b) *Justified*$_e(\neg(T_k \Rightarrow$ *Justified*$_e$(GÖDEL))).

Then the rest of part II will derive a contradiction from b), thus showing that the assumption that COMPETENCE is both true and justified must be false.

6.6.1   Part I of the Proof

(1) $T_k \Rightarrow$ *Justified*$_e$(GÖDEL) (assumption of part I—to be refuted)

(2) *Justified*$_e$(GÖDEL). Reason: For the "reductio" proof of our incompleteness theorem, we are assuming both COMPETENCE and that this belief is justified by evidence e. But COMPETENCE, when written out in our notation, is just: "on any empirical evidence e, and for any scientific proposition **p**, *Justified*$_e$(**p**) iff $T_k \Rightarrow$ *Justified*$_e$(**p**)," and by 1, $T_k \Rightarrow$ *Justified*$_e$(GÖDEL), so *Justified*$_e$(GÖDEL).

(3) It is justified$_e$ to believe $T_k \Rightarrow$ *Justified*$_e$(GÖDEL). Reason: we just showed that *Justified*$_e$(GÖDEL). Then by the assumption (that we are making throughout) that *Justified*$_e$(COMPETENCE) and axiom A3, we are justified$_e$ in believing $T_k \Rightarrow$ *Justified*$_e$(GÖDEL).

(4) We are justified$_e$ in believing "$\neg(Tk \Rightarrow$ *Justified*$_e$(GÖDEL))." Reason: by (2), we are justified$_e$ in believing *Justified*$_e$(GÖDEL). By the GÖDEL PROPERTY, *Justified*$_e$(GÖDEL) iff *Justified*$_e(\neg(T_k \Rightarrow$ *Justified*$_e$(GÖDEL))), and since this equiv-alence is known to us, and we are justified$_e$ in believing the left side, we are justified$_e$ in believing the right side—that is, we are justified$_e$ in believing *Justified*$_e$ $(\neg(Tk \Rightarrow$ *Justified*$_e$(GÖDEL)))—that is, *Justified*$_e$(*Justified*$_e$(*Justified*$_e(\neg(T_k \Rightarrow$

Justified$_e$(GÖDEL)))). So, by axiom A1), we are justified$_e$ in believing ¬(T$_k$ ⇒ *Justified$_e$*(GÖDEL)).

But (3) and (4) violate our consistency axiom, A2)! Thus (still assuming that COMPETENCE is both true and justified on evidence e), we conclude that the assumption of our subproof is false: it is not the case that T$_k$ ⇒ *Justified$_e$*(GÖDEL). But this is reasoning that we can easily go through if we have discovered COMPETENCE to be true! So, without any additional empirical evidence, we have justified$_e$:

"¬(T$_k$ ⇒ *Justified$_e$*(GÖDEL))"

So we have found that *Justified$_e$*(¬(T$_k$ ⇒ *Justified$_e$*(GÖDEL))). To complete the proof of our incompleteness theorem, we therefore now need a proof that this too leads to a contradiction. Here it is:

6.6.2 Part II

(1) *Justified$_e$*(¬(T$_k$ ⇒ *Justified$_e$*(GÖDEL))). (PROVED IN PART I)

(2) By the GÖDEL PROPERTY, (1) is equivalent to *Justified$_e$*(GÖDEL), and we know this equivalence, so it suffices to show that *Justified$_e$*(GÖDEL) leads to a contradiction. So assume *Justified$_e$*(GÖDEL). Then using also the assumption that we are making throughout, that *Justified$_e$*(COMPETENCE) and Axiom A3), *Justified$_e$*(T$_k$ ⇒ *Justified$_e$*(GÖDEL)). But we assumed *Justified$_e$*(¬(T$_k$ ⇒ *Justified$_e$*(GÖDEL))), and this violates our consistency axiom A2). This completes the proof of our anti-Chomskian incompleteness theorem.

Notes

1. However, I have argued that the philosophical, as opposed to the mathematical, significance of Tarski's achievement has been both overestimated and misrepresented. See Putnam (1985a).

2. I am deliberately ignoring the "use-mention distinction" to simplify exposition.

3. Equations of the form P = 0, to be solved in natural numbers, where P is a polynomial with integral coefficients, are called Diophantine equations. "Exponential Diophantine equations" are equations of the form P = 0, to be solved in natural numbers, where P is an expression which is like a polynomial with integral coefficients except for having some variable exponents (e.g., the Fermat equation $x^n + y^n - z^n = 0$ is exponential Diophantine).

4. N.B. the number in the ith position is called "$(\underline{s})_{i-1}$" and not "$(\underline{s})_i$" because Kleene—whose notation I am employing—calls the first position "$(\underline{s})_0$" and not "$(\underline{s})_1$."

5. Although some would regard this assumption as self-evident, those of us who allow "quasi-empirical" methods in mathematics should not accept it. On the latter, see Putnam (1975).

6. It suffices here to assume this for case in which p itself contains (via use or mention) no more than two occurrences of "Justified". Unlike Chomsky, I shall not assume that we have the competence to understand arbitrarily long sentences.

References

Paris, J., and L. Harrington. 1977. A mathematical incompleteness in Peano arithmetic. In *Handbook of Mathematical Logic*, ed. J. Barwise, 1133–1142. Amsterdam: North-Holland.

Putnam, H. 1960. An unsolvable problem in number theory. *Journal of Symbolic Logic* 25:220–232.

Putnam, H. 1975. What is mathematical truth? In *Philosophical Papers: Mathematics, Matter and Method*, Vol. 1, 60–78. Cambridge: Cambridge University Press.

Putnam, H. 1985a. A comparison of something with something else. *New Literary History* 17(1):61–79.

Putnam, H. 1985b. Reflexive reflections. *Erkenntnis* 22:143–153.

Putnam, H. 1994. *Words and Life*, ed. J. Conant. Cambridge: Harvard University Press.

Putnam, H. 2000. Nonstandard models and Kripke's proof of the Gödel theorem. *Notre Dame Journal of Formal Logic* 41(1):53–58. Reprinted in *Philosophy in an Age of Science*, ed. M. De Caro and D. Macarthur. 2012. Cambridge: Harvard University Press.

Acknowledgment

This chapter was previously published in the *Logic Journal of the IGPL*, vol. 14, no. 5 (October 2006), pp. 745–759.

7 The Open Texture of Computability

Stewart Shapiro

[W]e get to know the meaning of ["intuitively evident curve"] through a demonstrative definition. ... This means that we call anything a "curve" which is somewhat similar to a paradigm
(say, to a drawn, crooked line) without specifying precisely the kind of similarity; therefore
this concept is not sharply delineated. Consequently, there will be cases where one will waver
between calling something a curve or not. ... The concepts of mathematics, however, are
precisely defined.
—Friedrich Waismann (1959, 165)

7.1 Proving Things about Intuitive Notions

Church's thesis (CT) is of course the statement that a number-theoretic function is
effectively computable if and only if it is recursive. It began its public life with
Alonzo Church's 1936 proposal:

We now define the notion ... of an *effectively calculable* function of positive integers by
identifying it with the notion of a recursive function of positive integers ... This definition is
thought to be justified by the considerations which follow, so far as positive justification can
ever be obtained for the selection of a formal definition to correspond to an intuitive one.
(Church 1936, section 7)

At the time, and for at least the next half-century, there was a near consensus that
CT is not subject to mathematical proof or refutation. That is, almost everyone held
that mathematicians did not and could not attempt to derive CT or its negation
from accepted or previously established principles of mathematical domains. In a
retrospective article, Church's student Stephen Cole Kleene (1952, 317, 318–19) gave
a standard reason for this:

Since our original notion of effective calculability of a function (or of effective decidability
of a predicate) is a somewhat vague intuitive one, [CT] cannot be proved ...
  While we cannot prove Church's thesis, since its role is to delimit precisely an hitherto
vaguely conceived totality, we require evidence that it cannot conflict with the intuitive notion
which it is supposed to complete; i.e., we require evidence that every particular function which

our intuitive notion would authenticate as effectively calculable is ... recursive. The thesis may be considered a hypothesis about the intuitive notion of effective calculability, or a mathematical definition of effective calculability; in the latter case, the evidence is required to give the theory based on the definition the intended significance.

Kleene's argument here is straightforward. Even though computability is a property of mathematical objects—number theoretic functions—it is a vague, intuitive notion from ordinary language. Most of the founders, certainly Church, Kleene, and Alan Turing, were thinking about what can be computed by a suitably idealized human following an algorithm (see, for example, Copeland 1997). So the notion of computability seems to invoke psychological or other anthropocentric notions. Some later writers invoke a different notion of computability, which relates to idealized mechanical computing devices. This latter notion is prima facie physical, at least in part. In contrast to both of these intuitive notions, recursiveness is a precise property of number-theoretic functions, definable within pure number theory. So there is no sense of *proving* that those two are extensionally the same.

If computability is vague, then proving Church's thesis would be like trying to prove that a family is rich if and only if its total net worth is at least \$973,400, or that a bath is hot if and only if its mean temperature is at least 38.64° centigrade. But to make this case, we would need an argument that computability is vague. Are there any borderline computable functions? Can we construct a sorites series from a clearly computable function to a clearly noncomputable function? This would broach the question of what vagueness is, which is currently subject to much philosophical controversy.

Perhaps vagueness is beside the point. Church's and Kleene's point may be that computability is an *intuitive* notion. Sometimes the word "pre-theoretic" is used. How can one prove that an intuitive, pre-theoretic notion is coextensive with one that enjoys a rigorous or otherwise formal definition? In general, how do intuitive, mathematical notions relate to their rigorously defined successors?

If "intuitive" notions are somehow disqualified from the pristine sphere of mathematical demonstration, there would not have been any mathematics, or at least no mathematical proofs, before the advent of formal deductive systems. If we are to make sense of mathematics before, say, 1900, and of much mathematics today, we had better allow intuitive, pre-theoretic notions into the fold.

Even from the beginning, it was only a *near* consensus that CT is not subject to mathematical demonstration. In a letter to Kleene, Church noted that Kurt Gödel opposed the prevailing view:[1]

In regard to Gödel and the notions of recursiveness and effective calculability, the history is the following. In discussion with him ... it developed that there is no good definition of effective calculability. My proposal that lambda-definability be taken as a definition of it he regarded as thoroughly unsatisfactory ...

His [Gödel's] only idea at the time was that it might be possible, in terms of effective calculability as an undefined term, to state a set of axioms which would embody the generally accepted properties of this notion, and to do something on that basis.

It is not easy to interpret these remarks, but Gödel seems to have demanded a *proof*, or something like a proof, of CT. A conceptual analysis of computability would suggest axioms for the notion. Then, perhaps, one could derive that every computable function is recursive, and vice versa, from those axioms.[2] I presume that this might count as a demonstration, or proof, of CT.

Gödel was soon convinced that (something equivalent to) CT is true. In a 1946 address (published in Davis 1965, 84–88), he remarked that

Tarski has stressed in his lecture (and I think justly) the great importance of the concept of general recursiveness (or Turing's computability). It seems to me that this importance is largely due to the fact that with this concept one has for the first time succeeded in giving an absolute definition of an interesting epistemological notion ... (Gödel 1946, 84)

Although it is not clear whether Gödel regarded Turing's original (1936) treatment of computability as constituting, or perhaps suggesting, or leading to, a rigorous *proof* of CT, it seems that Gödel was satisfied with Turing's treatment (see Kleene 1981, 1987; Davis 1982; and my review of those, Shapiro 1990). In a 1964 postscript to Gödel (1934), he wrote that "Turing's work gives an analysis of the concept of 'mechanical procedure' (alias 'algorithm' or 'computation procedure' or 'finite combinatorial procedure'). This concept is shown to be equivalent to that of a Turing machine." The word "shown" here might indicate something in the neighborhood of "proved," but perhaps we should not be so meticulous in interpreting this remark.

In any case, the received view that CT is not subject to mathematical resolution was eventually challenged by prominent philosophers, logicians, and historians. Robin Gandy (1988) and Elliott Mendelson (1990) claimed that CT is susceptible of rigorous, mathematical proof; Gandy went so far as to claim that CT has already been proved. He cites Turing's (1936) study of a human following an algorithm as the germ of the proof. Gandy referred to (a version of) CT as "Turing's theorem." Wilfried Sieg (1994) reached a more guarded, but similar conclusion. For Sieg, "Turing's theorem" is the proposition that if f is a number-theoretic function that can be computed by a being satisfying certain determinacy and finiteness conditions, then f can be computed by a Turing machine. Turing (1936) contains arguments that humans satisfy some of these conditions, but, apparently, Sieg (1994) considered this part of the text to be less than proof. Sieg (2002a, 2002b) claims to have completed the project of demonstrating the equivalence, via a painstaking analysis of the notions involved:

My strategy ... is to bypass theses altogether and avoid the fruitless discussion of their (un-) provability. This can be achieved by *conceptual analysis*, i.e., by sharpening the informal notion, formulating its general features axiomatically, and investigating the axiomatic framework ...
The detailed conceptual analysis of effective calculability yields rigorous characterizations that dispense with theses, reveal human and machine calculability as axiomatically given mathematical concepts, and allow their systematic reduction to Turing computability. (Sieg 2002a, 390, 391)

Sieg's use of the term "sharpening" raises the aforementioned matter of vagueness. If the intuitive notion is in fact vague, how can it be coextensive with a sharp notion? A prominent logician once suggested to me the possibility that it can be shown—demonstrated somehow—that even if a certain mathematical notion is vague when it is first conceived, there is a unique sharp notion that underlies it.

Gödel, the most prominent logician of the twentieth century, had a similar view of things, invoking his famous (or infamous) analogy with perception:

If we begin with a vague intuitive concept, how can we find a sharp concept to correspond to it faithfully? The answer is that the sharp concept is there all along, only we did not perceive it clearly at first. This is similar to our perception of an animal first far away and then nearby. We had not perceived the sharp concept of mechanical procedures before Turing, who brought us to the right perspective. And then we do perceive clearly the sharp concept.
If there is nothing sharp to begin with, it is hard to understand how, in many cases, a vague concept can uniquely determine a sharp one without even the *slightest* freedom of choice.
"Trying to see (i.e., understand) a concept more clearly" is the correct way of expressing the phenomenon vaguely described as "examining what we mean by a word." (quoted in Wang 1996, 232, 233; see also Wang 1974, 84–85)

It is not clear how much "freedom of choice" there was concerning the development of computability. For that matter, it is not clear what it is to have "freedom of choice" when examining certain concepts. This will occupy us below. Gödel mentions two other cases of initially vague notions for which, at least with hindsight, we can see that the formal development could not have gone in any other way:

The precise concept meant by the intuitive idea of velocity is ds/dt, and the precise concept meant by "size" ... is clearly equivalent with the Peano measure in the cases where either concept is applicable. In these cases the solutions again are *unquestionably* unique, which here is due to the fact that only they satisfy certain axioms which, on closer inspection, we find to be undeniably implied by the concept we had. For example, congruent figures have the same area, a part has no larger size than the whole, etc. (quoted in Wang 1996, 233)

It is an intriguing idea that a conceptual analysis, followed by rigorous mathematical deduction, can simultaneously establish/prove its conclusion *and* clear away vagueness in the underlying concepts, showing them to have sharp underpinnings all along. This is accomplished, supposedly, by formulating some principles that hold of the original, intuitive concepts, and showing that only one property satisfies these "axioms." Recursiveness might be the result of a "concept expansion" of computability, in the sense of Buzaglo (2002).

In any case, the Gödel/Mendelson/Gandy/Sieg position(s) generated responses (e.g., Folina 1998, Black 2000), and the debate continues. As the foregoing sketch indicates, the issues engage some of the most fundamental questions in the philosophy of mathematics. What is it to prove something? What counts as a proof? For that matter, what is mathematics about? If the subject matter of mathematics is a realm of abstracta that are causally separated from the physical world and the mathematician, then what do we mean when we say that a function is, or is not, computable by a human following an algorithm, or by a machine? Why are these empirical, psychological elements interfering in the austere and serene realms of mathematics? How do you mathematically prove things about the empirical world of humans following algorithms or of mechanical computing devices? How do proofs eliminate vagueness?

The Gödel/Mendelson/Gandy/Sieg position(s) also suggest some curious historical questions. If Turing's (1936) paper does constitute a proof, or even a sketch or a germ of a proof, then why did so many people fail to see it that way? Aren't proofs supposed to be compelling for any rational agent that understands the language? Some prominent figures, such as Jean Porte (1960) and László Kalmár (1959), continued to hold that CT is *false* as late as twenty-five years after Turing's work was published, and even Rózsa Péter (1957) maintained some doubts (of which more later). Almost everyone else agreed that CT is true, but with a few notable exceptions, most accepted the once-received view that it is not the sort of thing that can be proved. One would think that if Turing (1936) constitutes the seed of a proof, then the mathematicians of the day, and the next fifty years, would recognize it as such. These folks should be able to detect proofs if anybody can. Mathematicians should be able to recognize the pursuit of their own subject, shouldn't they?

7.2   Analyses of "Proof"?

This is not the place to address all of the philosophical issues raised by our present question, but we cannot very well duck such issues as beyond the scope of this paper. So what is a proof? The emerging foundational studies—the very environment that led to the work on computability—produced several closely related explications of mathematical proof. The most straightforward of these begins by defining a *derivation* to be a sequence of well-formed-formulas in a formal language, constructed according to certain rules, specified in advance. A derivation constitutes, or at least represents, a *proof* if the specified deductive system is sound (in the sense that every argument that it sanctions is valid) and if the premises are interpreted as statements that are either self-evident or previously established, and if the conclusion was not previously established. Call such a sequence a *formal proof.*

So what would constitute a formal proof of Church's thesis? Presumably, it would begin with a standard formalization of number-theory. One would add a predicate for computability, together with some axioms for it. The axioms should either be unquestionably true—self-evident—or previously established. Then we would produce a sequence of formulas, each of which would either be an axiom (of number theory or of computability), or would follow from previous lines by the unquestionably valid, formally correct rules of the deductive system. The last line would be CT.

This model seems to fit Gödel's early suggestion to Church that logicians should try to "state a set of axioms which would embody the generally accepted properties of [effective calculability] and ... do something on that basis." The "something" would be the formalized, or at least formalizable derivation.

To labor the obvious, the notion of "proof" predates the development of formal deductive systems, and the vast majority of mathematical demonstrations are not rigorous derivations in formal deductive systems. What counts as an *unformalized* proof is an intuitive and vague matter. So we seem to have broached the very same kinds of questions that are raised by CT. We might define "*Hilbert's thesis*" to be the statement that a text constitutes a proof if and only if it corresponds to a formal proof (although any of half a dozen other names would have done just as well— including that of Alonzo Church).

On the present explication, whether an unformalized text constitutes a proof presumably depends on how close the text is to a formalization, and how plausible the resulting formalized axioms and premises are, with respect to the intuitive notions invoked in it. This perspective might allow one to think of Turing's text as a formalizable proof—or the germ of one—despite the fact that some people were not convinced, and despite the fact that most mathematicians did not, and many still do not, recognize it as such. The uncertainty is charged to the connection between an informal text in ordinary language and a formalization thereof.

This example, and thousands of others, raises a general question of how we tell whether a given piece of live mathematical reasoning corresponds to a given actual or envisioned formal proof. Clearly, there can be some slippage here: such is informal reasoning, and such is vagueness. How does one guarantee that the stated axioms or premises of the formal proof are in fact necessary for the intuitive, pre-theoretic notions invoked in the informal text? That is, how do we assure ourselves that the formalization is faithful? This question cannot be settled by a *formal* derivation. That would start a regress, at least potentially. We would push our problem to the axioms or premises of *that* derivation. Moreover, any formalization of a real-life argument reveals missing steps, or gaps, and plugging those would sometimes require theses much like Church's thesis.

In a collection of notes entitled "What Does a Mathematical Proof Prove?" (published posthumously in 1978, 61–69), Imre Lakatos makes essentially the same point in a more general setting. He makes a distinction between the pre-formal development and the formal development of a branch of mathematics.[3] After a branch of mathematics has been successfully formalized, one can still raise sensible questions concerning the relationship between the formal deductive system and the original, pre-formal mathematical ideas. To follow Gödel's examples, how do the formal definitions of velocity and area relate to their intuitive, pre-formal counterparts? Can we be sure that the formal system accurately reflects the original mathematical structures? These residual questions cannot be settled with a derivation in a further formal deductive system, not without begging the question or starting a regress— there would be new, but similar, questions concerning the new deductive system.

According to a second, and closely related, explication of proofhood, a proof is a sequence of statements that can be "translated" into a derivation in Zermelo-Fraenkel set theory (ZF). Call this a *ZF-proof*. The staunch naturalist Penelope Maddy (1997, 26) sums up the role of set theory, in this foundational respect:

[I]f you want to know if there is a mathematical object of a certain sort, you ask (ultimately) if there is a set-theoretic surrogate of that sort; if you want to know if a given statement is provable or disprovable, you mean (ultimately), from the axioms of the theory of sets.

The ZF rendition of "proof" has essentially the same problems, or features, as the above notion of "formal proof." Here we pay attention to the "translation." What should be preserved by a decent translation from an informal mathematical text into the language of set theory? Despite the use of the word "translation," it is surely too much to demand that the ZF-version has the same *meaning* as the original text. How can we capture the meaning of, say, a statement about analytic complex-valued functions by using only the membership symbol? Presumably, the central mathematical and logical relations should be preserved in the translation. But what are those? Can we leave this matter at an intuitive level, claiming that we know a good "translation" when we see it?

Let us see how the scenario would play itself out in the present case. A ZF-proof of Church's thesis would begin with set-theoretic "definitions" of "computability" and at least one of the notions of "recursiveness," "Turing computability," "λ-definability," etc. There are, or easily could be, good formulations of the latter in ZF, at least at this point in history. Most of the mathematical community is comfortable with the set-theoretic renditions of standard mathematical theories, and recursive function theory is as standard as it gets. However, formulating the notion of "computability" in the language of ZF is another story. How could we assure ourselves that the proposed set-theoretic predicate really is an accurate formulation of the intuitive, pre-theoretic notion of computability? Would we prove that? How? In ZF?

In effect, a statement that a proposed predicate in the language of set theory (with its single primitive) does in fact coincide with computability would be the same sort of thing as CT, in that it would propose that a precisely defined—now set-theoretic— property is equivalent to an intuitive one. We would be back where we started, philosophically.[4] Clearly, in claiming that CT is capable of proof, Mendelson and Gandy (not to mention Gödel) are not asserting the existence of a ZF-proof for CT (see Mendelson 1990, 223).

I take it as safe to claim that if there is to be a mathematical proof of CT, the proof cannot be *fully* captured with a formal proof or a ZF-proof. Following Lakatos, there would be an intuitive or perhaps philosophical residue concerning the adequacy of the formal or ZF derivation to the original, pre-theoretic notion of computability. So if one *identifies* mathematical proof with formal proof or with ZF-proof, then one can invoke *modus tolens* and accept the conclusion that CT is not subject to mathematical proof. It is more natural, however, to hold that (i) CT is not entirely a formal or ZF matter, but (ii) this does not make CT any less mathematical, nor does it rule out a proof of CT. Mendelson, too, claims that there is more to mathematics than formal proofs and ZF proofs. If nothing else, mathematics, as such, is concerned with the adequacy of "translations" to and from the language of ZF. The general theme here can be illustrated with other, less controversial cases, to which we now turn.

7.3   Theses Everywhere

My two earlier papers (Shapiro 1981, 1993) on Church's thesis and Mendelson (1990) present a number of other mathematical contexts in which an intuitive, pre-theoretic notion is identified with a more precisely defined one. These other "theses" are not subject to doubt anymore, nor is their status as mathematics in question. Of course, this is not to say that they are *proved*, but the theses do serve as premises in informal reasoning, and as central parts of mathematics.

Let us call "Weierstrass's thesis" the proposition that the pre-theoretic or intuitive notion of a continuous function is (more or less) extensionally equivalent to the notions yielded by the now standard ε-δ definition. It is clear that there is an intuitive such notion or notions of continuous function, and that mathematicians worked with it, or them, well before the rigorous definition was proposed and accepted.

Moreover, the definitions *are* accepted, almost without opposition (but see Bell 1998), despite the fact that they have some consequences that conflict with intuition. Prominent among those is the existence of a continuous curve that is nowhere differentiable.

We saw Gödel's mention of the notions of velocity and area. Although ancient mathematicians did not identify magnitudes like lengths, areas, and volumes with real numbers, as we do today, they worked with a notion of ratios of magnitudes, and proved many theorems about such ratios. Mendelson cites the identification of functions with sets of ordered pairs, Tarski's definition of truth (in formalized languages not containing a truth predicate, anyway), the model-theoretic definition of validity, and the Cauchy-Weierstrass ε-δ definition of limit. The previous section broached two "theses" concerning the notion of "proof," namely formal proof and ZF-proof.

As far as I know, the epistemological status of such theses, and the extent to which they are and are not subject to proof, has not been settled. These are key instances of what Georg Kreisel (1967) calls "informal rigor" (see also Kreisel 1987).

7.4   Open Texture

We can gain some insight into the matter by considering a thesis of Friedrich Waismann (1945) concerning empirical terms in ordinary language. The extension of the thesis to mathematics and mathematical proof is interesting and instructive.

Let P be a predicate from natural language. According to Waismann, P exhibits *open texture* if there are possible objects p such that nothing in the established use of P, or the non-linguistic facts, determines that P holds of p or that P fails to hold of p. In effect, Pp is left open by the use of the language, to date.

Here is one of the thought experiments Waismann invokes to characterize this notion:

Suppose I have to verify a statement such as "There is a cat next door"; suppose I go over to the next room, open the door, look into it and actually see a cat. Is this enough to prove my statement? ... What ... should I say when that creature later on grew to a gigantic size? Or if it showed some queer behavior usually not to be found with cats, say, if, under certain conditions it could be revived from death whereas normal cats could not? Shall I, in such a case, say that a new species has come into being? Or that it was a cat with extraordinary properties? ... The fact that in many cases there is no such thing as a conclusive verification is connected to the fact that most of our empirical concepts are not delimited in all possible directions. (Waismann 1945, 121–122)

The context of this passage is a discussion of a crude form of phenomenalism, but the interest and importance of open texture goes well beyond a diagnosis of the failure of that program. The last observation in the passage is the key: our empirical concepts are not delimited in all possible directions.[5] I would add that neither are some of our mathematical concepts.

As Waismann sees things, language users introduce empirical terms to apply to certain objects or kinds of objects, and of course the terms are supposed to fail to apply to certain objects or kinds of objects. To oversimplify, a predicate may be introduced, via ostension, with paradigm cases: these and all things like them are *P*'s. Perhaps there are also some explicit or at least implicit anti-paradigms: those and all things like them are non-*P*'s. Or a term may be introduced with a description, which of course uses other words, which may themselves be subject to open texture. But no matter how a term gets introduced and acquires an established use, we can never be sure that every possible situation is covered, one way or the other.

According to many accounts of vagueness, borderline cases are those that are left undecided by established usage. So vague predicates seem to be instances of open texture.[6] Waismann holds that open texture applies well beyond the phenomenon of vagueness (or else the phenomenon of vagueness extends further than one would think). Some philosophical accounts have it that natural kind terms somehow pick out properties that are sharp, in the sense that they have fixed extensions in all metaphysically possible worlds. On such views, the progress of science (or metaphysics) tells us, or will tell us, whether various hitherto unconsidered cases fall under the kind in question, and will correct any mistakes we now make with the terms. Waismann would reject all such views, and, in fact, he illustrates the thesis with what is usually taken to be a natural kind term:

The notion of gold seems to be defined with absolute precision, say by the spectrum of gold with its characteristic lines. Now what would you say if a substance was discovered that looked like gold, satisfied all the chemical tests for gold, whilst it emitted a new sort of radiation? "But such things do not happen." Quite so; but they *might* happen, and that is enough to show that we can never exclude altogether the possibility of some unforeseen situation arising in which we shall have to modify our definition. Try as we may, no concept is limited in such a way that there is no room for any doubt. We introduce a concept and limit it in *some* directions; for instance we define gold in contrast to some other metals such as alloys. This suffices for our present needs, and we do not probe any farther. We tend to *overlook* the fact that there are always other directions in which the concept has not been defined. ... we could easily imagine conditions which would necessitate new limitations. In short, it is not possible to define a concept like gold with absolute precision; i.e., in such a way that every nook and cranny is blocked against entry of doubt. That is what is meant by the open texture of a concept. (Waismann 1945, 122–123)

The phrase "open texture" does not appear in Waismann's treatment of the analytic-synthetic distinction in a lengthy article published serially in *Analysis* (1949, 1950, 1951a, 1951b, 1952, 1953), but the notion—or a closely related one—clearly plays a central role there. He observes that language is an evolving phenomenon. As new situations are encountered, and as new scientific theories develop, the extensions of predicates change. Sometimes the predicates become sharper, which is what someone who accepts open texture would predict. As new cases are encountered, the predicate in question is extended to cover them, one way or the other. When things like this happen, there is often no need to decide—and no point in deciding—whether the application of a given predicate to a novel case or a shift in its extension represents a change in its meaning or a discovery concerning the term's old meaning/extension. The contrary thesis, that there is something like the one and only correct way to go on consistent with the meaning of the term, misrepresents the nature of language:

Simply ... to refer to "the" ordinary use [of a term] is naive ... [The] whole picture is in a state of flux. One must indeed be blind not to see that there is something unsettled about language; that it is a living and growing thing, adapting itself to new sorts of situations, groping for new sorts of expression, forever changing. (Waismann 1951b, 122–123)

Toward the end of the series, he writes: "What lies at the root of this is something of great significance, the fact, namely, that language is never complete for the expression of all ideas, on the contrary, that it has an essential *openness*" (Waismann 1953, 81–82).[7]

The official definition of open texture limits it to the application of predicates (or their negations) to hitherto unconsidered, and even undreamt of, cases. The dynamic nature of language goes well beyond this. Waismann notes that sometimes there are outright *changes* in the application of various words and expressions. Major advances in science sometimes—indeed usually—demand revisions in the accepted use of common terms: "breaking away from the norm is sometimes the *only way* of making oneself understood" (1953, 84). He illustrates the point in some detail with the evolution of the word "simultaneous" (Waismann 1952). The main innovative theses of the theory of relativity actually violated the previous meaning of that word. How are we to understand this linguistic fallout of the theory of relativity? Are we to say that a brand new word, with a new meaning, is coined with the same spelling as an old word, or should we say that an old word has found some new and interesting applications? Did Einstein discover a hidden and previously unnoticed relativity in the established meaning of the established word "simultaneous" (or its German equivalent), even though he was not a linguist by training, and showed no special interest in that subject? Or did Einstein coin a new theoretical term, to replace an old term whose use had scientifically false presuppositions?

According to Waismann, there is often no need, and no reason, to decide what counts as a change in meaning and what counts as the extension of an old meaning to new cases—going on as before, as Wittgenstein might put it. Waismann said, in an earlier installment in the series: "there are no *precise rules* governing the use of words like 'time,' 'pain,' etc., and that consequently to speak of the 'meaning' of a word, and to ask whether it has, or has not changed in meaning, is to operate with too blurred an expression" (Waismann 1951a, 53).

As noted, Waismann only applies his notion of open texture to empirical terms. Are the standard terms of mathematics exceptions to his account of language as in flux? One might think that with mathematics, at least, we have precision in the use of our terms. Consider, for example, the notion of a prime (natural) number. Strict finitism aside, can we really envision the possibility of encountering a natural number n for which it is somehow indeterminate whether or not n is prime? Don't we *prove* that every natural number (other than zero or one) is either prime or composite?

Of course, my inability to conceive of a situation is no proof that it is not possible. Nevertheless, it seems that the notion of prime natural number is not subject to open texture. However, I submit that this example is more the exception than the rule. The sort of precision we are used to—and celebrate—in mathematics applies, perhaps, to contemporary formalized mathematics and to branches of mathematics that have been rendered in ZF—provided, once again, that no questions about the adequacy of the formalization, or the adequacy of ZF, are raised (as discussed in section 7.2 above). Nevertheless, open texture is indeed found in the informal practice and development of mathematics. The boundaries of the notion of "natural number" are, perhaps, as sharp as can be. No room for doubt or flux with that notion. But what of the more general notion of "number"? Although we now have no doubts that complex numbers are numbers, this was once controversial. If it is a matter of simple definition, applying an established notion, why should there ever have been controversy? And what of quaternions? Are those numbers? Perhaps there is no real need to decide whether quaternions are numbers. As Waismann might put it, in asking this question we operate with too blurred an expression. In this case, the expression is "number," which is as mathematical as it gets.

Mendelson (1990, 232) argues that the notions that go into the supposedly sharp notion of recursive function are, or at least once were, subject to the same vagueness or indeterminacy that supposedly plagues the notion of effective computability:

> The concepts and assumptions that support the notion of partial-recursive function are, in an essential way, no less vague and imprecise than the notion of effectively computable function; the former are just more familiar and are part of a respectable theory with connections to other parts of logic and mathematics ... Functions are defined in terms of sets, but the concept of set is no clearer than that of function ... Tarski's definition of truth is formulated in set-theoretic terms, but the notion of set is no clearer than that of truth.

Mendelson does not elaborate on this remark, but he is correct that the notion of set has a long and sometimes troubled history, and I think it must be admitted that things are not crystal clear even now. There is a logical notion, based on unrestricted comprehension—Gottlob Frege's Basic Law V—which turned out to be inconsistent. And there is a more mundane and less problematic notion of a collection of previously given entities. George Boolos (1989) argues that there is no single, intuitive notion of set that underlies Zermelo-Fraenkel set theory. It is a more or less ad hoc mixture of two notions. The currently unresolved status of propositions like the continuum hypothesis, and the wide variety of philosophical and mathematical approaches to that matter, among set theorists, at least suggest that we do not yet hold a single, sharply delineated notion.

7.5   Proofs and Refutations

Before returning to computability, let us briefly re-examine Lakatos's favorite example, developed in delightful detail in *Proofs and Refutations* (1976). He presents a lively dialogue involving a class of rather exceptional mathematics students. The dialogue is a rational reconstruction of the history of what may be called Euler's theorem:[8]

Consider any polyhedron. Let V be the number of its vertices, E the number of its edges, and F the number of its faces. Then $V-E+F = 2$.

The reader is first invited to check that the equation holds for standard polyhedra, such as rectangular solids, pyramids, tetrahedra, icosahedra, and dodecahedra. One would naturally like this inductive evidence confirmed with a proof, or else refuted by a counterexample. Lakatos provides plenty of examples of both.

The teacher begins with a proof of Euler's theorem. We are told to think of a given polyhedron as hollow, with its surface made of thin rubber. Remove one face and stretch the remaining figure onto a flat wall. Then add lines to triangulate all of the polygonal faces, noting that in doing so we do not change $V-E+F$. For example, drawing a line between two vertices of the same polygon adds 1 face and 1 edge, no vertices. When the figure is fully triangulated, start removing the lines one or two at a time, doing so in a way that does not alter $V-E+F$. For example, if we remove two lines on the outer boundary along with the included vertex, we decrease V by 1, E by 2, and F by 1. At the end, we are left with a single triangle, which, of course, has 3 vertices, 3 edges, and 1 face. So for that figure, $V-E+F = 1$. If we add back the face we removed at the start, we find that $V-E+F = 2$ for the original polyhedron. QED.

The class then considers counterexamples to Euler's conjecture: a picture frame, a cube with a cube-shaped hole in one if its faces, a hollow cube with cube-shaped hole in its interior, and a "star polyhedron" whose faces protrude from each other in space. One of the students even proposed that a sphere and a torus each qualify as a polyhedron, and are thus counterexamples to Euler's theorem: since a sphere and a torus have a single face with no vertices or edges, $V-E+F = 1$.

Each counterexample violates (or falsifies) at least one of three main "lemmas" of the teacher's proof. In some cases, the three-dimensional figure in question cannot be stretched flat onto a surface after the removal of a face. In other cases, the stretched plane figure cannot be triangulated without changing the value of $V-E+F$ (or cannot be triangulated at all), and in still other cases, the triangulated figure cannot be decomposed without altering the value of $V-E+F$.

The dialogue then gets most interesting, all the more so given that it more or less follows some threads in the history of mathematics. Some students declare that the counterexamples are "monsters" and do not refute Euler's theorem. One route is to insist that the figures in question are not really polyhedra. A philosopher in the crowd might argue that an analysis of "polyhedron," drawing on established, robust intuitions, would reveal this. Then the class could get entangled in a debate over the meaning of this word in ordinary language (be it English, Greek, Latin, etc.) or, even worse, a metaphysical debate over the proper analysis of the underlying concept that the word picks out. The class briefly considers—and just as briefly dismisses—a desperate attempt along those lines: one *defines* a polyhedron to be a figure that can be stretched onto a surface once a face is removed, and then triangulated and decomposed in a certain way. That would make the teacher's "proof" into a stipulative definition of the word "polyhedron." A second maneuver is to overly restrict the theorem so that the proof holds: the proper theorem is that for any convex, "simple" polyhedron, $V-E+F = 2$. An advocate of this maneuver is content to ignore the interesting fact that $V-E+F = 2$ does hold for some concave, and some non-simple, polyhedra. A third line is to take the counterexamples to refute Euler's theorem, and to declare that the notion of "polyhedron" is too complex and unorderly for decent mathematical treatment. Those inclined this way just lose interest in the notion. A fourth line accepts the counterexamples as refuting Euler's theorem, and looks for a generalization that covers the Eulerian and non-Eulerian polyhedra in a single theorem.

The third and fourth lines, of course, reject the teacher's (purported) proof, either at all or in the generality in which it was intended. The fourth line takes the proof as pointing toward the proper generalization. This leads to further rounds of the procedure. Someone proposes a proof of a generalization of Euler's theorem, and then counterexamples to that proof are found—some even more bizarre "polyhedra" are considered.

The situation in Lakatos's dialogue—or, better, the history it reconstructs—illustrates Waismann's account of language, even though it concerns mathematics and not empirical science or ordinary language. The start of the dialogue refers to a period in which the notion of polyhedron had an established use in the mathematical community (or communities). Nevertheless, the word, or notion, or concept, had no established, formal *definition*. Surely, a necessary condition for a figure to be a polyhedron is that it be bounded by plane polygons (i.e., closed networks of edges all of which lie in the same plane and enclose a single area). The above "examples" of a sphere and a torus are thus easily dismissed (and they are not really taken seriously in Lakatos's dialogue). But there were no established sufficient conditions for being a polyhedron.

In short, the mathematicians of the time, and previous generations of mathematicians, had a notion of "polyhedron" governed by open texture. This did not prevent them from working with the notion, and proving things about polyhedra. Consider, for example, the ancient theorem that there are exactly five Platonic solids. I submit that, at the time, it simply was not determinate whether picture frames and cubes with cube-shaped holes in their center, etc., count as polyhedra. When the cases did come up, and threatened to undermine a lovely generalization discovered by the great Euler, a decision had to be made. As Lakatos shows, different decisions were made, or at least proposed.

Those who found the teacher's proof compelling (at least initially) could look to its details—to what Lakatos calls its "hidden lemmas"—to shed light on just *what a polyhedron is*. Surely it is pure dogma, in the most pejorative sense, to simply declare that, by definition, a polyhedron just is a three-dimensional figure for which the proof works. As noted, an attempt along those lines is quickly dismissed in the dialogue. But one can get some guidance as to what one thinks a polyhedron is by examining the details of what looks like a compelling proof.

On the other hand, those mathematicians who found the counterexamples compelling can look to the details of the proof, and to the counterexamples, to formulate a more general definition of "polyhedron," in order to find the characteristics that make some polyhedra, and not others, Eulerian. In this case, at least, both approaches proved fruitful. We can look back on the history and see how much was learned about the geometry of Euclidean space.

At the end of the dialogue, a most advanced student proposes a purely set-theoretic definition of "polyhedron." Accordingly, a polyhedron just is a set of things called "vertices," "edges," and "faces" that satisfy some given formal conditions. The student insists that it really does not matter what the "vertices," "edges," and "faces" are, so long as the stated conditions are satisfied. That is, the theorem has been removed from the topic of space altogether. The student then gives a fully formal (or at least easily formalizable) proof of a generalization of Euler's theorem from these definitions. The only residual question left, it seems to me, is the extent to which the set-theoretic definition captures the essence of the original, pre-theoretic (or at least pre-formal) concept of polyhedron. Lakatos had that exactly right.

The advanced student's orientation is of a piece with the algebraic account of mathematics that has been popular since the start of the twentieth century. The following occurs in a letter that Hilbert wrote to Frege:[9]

... it is surely obvious that every theory is only a scaffolding or schema of concepts together with their necessary relations to one another, and that the basic elements can be thought of in any way one likes. If in speaking of my points, I think of some system of things, e.g., the system: love, law, chimney-sweep ... and then assume all my axioms as relations between these things, then my propositions, e.g., Pythagoras' theorem, are also valid for these things ... [A]ny theory can always be applied to infinitely many systems of basic elements.

Frege complained that Hilbert's orientation loses touch with geometry, just as some might complain that the bright student has lost touch with the intuitive notion of polyhedron. His "definition" has nothing to do with figures in three-dimensional space. One might retort that the connection with space was never part of the mathematical notion. All that ever mattered were the formal relations embodied in the concepts.

I submit that the wise course is to follow Waismann, and suggest that the very question of what, exactly, goes into the original, pre-theoretic notions is to operate with "too blurred" an expression. One can perhaps claim, now, that the final, austere and rigorous set-theoretic definition of "polyhedron"—as a set of "vertices," "edges," and "faces" under certain conditions—is not subject to open texture. Its boundaries are as determinate as one could wish—assuming that there is no flexibility concerning the logic or the underlying set-theoretic model theory. But this is not to say that the original, pre-theoretic notion of "polyhedron" was similarly determinate, nor is it to say that the pre-theoretic notion (or notions) exactly matched the formal definition. This last is yet another example of the same sort of thing as Church's thesis is, and so we are ready to resume our main theme.

7.6   Turing's Theorem

Our main question, of course, concerns the so-called "intuitive," or "pre-theoretic," notion of computability, and its relationship to recursiveness. I do not want to get hung up in a meaning analysis, but I take the suffix "-able" to mean something like "capable of" or "it is possible to." To say that an item is edible is to say that it is capable of being eaten—presumably without toxic effects. To say that a concept is definable is to say that it is capable of definition. And to say that a number-theoretic function is computable is to say that it is capable of being computed: it is possible to compute the function.

Typically, the modal construction underlying the suffix is sensitive to the interests of those speaking or writing, and to their background assumptions concerning allowed abilities and the like. Say that a distance and time is "runnable" by a person if she can cover the distance in the given time on relatively flat ground by running. Is an eight-minute mile runnable by me? It depends on what, exactly, is being asked. If I warm up right now and go out and run a mile as fast as I can, it will take me much longer than eight minutes, probably ten or eleven. So, in that sense, an eight minute mile is not runnable by me. On the other hand, if I were to spend six months on a training regimen, which would involve working out diligently with a trainer four or five days each week and losing about thirty pounds (and avoiding injury), then I probably could manage an eight-minute mile again. And I am probably capable of executing this regimen. So in a sense, an eight-minute mile is runnable after all.

So what are the corresponding parameters of the pre-theoretic notion of computability? What tools and limitations are involved? I would suggest that in the 1930s, and probably for some time afterward, this concept was not delineated with enough precision to decide every possible consideration concerning tools and limitations. In other words, "computability" exhibited open texture. And just as with Lakatos's example of a polyhedron, the mathematical work, notably Turing's (1936) argument and the efforts of the other founders—people like Church, Turing, Emil Post, Kleene, and Péter—sharpened the notion to what we have today. In other words, the mathematical work served to set the parameters and thus sharpen the original pre-theoretic notion.

Turing's own text makes it clear that he focuses on computation by a human being following an algorithm and not, say, a digital computing device. Following Sieg (1994), let us use the term "computor" to designate a person engaged in computation. So our question concerns what tools and abilities we are to allot to the computor in characterizing the notion of computability.

Some of the issues here can be illustrated with the so-called "easy" half of Church's thesis, the statement that every recursive function is computable. We confront, first, some more or less standard matters of feasibility. The following double recursion defines an Ackermann function f, on the natural numbers, in terms of the successor function s:

$\forall y(fy0=s0)$

$\forall x(f0sx=ssf0x)$

$\forall y\forall x(fsysx=fyfsyx)$.

The defined function is recursive, but not primitive recursive. Boolos (1987) points out that the value of $f5,5$ is larger than the number of particles in the known universe. In a real sense, the Ackermann function *cannot* be computed, in much the same sense that a two-minute mile (or a 0.000000001 minute mile) is not runnable—by me or anyone else. No human computor will live long enough to complete this instance of the algorithm. With the indicated small inputs, the function cannot be computed without using more material than is available in the known universe. So here is a recursive function that is not computable.

Porte (1960) presented another example of a horribly infeasible, recursive function, and concluded that it is "not humanly computable, and therefore not effectively computable," as Mendelson (1963, section 1) put it in a review. And we did just note that we are particularly interested in *human* computability, didn't we?

Of course, the situation is quite standard, and so is the response. Mendelson put it well:

Human computability is not the same as effective computability. A function is considered effectively computable if its value can be computed in an effective way in a finite number of steps, but there is no bound on the number of steps required for any given computation. Thus, the fact that there are effectively computable functions which may not be humanly computable has nothing to do with Church's thesis. (1963, 202)

In other words, the notion of computability invoked in Church's thesis invokes idealizations on the abilities of our computors. We do not allow computations to fail due to the computor losing consciousness or running out of material. Similar idealizations have been invoked as long as there has been mathematics. Euclid's first postulates reads, "to draw a straight line from any point to any point" and the third is "to describe a circle with any center and distance." There are no bounds on how close the two points have to be or how small or large the radius can be. Still, I think it must be admitted that the idealization does represent a *sharpening* of the pretheoretic notion of computability. Otherwise, people like Porte should be charged with being confused, of not knowing what they are talking about, as late as 1960.

Note that we could idealize even more and allow infinitely long algorithms. This would give a different, but not very interesting notion: every number-theoretic function would be computable in that sense of "computable." Similarly, every number-theoretic function can be "computed" with a Turing machine with infinitely many states.

The fact that we are idealizing somewhat on time, attention span, and materials does not, by itself, sharpen the notion all the way to the hard rails of recursiveness. Some open texture still remains, depending on how far the idealization is to go. An idealized person, considered in isolation, is more like a finite-state machine than a Turing machine. Even if we waive the fact that the brain has only so many neurons, we do insist on a finite memory. A computor, considered in isolation, has nothing corresponding to the Turing machine tape. Of course, in discussing computation, it is customary to allow the computor to use pencil and paper for doing scratch work. Suppose that we limit the computor to a certain, fixed, amount of paper, say one standard A4 or letter-sized sheet for each particle in the universe, and we assume, as seems reasonable, that she cannot write more than 10,000 characters on each one (given normal limits on eyesight). We would still only have a (very large) finite-state machine, and not a Turing machine. The idealization relevant to Church's thesis is that the computor has a truly unbounded amount of paper available. We assume that there is no possible circumstance in which she runs out of scratch paper or pencils.[10]

There are other issues. It might be reasonable, for some purposes, to set *some fixed* bound on how fast a function can grow before we will call it "computable." We might require a function to be computable in polynomial time, or exponential time, or hyperexponential time, or in polynomial space, or whatever. This would disqualify the Ackermann functions. But the standard notion of computability recognizes no such bounds, other than mere finitude.

Again, I do not claim that the current conception of computability is incoherent, nor that once it is formulated, it corresponds—exactly—to recursiveness. Church's thesis is certainly true. But this is not to say that the original, pre-theoretic or intuitive notion of computability was as sharp as this.

In his later article, Mendelson observes that there is little doubt that the so-called "east half" of CT is established beyond all doubt:

The so-called initial functions are clearly ... computable; we can describe simple procedures to compute them. Moreover, the operations of substitution and recursion and the least-number operator lead from ... computable functions to ... computable functions. In each case, we can describe procedures that will compute the new functions. (1990, 233)

Mendelson concludes that this "simple argument is as clear a proof as I have seen in mathematics, and it is a proof in spite of the fact that it involves the intuitive notion of ... computability." I would add that this argument, or something like it, does or did convince just about all of the folks working in computability. This probably explains why there is not much challenge to this half of CT, once issues of feasibility and bounds on memory and the like are taken off the table.

Nevertheless, I submit that both conceptually and in the historical context, this argument for the easy half of CT served, and continues to serve, to *sharpen* the intuitive notion. A study of the reasoning proposed in Mendelson's argument shows where the idealization from actual human (or machine) abilities comes in. The argument takes no account on the length of the sequence of functions used to define a recursive function. We see that we are to ignore, or reject, the possibility of a computation failing because the computor runs out of memory or materials. Similarly, the correctness of the argument depends on our not caring about how much time a computation takes, or how much space we need for it. So the Ackermann functions are included.

The idealization away from considerations of feasibility, bounded states, and the like, is what Lakatos might call a "hidden lemma" of Mendelson's proof. A critic of the argument, or of Church's thesis, has options. She can cite an Ackermann function as a Lakatos-style refutation, calling for monster-barring, or monster-adjustment, or a retreat to the safety of finite-state machines, or polynomial space computability, or the like. A critic of this critic could retort that feasibility and limits on space and memory were *never* part of the pre-theoretic notion. He might boldly claim that a conceptual analysis would reveal this. A third person could take the apparent stand-off here as impetus to generalize the notion of computability, yielding notions like finite state computability, push-down computability, polynomial space computability, etc. With Waismann, I do not see a strong need to adjudicate disputes concerning which formalized notion gives the true essence of the intuitive, pre-theoretic notion. To even ask the question is to operate with too blurred a notion.

In light of the proof, and with hindsight, it remains eminently reasonable to focus on the idealized notion of computability, just as it was reasonable to focus on the sharply defined notions of polyhedron, continuity, area, and the like. Arguments like the one Mendelson cites help to clear away the vagueness. We look to see what the proof proves, and thereby gain insight on how the pre-theoretic notion should be sharpened. After the fact, one might think that the argument proves something determinate about a previously sharp notion. I submit that this would be a mistake. I'd say that the proof serves, or at least helps, to fix the intuitive notion.

Wittgenstein is notorious for saying that a mathematical proof somehow fixes the sense of what is proved. Here is a sample:

A psychological disadvantage of proofs that construct *propositions* is that they easily make us forget that the *sense* of the result is not to be read off from this by itself, but from the *proof*.

We have won through to a piece of knowledge in the proof? And the final proposition expresses this knowledge? Is this knowledge now independent of the proof (is the navel string cut)? ... Why should I not say: in the proof I have won through to a *decision*? The proof places this decision in a system of decisions.

I go through the proof and say: Yes, this is how it *has* to be; I must fix the use of my language in *this* way. I want to say that the *must* corresponds to a track which I lay down in language.

When I say that a proof introduces a new concept, I meant something like: the proof puts a new paradigm among the paradigms of the language. ... One would like to say: the proof changes the grammar of our language, changes our concepts. It makes new connections, and it creates the concept of these connections. (It does not establish that they are there; they do not exist until it makes them.) (Wittgenstein 1978, part III: 25, 27, 30, 31)

The examples that Wittgenstein discusses here come from fairly elementary arithmetic, analysis, and perhaps some basic set theory. When it comes to branches of mathematics like those—branches that are no longer subject to open texture—his remarks are, I think, absurd. Wiles's proof of Fermat's last theorem does not, in any interesting way, change what we mean (or meant) by the expression of the result. The statement means the same to us as it did to Fermat. To be sure, Wiles's proof relies on some connections to branches of mathematics that Fermat did not dream of, but the very meaning of the proposition in question does not change as a result of those connections.

Nevertheless, something in the neighborhood of Wittgenstein's remarks sometimes holds in cases where there is open texture. The acceptance of a proof, as a proof, can serve to sharpen the notions and thus, perhaps, to change their meaning (if this is not to operate with too blurred an expression). In the case at hand, the acceptance of the proof of the easy half of Church's thesis serves to set the limits on feasibility to where they are today.

There is a further question, in the same or a nearby ballpark, concerning what computability is a property of. What are the sorts of things that are, or are not, computable? The first guess, perhaps, is that computability is a property of functions from the natural numbers to the natural numbers, or perhaps functions on the standard numerals. But there seems to be a way to diagonalize out of any (effectively) denumerable sequence of computable functions. Suppose that $f_1, f_2, \ldots$ are all computable. Then consider the function f, defined as follows:

$fn = f_n n + 1.$

Intuitively, f is computable, and yet it cannot occur in the list. This would seem to tell against any attempt to identify computability with any effectively denumerable property. One conclusion, perhaps, is that there is no way to determine, effectively, if a given function is computable.

The practice now is to think of computability as a property of *partial* functions, functions from a subset of the natural numbers (or the numerals) to the natural numbers. Then the above diagonal argument breaks down. There is indeed an effective list $\phi_1, \phi_2, \ldots$ of all partial recursive functions. We can define a partial recursive function ϕ as follows:

if n is in the domain of ϕ_n, then $\phi n = \phi_n n + 1$; otherwise ϕn is undefined (i.e., n is not in the domain of ϕ).

Clearly, ϕ is computable: given n, start computing $\phi_n n$. If the result terminates, then add one to the result and halt. There is no contradiction in the assumption that ϕ occurs in our list. All we can conclude is that if ϕ is ϕ_m, then m is not in the domain of ϕ.

The focus on partial functions was clearly a brilliant innovation. Apparently, this played a key role in Gödel's thinking. We had occasion to quote his 1946 Princeton lecture earlier. He noted that the importance of Turing's analysis of computability

is largely due to the fact that with this concept one has for the first time succeeded in giving an absolute definition of an interesting epistemological notion, i.e., one not depending on the formalism chosen. In all other cases treated previously, such as demonstrability or definability, one has been able to define them only relative to a given language, and for each individual language it is clear that the one thus obtained is not the one looked for. For the concept of computability, however, the situation is different. By a kind of miracle it is not necessary to distinguish orders, and the diagonal procedure does not lead outside the defined notion. (Gödel 1946, 84)

Nevertheless, one might think that there is something counterintuitive about calling something an "algorithm" if there is no way to tell, in advance, whether or not it will terminate on a given input. Or perhaps it is counterintuitive to call a partial function "computable" if there is no way to determine, effectively, whether a given number is in its domain or not. One might think that success is built into the intuitive notion of a computation.[11] Such considerations may have led to the extensive study of so-called "provably recursive functions." Let S be a formalization of arithmetic, sufficient to develop recursive function theory. Say that a (total) function f is *provably recursive in S*, if there is a Turing machine M that computes f, and there is a derivation in S that the partial function computed by M is total (i.e., that M halts on every input).

I submit that one can be forgiven for thinking that the notion of "provably recursive," perhaps in some specified system, such as Dedekind-Peano arithmetic, is a better model of the intuitive notion of computability than the notion of "partial recursive function." Or at least that it is better is some ways. To be sure, this notion is not as clean as the more standard one. There is, after all, the reference to the deductive system S, and the nasty threat of diagonalization. But is there something in the intuitive, or pre-theoretic notion that indicates that the general notion of *partial* recursive function is *the* right one?

Apparently, Gödel thought so, continuing a theme we encountered earlier:

The precise notion of mechanical procedure is brought out clearly by Turing machines producing partial rather than general [i.e., total] recursive functions. In other words, the intuitive notion does not require that a mechanical procedure should always terminate or succeed. A sometimes unsuccessful procedure, if sharply defined, still is a procedure, that is, a well-determined manner of proceeding. Hence we have an excellent example here of a concept which did not appear sharp to us, but has become so as a result of careful reflection. The resulting definition of the concept of mechanical by the sharp concept of "performable by a Turing machine" is both correct and unique. ... Moreover it is absolutely impossible that anybody who understands the question and knows Turing's definition should decide for a different concept. (quoted in Wang 1974, 84)

The last remark is probably correct, despite the opposition that Church's thesis once generated. It is also agreed that the mathematical work in the '30s and '40s served to sharpen the notion to the one we use today. The question here is whether the original, intuitive or pre-theoretic notion was as precise as the one that emerged at the end of that period. I submit that it was not. A community that opted for one of the other notions, such as that of Turing-computable-in-polynomial-time, or provably-recursive-in-Peano-Dedekind-arithmetic, or finite-state computable, cannot be accused of a failure to understand what they are talking about.

Let us now turn to the so-called harder and, at one time, more controversial half of Church's thesis, the statement that every computable function is recursive. Here we return to the question of what tools and abilities to allot to our idealized human computors.

The notion of computability is surely deterministic. Our computor is not allowed to act randomly, willy nilly, at any point during the computation. Rather, she is supposed to execute a fixed algorithm. OK, then what is an algorithm? Presumably, an algorithm is a set of instructions that tells the computor what to do at every stage. Is *that* notion sufficiently sharp, pre-theoretically?

Kalmár accepted the aforementioned near-consensus view that "Church's thesis is not a mathematical theorem which can be proved or disproved in the exact mathematical sense" (1959, 72). But he came to the opposite conclusion on the main question, giving a "plausibility argument" *against* CT. Let f be a two-place (total) function from natural numbers to natural numbers. Define the "improper minimalization" of f to be the function f' such that

$$f'(x) = \begin{cases} \text{the least natural number } y \text{ such that } f(x,y) = 0, \text{ if there is such a } y; \\ 0, \text{ if there is no natural number } y \text{ such that } f(x,y) = 0. \end{cases}$$

Let ϕ be a recursive function whose improper minimalization ψ is not recursive.[12] Kalmár proposes the following "method" to "calculate the value $\psi(p)$ in a finite number of steps":

Calculate in succession the values $\phi(p,0)$, $\phi(p,1)$, $\phi(p,2)$, … and simultaneously try to prove by all correct means that none of them equals 0, until we find either a (least) natural number q for which $\phi(p, q)=0$ or a proof of the proposition stating that no natural number y with $\phi(p, y)=0$ exists; and consider in the first case this q, in the second case 0 as result of the calculation. (Kalmár 1959, 76–77)

As Kalmár concedes, this "method" will not "compute" the function ψ unless it is the case that for each p, if there is no y such that $\phi(p, y)=0$, then it can be proved by correct means that there is no y such that $\phi(p, y)=0$. But he finds this assumption concerning human abilities "plausible." His "method" also assumes that we (or at least our idealized counterparts) can reliably detect proofs, when those go by "correct means." These assumptions are what Lakatos might call "hidden lemmas" of Kalmár's "proof."

I do not mean to suggest, for even one minute, that there is a legitimate sense in which Kalmár's method counts as an algorithm. Church's thesis is true. Even at the time, Mendelson (1963, section 3) had no trouble dismissing the example. But is there something unambiguous in the *pre-theoretic* notion, or notions, of computability, in use in the '30s and a few decades after, that rules out Kalmár's "method" definitively?

The question here is why Kalmár thought that this "method" constitutes an algorithm that is relevant to Church's thesis. To say the least, he was an intelligent mathematician, and was not prone to deny what is obvious, a mere matter of understanding the meaning of a word in use. The situation here is a sort of direct opposite to that, noted above, with the proof of the easy half of Church's thesis. By examining the details of Kalmár's argument, and why we are going to *reject* its conclusion, we come to see what we are to mean by "algorithm." We sharpen the concept of computability through the rejection.

Notice that Kalmár's instructions *do* tell the computor what to do at each stage, provided that she is a competent mathematician. She is told to try to prove a certain theorem. Mathematicians are trained to do just that—to try and prove theorems. If Kalmár's "plausible" assumption, noted above, is correct, then his "method" will indeed terminate with the correct answer, if the computor is diligent enough and has unlimited time and materials at her disposal.

The problem, of course, is that the "method" does not tell the computor *exactly* what to do at each stage. It does not specify what to write down, which proof tricks to try. Kalmár's "procedure" is too open-ended to count as an algorithm.

Apparently, at the time, things were not as clear on this score as they are now. Chapter 19 of Péter's landmark textbook at least tentatively *endorses* Kalmár's "plausibility" argument against Church's thesis (1957, section 19.2). The next chapter turns to Church's thesis. It opens:

> Now I should like to quote some of the arguments used in attempts to make plausible the identification of the "calculable functions" with the general recursive functions.
> The assertion that the values of a function are everywhere calculable in a finite number of steps has meaning only under the condition that this calculation does not depend on some individual arbitrariness but constitutes a procedure capable of being repeated and communicated to other people at any time. Hence it must be a mechanical procedure, and thus one can imagine, in principle, a machine able to carry through the single steps of the calculation.

One would think that Kalmár's "method" for calculating improper minimalizations is thereby disqualified. Different mathematicians will respond differently to the instruction: "try to prove such and such a theorem," and no one has argued that this "method" can be mechanized. We know that it can't be. Still, Péter does not object to Kalmár's method, at least not yet. She goes on to give a detailed, painstaking analysis of computation, relating the notion to Turing machines. The analysis is clearly in the spirit of Turing (1936). The chapter closes thus:

If we assume that in the concept of a function calculable by the aid of a Turing machine we have succeeded in capturing the concept of the most general number-theoretic function whose values are everywhere calculable, then the results obtained above in fact characterize the general recursive functions as the functions calculable in the most general sense; and under this interpretation, the function [defined by Kalmár] ... is an example of a function not calculable in the most general sense. (Péter 1957, section 20.13)

So far, so good. Although she does say "if," it seems that she has rejected the computability of Kalmár's function. But Péter hedges:

But, however plausible it may seem that this interpretation correctly reflects real mathematical activity, we are nevertheless dealing here with a certain demarcation of the concept of calculability, and the future evolution of mathematics may bring about methods of calculation completely unexpected nowadays.

Waismann could not put it better. Péter declares that, at the time, the notion of computability was still subject to open texture, or, at any rate, she did feel herself to be in a position to rule out any further sharpening of the notion.[13]

In the ensuing decades, the community of logicians has come to see the notion of computability as sufficiently sharpened. It is now reasonable to hold that Church's thesis is established, if not proved. More recently, Turing's argument has been supplemented and extended by the deep analyses by Gandy and Sieg. In effect, they have fulfilled Gödel's suggestion above section 7.1: "to state a set of axioms which would embody the generally accepted properties of this notion, and to do something on that basis" (quoted in David 1982, 9). The Sieg-Gandy axioms have something of the flavor of the final definition of "polyhedron" in Lakatos (1976). A "computation" is a certain kind of function on hereditarily finite sets. Yet the axioms on computations are perfectly reasonable. Indeed, they are obvious truths about the notion of computability in question, or at least they are now.

Gandy and Sieg have also analyzed the concept of machine computability, in painstaking detail, and Sieg has shown that notion to be coextensive to recursiveness, and thus with human computability. Here, too, we can see the sharpening of a concept originally subject to open texture. It is sometimes pointed out that there are models of current physical theories in which a certain quantity, such as the temperature at a given point or the number of electrons in a given area, is not recursive. So, one might think, a machine that detects the value of such a quantity might count as "computing" a nonrecursive function.[14] After all, its instructions are clear and the device is physically determined (at least up to quantum effects). Yet, this does not count as a computing device. Or so it seems to us now, armed with our current concepts of "computability" and "algorithm."

For a second example, it may be possible, in some sense, for a device to detect, in a finite time, what would be the result of an infinitely long "computation" of another machine, provided that the structure of space-time cooperates (and an actual infinity of materials were available). In a sense, our device can determine the result of a "super-task." Such a device would thus be able to solve the halting problem, in a finite time. The conditions on the Sieg-machines rule out such "devices," since they compute nonrecursive functions. Moreover, the conditions in question are eminently reasonable. But can one say that the rogue "devices" are definitively ruled out by the intuitive, pre-theoretic notion(s) of machine computation? Perhaps, but it might be better to say, with Waismann, that the question itself operates with too blurred an expression. I submit that here, too, a better interpretation is that the Gandy-Sieg analysis serves to sharpen the notion.

In sum, the notions of (idealized) human computability and (idealized) machine computability are now about as sharp as anything gets in mathematics. There is not much room for open texture anymore—or so it seems, anyway. The present conclusion is that the notion of computability in use now is the result of the last seventy years of examining texts like Turing (1936), of reacting to proofs and refutations, and of the overwhelming success of the theory of computability. It is not accurate to think of the historical proofs of CT and related theses as establishing something about absolutely sharp pre-theoretic notions. Rather, the analytical and mathematical work served to sharpen the very notions themselves. Once again, this is the norm in mathematics.

Acknowledgments

This paper is a sequel to my "Computability, Proof, and Open-Texture" (Shapiro 2006). To keep it self-contained, there is some overlap with that article, highlighting the main points. Thanks to the members of the audiences at the conference which this volume commemorates, especially Carl Posy, Oron Shagrir, and Mark Steiner. Thanks also to the workshop on the foundations of mathematics held at Notre Dame in October of 2005 and to the mathematics workshop at the Arché Research Centre at the University of St. Andrews, which devoted sessions to this project. I am indebted to conversations with Timothy Smiley, Crispin Wright, and Peter Clark.

Notes

1. The letter, which was dated November 29, 1935, is quoted in Davis (1982, 9). Gödel's own work yielded a notion now known as Gödel-Herbrand definability, which constitutes another "definition" of computability that is equivalent to Turing computability, λ-definability, etc.

2. In a panel discussion, Harvey Friedman once suggested a similar strategy for resolving the issue of CT in a mathematically satisfactory manner.

3. Lakatos distinguishes both of these from what he calls the "post-formal" development of a branch of mathematics. This occurs when the formalization is itself used to shed light on the logical and semantic relations among the informal notions, producing such things as independence proofs.

4. If there were a theorem in ZF equating a set-theoretic predicate with (the set-theoretic surrogate for) recursiveness, we would have more evidence for CT, or else evidence that the set-theoretic formulation is correct (or both). The indicated theorem would be the same sort of thing as the equivalence of recursiveness and Turing computability.

5. Mark Wilson's (2006) onslaught against the "classical picture" of concepts is of a piece with Waismann's thesis here.

6. Waismann distinguishes open texture from vagueness. According to Waismann, vague terms are *actually* used in a "fluctuating way," while the actual use—to date—of other open textured terms may be uniform, or sufficiently uniform. "Open texture ... is something like *possibility of vagueness*" (1945, 123).

7. The publication of this series coincides with Quine's (1951) celebrated attack on the very notion of analyticity. It would take us too far afield to explore the similarities and differences.

8. Much of the actual history is recounted in Lakatos's footnotes.

9. The correspondence between Frege and Hilbert is published in Frege (1976) and translated in Frege (1980).

10. A Mac, PC, or mainframe is also more like a finite-state device than a Turing machine, since it does not have unlimited memory. To get something equivalent to a Turing machine, we could consider a PC together with a supply of external disks (tapes, floppies, memory sticks, etc.) together with a clerk who keeps track of which disk is inserted into the machine. The clerk responds to instructions like "remove the current disk and insert the previous one." We need not assume that the clerk has access to an actual infinity of disks. It is enough that he live near a disk factory and can obtain more, when needed. Thanks to John Case for this metaphor. However, we do have to assume that the factory will never run out of materials to make more disks.

11. Thanks to Timothy Smiley.

12. The proper minimalization of a two-place (total) function f is the partial function whose value at x is the least y such that $f(x, y)=0$, if there is such a y, and is undefined otherwise. The operation plays an important role in the theory of partial recursive functions.

13. Péter was not quite finished with Kalmár's function. In the next chapter (section 21.8), she calls for a generalization of the notion of (Herbrand-Gödel) recursiveness, and then cites a theorem, due to Kalmár, that the above improper minimalization function is the unique solution to a certain system of equations. She suggests, tentatively, that this result "will perhaps in the course of time rouse more doubts as to the complete generality of the concept of the general recursive function." In a review of Péter (1957), Raphael M. Robinson (1958) reads this as expressing doubts about Church's thesis. Robinson "does not regard it as surprising that a function determined in a non-effective way from a system of functional equations should fail to be general recursive." It seems to me, however, that Péter's remarks here are directed at the intuitive, informal notion of a *function defined by recursion*—the other notion invoked in CT. Recursiveness, too, may be subject to open texture.

14. Thanks to Peter Clark.

References

Bell, J. 1998. *A Primer of Infinitesimal Analysis*. Cambridge: Cambridge University Press.

Black, R. 2000. Proving Church's thesis. *Philosophia Mathematica* 8:244–258.

Boolos, G. S. 1987. A curious inference. *Journal of Philosophical Logic* 16:1–12.

Boolos, G. S. 1989. Iteration again. *Philosophical Topics* 17:5–21.

Buzaglo, M. 2002. *The Logic of Concept Expansion*. Cambridge: Cambridge University Press.

Church, A. 1936. An unsolvable problem of elementary number theory. *American Journal of Mathematics* 58:345–63. Reprinted in Davis, *The Undecidable,* 89–107.

Copeland, B. J. 1997. "The Church-Turing thesis." *Stanford Encyclopedia of Philosophy*, ed. E. Zalta. http://plato.stanford.edu/entries/church-turing.

Davis, M. 1965. *The Undecidable: Basic Papers on Undecidable Propositions, Unsolvable Problems and Computable Functions.* Hewlett, NY: Raven Press.

Davis, M. 1982. Why Gödel didn't have Church's thesis. *Information and Control* 54:3–24.

Folina, J. 1998. Church's thesis: Prelude to a proof. *Philosophia Mathematica* 6(3):302–23.

Frege, G. 1976. *Wissenschaftlicher Briefwechsel*, ed. G. Gabriel, H. Hermes, F. Kambartel, and C. Thiel. Hamburg: Felix Meiner.

Frege, G. 1980. *Philosophical and Mathematical Correspondence.* Oxford: Blackwell.

Gandy, R. 1988. The confluence of ideas in 1936. In *The Universal Turing Machine*, ed. R. Herken, 55–111. New York: Oxford University Press.

Gödel, K. 1934. On undecidable propositions of formal mathematical systems. Reprinted in Davis, *The Undecidable*, 39–74.

Gödel, K. 1946. Remarks before the Princeton Bicentennial Conference on problems in mathematics. Reprinted in Davis, *The Undecidable*, 84–88.

Kalmár, L. 1959. An argument against the plausibility of Church's thesis. *Constructivity in Mathematics*, 72–80. Amsterdam: North-Holland.

Kleene, S. C. 1952. *Introduction to Metamathematics.* Amsterdam: North-Holland.

Kleene, S. C. 1981. Origins of recursive function theory. *Annals of the History of Computing* 3(1):52–67.

Kleene, S. C. 1987. Reflections on Church's thesis. *Notre Dame Journal of Formal Logic* 28:490–98.

Kreisel, G. 1967. Informal rigour and completeness proofs. In *Problems in the Philosophy of Mathematics*, ed. I. Lakatos, 138–186. Amsterdam: North-Holland.

Kreisel, G. 1987. Church's thesis and the ideal of informal rigour. *Notre Dame Journal of Formal Logic* 28:499–519.

Lakatos, I. 1976. *Proofs and refutations*, ed. J. Worrall, and E. Zahar. Cambridge: Cambridge University Press.

Lakatos, I. Worrall, J., and G. Currie, ed. 1978. *Mathematics, Science and Epistemology.* Cambridge: Cambridge University Press.

Maddy, P. 1997. *Naturalism in Mathematics.* Oxford: Oxford University Press.

Mendelson, E. 1963. On some recent criticisms of Church's thesis. *Notre Dame Journal of Formal Logic* 4:201–205.

Mendelson, E. 1990. Second thoughts about Church's thesis and mathematical proofs. *The Journal of Philosophy* 87:225–233.

Péter, R. 1957. *Rekursive Funktionen*, 2nd ed. Budapest: Verlag der Ungarischen Akademie der Wissenschaften. Translated as *Recursive Functions.* New York: Academic Press, 1967.

Porte, J. 1960. *Quelques pseudo-paradoxes de la 'calculabilité effective.'* Actes du 2me Congrés International de Cybernetique, 332–334. Namur, Belgium: Association Internationale de Cybernétique.

Quine, W. V. O. 1951. Two dogmas of empiricism. *Philosophical Review* 60:20–43.

Robinson, R. M. 1958. Review of Péter 1957. *Journal of Symbolic Logic* 23:362–363.

Shapiro, S. 1981. Understanding Church's thesis. *Journal of Philosophical Logic* 10:353–65.

Shapiro, S. 1990. Review of Kleene 1981, Davis 1982, and Kleene 1987. *Journal of Symbolic Logic* 55:348–350.

Shapiro, S. 1993. Understanding Church's thesis, again. *Acta Analytica* 11:59–77.

Shapiro, S. 2006. Computability, proof, and open-texture. In *Church's Thesis after 70 Years*, ed. A. Olszewski, J. Woleński, and R. Janusz, 420–55. Frankfurt: Ontos Verlag.

Sieg, W. 1994. Mechanical procedures and mathematical experience. In *Mathematics and Mind*, ed. A. George, 71–140. Oxford: Oxford University Press.

Sieg, W. 2002a. Calculations by man and machine: Conceptual analysis. In *Reflections on the Foundations of Mathematics: Essays in Honor of Solomon Feferman*, ed. W. Sieg, R. Sommer, and C. Talcott, 390–409. Natick, MA: Association for Symbolic Logic.

Sieg, W. 2002b. Calculations by man and machine: Mathematical presentation. In *In the Scope of Logic, Methodology and Philosophy of Science*, Vol. 1, ed. P. Gärdenfors, J. Woleński, and K. Kijania-Placek, 247–62. Dordrecht: Kluwer Academic.

Turing, A. M. 1936. On computable numbers, with an application to the *Entscheidungsproblem*. *Proceedings of the London Mathematical Society* 42:230–65. Reprinted in Davis, *The Undecidable*, 116–53.

Waismann, F. 1945. Verifiability. In *Proceedings of the Aristelian Society* 19(Suppl.):119–150. Reprinted in *Logic and Language*, ed. A. Flew, 117–144. Oxford: Basil Blackwell, 1968.

Waismann, F. 1950. Analytic-synthetic II. *Analysis* 11:25–38.

Waismann, F. 1951a. Analytic-synthetic III. *Analysis* 11:49–61.

Waismann, F. 1951b. Analytic-synthetic IV. *Analysis* 11:115–124.

Waismann, F. 1952. Analytic-synthetic V. *Analysis* 13:1–14.

Waismann, F. 1953. Analytic-synthetic VI. *Analysis* 13:73–89.

Waismann, F. 1959. *Introduction to Mathematical Thinking: The Formation of Concepts in Modern Mathematics*. New York: Harper and Row. First published 1951, Frederick Unger Publishing.

Waismann, F. 1968. Verifiability. In *Logic and Language*, ed. A. Flew. Oxford: Basil Blackwell.

Wang, H. 1974. *From Mathematics to Philosophy*. London: Routledge & Kegan Paul.

Wang, H. 1996. *A Logical Journey: From Gödel to Philosophy*. Cambridge: MIT Press.

Wilson, Mark. 2006. *Wandering Significance*. Oxford: Oxford University Press.

Wittgenstein, L. 1978. *Remarks on the Foundations of Mathematics*. Trans. G. E. M. Anscombe. Cambridge, MA: MIT Press.

8 Gödel's Philosophical Challenge (to Turing)

Wilfried Sieg

"To Turing" is flanked by parentheses in the title, as the philosophical challenge issued by Gödel's mathematical results, the incompleteness theorems, was not only a challenge to Turing but also to Gödel himself; it certainly should be taken up by us. At issue is whether there is a rigorous argument from these results to the claim that machines can never replace mathematicians or, more generally, that the human mind infinitely surpasses any finite machine. Gödel made the former claim in 1939; the latter assertion was central in his Gibbs lecture of 1951. In his note of 1972, Gödel tried to argue for that assertion with greater emphasis on subtle aspects of mathematical experience in set theory. He explored, in particular, the possibility of a humanly effective, but nonmechanical, process for presenting a sequence of ever-stronger axioms of infinity.

To understand the claims in their broad intellectual context, one is almost forced to review the emergence of a rigorous notion of computability in the early part of the twentieth century. Gödel's role in that emergence is "dichotomous," as John Dawson noted in a lecture (2006). There are crucial impulses, like the definition of general recursive functions in the 1934 Princeton lectures. This definition was the starting point for Kleene's work in recursion theory and served as the rigorous mathematical notion in Church's first published formulation of his "thesis" (Church 1935). There is, however, neither a systematic body of recursion theoretic work nor an isolated central theorem that is associated with Gödel's name. The reason for that seems to be clear: Gödel was not interested at all in developing the theory, but rather in securing its conceptual foundation. He needed such a foundation for two central and related purposes, namely, (i) to formulate the incompleteness theorems in *mathematical generality for all formal theories* (containing arithmetic) and (ii) to articulate and sharpen *philosophical consequences of the undecidability and incompleteness results*.

The philosophical consequences, as I indicated, are concerned with the superiority of the human mind over machines in mathematics. This takes for granted that a convincing solution to the issue indicated under (i) has been found and that such a solution involves suitably characterized machines. The first two parts of this essay, entitled "Primitive and General Recursions" and "Finite Machines and Computors," present the general foundational context. It is only then that the central philosophical issue is addressed in the third part, "Beyond Mechanisms and Discipline." Gödel's and Turing's views on mind are usually seen in sharp opposition to each other. Indeed, Gödel himself claimed to have found a "philosophical error in Turing's work," but his argument for such an error rests on the (incorrect) assumption that Turing in 1936 tried to establish that mental procedures do not go beyond mechanical ones. If one focuses on the real challenge presented by the incompleteness theorems, then one finds that Gödel and Turing pursue parallel approaches with complementary programmatic goals, but dramatically different methodological perspectives. Concrete work to elucidate the situation is suggested in the last part of this essay, "Finding Proofs (with Ingenuity)."

8.1   Primitive and General Recursions

It was of course Kronecker who articulated forcefully in the 1870s the requirement that mathematical objects should be finitely presented, that mathematical notions should be decidable, and that the values of functions should be calculable in finitely many steps. And it was of course Dedekind who formulated in his essay *Was sind und was sollen die Zahlen?* the general schema of primitive recursion. At the turn from the nineteenth to the twentieth century, Hilbert transferred Kronecker's normative requirements from mathematics to the frameworks in which mathematical considerations were to be presented; that is, to axiomatic theories (see Hilbert 1900). This shift was accompanied by a methodologically sound call for proofs to establish the theories as consistent.[1] A syntactic and, in Hilbert's view, "direct" consistency proof was given in Hilbert 1905 for a purely equational theory. The approach was fairly criticized by Poincaré and, for a long time, not pursued any further by Hilbert. Only in 1921 did Hilbert come back to this particular argument and use it as the starting point of novel proof theoretic investigations, now with a finitist foundation that included recursion equations for all primitive recursive functions as basic principles.[2]

In order to carry out these proof theoretic arguments, functions in formal theories have to be calculable; indeed, calculable from a finitist perspective. That is clear from even a rough outline of the consistency proof Hilbert and Bernays obtained in early 1922 and presented in (Hilbert 1923). It concerns the quantifier-free theory we call primitive recursive arithmetic (PRA) and proceeds as follows. The linear proofs are first transformed into tree structures; then all variables are systematically replaced by numerals, resulting in a configuration of purely numeric statements that all turn out to be true and, consequently, cannot contain a contradiction. Yet to recognize the truth of the numeric formulae one has to calculate, from a finitist perspective, the value of functions applied to numerals.[3] This was a significant test of the new proof theoretic techniques, but the result had one drawback: a consistency proof for the finitist system PRA was not needed according to the programmatic objectives, but a treatment of quantifiers was required. Following Hilbert's *Ansatz* of eliminating quantifiers in favor of ε-terms, Ackermann carried out the considerations for "transfinite" theories, that is, for the first-order extension of PRA (correctly, as it turned out, only with just quantifier-free induction). Herbrand obtained in 1931 the result for essentially the same system, but with recursion equations for a larger class of finitistically calculable functions; that is how Herbrand described the relation of his result to that of Ackermann in a letter of 7 April, 1931, to Bernays.

As to the calculability of functions, Hilbert and Bernays had already emphasized in their lectures from the winter semester 1921–22: "For every single such definition by recursion it has to be determined that the application of the recursion formula indeed yields a number sign as function value—for each set of arguments." Such a determination was taken for granted for primitive recursive definitions. We find here, in a rough form, Herbrand's way of characterizing broader classes of finitistically calculable functions according to the schema in his 1931 letter:

In arithmetic we have other functions as well, for example functions defined by recursion, which I will define by means of the following axioms. Let us assume that we want to define all the functions $f_n(x_1, x_2, \ldots, x_{pn})$ of a certain finite or infinite set F. Each $f_n(x_1, \ldots)$ will have certain defining axioms; I will call these axioms (3F). These axioms will satisfy the following conditions:

(i) The defining axioms for f_n contain, besides f_n, only functions of lesser index.

(ii) These axioms contain only constants and free variables.

(iii) We must be able to show, by means of intuitionistic proofs, that with these axioms it is possible to compute the value of the functions univocally for each specified system of values of their arguments. (Letter to Gödel of 7 April, 1931; in Gödel 2003)

Having given this schema, Herbrand mentions that the non–primitive recursive Ackermann function falls under it. Recall also that Herbrand, as well as Bernays and von Neumann, used at the time "intuitionistic" as synonymous with "finitist."

In two letters from early 1931, Herbrand and Gödel discussed the impact of the incompleteness theorems on Hilbert's program. Gödel claimed that some finitist arguments might not be formalizable even in the full system of *Principia Mathematica*; in particular, he conjectured that the finitist considerations required for guaranteeing the unicity of the recursion axioms are among them. In late 1933, Gödel gave a lecture in Cambridge, Massachusetts, and surveyed the status of foundational investigations. This fascinating lecture describes finitist mathematics and reveals a number of mind changes: (i) when discussing calculable functions, Gödel emphasizes their recursive definability, but no longer the finitist provability requirement; and (ii) when discussing Hilbert's program, Gödel asserts that *all* finitist considerations can be formalized in elementary number theory (Gödel 1933). He supports his view by saying that finitist considerations use only the proof and definition principle of complete induction; the class of functions definable in this way includes all those given by Herbrand's schema. I take Gödel's deliberate decision to disregard the provability condition as a first and very significant step toward the next major definition; that is, that of general recursive functions.

Only a few months after his lecture in Cambridge, Gödel was presented with Church's proposal of identifying the calculability of number-theoretic functions with their λ-definability. Gödel, according to Church in a letter of 29 November, 1935 to Kleene, viewed the proposal as thoroughly unsatisfactory and proposed "to state a set of axioms which would embody the generally accepted properties of this notion [i.e., effective calculability], and to do something on that basis" (in Sieg 1997, 463). However, instead of formulating axioms for that notion in his Princeton lectures, Gödel took a second important step in modifying Herbrand's definition further. He considered as *general recursive* those total number theoretic functions whose values can be computed in an equational calculus, starting with general recursion equations and proceeding with very elementary replacement rules. In a 1964 letter to van Heijenoort, Gödel asserted, "... it was exactly by specifying the rules of computation that a mathematically workable and fruitful concept was obtained."[4]

Though Gödel had obviously defined a broad class of calculable functions, at the time he did *not* think of general recursiveness as a rigorous explication of calculability.[5] Only in late 1935 did it become plausible to him, as he put it on May 1, 1968, in a letter to Kreisel, "that my [incompleteness] results were valid for all formal systems." The plausibility of this claim rested on an observation concerning computability in the *Postscriptum* to his note "On the length of proofs." Here is the observation for systems S_i of i-th order arithmetic, i>0:

It can, moreover, be shown that a function computable in one of the systems S_i, or even in a system of transfinite order, is computable already in S_1. Thus the notion "computable" is in a certain sense "absolute," while almost all metamathematical notions otherwise known (for example, provable, definable, and so on) quite essentially depend upon the system adopted. (Gödel 1936, 399)

Ten years later, in his contribution to the Princeton bicentennial conference, Gödel formulated the absoluteness claim not just for higher-type extensions of arithmetic, but for *any* formal system containing arithmetic and, in particular, for set theory. The philosophical significance of general recursiveness is almost exclusively attributed to its absoluteness. Connecting his remarks to a previous lecture given by Tarski, Gödel started his talk with:

Tarski has stressed in his lecture (and I think justly) the great importance of the concept of general recursiveness (or Turing's computability). It seems to me that this importance is largely due to the fact that with this concept one has for the first time succeeded in giving an absolute definition of an interesting epistemological notion, i.e., one not depending on the formalism chosen. (Gödel 1946, 150)

In 1965 Gödel added a footnote to this remark clarifying the precise nature of the absoluteness claim:

To be more precise: a function of integers is computable in any formal system containing arithmetic if and only if it is computable in arithmetic, where a function f is called computable in S if there is a computable term representing f.

The metamathematical absoluteness claim as formulated in 1936 can readily be established for the specific theories of higher-order arithmetic. However, in order to prove the claim that functions computable in *any formal system containing arithmetic* are general recursive, the formal nature of the systems has to be rigorously characterized and then exploited. One can do that, for example, by imposing on such systems the recursiveness conditions of Hilbert and Bernays, formulated in Supplement II of the second volume of their *Grundlagen der Mathematik* (1939). Proceeding in this way one commits a subtle circularity, however, in case one insists simultaneously that the general recursive functions allow the proper mathematical characterization of *formality*.[6]

In Gödel's Princeton remark "Turing's computability" is mentioned, but is listed parenthetically behind general recursiveness without any emphasis that it might have a special role. That notion becomes a focal point in Gödel's reflections only in the 1951 Gibbs lecture. There, he explores the implications of the incompleteness theorems, not in their original formulation, but rather in a "much more satisfactory form" that is "due to the work of various mathematicians" (304–305). He stresses, "The greatest improvement was made possible through the precise definition of the concept of finite procedure, which plays such a decisive role in these results."[7] Gödel points out that there are different ways of arriving at a precise definition of finite procedure, which all lead to exactly the same concept. However, and here is the observation on Turing,

The most satisfactory way … [of arriving at such a definition] is that of reducing the concept of finite procedure to that of a machine with a finite number of parts, as has been done by the British mathematician Turing. (Gödel 1951, 304–305)

Gödel does not expand on this brief remark; in particular, he gives no hint of how *reduction* is to be understood. There is also no explanation of why such a reduction is the most satisfactory way of getting to a precise definition or, for that matter, of why the concept of a machine with a finite number of parts is equivalent to that of a Turing machine. At this point, it seems, the ultimate justification lies in the pure and perhaps rather crude fact that finite procedures can be effected by finite machines.[8]

Gödel claims in the Gibbs lecture (1951, 311) that the state of philosophy "in our days" is to be faulted for not being able to draw in a mathematically rigorous way the philosophical implications of the "mathematical aspect of the situation," that is, the situation created by the incompleteness results. I have argued that not even the mathematical aspect had been clarified in a convincing way; after all, it crucially depended on very problematic considerations concerning a precise notion of computability.

8.2   Finite Machines and Computors

To bring out very clearly that the appeal to a reduction is a most significant step for Gödel, let me go back to the informative manuscript (Gödel 193?) from the late 1930s. In it Gödel examines general recursiveness and Turing computability, but under a methodological perspective that is completely different from the one found in the Gibbs lecture. After having given a perspicuous presentation of his equational calculus, Gödel claims outright that it provides "the correct definition of a computable function." Thus, he seems to be fully endorsing Church's thesis concerning general recursive functions. He adds a remark on Turing and asserts, "That this really is the correct definition of *mechanical* computability was established beyond any doubt by Turing" (Gödel 193?, 168). How did Turing establish this claim? Here is Gödel's answer:

He [Turing] has shown that the computable functions defined in this way [via the equational calculus] are exactly those for which you can construct a machine with a finite number of parts which will do the following thing. If you write down any number $n_1, \ldots, n_r$ on a slip of paper and put the slip of paper into the machine and turn the crank, then after a finite number of turns the machine will stop and the value of the function for the argument $n_1, \ldots, n_r$ will be printed on the paper. (168)

The mathematical theorem stating the equivalence of Turing computability and general recursiveness plays a pivotal role at this time: Gödel does *not* yet focus on Turing's analysis as being the basis for a reduction of mechanical calculability to (Turing) machine computability.[9]

The appreciation of Turing's work indicated in the Gibbs lecture for the first time is deepened in other writings of Gödel. Perhaps it would be better to say that Turing's work appears as a topic of perceptive, but also quite aphoristic remarks. Indeed, there are only three such remarks that were published during Gödel's lifetime after 1951: the *Postscriptum* to the 1931 incompleteness paper, the *Postscriptum* to the 1934 Princeton lecture notes, and the 1972 note "A Philosophical Error in Turing's Work." The latter note appeared in a slightly different version in Wang's book from 1974. In the following I will refer to the "1972 note" and the "1974 note," though I am convinced that the first note is the later one.

The brief *Postscriptum* added to Gödel's paper of 1931 in 1963 emphasizes the centrality of Turing's work for both incompleteness theorems; here is the text:

In consequence of later advances, in particular of the fact that due to A. M. Turing's work a precise and unquestionably adequate definition of the general notion of formal system can now be given, a completely general version of Theorems VI and XI is now possible. That is, it can be proved rigorously that in *every* consistent formal system that contains a certain amount of finitary number theory there exist undecidable arithmetic propositions and that, moreover, the consistency of any such system cannot be proved in the system. (Gödel 1931, 195)

In the more extended *Postscriptum* written a year later for his Princeton lecture notes, Gödel repeats this remark almost verbatim, but then states a reason why Turing's work provides the basis for a "precise and unquestionably adequate definition of the general concept of formal system":

Turing's work gives an analysis of the concept of "mechanical procedure" (alias "algorithm" or "computation procedure" or "finite combinatorial procedure"). This concept is shown to be equivalent with that of a "Turing machine." (1934, 369–370)

In a footnote attached to the final sentence in the passage above, Gödel refers to Turing (1936) and points to its ninth section, where Turing argues for the adequacy of his machine concept. Gödel emphasizes that previous equivalent definitions of computability, including general recursiveness and λ-definability, "are much less suitable for our purposes" (370). However, he does not elucidate the special character of Turing computability in this context or any other context I am aware of, and he does not indicate either how he thought an analysis proceeded or how the equivalence between the (analyzed) concept and Turing computability could be shown. In the next paragraph, I will give a very condensed version of Turing's important argument, though I note right away that Turing did not view it as *proving* an equivalence result of the sort Gödel described.[10]

Call a human computing agent who proceeds mechanically a *computor*; such a computor operates deterministically on finite, possibly two-dimensional configurations of symbols when performing a calculation.[11] Turing aims to isolate the *most basic steps* taken in calculations, that is, steps that need not be further subdivided. This goal requires that the configurations on which the computor operates be *immediately recognizable*. Joining this demand with the evident limitation of the computor's sensory apparatus leads to the "boundedness" of configurations and the "locality" of operations:

(B) There is a fixed finite bound on the number of configurations a computor can immediately recognize; and

(L) A computor can change only immediately recognizable (sub-) configurations.

Since Turing considers the two-dimensional character of configurations as inessential for mechanical procedures, the calculations of the computor, satisfying the boundedness and locality restrictions, are directly captured by Turing machines operating on strings; the latter can provably be mimicked by ordinary two-letter Turing machines.[12]

So it seems we are led naturally and convincingly from calculations of a computor on two-dimensional paper to computations of a Turing machine on a linear tape. Are Turing machines in the end, as Gandy put it, nothing but *codifications* of computors? Is Gandy right when claiming in (1980, 124) that Turing's considerations provide (the outline of) a proof for the claim, "What can be calculated by an abstract human being working in a routine way is computable"? Does Turing's argument thus secure the conclusiveness and generality of the limitative mathematical results, respect their broad intellectual context, and appeal only to mechanical procedures that are carried out by humans without the use of higher cognitive capacities?

Turing himself found his considerations mathematically unsatisfactory. Indeed, he took two problematic steps by (i) starting the analysis with calculations on two-dimensional paper (this is problematic as possibly more general configurations and procedures should be considered) and (ii) dismissing, without argument, the two-dimensional character of paper as "no essential of computation" (250). However, a restricted result *is* rigorously established by Turing's considerations: *Turing machines can carry out the calculations of computors*—as long as computors not only satisfy (B) and (L), but also operate on linear configurations; this result can be extended to extremely general configurations, K-graphs.[13] But even then there is no *proof* of Turing's thesis.

The methodological difficulties can be avoided by taking an alternative approach, namely, to characterize a *Turing computor* axiomatically as a discrete dynamical system and to show that any system satisfying the axioms is computationally reducible to a Turing machine. (See Sieg 2002 and 2009a.) No appeal to a thesis is needed; rather, that appeal has been replaced by the task of recognizing the correctness of axioms for an intended notion. This way of extracting from Turing's analysis clear axiomatic conditions and then establishing a representation theorem seems to follow Gödel's suggestion to Church in 1934; it also seems to fall, in a way, under the description Gödel gave of Turing's work, when arguing that it analyzes the concept "mechanical procedure" and that "this concept is shown to be equivalent with that of a Turing machine."[14]

With the conceptual foundations in place, we can examine how Gödel and Turing thought about the fact that humans transcend the limitations of any particular Turing machine (with respect to the first incompleteness theorem). They chose quite different paths: Gödel was led to argue for the existence of humanly effective, non-mechanical procedures and continued to identify finite machines with Turing machines; thus, he "established" our topical claim that the human mind infinitely surpasses any finite machine. Turing, by contrast, was led to the more modest demand of releasing computors and machines from the strict discipline of carrying out procedures mechanically and providing them with room for initiative. Let us see what that amounts to.

8.3   Beyond Mechanisms and Discipline

Gödel's paper (193?) begins by referring to Hilbert's famous words, "for any precisely formulated mathematical question a unique answer can be found" (164). He takes those words to mean that for any mathematical proposition A there is a proof of either A or not-A, "where by 'proof' is meant something which starts from evident axioms and proceeds by evident inferences" (164). He argues that the incompleteness theorems show that something is lost when one takes the step from this notion of proof to a formalized one: "... it is not possible to formalise [*sic!*] mathematical evidence even in the domain of number theory, but the conviction about which Hilbert speaks remains entirely untouched. Another way of putting the result is this: it is not possible to mechanise [*sic!*] mathematical reasoning" (164). And that means for Gödel that "it will never be possible to replace the mathematician by a machine, even if you confine yourself to number-theoretic problems" (164–165). Gödel took this deeply rationalist and optimistic perspective still in the early 1970s: Wang reports that Gödel rejected the possibility that there are number theoretic problems undecidable for the human mind.[15]

Gödel's claim that it is impossible to mechanize mathematical reasoning is supported in the Gibbs lecture by an argument that relies primarily on the second incompleteness theorem; see the detailed analyses in Feferman (2006a) and Sieg (2007, section 2). This claim raises immediately the question, "What aspects of mathematical reasoning or experience defy formalization?" In his 1974 note, Gödel points to two "vaguely defined" (325) processes that may be sharpened to systematic and effective, but nonmechanical procedures; namely, the process of defining recursive well-orderings of integers for larger and larger ordinals of the second number class, and that of formulating stronger and stronger axioms of infinity. The point is reiterated in the modified formulation of the 1972 note, where Gödel considers another version of his first theorem that may be taken "as an indication for the existence of mathematical yes or no questions undecidable for the human mind" (305). However, he points to a *fact* that in his view weighs against such an interpretation: "There *do* exist unexplored series of axioms which are analytic in the sense that they only explicate the concepts occurring in them." As an example he presents again axioms of infinity, "which only explicate the content of the general concept of set." These reflections on axioms of infinity and their impact on provability are foreshadowed in (Gödel 1947), where Gödel asserts that the current axioms of set theory "can be supplemented without arbitrariness by new axioms which are only the natural continuation of the series of those [axioms of infinity] set up so far" (182).

Though Gödel calls the existence of an unexplored series of axioms a *fact*, he asserts also that the process of forming such a series does not yet form a "well-defined procedure which could actually be carried out (and would yield a non-recursive number-theoretic function)," because it would require "a substantial advance in our understanding of the basic concepts of mathematics" (306). A prima facie startlingly different reason for not yet having a precise definition of such a procedure is given in the 1974 note: it would require "a substantial deepening of our understanding of the basic operations of the mind" (325). That is, however, only prima facie different, as Gödel's 1972 note connects such a procedure with the dynamic development of the human mind:

[M]ind, in its use, is not static, but constantly developing, i.e., that we understand abstract terms more and more precisely as we go on using them, and that more and more abstract terms enter the sphere of our understanding. (306)[16]

Gödel continues:

There may exist systematic methods of actualizing this development, which could form part of the procedure. Therefore, although at each stage the number and precision of the abstract terms at our disposal may be *finite*, both … may *converge toward infinity* in the course of the application of the procedure.

The procedure mentioned as a plausible candidate for satisfying this description is again the process of forming ever stronger axioms of infinity.

The notes from 1972 and 1974 are very closely connected, but there is a subtle and yet, it seems to me, substantive difference. In the 1974 note the claim that the number of possible states of mind may converge to infinity is a consequence of the dynamic development of mind. That claim is followed by a remark that begins in a superficially similar way as the first sentence of the above quotation, but ends with a quite different observation:

Now there may exist systematic methods of accelerating, specializing, and uniquely determining this development, e.g. by asking the right questions on the basis of a mechanical procedure. (325)

I don't fully understand these enigmatic observations, but three points can be made. First, mathematical experience has to be invoked when asking the right questions; second, aspects of that experience may be codified in a mechanical procedure and serve as the basis for asking the right questions; third, the answers may involve abstract terms that are introduced by the nonmechanical mental procedure. We should not dismiss or disregard Gödel's methodological remark that "asking the right questions on the basis of a mechanical procedure" may be part of a systematic method to push forward the development of mind.[17] Even this very limited understanding allows us to see that Gödel's reflections overlap with Turing's proposal for investigating matters in a broadly empirical and directly computational manner.

Much of Turing's work of the late 1940s and early 1950s deals explicitly with mental processes. But nowhere is it claimed that the latter cannot go beyond mechanical ones. Mechanical processes are still made precise as Turing machine computations; in contrast, machines that might exhibit intelligence have a more complex structure than Turing machines and, most importantly, interact with their environment. Conceptual idealization and empirical adequacy are now being sought for quite different purposes, and one might even say that Turing is actually trying to capture what Gödel described when searching for a broader concept of humanly effective calculability, namely, "that mind, in its use, is not static, but constantly developing." In his paper "Intelligent Machinery," Turing states:

If the untrained infant's mind is to become an intelligent one, it must acquire both discipline and initiative. So far we have been considering only discipline [via the universal machine]. ... But discipline is certainly not enough in itself to produce intelligence. That which is required in addition we call initiative. This statement will have to serve as a definition. Our task is to discover the nature of this residue as it occurs in man, and to try and copy it in machines. (Turing 1948, 21)[18]

How, in particular, can we transcend discipline when doing mathematics? Turing already provided a hint in his 1939 paper, where ordinal logics are introduced to expand formal theories in a systematic way (see Feferman 1988 and 2006b for informative discussions). In that paper, his PhD thesis written under the direction of Church, Turing distinguishes between *ingenuity* and *intuition*. He observes that in formal logics their respective roles take on a greater definiteness. Intuition is used for "setting down formal rules for inferences which are always intuitively valid," whereas ingenuity is to "determine which steps are the more profitable for the purpose of proving a particular proposition" (209). He notes:

In pre-Gödel times it was thought by some that it would be possible to carry this programme to such a point that all the intuitive judgements of mathematics could be replaced by a finite number of these rules. The necessity for intuition would then be entirely eliminated. (Turing 1939, 209)

That intuition cannot be eliminated, on account of the first incompleteness theorem, is emphasized in Turing's letters to Max Newman from around 1940, reprinted in Copeland (2004, 211–216). After all, one can determine that the Gödel sentence is true, despite the fact that it is independent. Providing a general reason for such a determination, Turing writes, "... there is a fairly definite idea of a true formula which is quite different from the idea of a provable one" (215). Eight years later, in 1948, Turing formulated at the very outset reasons given by some for asserting that "it is not possible for machinery to show intelligent behaviour" (107). One of the reasons is directly related to the limitative theorems, which are assumed to show that when machines are used for "determining the truth or falsity of mathematical theorems ... then any given machine will in some cases be unable to give an answer at all" (108). This inability of any particular machine is contrasted with human intelligence that "seems to be able to find methods of ever-increasing power for dealing with such problems 'transcending' the methods available to machines" (Turing 1948, 108).

It is thus not surprising that Turing takes in his 1950 paper (444–5) the *mathematical objection* to his view quite seriously. He considers the objection as based on the limitative results, in particular Gödel's theorems, which are understood by some as proving "a disability of machines to which the human intellect is not subject" (445). Turing gives two responses. The short one states that the objection takes for granted, without any sort of proof that the human intellect is not subject to the limitations to which machines provably are. However, Turing thinks that the objection cannot be dismissed quite so lightly, and proceeds to a second response, which acknowledges the superiority of the human intellect with respect to a single machine (we can recognize the truth of "its" Gödel sentence). But Turing views that as a petty triumph. The reason for this is formulated succinctly as follows:

There would be no question of triumphing simultaneously over *all* machines. In short, then, there might be men cleverer than any given machine, but then there might be other machines cleverer again, and so on. (Turing 1950, 445)

Turing does not offer a proof of the claim that there is "no question of triumphing simultaneously over *all* machines." It is precisely here that Gödel's "fact" concerning a humanly effective, but nonmechanical procedure seems to be in conflict with Turing's assertion.[19] If the "fact" were a fact, then it would sustain the objection successfully. Can one go beyond claim and counterclaim? Or, even better, can one use the tension as an inspiration for concrete work that elucidates the situation?

8.4 Finding Proofs (with Ingenuity)

Let us return, as a first positive step toward bridging the gap between claim and counterclaim, to Turing's distinction between ingenuity and intuition. Intuition is explicitly linked to the incompleteness of formal theories and provides an entry point to exploiting, through computational work, a certain parallelism between Turing's and Gödel's considerations, when the latter are based on mechanical procedures. Copying the *residue* in machines is the common task at hand. It is a difficult one in the case of mathematical thinking and, Gödel would argue, an impossible one, if machines are particular Turing machines. Turing would agree, of course. Before we can start copying, we have to discover partially the nature of the residue; one might hope to begin doing that through proposals for finding proofs in mathematics.

In his lecture to the London Mathematical Society and in "Intelligent Machinery," Turing calls for heuristically guided intellectual searches and for initiative that includes, in the context of mathematics, proposing new intuitive steps. Such searches and the discovery of novel intuitive steps would be at the center of "research into intelligence of machinery" (127). Let me draw a diagram: the formal theory FT_i has been expanded to the proof theoretically stronger theory FT_{i+1}; the theories are presented via Turing machines M_i and M_{i+1}, respectively.

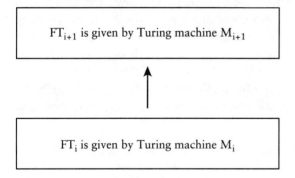

The transition from one theory to the next and, correspondingly, from one Turing machine to the next is nonmechanical for Gödel as well as for Turing. In Gödel's case, unfolding the explication of the concept of set by a nonmechanical method is the basis for a humanly effective procedure. Even if Gödel's method would take into account a mechanical procedure of the character described in note 17, in the end, it would present a new and stronger axiom of infinity; it is in this sense that the method could be viewed as *uniform*. For Turing, it seems, the addition of intuitive steps (outside of his ordinal logics) is principally based on the analysis of machine learning and computer experimentation.[20] It would be closely tied to the particulars of a situation without the connecting thread of Gödel's method and, thus, it would not be uniform. In addition, Turing emphasizes at a number of places that a random element be introduced into the development of machines, thus providing an additional feature that releases them from strict discipline and facilitates a step from M_i to M_{i+1}.

What is striking is that both Gödel and Turing make "completeness claims": at the end of the second paragraph of section 8.3 above, Gödel's remark from his 1947 paper is quoted, namely that every set theoretic statement is decidable from the current axioms together with "a true assertion about the largeness of the universe of all sets"; in note 19, Turing's remark is quoted that by choosing a suitable machine one can approximate "truth" by "provability" and "in a sense approximate it [truth] as well as you please." That is highly speculative in both cases; slightly less speculatively, Turing conjectured:

As regards mathematical philosophy, since the machines will be doing more and more mathematics themselves, the centre of gravity of the human interest will be driven further and further into philosophical questions of what can in principle be done etc. (1947, 103)

This expectation has not been borne out yet, and Gödel would not be surprised. However, he could have cooperated with Turing on the "philosophical questions of what can in principle be done" and, to begin with, they could have agreed terminologically that there is a human mind whose working is not reducible to the working of any particular brain. They could have explored, and possibly argued about, Turing's contention "that machines can be constructed which will simulate the behaviour of the human mind very closely" (1951a, 472). Indeed, Turing had taken a step toward a concept of human mind when he emphasized at the end of "Intelligent Machinery," "the isolated man does not develop any intellectual power," and then argues:

It is necessary for him to be immersed in an environment of other men, whose techniques he absorbs during the first twenty years of his life. He may then perhaps do a little research of his own and make a very few discoveries which are passed on to other men. From this point of view the search for new techniques must be regarded as carried out by the human community as a whole, rather than by individuals. (127)

Turing calls this, appropriately enough, a *cultural search,* in contrast to the more limited *intellectual searches* possible for individual men or machines. To build machines that think serves also another purpose, as Turing explained in a 1951 radio broadcast: "The whole thinking process is still rather mysterious to us, but I believe that the attempt to make a thinking machine will help us greatly in finding out how we think ourselves." (Turing 1951b, 486)

For the study of human thinking, mathematics is a marvelous place to start. Where else do we find an equally rich body of rigorously organized knowledge that is structured for both intelligibility and discovery? Turing, as we saw above, had high expectations for machines' progress in doing mathematics; but it is still extremely difficult for them to "mathematize" on their own. Newman, in a radio debate with Braithwaite, Jefferson, and Turing, put the general problem very well:

Even if we stick to the reasoning side of thinking, it is a long way from solving chess problems to the invention of new mathematical concepts or making a generalisation [*sic!*] that takes in ideas that were current before, but had never been brought together as instances of a single general notion. (Turing 1952, 498)

The important question is whether we can gain, by closely studying *mathematical practice*, a deeper understanding of fundamental concepts, techniques and methods of mathematics and, in that way, advance our understanding of the capacities of the mathematical mind as well as of basic operations of the mind. This question motivates a more modest goal, namely, formulating strategies for an automated search: not for proofs of new results, but for proofs that reflect logical and mathematical understanding, proofs that reveal their intelligibility and that force us to make explicit the *ingenuity* required for a successful search.[21] The logical framework for such studies must include a s*tructural theory of proofs* that extends proof theory through (i) articulating structural features of derivations and (ii) exploiting the meaning of abstract concepts; both aspects are crucial for finding humanly intelligible proofs.[22] We will hopefully find out what kind of broad strategies and heuristic ideas will emerge, and what is the necessary ingenuity. In this way we will begin to uncover part of Turing's residue and part of what Gödel considered as humanly effective, but not mechanical, in each case "by asking the right questions on the basis of a mechanical procedure" (Gödel 1974, 325).

The very last remark in Turing (1954) comes back, in a certain sense, to the mathematical objection. Turing views the limitative results as being "mainly of a negative character, setting bounds to what we can hope to achieve purely by reasoning." Characterizing in a new way the *residue* that has to be discovered and implemented to construct intelligent machinery, Turing continues, "These, and some other results of mathematical logic may be regarded as going some way towards a demonstration, within mathematics itself, of the inadequacy of 'reason' unsupported by common sense" (23). This is as close as Turing could come to agree with Gödel's dictum "The human mind infinitely surpasses any finite machine," if "finite machine" is identified with "Turing machine."

Acknowledgments

Versions of this note were read at the Computability in Europe conference in 2006, as the Gödel lecture at the Colloquium Logicum conference in 2006, and in the logic seminar of the mathematics department at the University of Lisbon. It is closely based on previous papers of mine (Sieg 2006, 2007), but I argue here for a parallelism between Gödel's and Turing's considerations for transcending purely mechanical processes in mathematics. I revised and completed the manuscript in March 2009, while I was a fellow at the Swedish Collegium for Advanced Study in Uppsala, but made some stylistic changes two years later. Finally, remarks by Jack Copeland and Oron Shagrir stimulated a sharpening and expansion of points in the last section; that version served as the basis for my talk, "Church's Thesis: Logic, Mind and Nature," at the Studia Logica Conference in Krakow in June 2011.

Notes

In Milan Kundera's *Ignorance* (Harper Collins, 2002) one finds on page 124, "We won't understand a thing about human life if we persist in avoiding the most obvious fact: that a reality no longer is what it was when it was; it cannot be reconstructed." These remarks of Kundera, born in Gödel's hometown Brno, apply even to attempts of understanding and reconstructing a limited aspect of past intellectual life.

1. This is in the logicist tradition of Dedekind; cf. Sieg and Schlimm (2005) and Sieg (2009b).

2. For the development of Hilbert's foundational investigations, it has to be mentioned that the Göttingen group had in the meantime assimilated Whitehead and Russell's *Principia Mathematica*; that is clear from the carefully worked-out lecture notes from the winter term 1917–18; cf. my paper Sieg (1999)

3. That was done in Hilbert and Bernays (1921–22); a summary is found in section II of Ackermann (1925), entitled "The Consistency Proof before the Addition of the Transfinite Axioms." Ackermann does not treat the induction rule, but that can easily be incorporated into the argument following Hilbert and Bernays. These early proof theoretic results are presented, refined, and extended in Hilbert and Bernays (1934).

4. For brief descriptions of the equational calculus see Gödel (1934, 368–369) or his (193?, 166–168).

5. Cf. his letter to Martin Davis quoted in Davis (1982, 9).

6. This is analyzed in section 2 of Sieg (1994) and, with an illuminating Churchian perspective, in section 4 of Sieg (1997).

7. In a footnote, Gödel explains that the concept of "finite procedure" is considered to be equivalent to the concept of a "computable function of integers," that is, a function f "whose definition makes it possible actually to compute $f(n)$ for each integer n" (1934, 348).

8. In his 1933 paper, Gödel describes the constructivity requirements on theories and explicates the purely formal character of inference rules. The latter "refer only to the outward structure of the formulas, not to their meaning, so that they could be applied by someone who knew nothing about mathematics, or by a machine." He also asserts there, "thus the highest possible degree of exactness is obtained" (45).

9. In spring 1939, Gödel gave a logic course at Notre Dame and argued for the superiority of the human mind over machines via the undecidability of the decision problem for predicate logic; the latter is put into the historical context of Leibniz's *Calculemus*! He claims: "So here already one can prove that Leibnitzens [*sic!*] program of the 'calculemus' cannot be carried through, i.e. one knows that the human mind will never be able to be replaced by a machine already for this comparatively simple question to

decide whether a formula is a tautology or not." The conception of machine is as in (193?)—an office calculator with a crank.

10. I have analyzed Turing's argument in other papers, e.g., in Sieg (1994) and (2002). My subsequent discussion takes Turing machines in the way in which Post defined them in 1947, namely, as production systems. This has the consequence that states of mind are physically represented, quite in Turing's spirit; cf. part III of section 9 in his paper (1936) and the marvelous discussion in Turing (1954).

11. That captures exactly the intellectual problematic and context: the *Entscheidungsproblem* was to be solved mechanically by us; formal systems were to guarantee intersubjectivity on a minimal, mechanically verifiable level between us.

12. It should be noted that step-by-step calculations in the equational calculus cannot be carried out by a computor satisfying these restrictive conditions: arbitrarily large numerals have to be recognized and arbitrarily complex terms have to be replaced by their numerical values—in one step.

13. The underlying methodological matters are discussed in Sieg and Byrnes (1996), where K-graphs were introduced as a generalization of the graphical structures considered in Kolmogorov and Uspenski (1963).

14. In Martin (2005), a particular (and insightful) interpretation of Gödel's view on mathematical concepts is given. It is developed with special attention to the concept of set, but it seems to be adaptable to the concept of computability. Cf. the summary on 223–224.

15. Wang (1974, 324–325). For a broad discussion of Gödel's reflections on "absolutely unsolvable problems," cf. Feferman (2006a) and Kennedy and van Atten (2004, 2009).

16. Gödel's brief exploration of the issue of defining a nonmechanical but effective procedure is preceded in this note by a severe critique of Turing. He *assumes* that Turing's argument in the 1936 paper was to show that "mental procedures cannot go beyond mechanical procedures" and considers it inconclusive, because Turing neglects the dynamic nature of mind. However, simply carrying out a mechanical procedure does not, and indeed should not, involve an expansion of our understanding. Turing viewed the restricted use of mind in computations undoubtedly as static. I leave that misunderstanding out of the systematic considerations in the main text. The appeal to finiteness of states of mind when comparing Gödel's and Turing's perspectives is also pushed into the background, as it is not crucial at all for the central issues under discussion: there does not seem to be any disagreement.

17. There seems to also be a connection to remarks in his 1947 paper, where Gödel points out that there may be "another way" (apart from judging its intrinsic necessity) to decide the truth of a new axiom (182–3). This other way consists in inductively studying its success, "that is, its fruitfulness in consequences and in particular in 'verifiable' consequences, i.e., consequences demonstrable without the new axiom, whose proofs by means of the new axiom, however, are considerably simpler and easier to discover, and make it possible to condense into one proof many different proofs" (182–183).

18. In his (1950), Turing pointed out, in a similar spirit: "Intelligent behaviour presumably consists in a departure from the completely disciplined behaviour involved in computation, but a rather slight one, which does not give rise to random behaviour, or to pointless repetitive loops" (459).

19. "Seems," as Turing pits individual men against particular machines, whereas Gödel pits the "human mind" against machines. This aspect is also briefly discussed in the first letter to Newman in Copeland (2004): if one moves away from considering a particular machine and allows machines with different sets of proofs, then "by choosing a suitable machine one can approximate 'truth' by 'provability' better than with a less suitable machine, and can in a sense approximate it as well as you please" (215).

20. Copeland gives much the same interpretation. He remarks: "In his post-war writing on mind and intelligence ... the term 'intuition' drops from view and what comes to the fore is the closely related idea of *learning*—in the sense of devising and discovering—new methods of proof" (2006, 168).

21. This involves undoubtedly reactions to Turing's remarks and impatient questions in a letter to Newman: "In proofs there is actually an enormous amount of sheer slogging, a certain amount of ingenuity, while in most cases the actual 'methods of proof' are quite well known. Cannot we make it clearer where the slogging comes in, where there is ingenuity involved, and what are the methods of proof?" (Copeland 2004, 213)

Abramson (2008) emphasizes insightfully the significance of Lady Lovelace's objection. In the context here, his emphasis pointed out to me that Turing views "the mere working out of consequences from data and general principles" as a "virtue" and as a "source for surprises." Turing articulates that important perspective after having called "false" the assumption that "as soon as a fact is presented to a mind all consequences of the fact spring into the mind simultaneously with it" (1950, 451).

22. I have been pursuing a form of such a structural proof theory for quite a number of years. Central considerations and results are presented in Sieg (2010); there I also pointed out connections with Greek mathematics and the radical transformation of mathematics in the nineteenth century, as described in Stein (1988). A fully automated proof search method for (classical) first-order logic has been implemented in the AProS system. The overall project, addressing strategic search and dynamic tutoring, is now also being extended to elementary set theory; it is described at http://www.phil.cmu.edu/projects/apros, and AProS is downloadable from that site.

References

Abramson, D. 2008. Turing's responses to two objections. *Minds and Machines* 18 (2):147–167.

Ackermann, W. 1925. Begründung des 'tertium non datur' mittels der Hilbertschen Theorie der Widerspruchsfreiheit. *Mathematische Annalen* 93:1–36.

Church, A. 1935. An unsolvable problem of elementary number theory. *Bulletin of the AMS* 41:332–333.

Copeland, B. J. 2004. *The Essential Turing: The Ideas That Gave Birth to the Computer Age.* Oxford: Clarendon Press.

Copeland, B. J. 2006. Turing's thesis. In A. Olszewski, J. Wolenski, and R. Janusz, *Church's Thesis after 70 Years*, 147–174. Frankfurt: Ontos Verlag.

Davis, M. 1982. Why Gödel did not have Church's thesis. *Information and Control* 54:3–24.

Dawson, J. W., Jr. 2006. Gödel and the origin of computer science. In *Logical Approaches to Computational Barriers*, ed. A. Beckmann, U. Berger, B. Löwe, and J. V. Tucker, 133–136. Proceedings of the Second Conference on Computability in Europe, Swansea, UK. Berlin: Springer Verlag.

Dedekind, R. 1888. *Was sind und was sollen die Zahlen?* Braunschweig: Vieweg.

Feferman, S. 1988. Turing in the land of O(z). In *The Universal Turing Machine: A Half-Century Survey*, ed. R. Herken, 113–147. Oxford: Oxford University Press.

Feferman, S. 2006a. Are there absolutely unsolvable problems? Gödel's dichotomy. *Philosophia Mathematica* 14(2):134–152.

Feferman, S. 2006b. Turing's Thesis. *Notices of the American Mathematical Society* 53(10):1200–1205.

Gandy, R. 1980. Church's thesis and principles for mechanisms. In *The Kleene Symposium*, ed. J. Barwise, H. J. Keisler, and K. Kunen, 123–148. Amsterdam: North-Holland.

Gödel, K. 1931. Über formal unentscheidbare Sätze der Principia Mathematica und verwandter Systeme, I, *Monatshefte für Mathematik und Physik*, 38:173–98. English translation in Gödel, *Collected Works I*, 144–195.

Gödel, K. 1933. The present situation in the foundations of mathematics. In Gödel, *Collected Works III*, 45–53.

Gödel, K. 1934. On undecidable propositions of formal mathematical systems. In Gödel, *Collected Works I*, 346–371.

Gödel, K. 1936. Über die Länge von Beweisen. English translation in Gödel, *Collected Works I*, 396–399.

Gödel, K. 1939. Finding aid. Notre Dame lecture on logic. In Gödel 2003, 527–528.

Gödel, K. 193?. Undecidable Diophantine propositions. In Gödel, *Collected Works III*, 164–175.

Gödel, K. 1946. Remarks before the Princeton bicentennial conference on problems in mathematics. In Gödel, *Collected Works II*, 150–153.

Gödel, K. 1947. What is Cantor's continuum problem? In Gödel, *Collected Works II*, 167–187.

Gödel, K. 1951. Some basic theorems on the foundations of mathematics and their implications. In Gödel, *Collected Works III*, 304–323.

Gödel, K. 1964. *Postscriptum* for Gödel (1934). In Gödel, *Collected Works I*, 369–371.

Gödel, K. 1972. Some remarks on the undecidability results. In Gödel, *Collected Works II*, 305–306.

Gödel, K. 1974. Note in Wang, *From Mathematics to Philosophy*, 325–326.

Gödel, K. 1986. *Collected Works, Vol. I: Publications 1929–1936*, ed. S. Feferman, J. W. Dawson Jr., S. C. Kleene, G. H. Moore, R. M. Solovay, and J. van Heijenoort. Oxford: Oxford University Press.

Gödel, K. 1990. *Collected Works, Vol. II: Publications 1938–1974*, ed. S. Feferman, J. W. Dawson Jr., S. C. Kleene, G. H. Moore, R. M. Solovay, and J. van Heijenoort. Oxford: Oxford University Press.

Gödel, K. 1995. *Collected Works, Vol. III: Unpublished Essays and Lectures*, ed. S. Feferman, J. W. Dawson Jr., W. Goldfarb, C. Parsons, and R. M. Solovay. Oxford: Oxford University Press.

Gödel, K. 2003. *Collected Works, Vol. V: Correspondence, H–Z*, ed. S. Feferman, J. W. Dawson Jr., W. Goldfarb, C. Parsons, and W. Sieg. Oxford: Clarendon Press.

Herbrand, J. 1931. On the consistency of arithmetic. In *Logical Writings*, ed. W. Goldfarb, 282–298. Cambridge: Harvard University Press, 1971.

Hilbert, D. 1900. Über den Zahlbegriff. *Jahresbericht der Deutschen Mathematiker Vereinigung* 8:180–194.

Hilbert, D. 1905. Über die Grundlagen der Logik und der Arithmetik. in *Verhandlungen des dritten Internationalen Mathematiker-Kongresses in Heidelberg vom 8, bis 13 August*, ed. A. Krazer. Leipzig: Teubner, 174–185. English translation in *From Frege to Gödel: A Source Book in Mathematical Logic, 1879–1931*, ed. J. van Heijenoort, 129–138. Cambridge: Harvard University Press.

Hilbert, D. 1923. Die logischen Grundlagen der Mathematik. *Mathematische Annalen* 88:151–165.

Hilbert, D., and P. Bernays. 1921–22. Grundlagen der Mathematik. Lecture notes for a course at the Georg-August Universität, Göttingen. Göttingen: Library of the Mathematisches Institut.

Hilbert, D., and P. Bernays. 1934. *Grundlagen der Mathematik I*. Berlin: Springer Verlag.

Hilbert, D., and P. Bernays. 1939. *Grundlagen der Mathematik II*. Berlin: Springer Verlag.

Kennedy, J., and M. van Atten. 2004. Gödel's modernism: On set-theoretic incompleteness. *Graduate Faculty Philosophy Journal* 25 (2):289–349.

Kennedy, J., and M. van Atten. 2009. "Gödel's modernism: On set-theoretic incompleteness" revisited. In *Logicism, Intuitionism, and Formalism—What Has Become of Them?* ed. S. Lindström, K. Segerberg, and V. Stoltenberg-Hansen, 303–55. Berlin: Springer Verlag.

Kolmogorov, A., and V. Uspenski. 1963. On the definition of an algorithm. *AMS Translations* 21 (2):217–245.

Martin, D. A. 2005. Gödel's conceptual realism. *Bulletin of Symbolic Logic* 11 (2):207–224.

Post, E. L. 1947. Recursive unsolvability of a problem of Thue. *Journal of Symbolic Logic* 12:1–11.

Sieg, W. 1994. Mechanical procedures and mathematical experience. In *Mathematics and Mind*, ed. A. George, 71–117. Oxford University Press.

Sieg, W. 1997. Step by recursive step: Church's analysis of effective calculability. Bulletin of Symbolic Logic 3(2):154–180. Reprinted in A. Olszewski, J. Wolenski, and R. Janusz, *Church's Thesis after 70 Years*, 456–490. Frankfurt: Ontos Verlag.

Sieg, W. 1999. Hilbert's programs: 1917–1922. *Bulletin of Symbolic Logic* 5(1):1–44.

Sieg, W. 2002. Calculations by man and machine: Conceptual analysis. In *Reflections on the Foundations of Mathematics. Essays in Honor of Solomon Feferman*, ed. W. Sieg, R. Sommer, and C. Talcott, 390–409. Lecture Notes in Logic, Vol. 15. Natick, MA: Association for Symbolic Logic.

Sieg, W. 2006. Gödel on computability. *Philosophia Mathematica* 14 (2):189–207.

Sieg, W. 2007. On mind and Turing's machines. *Natural Computing* 6:187–205.

Sieg, W. 2009a. On computability. In *Philosophy of Mathematics*, ed. A. D. Irvine, 535–630. Amsterdam: North-Holland.

Sieg, W. 2009b. Hilbert's proof theory. In *Handbook of the History of Logic: Logic from Russell to Church*, Vol. 5, ed. D. M. Gabbay and J. Woods, 321–384. Amsterdam: North-Holland.

Sieg, W. 2010. Searching for proofs (and uncovering capacities of the mathematical mind). In *Proofs, Categories and Computations*, ed. S. Feferman, and W. Sieg, 189–215. London: College Publications.

Sieg, W., and J. Byrnes. 1996. K-graph machines: Generalizing Turing's machines and arguments. *Gödel '96: Logical foundations of mathematics, computer science and physics*, ed. P. Hájek. Lecture notes in logic, Vol. 6, 98–119. Berlin: Springer Verlag.

Sieg, W., and D. Schlimm. 2005. Dedekind's analysis of number: Systems and axioms. *Synthese* 147:121–170.

Stein, H. 1988. Logos, logic, and logistiké: Some philosophical remarks on nineteenth-century transformation of mathematics. In *History and Philosophy of Modern Mathematics*, ed. W. Aspray and P. Kitcher, 238–259. Minnesota Studies in the Philosophy of Science, Vol. XI. Minneapolis: University of Minnesota Press.

Turing, A. M. 1936. On computable numbers, with an application to the Entscheidungsproblem. *Proceedings of the London Mathematical Society*, 42(2):230–265.

Turing, A. M. 1939. Systems of logic based on ordinals. *Proceedings of the London Mathematical Society*, 45(2):161–228.

Turing, A. M. 1947. Lecture to the London Mathematical Society on February, 20, 1947. In D. C. Ince, *Collected Works of A. M. Turing: Mechanical Intelligence,* Vol. 1, 87–105. Amsterdam: North-Holland

Turing, A. M. 1948. Intelligent Machinery. In D. C. Ince, *Collected Works of A. M. Turing: Mechanical Intelligence,* Vol. 1, 107–127. Amsterdam: North-Holland.

Turing, A. M. 1950. Computing machinery and intelligence. *Mind* 59:433–460.

Turing, A. M. 1951a. Intelligent machinery: A heretical theory. Radio broadcast. Printed in Copeland, *The Essential Turing*, 472–475.

Turing, A. M. 1951b. Can digital computers think? Radio broadcast. Printed in Copeland, *The Essential Turing,* 482–486.

Turing, A. M. 1952. Can automatic calculating machines be said to think? Radio broadcast discussion with A. M. Turing, R. Braithwaite, G. Jefferson, and M. Newman. In Copeland, *The Essential Turing,* 494–506.

Turing, A. M. 1954. Solvable and unsolvable problems. *Science News* 31:7–23.

Wang, H. 1974. *From Mathematics to Philosophy*. London: Routledge & Kegan Paul.

9 Interactive Computing and Relativized Computability

Robert Irving Soare

In the 1930s, following Gödel's incompleteness theorem, the formal definitions of a computable function were proposed by several researchers and used to produce unsolvable problems. In what follows, we compare these formal definitions and contributions.

Turing's *automatic machine (a-machine)*, now called simply a Turing machine, gave one such definition (1936). Turing (1939) very briefly hinted at an *oracle machine (o-machine)*, an extended *a*-machine which could consult an *oracle*, an external database, during the computation. Turing entered the British cryptographic service in 1939 and left computability theory forever. Post realized the importance of oracle computability and developed it between 1943 and 1954 into the theory of relative computability we know today. We examine carefully Post's contributions and the general concept of an *o*-machine.

The concept of a machine communicating with a database or oracle and the implementation of online or interactive computing in the real world are among the most important ideas in computability theory, but have often been pushed aside by an overemphasis on offline computing and Turing plain automatic machines (*a*-machines). Oracle computations are the basis of most of the work in computability theory and its applications to algebra, analysis, and differential geometry. They are also a model for much of the online and interactive computing used in real-world computing.

In the final sections, we consider three misalignments in computability theory, issues pushed aside from their rightful scientific and historical place by lesser issues that took the center of attention. We discuss how to realign these issues closer to the opinion of Gödel and Turing and closer to the scientific and historical evidence. Some conclusions are given at the end.

9.1   Introduction

The central concept of computability theory is the notion of a Turing oracle machine, or *o*-machine (Turing 1939), not the plain Turing automatic machine, or *a*-machine (Turing 1936). It is central to the theoretical development of computability and to applications to computing in the real world. We explore this importance. We also challenge a number of traditional views as often presented in the literature since 1940.

9.1.1   Terminology: Incompleteness and Incomputability

The two principal accomplishments in computability and logic in the 1930s were the discovery of incompleteness by Gödel (1931) and of incomputability by Church and Turing, each independently and each in 1936 (Church 1936a; Turing 1936). We use the term "noncomputable" or "incomputable" for individual instances, but we often use the term "incomputability" for the general concept because it is linguistically and mathematically parallel to "incomplete." The term "incomputable" appeared in English as early as 1606 with the meaning that which "cannot be computed or reckoned; incalculable," according to the *Oxford English Dictionary*. *Webster's* dictionary defines it as "greater than can be computed or enumerated; very great." Neither dictionary lists an entry for "noncomputable," although it has often been used in computability theory to mean "not computable" for a specific function or set, analogously to how "nonmeasurable" is used in analysis.

9.1.2   The Goal of *Incomputability*, not Computability

For several thousand years, the study of algorithms had led to new theoretical algorithms and sometimes new devices for *computability* and calculation. In the 1930s, for the first time the goal was the refutation of Hilbert's two programs, a finite consistency proof for Peano arithmetic, and the *Entscheidungsproblem* (decision problem). For the latter, two main discoverers of computability, Alonzo Church and Alan Turing, wanted to give formal definitions of a computable function so that they could diagonalize over all computable functions and produce an *incomputable* (unsolvable) problem. The specific models of computable functions produced by 1936, Turing *a*-machines, λ-definable functions, and recursive functions, would all have deep applications to the design and programming of computing machines, but not until after 1940. Meanwhile, the researchers spent the remainder of the 1930s investigating more of the new world of incomputability they had created by diagonal arguments, just as Georg Cantor had spent the last quarter of the nineteenth century exploring the world of uncountable sets that he had created by the diagonal method. In section 9.1 and section 9.2, we consider this historical development from 1931 to 1939, and we introduce quotes from Gödel to show convincingly that he believed "the correct definition of mechanical computability was established beyond any doubt by Turing" (Gödel 1995, 166) and only by Turing.

9.1.3 Computing Relative to an Oracle or Database

In 1936, Turing's *a*-machines and Church's use of Gödel's recursive functions solved an immediate problem by producing a definition of a computable function with which one could diagonalize and produce undecidable problems in mathematics. The Turing *a*-machine is a good model for offline computing, such as a calculator or a batch processor where the process is initially given a procedure and an input and continues with no further outside information.

However, many modern computer processes are *online processes,* in that they consult an external database of other resources during the computation process. For example, a laptop computer might consult the World Wide Web via an Ethernet or wireless connection while it is computing. These processes are sometimes called *online* or *interactive* or *database* processes, depending on the way they are set up. In modern computer terminology, "online" indicates a state of connectivity, while "offline" indicates a disconnected state. Usually "online" refers to the Internet or World Wide Web.

Turing spent 1936–1938 at Princeton writing a PhD thesis under Church on ordinal logics. A tiny and obscure part of his paper (1939, section 4) included a description of an *oracle machine* (*o*-machine), roughly a Turing *a*-machine which could interrogate an *"oracle" (external database)* during the computation. The one-page description was very sketchy, and Turing never developed it further.

Emil Post (1944, section 11) considerably expanded and developed relative computability and Turing functionals. These concepts were not well understood when Post began, but in Post (1943, 1944, 1948) and Kleene and Post (1954) they emerged into their modern state. These are summarized below in section 9.5.6, "The Post–Turing Thesis." This remarkable role played by Post has been underemphasized in the literature, but is discussed here in section 9.5.

The theory of relative computability developed by Turing and Post and the *o*-machines provides a precise mathematical framework for interactive or online computing, just as Turing *a*-machines provide one for offline computing processes such as batch processing. Oracle computing processes are those most often used in theoretical research as well as in real-world computing, where a laptop computer may communicate with a database like the World Wide Web. Often the local computer is called the "client" and the remote device the "server."

In sections 9.4 and 9.5, we study Turing's oracle machines (*o*-machines) and Post's development of them into relative computability. It is surprising that so much attention has been paid to the Church–Turing thesis over the last seventy years, and so little to the Post–Turing thesis on relative reducibility, particularly in view of the importance of relative computability (Turing o-machines) in comparison with plain computability (Turing a-machines) in both theoretical and practical areas.

9.2 Computability and Incomputability

Mathematicians have studied algorithms and computation since ancient times, but the modern study of computability and incomputability began around 1900. David Hilbert was deeply interested in the foundations of mathematics. Hilbert in 1899 gave an axiomatization of geometry and showed in 1900 that the question of the consistency of geometry reduced to that for the real-number system, and that, in turn, to arithmetic by results of Dedekind (at least in a second-order system). Hilbert in 1904 proposed proving the consistency of arithmetic by what emerged by 1928 as his *finitist program*. He proposed using the finiteness of mathematical proofs in order to establish that contradictions could not be derived. This tended to reduce proofs to manipulation of finite strings of symbols devoid of intuitive meaning, which stimulated the development of mechanical processes to accomplish this. Hilbert's second major program concerned the *Entscheidungsproblem* (decision problem). Kleene (1987b) wrote, "The *Entscheidungsproblem* for various formal systems had been posed by Schröder in 1895, Löwenheim in 1915, and Hilbert in 1918." It was apparently formulated by Behmann in 1921. The decision problem for first-order logic emerged in the early 1920s in lectures by Hilbert and was stated in Hilbert and Ackermann (1928). It was to give a decision procedure (*Entscheidungsverfahren*) "that allows one to decide the validity of the sentence" (1928). Hilbert characterized this as the fundamental problem of mathematical logic. Davis (1965, 108) wrote, "This was because it seemed clear to Hilbert that with the solution of this problem, the *Entscheidungsproblem*, it should be possible, at least in principle, to settle all mathematical questions in a purely mechanical manner." Von Neumann in 1927 doubted that such a procedure existed but had no idea how to prove it.

9.2.1 Gödel's Incompleteness Theorem

Hilbert retired in 1930 and was asked to give a special address in the fall of 1930 in Königsberg, the city of his birth. Hilbert spoke on natural science and logic, the importance of mathematics in science, and the importance of logic in mathematics. He asserted that there are no unsolvable problems and stressed,

Wir müssen wissen. (We must know.)

Wir werden wissen. (We will know.)

At a mathematical conference preceding Hilbert's address, a quiet, obscure young man, Kurt Gödel, only a year a beyond his PhD, announced a result which would forever change the foundations of mathematics. He formalized the liar paradox, "This statement is false," to prove roughly that for any effectively axiomatized, consistent extension T of number theory (Peano arithmetic) there is a sentence σ which asserts its own unprovability in T. John von Neumann, who was in the audience, immediately understood the importance of Gödel's incompleteness theorem. He was at the conference representing Hilbert's proof theory program and recognized that Hilbert's program was over. In the next few weeks von Neumann realized that by arithmetizing the proof of Gödel's first theorem, one could prove an even better one, that no such formal system T could prove its own consistency. A few weeks later he brought his proof to Gödel, who thanked him and informed him politely that he had already submitted the second incompleteness theorem for publication. Von Neumann immediately recognized that Hilbert's formalist program was dead. Gödel himself was a bit more skeptical at the end of his paper (1931), but probably came around to that viewpoint by 1933.

Gödel's incompleteness theorem (1931) not only had a dramatic effect on Hilbert's first program for finite consistency, but it also had a significant influence on progress toward refuting Hilbert's second theme, the *Entscheidungsproblem*. Gödel had successfully challenged Hilbert's first proposal. This made it easier to challenge Hilbert on the second topic of the decision problem. Both refutations used diagonal arguments. Of course, diagonal arguments had been known since Cantor's work, but Gödel showed how to arithmetize the syntactic elements of a formal system and diagonalize within that system. Crucial elements in computability theory, such as the Kleene μ-recursive functions, or the self-reference in Kleene's recursion theorem, all depend upon giving code numbers to computations and elements within a computation, and in calling algorithms by their code numbers (Gödel numbers). These ideas spring from Gödel's (1931) incompleteness proof. The universal Turing machine and Turing's unsolvable problems do not use arithmetization, but a more direct diagonalization.

9.2.2 Alonzo Church

By 1931, computability was a young man's game. Hilbert had retired and after 1930 had no new influence on the field, although his previous work had great influence. As the importance of Gödel's incompleteness theorem began to sink in and researchers began concentrating on the *Entscheidungsproblem,* the major figures were all young. Alonzo Church (b. 1903), Kurt Gödel (b. 1906), and Stephen Cole Kleene (b. 1909) were all under thirty. Alan Turing (b. 1912), perhaps the most influential of all on computability theory, was not even twenty. Only Emil Post (b. 1897) was over thirty, and he was not yet thirty-five. These young men were about to leave Hilbert's

ideas behind and open the path of computability for the next two-thirds of the
twentieth century, which would solve the theoretical problems involving and show
the way toward practical computing devices.

Church completed his PhD at Princeton in 1927 under Oswald Veblen, who
himself had written a PhD thesis entitled "A system of Axioms for Geometry"
under E. H. Moore at the University of Chicago in 1903. Church spent one year at
Harvard and one year at Göttingen and Amsterdam. He returned to Princeton as
an assistant professor of mathematics in 1929. In 1931, Church's first student,
Stephen C. Kleene, arrived at Princeton. Church had begun to develop a formal
system now called the λ-calculus. In 1931, Church knew only that the successor
function was λ-definable. Kleene began proving that certain well-known functions
were λ-definable. By the time Kleene received his PhD in 1934, he had shown that
all the usual number theoretic functions were λ-definable. On the basis of this evidence and his own intuition, Church proposed to Gödel around March 1934 the
first version of his thesis on functions which are *effectively calculable,* the term in
the 1930s for a function which is computable in the informal sense. (See Davis
1965, 8–9.)

9.2.3   Church's First Thesis

(We state the various theses in the LaTeX *definition* mode for easy numerical reference. We are defining the statement of each *thesis* as it emerged, not its accuracy in
formally representing effective calculability. Later we shall present the extensional
and intensional evidence for them.)

Definition 9.1   Church's thesis (first version; 1934)   *A function is effectively calculable if and only if it is λ-definable.*

When Kleene first heard this thesis, he tried to refute it by a diagonal argument,
but since the λ-definable functions were only partial functions, the diagonal was one
of the rows. Instead of a contradiction, Kleene had proved a beautiful new theorem,
the Kleene recursion theorem, whose proof is a diagonal argument which fails (see
Soare 1987, 36). Although Kleene was convinced by Church's first thesis, Gödel was
not. Gödel rejected Church's first thesis as "thoroughly unsatisfactory."

9.2.4   Herbrand–Gödel Recursive Functions

From 1933 to 1939, Gödel spent time both in Vienna pursuing his academic career
and at Fine Hall in Princeton, which housed both the Princeton University faculty
in mathematics and the Institute for Advanced Study, of which he was a member.
Gödel spent the first part of 1934 at Princeton. The primitive recursive functions he
had used in his 1931 paper did not constitute all computable functions. He expanded

on a concept of Herbrand and brought it closer to the modern form. At Princeton in the spring of 1934, Gödel lectured on the Herbrand–Gödel recursive functions, which came to be known as the *general recursive functions* to distinguish them from the primitive recursive functions which at that time were called "recursive functions." Soon the prefix "primitive" was added to the latter, and the prefix "general" was generally dropped from the former. Gödel's definition gave a remarkably succinct system whose simple rules reflected the way a mathematician would informally calculate a function using recursion.

Church and Kleene attended Gödel's lectures on recursive functions. J. B. Rosser and Kleene took notes, which appeared as Gödel (1934). After seeing Gödel's lectures, Church and Kleene changed their formalism (especially for Church's thesis) from "λ-definable" to "Herbrand–Gödel general recursive." Kleene 1981 wrote,

I myself, perhaps unduly influenced by rather chilly receptions from audiences around 1933–35 to disquisitions on λ-definability, chose, after general recursiveness had appeared, to put my work in that format.

Nevertheless, λ-definability is a precise calculating system and has close connections to modern computing, such as functional programming.

9.2.5   Stalemate over Church's Second Thesis

Church reformulated his thesis, with Herbrand–Gödel recursive functions in place of λ-definable ones. This time, without consulting Gödel, Church presented to the American Mathematical Society on April 19, 1935, the famous proposition described in his 1936 paper.

In this paper, a definition of *recursive function of positive integers* that is essentially Gödel's is adopted. It is maintained that the notion of an effectively calculable function of positive integers should be identified with that of a recursive function.

It has been known since Kleene (1952) as *Church's thesis* in the following form.

Definition 9.2   Church's thesis (1936a)   *A function on the positive integers is effectively calculable if and only if it is recursive.*

As further evidence, Church and Kleene had shown the formal equivalence of the Herbrand–Gödel recursive functions and the λ-definable functions. Kleene introduced a new equivalent definition, the μ-recursive functions, defined by the five schemata for primitive recursive functions, plus the least number operator μ. The μ-recursive functions had the advantage of a short standard mathematical definition, but the disadvantage that any function not primitive recursive could be calculated only by a tedious arithmetization, as in Gödel's incompleteness theorem.

9.2.6   Gödel's Thoughts on Church's Thesis

In spite of this evidence, Gödel still did not accept Church's thesis by the beginning of 1936. Gödel had become the most prominent figure in mathematical logic. It was his approval that Church wanted most. Church had solved the *Entscheidungsproblem* only if his characterization of effectively calculable functions was accurate. Gödel had considered the question of characterizing the calculable functions when he wrote,

[Primitive] recursive functions have the important property that, for each given set of values for the arguments, the value of the function can be computed by a finite procedure. (1934, 44)

The converse seems to be true, if, besides recursion according to scheme (V) [primitive recursion], recursions of other forms (e.g., with respect to two variables simultaneously) are admitted. This cannot be proved, since the notion of finite computation is not defined, but it serves as a heuristic principle. (44, n.3)

The second paragraph, Gödel's footnote 3, gives crucial insight into his thinking about the computability thesis and his later pronouncements about the achievements of Turing versus others. Gödel says later that he was not sure his system of Herbrand–Gödel recursive functions comprised all possible recursions. His final sentence suggests that he may have believed such a characterization "cannot be proved," but is a "heuristic principle."

This suggests Gödel was waiting not only for a formal *definition*, such as Turing machines, which came later, but also for a *demonstration* that this formal definition captured the informal notion of effectively calculable. Turing later gave this, and Gödel immediately and enthusiastically accepted it, but Gödel never found it in Church's work. Here he even suggests that such a precise mathematical characterization of the informal notion cannot be proved, which makes his acceptance of Turing's paper (1936) even more impressive.

9.3   Turing Breaks the Stalemate

9.3.1   Turing Machines

At the start of 1936, those gathered at Princeton—Gödel, Church, Kleene, Rosser, and Post nearby at City College in New York—constituted the most distinguished and powerful group in the world investigating the notion of a computable function and Hilbert's *Entscheidungsproblem*, but they could not agree on whether recursive functions constituted all effectively calculable functions. At that moment stepped forward a twenty-two-year-old youth, far removed from Princeton. Well, this was not just *any* youth. Alan Turing had already proved the central limit theorem in probability theory, not knowing it had been previously proved, and as a result had been elected a Fellow of King's College, Cambridge.

The work of Hilbert and Gödel had become well-known around the world. At Cambridge University, the topologist M. H. A. (Max) Newman gave lectures on Hilbert's *Entscheidungsproblem* in 1935. Alan Turing attended. Turing's mother had owned a typewriter which fascinated him as a boy. He designed his *automatic machine (a-machine)* as a kind of idealized typewriter with an infinite carriage, over which the reading head passes with the ability to read, write, and erase one square at a time before moving to an immediately adjacent square, just like a typewriter.

9.3.2 Turing's Thesis

Definition 9.3 Turing's thesis *A function is intuitively computable (effectively calculable) if and only if it is computable by a Turing machine; that is, an automatic machine (a-machine), as defined in Turing (1936).*

Turing showed his proof of the insolubility of the *Entscheidungsproblem* to the astonished Max Newman in April 1936. The *Proceedings of the London Mathematical Society* was reluctant to publish Turing's paper because Church's paper had already been submitted to another journal on similar material. Newman persuaded them that Turing's work was sufficiently different, and they published Turing's paper in volume 42 on November 30, 1936, and December 23, 1936. There has been considerable misunderstanding in the literature about exactly when Turing's seminal paper was published. This is important because of the appearance in 1936 of related papers by Church, Kleene, and Post, and Turing's priority is important here. Many papers, such as Kleene (1943, 73; 1987a; 1987b), Davis (1965, 72), Post (1943, 20), Gödel (1986, 456), and others, mistakenly refer to this paper as "Turing (1937)," perhaps because the volume 42 is 1936–37, covering 1936 and part of 1937, or perhaps because of the two-page minor correction (1937a). Others, such as Kleene (1952, 1981, 1981b), Kleene and Post (1954, 407), Gandy (1980), Cutland (1980), and others, correctly refer to it as "(1936)," or sometimes "(1936–37)." The journal states that Turing's manuscript was "Received 28 May, 1936–Read 12 November, 1936." It appeared in two sections, the first section on pages 230–240 in Volume 42, Part 3, issued on November 30, 1936, and the second section on pages 241–265 in Volume 42, Part 4, issued December 23, 1936. No part of Turing's paper appeared in 1937, but the two page minor correction (1937a) did. Determining the correct date of publication of Turing's work is important to place it chronologically in comparison with Church (1936a), Post (1936), and Kleene (1936).

9.3.3 The Impact of Turing's 1936 Paper

Turing's work was very different from that of Church and from the Herbrand–Gödel recursive functions of Gödel (1934). First, Turing had invented an entirely new formal model, that of an *a*-machine. Consisting of a finite control with a finite number of states and operating on finite strings of 1's and blanks, it gave a mechanical and machine-based view of calculation. It was clear that his *a*-machines were calculable and closely represented how a machine might operate.

Perhaps even more important, Turing gave a compelling argument that all calculable functions are computable by an *a*-machine. Turing began section 9 of the 1936 paper with the following sentences.

No attempt has yet been made to show that the "computable" numbers include all numbers which would naturally be regarded as computable. All arguments which can be given are bound to be, fundamentally, appeals to intuition, and for this reason rather unsatisfactory mathematically. The real question at issue is "What are the possible processes which can be carried out in computing a number?"

Turing went on to analyze how a human being might carry out a calculation, and showed step by step that it can be simulated by an *a*-machine. In this masterful demonstration, which Robin Gandy considered as precise as most mathematical proofs, Turing analyzed the informal nature of functions computable by a finite procedure and demonstrated that they coincide with those computable by an *a*-machine. Gandy (1988, 82) observed, "Turing's analysis does much more than provide an argument for [the thesis,] *it proves a theorem*." Gandy (1988, 83–84) pointed out, "Turing's analysis makes no reference whatsoever to calculating machines. Turing machines appear as a result, a codification, of his analysis of calculations by humans."

Church (1936a) likewise attempted to support his thesis by demonstrating that every effectively calculable function is Herbrand–Gödel recursive. Gandy (1988, 79) and especially Sieg (1994, 80, 87) in their excellent analyses brought out this weakness in Church's argument. Sieg (80) wrote, "… this core does not provide a convincing analysis: steps taken in a calculus must be of a restricted character and they are assumed, for example by Church, without argument to be recursive." Sieg (1994, 78) noted, "It is precisely here that we encounter the major stumbling block for Church's analysis, and that stumbling block was quite clearly seen by Church," who wrote that without this assumption it is difficult to see how the notion of a system of logic can be given any exact meaning at all. It is exactly this stumbling block that Turing overcame by a totally new approach.

Turing's *a*-machine has compelling simplicity and logic, which makes it even today the most convincing model of computability. Equally important with the Turing machine was Turing's analysis of the intuitive conception of a "function produced by a mechanical procedure" and his demonstration that all were computable by an *a*-machine. Turing (1936, 243) introduced the *universal* Turing machine, which has great theoretical and practical importance. Today in mathematics and computer science, Turing machines are the primary formalism for defining computable functions. This is partly due to the machinistic nature of Turing machines, as opposed to recursive functions and arithmetization, but also because of the compelling analysis of calculability given by Turing.

9.3.4 Gödel's Opinion of Turing's Work

Gödel never accepted Church's thesis in definition 9.2, the confluence argument. Gödel was interested in the *intensional* analysis of finite procedure as given by Turing (1936). He had not accepted the argument of confluence as sufficient to justify Church's thesis. Gödel clearly expresses his opinion in his three-volume *Collected Works* (Gödel 1986, 1990, 1995). Let us examine there what Gödel has to say. In the following articles, Gödel considers all these as equivalent formal definitions. The question was whether they captured the *informal* concept of a function specified by a *finite procedure*. The best source for articles from Gödel is these three-volume *Collected Works*, which we have listed in the references by year of publication: Volume I (Gödel 1986); Volume II (Gödel 1990); and Volume III (Gödel 1995).

Gödel's Notes in the **Nachlass**

This article has an introductory note by Martin Davis (Gödel 1995, 156). Davis wrote, "This article is taken from handwritten notes in English, evidently for a lecture, found in the *Nachlass* in a spiral notebook." In the *Nachlass,* or collected papers, printed in Gödel (1995, 166), Gödel wrote,

When I first published my paper about undecidable propositions the result could not be pronounced in this generality, because for the notions of mechanical procedure and of formal system no mathematically satisfactory definition had been given at that time. ... The essential point is to define what a procedure is.

To formally capture this crucial informal concept, Gödel, who was giving an introductory lecture, began with a definition of the primitive recursive functions (which he quickly proved inadequate by a diagonal argument), and then his own Herbrand–Gödel recursive functions on page 167. (Gödel gave the Herbrand–Gödel recursive function definition rather than Turing machines because he knew they were equivalent. He intended his talk to be as elementary as possible for a general audience, which he knew would be more familiar with recursion.) Gödel continued on page 168, "That this really is the correct definition of mechanical computability was established beyond any doubt by Turing." The word "this" evidently refers to the recursive functions. Gödel knew that Turing had never proved anything about recursive functions. What did he mean? Gödel knew that by the work of Turing, Church, and Kleene, the formal classes of Turing computable functions, recursive functions, and λ-definable functions all coincide. Gödel was asserting that it was

Turing who had demonstrated that these formal classes captured the informal notion of a procedure. It was Turing's proof (1936) and the formal equivalences that had elevated Herbrand–Gödel recursive functions to a correct characteristic of effectively calculable functions, not that the Herbrand–Gödel recursive functions had elevated Turing computable functions. Indeed, Gödel had seen Church's thesis 9.2 expressed in terms of Herbrand–Gödel recursive functions, and had rejected it in 1935 and 1936 because he was not sure his own definition had captured the informal concept of procedure.

Gödel had begun with the recursive function as more easily explained to a general audience, but having introduced Turing, Gödel now went forward with Turing's work.

But Turing has shown more. He has shown that the computable functions defined in this way are exactly those for which you can construct a machine with finite number of parts which will do the following thing. If you write down any number $n_1, \dots, n_r$, on a slip of paper and put the slip into the machine and turn the crank then after a finite number of turns the machine will stop and the value of the function for the argument $n_1, \dots, n_r$ will be printed on the paper.

Princeton Bicentennial

To fully understand this article, one should be familiar with Gödel's "Über die Länge von Beweisen" ("On the length of proofs," 1936a; in Gödel 1986, 396–398). Gödel discussed what it means for a function to be computable in a formal system S and remarked that given a sequence of formal systems $S_i, S_{i+1}, \dots$, it is possible that passing from one formal system S_i to one of higher order S_{i+1} not only allows us to prove certain propositions that were not provable before, but also makes it possible to shorten by an extraordinary amount proofs already available.

For Gödel's Princeton bicentennial address (1946), see the *Collected Works*, Volume II (Gödel 1990, 150). Gödel muses on the remarkable fact of the absoluteness of computability, that it is not necessary to distinguish orders (different formal systems). Once we have a sufficiently strong system (such as Peano arithmetic), we can prove anything about computable functions that could be proved in a more powerful system. Once again, Gödel identifies those formal systems known to be equivalent, general recursiveness, Turing computability, and others, as a single formal system.

Tarski has stressed in his lecture (and I think justly) the great importance of the concept of general recursiveness (or Turing's computability). It seems to me that this importance is largely due to the fact that with this concept one has for the first time succeeded in giving an absolute definition of an interesting epistemological notion, *i.e.*, one not depending on the formalism chosen. ... A function of integers is computable in any formal system containing arithmetic if and only if it is computable in arithmetic. ...

In all other cases treated previously, such as demonstrability or definability, one has been able to define them only relative to a given language, and for each individual language it is clear that the one thus obtained is not the one looked for. For the concept of computability, however, although it is merely a special kind of demonstrability or decidability, the situation is different. By a kind of miracle it is not necessary to distinguish orders, and the diagonal procedure does not lead outside the defined notion. (1990, 150)

Gödel stated, *one* has "for the first time succeeded in giving an absolute definition of an interesting epistemological notion." Who is the *"one"* who has linked the informal notion of procedure or effectively calculable function to one of the formal definitions? This becomes irrefutably clear below in the discussion of Gödel's Letter to Kreisel (1968).

The Flaw in Church's Thesis

Gödel was the first to provide one of the formalisms later recognized as a definition of computability, the general recursive functions. However, Gödel himself never claimed to have made this link. Church claimed it in his announcement of Church's thesis in 1935 and 1936, but Gödel did not accept it then and gave no evidence later of believing that Church had done this. Modern scholars found weaknesses in Church's attempted proof (1936a) that the recursive functions constituted all effectively calculable functions.

If the basic steps are stepwise recursive, then it follows easily by the Kleene normal form theorem, which Kleene had proved and communicated to Gödel before November 1935 (see Kleene 1987b, 57), that the entire process is recursive. The fatal weakness in Church's argument was the core assumption that the atomic steps were stepwise recursive, something he did not justify. Gandy (1988, 79) and especially Sieg (1994, 80, 87) in their excellent analyses brought out this weakness in Church's argument. Sieg (80) wrote, "This core does not provide a convincing analysis: steps taken in a calculus must be of a restricted character and they are assumed, for example by Church, without argument to be recursive." Sieg (78) comments, "It is precisely here that we encounter the major stumbling block for Church's analysis, and that stumbling block was quite clearly seen by Church," who wrote that without this assumption it is difficult to see how the notion of a system of logic can be given any exact meaning at all. It is exactly this stumbling block that Turing overcame by a totally new approach.

Gödel on Church's Thesis

Gödel may not have found errors in Church's demonstration, but he never gave any hint that he thought Church had been the first to show that the recursive functions coincided with the effectively calculable ones. On the contrary, Gödel said,

As for previous equivalent definitions of computability, which, however, are much less suitable for our purpose [i.e., verifying the computability thesis], see A. Church 1936a, 256–358. (Gödel 1946, 84; and Gödel 1986, 150–153)

Gödel's Letter to Kreisel

In a letter to Georg Kreisel of May 1, 1968, Gödel wrote:

But I was completely convinced only by Turing's paper. (Sieg 1994, 88)

Gödel, Collected Works, Volume III

In his introduction to this volume, Martin Davis wrote,

On 26 December 1951, at a meeting of the American Mathematical Society at Brown University, Gödel delivered the twenty-fifth Josiah Willard Gibbs Lecture, "Some basic theorems on the foundations of mathematics and their implications." (Gödel 1995, 304–305)

It is probable, as Wang suggests (1987, 117–118), that the lecture was the main project Gödel worked on in the fall of 1951.

In his Gibbs lecture (1951), Gödel wrote,

Research in the foundations of mathematics during the past few decades has produced some results of interest, not only in themselves, but also with regard to their implications for the traditional philosophical problems about the nature of mathematics. The results themselves, I believe, are fairly widely known, but nevertheless I think it will be useful to present them in outline once again, especially in view of the fact that due to the work of various mathematicians, they have taken on a much more satisfactory form than they had had originally. The greatest improvement was made possible through the precise definition of the concept of finite procedure ["equivalent to the concept of a 'computable function of integers'"], which plays a decisive role in these results. There are several different ways of arriving at such a definition, which, however, all lead to exactly the same concept. The most satisfactory way, in my opinion, is that of reducing the concept of a finite procedure to that of a machine with a finite number of parts, as has been done by the British mathematician Turing.

In this one paragraph,

1. Gödel stressed the importance of the results to mathematics and philosophy.

2. Gödel gave full credit to Turing and his "machine with a finite number of parts" for capturing the concept of finite procedure.

3. Gödel never mentions Church or Gödel's own definition of recursive functions.

This is one of the most convincing and explicit demonstrations of Gödel's opinion of Turing's work.

Gödel's Postscriptum, *June 3, 1964, to Gödel (1934)*

In consequence of later advances, in particular of the fact that, due to A. M. Turing's work, a precise and unquestionably adequate definition of the general concept of formal system can now be given, the existence of undecidable arithmetical propositions and the non-demonstrability of the consistency of a system in the same system can now be proved rigorously for *every* consistent formal system containing a certain amount of finitary number theory. (Davis 1965, 71; Gödel 1986, 369–370)

Turing's work gives an analysis of the concept of "mechanical procedure" (alias "algorithm" or "computation procedure" or "finite combinatorial procedure"). This concept is shown to be equivalent with that of a "Turing machine."

9.3.5 Hao Wang Reports on Gödel

Hao Wang was a very close friend and professional colleague of Gödel, whom he called "G" in the following passage. Wang (1987, 96) wrote about Gödel's opinion of Turing's work:

Over the years G habitually credited A. M. Turing's paper of 1936 as the definitive work in capturing the intuitive concept [of computability], and did not mention Church or E. Post in this connection. He must have felt that Turing was the only one who gave persuasive arguments to show the adequacy of the precise concept. ... In particular, he had probably been aware of the arguments offered by Church for his "thesis" and decided that they were inadequate. It is clear that G and Turing (1912–1954) had great admiration for each other.

9.3.6 Kleene's Remarks about Turing

Turing's computability is intrinsically persuasive ... [but] λ-definability is not intrinsically persuasive ... [and] general recursiveness scarcely so (its author Gödel being at the time not at all persuaded).
—Stephen Cole Kleene (1981b, 49)

Turing's machine concept arises from a direct effort to analyze computation procedures as we know them intuitively into elementary operations. Turing argued that repetitions of his elementary operations would suffice for any possible computation.

For this reason, Turing computability suggests the thesis more immediately than the other equivalent notions, and so we choose it for our exposition.
—Stephen Cole Kleene (1967, 233)

9.3.7 Church's Remarks about Turing

[Computability by a Turing machine] has the advantage of making the identification with effectiveness in the ordinary (not explicitly defined) sense evident immediately—i.e., without the necessity of proving preliminary theorems.
—Alonzo Church (1937a), Review of Turing (1936)

In modern times it is sometimes stated as follows, recognizing that Church (1935, 1936a) got it first, but that Turing (1936) got it right, in the opinion of Gödel and many modern scholars.

Definition 9.4   Church–Turing thesis   *A function is intuitively computable if and only if it is computable by a Turing machine, or equivalently if it is specified by a recursive function.*

We strongly believe that it should not be called any of the three (Church's thesis, Turing's thesis, or the Church–Turing thesis) but rather should be called the *computability thesis,* as we argue in sections 9.13 and 9.14, just as the calculus is named for neither of its discoverers, Newton and Leibniz.

9.4   Turing's Oracle Machines

After introducing definitions of computable functions—Turing *a*-machines, recursive functions, and λ-definable functions—the originators continued during 1936–1939 to explore *incomputable* phenomena, rather than computable applications of these devices, which came only a decade or more later. Church and Kleene (1936) as well as Church (1938) and Kleene (1938) studied computable well-orderings and defined recursive ordinals, which were later used to extend the jump operation to the arithmetic hierarchy and beyond to the hyperarithmetic hierarchy up to the first nonrecursive ordinal ω_1^{CK}.

Turing spent 1936–1938 at Princeton working on a PhD with Church. His thesis was completed in 1938 and published in Turing (1939). Church and other mathematicians had found Gödel's incompleteness theorem unsettling. By Gödel's proof, an effective extension T_1 of Peano arithmetic cannot prove its own consistency con_{T_1}. However, we can add the arithmetical statement con_{T_1} to T_1 to get a strictly stronger theory T_2. Continuing, we can get an increasing hierarchy of theories $\{T_\alpha\}_{\alpha \in S}$ over a set S of ordinals. Turing's PhD thesis (1939) concerned such an increasing array of undecidable theories.

9.4.1   Turing Hinted at Oracle Machines

In one of the most important and most obscure parts of all of computability theory, Turing wrote in his ordinal logics paper (1939, section 4) a short statement about oracle machines:

Let us suppose we are supplied with some unspecified means of solving number-theoretic problems; a kind of oracle as it were. … This oracle cannot be a machine.
  With the help of the oracle we could form a new kind of machine (call them *o*-machines), having as one of its fundamental processes that of solving a given number-theoretic problem.

This is virtually all Turing said of oracle machines. His description was only a page long, and half of that was devoted to the unsolvability of related problems, such as whether an o-machine will output an infinite number of 0s or not.

In 1939 Turing left this topic never to return. It mostly lay dormant for five years until it was developed in a beautiful form by Post (1944, 1948), and other papers as we shall explain in section 9.5. Before doing so, we conclude this section with a modern treatment of oracle machines and Turing functionals, including some of the more important properties, even though these were mostly discovered much later, even after Post.

9.4.2   Modern Definitions of Oracle Machines

There are several equivalent ways that a Turing machine with oracle may be defined. We prefer the definition in Soare's book (1987, 46) of a machine with a head which reads the work tape and oracle tape simultaneously, but many other formulations produce the same class of functionals.

Definition 9.5   *A Turing oracle machine (o-machine) is a Turing machine with an extra "read-only" tape, called the oracle tape, upon which is written the characteristic function of some set A (called the oracle), and whose symbols cannot be printed over. The old tape is called the work tape and operates just as before. The reading head moves along both tapes simultaneously. As before, Q is a finite set of states, $S_1 = \{B, 0, 1\}$ is the oracle tape alphabet, $S_2 = \{B, 1\}$ is the work tape alphabet, and $\{R, L\}$ the set of head moving operations right and left. A Turing oracle program $\tilde{P}_e$ is now simply a partial map,*

$$\delta\colon Q \times S_1 \times S_2 \to Q \times S_2 \times \{R, L\},$$

where $\delta(q, a, b) = (p, c, X)$ indicates that the machine in state q reading symbol a on the oracle tape and symbol b on the work tape passes to state p, prints "c" over "b" on the work tape, and moves one space right (left) on both tapes if $X = R$ ($X = L$). The other details are just as previously in Soare (1987). The Turing oracle program $\tilde{P}_e$ takes some oracle A and defines a partial A-computable functional $\Phi_e^A(x) = y$. If the program yields output y while reading only the finite string $\sigma \prec A$, then we write $\Phi_e^\sigma(x) = y$.

Notation

(i) We let lower-case Greek letters φ, ψ represent partial functions from ω to ω and lower case Latin letters f, g, and h represent total functions.

(ii) We let upper-case Greek letters represent partial *functionals* from 2^ω to 2^ω. If $A \subseteq \omega$ then $\Psi^A(x)$ may be defined for some or all x. If $B \subseteq \omega$ we write $\Psi^A = B$ if $\Psi^A(x) = B(x)$ for all $x \in \omega$.

(iii) As in Soare (1987) we use $\{P_e\}_{e \in \omega}$ for an effective listing of Turing programs for Turing a-machines and let φ_e be the partial computable function defined by P_e. We let $\{\tilde{P}_e\}_{e \in \omega}$ be an effective listing of oracle Turing programs, and let Φ_e be the computable partial functional defined by $\tilde{P}_e$. If Φ_e^A is total and computes B, we say B is *computable in A* and write $B \leq_T A$. We refer to φ_e as a partial computable *function* ω to ω because its input and output are integers. On the other hand, Φ_e^A is called a partial computable *functional* because it takes a set A to a set B and is viewed as a map on Cantor Space 2^ω.

(iv) Since Rogers's book (1967), researchers have used $\varphi_e(x)$ or $\{e\}(x)$ for the partial computable function with program P_e. Since about 1970, researchers have used $\Phi_e^A(x)$ for the Turing functional with oracle program $\tilde{P}_e$ and have used $\phi_e^A(x)$ for the *use function,* the maximum element of A examined during the computation. Lachlan also used matched pairs Ψ, ψ, Γ, γ, and so forth for partial computable functionals and their use functions in many papers, and this is the general usage today. There is no confusion between the notation $\varphi_e(x)$ as a partial computable function and $\varphi_e^A(x)$ as a use function for $\Phi_e^A(x)$ because $\varphi_e(x)$ will never have an exponent A and the use function $\varphi_e^A(x)$ always will.

The Graph of a Partial Computable Function

Definition 9.6   *Given a partial computable (p.c.) function φ_e define the graph of φ_e as follows.*

$$g_e = graph(\varphi_e) := \{\langle x,y \rangle : \varphi_e(x) = y\} \tag{9.1}$$

Note that if φ_e is a partial computable (p.c.) function then $graph(\varphi_e)$ is a computable enumerable (c.e.) set. Likewise, given any (c.e.) set W_e we can find a single-valued c.e. subset $V_e \subseteq W_e$ which is the graph of a p.c. function. The notions of a Turing program to compute a p.c. function ψ and a description of its graph are interchangeable and equally powerful in describing ψ.

The Graph of an Oracle Computable Functional

Definition 9.7   *For an oracle machine program $\tilde{P}_e$ we likewise define the oracle graph of the corresponding computable functional Φ_e but now taking into consideration the finite strings read by the oracle head during the computation.*

$$G_e := oracle\ graph(\Phi_e) := \{\langle \sigma, x, y \rangle : \Phi_e^\sigma(x) = y\} \tag{9.2}$$

where σ ranges over $2^{<\omega}$.

Here $\Phi_e^\sigma(x) = y$ denotes that the oracle program $\tilde{P}_e$ with oracle σ on its oracle tape, and x on its input tape, eventually halts and outputs y, and does not read more of the oracle tape than σ during the computation. The crucial property of the oracle graph G_e and the one which makes a Turing functional Φ_e independent of any particular machine representation is the following.

9.4.3   The Oracle Graph Theorem

Theorem 9.1   (oracle graph theorem)   *Let the relation $\Phi_e^\sigma(x) = y$ be defined as in definition 9.5, and G_e be as in (9.2).*

(i) G_e is *single-valued* in the sense that

$$[\,\langle\sigma, x, y\rangle \in G_e \ \& \ \langle\sigma, x, z\rangle \in G_e \,] \quad \Rightarrow \quad y = z \tag{9.3}$$

(ii) G_e is c.e.

(iii) G_e is *monotonic* in the sense that

$$\langle\sigma, x, y\rangle \in G_e \quad \Rightarrow \quad (\forall \tau \succ \sigma)[\,\langle\tau, x, y\rangle \in G_e\,]. \tag{9.4}$$

Proof   (i) This follows by the convention in definition 9.5 (iii) of an o-machine that the machine can give an output only when it enters the halting state q_0 and thereafter it can make no moves or further output on that string and input. Therefore, for every pair (σ, x) there can be at most one y such that $\Phi_e^\sigma(x) = y$.

(ii) Clearly G_e is c.e. because $\langle\sigma, \mathrm{x}, \mathrm{y}\rangle \in G_e$ iff $(\exists s)[\Phi_{e,s}^\sigma(x) = y]$. This is Σ_1^0 and therefore c.e.

(iii) For property (9.4) apply the definition of an o-machine computation. If $\Phi_{e,s}^\sigma(x) = y$ then when the machine produces the output y it enters the halting state q_0, and will never make any more moves on input x. Therefore, for $\tau \succ \sigma$ the machine with τ on the oracle tape must eventually enter q_0 and output y by exactly the same computation, and will never make any more moves.

9.4.4   The Prefix-Free Graph F_e of Turing Functional Φ_e

Definition 9.8   *(i) A set of strings $S \subseteq 2^{<\omega}$ is prefix-free if S is an antichain with respect to the standard partial ordering $\prec$ on strings, i.e.,*

$$(\forall x)(\forall y)(\forall \sigma)(\forall \tau)[[\,\langle\sigma, x, y\rangle \in S \ \& \ \langle\tau, x, y\rangle \in S] \quad \Rightarrow \quad \sigma \mid \tau\,]]. \tag{9.5}$$

(ii) A set of axioms $S \subseteq 2^{<\omega} \times \omega \times \omega$ is prefix-free *if*

$$(\forall x)(\forall y)[\,\{\,\sigma : \langle\sigma, x, y\rangle \in S\,\} \ is \ a \ prefix-free \ set \ of \ strings\,]. \tag{9.6}$$

Of course, the oracle graph G_e cannot be prefix-free because motonicity (9.4) contradicts prefix-free (9.5) and (9.6). However, every functional Φ_e determines a prefix-free graph $F_e \subset G_e$ which we may regard as *basis* for G_e like a basis for a vector space.

Definition 9.9   *Given Φ_e define the prefix-free oracle graph*

$$F_e = \{ \langle \sigma, x, y \rangle : \Phi_e^\sigma(x) = y \quad with\ use \quad \varphi_e^\sigma(x) = |\sigma| \}. \tag{9.7}$$

This is prefix-free because of the next theorem.

Theorem 9.2 (unique use property)   *In (9.7) for every x, y, e, and oracle A there is at most one string $\sigma \prec A$ such that $\langle \sigma, x, y \rangle \in F_e$.*

Proof   The definition 9.9 and (9.7) of F_e means that we compute according to oracle program $\tilde{P}_e$ on input x and oracle A until if ever the machine reaches the halting state q_0 and gives some output y. At this point the machine halts forever. We put into F_e the triple $\langle \sigma, x, y \rangle$ where $\sigma \prec A$ is the amount of the oracle read so far. We cannot also add any $\rho \prec \sigma$ because if the program had halted on ρ it could never have read σ. Likewise, having halted on σ it could never have read any $\tau \succ \sigma$.

Of course, from any prefix-free oracle graph F_e we obtain the full oracle graph G_e by adding $\langle \tau, x, y \rangle$ to G for every $\langle \sigma, x, y \rangle \in F_e$ and $\tau \succ \sigma$, just as we can expand any map on a basis of a vector space to a map on the whole space. The prefix-free graph F_e contains all the essential information about the Turing functional Φ_e and is the key to understanding Turing computability.

9.4.5   Equivalent Definitions of Relative Computability

There are several different formal definitions of relative computability. This includes an oracle machine with a single reading head reading the work tape and oracle tape, or two independent reading heads, or other variations. In addition, several authors define relative computability from oracle A by adding the characteristic function of A either to the Herbrand–Gödel general recursive function definition or to the Kleene μ-recursive function definition. Each of these formal definitions produces a c.e. graph G_e and these definitions are all equivalent.

Furthermore, any Turing a-machine can clearly be simulated by a Turing o-machine as we note in the following theorem. Therefore, in presenting the subject we can bypass a-machines altogether, present o-machines, and then draw a-machines as special cases. This reinforces the claim that it is the o-machine, not the a-machine, which is the central concept of the subject.

Theorem 9.3   *If P_e is a Turing program for a Turing a-machine, then there is a Turing oracle program $\tilde{P}_i$ which on input x and any oracle A produces the same output y.*

Proof Let P_e be a Turing program to compute φ_e. Now P_e consists of a finite partial map which can be identified with a set of 5-tuples,

$$\delta: Q \times S_2 \to Q \times S_2 \times \{R,L\},$$

where Q is a finite set of states, $S_2 = \{B,1\}$ is the work tape alphabet, and $\{R,L\}$ the set of head moving operations right and left. Define an oracle program $\tilde{P}_i$ with transition function

$$\tilde{\delta}: Q \times S_1 \times S_2 \to Q \times S_2 \times \{R,L\},$$

for $S_1 = \{B,0,1\}$ the oracle tape alphabet as follows. For each line in P_e of the form $\delta(q, a) = (p, b, X)$ for $p, q \in Q$ and $a, b \in S_2$, we add to oracle program $\tilde{P}_i$ a line $\tilde{\delta}(q,c,a) = (p,b,X)$ for both $c = 0$ and $c = 1$. Hence, $\tilde{P}_i$ has exactly the same effect on input x as P_e regardless of the oracle A.

Notation for Functions and Functionals

The standard notation is that given above.

Remark *Note that the oracle Turing machine Φ_e is a finite object represented by an oracle program $\tilde{P}_e$ or an oracle graph G_e and has no oracle associated with it, but it can use any oracle A which may be attached. This is analogous to a laptop computer with no active connection to a database which may later be connected to the World Wide Web.*

Recently, some researchers have unfortunately used Φ_e to denote the standard partial computable function φ_e (a type 1 object). This is unwise because it blurs the distinction of types in which φ_e operates on integers (a type 1 object) and Φ_e is a functional on sets or on functions (a type 2 object). Furthermore, sometimes we would like to write Φ_e alone without its exponent A to identify it with $\tilde{P}_e$ or its oracle graph G_e as a finite object, like a laptop computer whose link with the web has temporarily been removed. Doing so clashes with the proposed use of Φ_e as a type 1 object. and leads to confusion with φ_e which is given by a different type of program. The functional Φ_e is defined by a program $\tilde{P}_e$ which is a finite set of 6-tuples operating on sets, while φ_e is defined by P_e a finite set of 5-tuples operating on integers. Furthermore, there is no justification for the necessity of Φ_e to denote φ_e since the current notation φ_e is quite satisfactory. We recommend against using Φ_e to denote φ_e the partial computable function.

9.5   Emil Post Introduces Relative Computability

The spirit of Turing's work was taken up by the American mathematician Emil Post, who had been appointed to a faculty position at City College of New York in 1932.

9.5.1   Post's Work in the 1930s

Post (1936) independently of Turing (but not independently of the work by Church and Kleene in Princeton) had defined a *"finite combinatory process"* which closely resembles a Turing machine. From this it is often and erroneously written (Kleene 1987b, 56; 1981, 61) that Post's contribution here was "essentially the same" as Turing's, but in fact it was much less. Post did not attempt to prove that his formalism coincided with any other formalism, such as general recursiveness, but merely expressed the expectation that this would turn out to be true, while Turing (1937b) proved the Turing computable functions equivalent to the λ-definable ones. Post gave no hint of a universal Turing machine. Most important, Post gave no analysis, as did Turing, of why the intuitively computable functions are computable in his formal system. Post offers only as a "working hypothesis" that his contemplated "wider and wider formulations" are "logically reducible to formulation 1." Lastly, Post, of course, did not prove the unsolvability of the *Entscheidungsproblem* because at the time Post was not aware of Turing's 1936 paper, and Post believed that Church (1936b) had settled the *Entscheidungsproblem*. Furthermore, Post wrote that Church's identification of effective calculability and recursiveness was a working hypothesis which is in "need of continual verification" (1936, 105). This irritated Church, who criticized it in his review (1937b) of Post (1936).

Post's contributions during the 1930s were original and insightful, corresponding in spirit to Turing's more than to Church's, but they were not as influential as those of Church and Turing. It was only during the next phase, from 1940 to 1954, that Post's remarkable influence was fully felt.

9.5.2   Post Fulfills Turing's Promise during 1940–1954

As Turing left the subject of pure computability theory in 1939, his mantle fell on the shoulders of Post. This was the mantle of clarity and intuitive exposition, the mantle of exploring the most basic objects such as computably enumerable sets, and most of all, the mantle of relative computability and Turing reducibility. During the next decade and a half, from 1940 until his death in 1954, Post played an extraordinary role in shaping the subject.

Post (1941, 1943) introduced a *second* and unrelated formalism called a *production* system and (in a restricted form) a *normal* system, which he explained again in (1944). Post's (normal) canonical system is a *generational* system, rather than a *computational* system as in general recursive functions or Turing computable functions, because it gives an algorithm for generating (listing) a set of integers rather than computing a function. This led Post to concentrate on *effectively enumerable sets* rather than computable functions. Post, like Church and Turing, gave a thesis (1943, 201), but stated it in terms of generated sets and production systems, which asserted that "any generated set is a normal set." That is, any effectively enumerable set in the intuitive sense could be produced as a normal set is his formal system. Although he had used other terminology earlier, by the 1940s Post had adopted the Kleene–Church terminology of "recursively enumerable set" for the formal equivalent of Post's effectively enumerable set.

Definition 9.10   Post's thesis (1943, 1944)   *A nonempty set is effectively enumerable (listable in the intuitive sense) iff it is recursively enumerable (the range of a recursive function) or equivalently iff it is generated by a (normal) production system.*

Post showed that every recursively enumerable set (one formally generated by a recursive function) is a normal set (one derived in his normal canonical system) and conversely. Therefore, normal sets are formally equivalent to recursively enumerable sets. Since recursively enumerable sets are equidefinable with partial computable functions, this definition of normal set gives a new formal definition of computability that is formally equivalent to the definitions of Church or Turing. (Equidefinable here means that from the definition of a partial computable function we can derive a c.e. set as its range, and from the definition of a c.e. set one can find a single valued c.e. subset which is the graph of a partial computable function.) Post's thesis is equivalent to Turing's thesis.

Post used the terms "effectively enumerable set" and "generated set" almost interchangeably, particularly for sets of positive integers. Post (1944, 285), like Church (1936a), defined a set of positive integers to be *recursively enumerable* if it is the range of a recursive function and then stated, "The corresponding intuitive concept is that of an *effectively enumerable* set of positive integers." (This is Church's [1936a] terminology also). Post explained his informal concept of a "generated set" of positive integers this way:

Suffice it to say that each element of the set is at some time written down, and earmarked as belonging to the set, as a result of predetermined effective processes. It is understood that once an element is placed in the set, it stays there. (1944, 286)

Post then restated Post's thesis 9.10 in the succinct form,

[E]very generated set of positive integers is recursively enumerable. (1944, 286)

He remarked that "this may be resolved into the two statements: every generated set is effectively enumerable, every effectively enumerable set of positive integers is recursively enumerable." Post continued, "Their converses are immediately seen to be true." Post's concentration on *c.e. sets* rather than partial computable *functions* may be even more fundamental than the thesis of Church and Turing characterizing computable functions because Sacks (1990) has remarked that often in higher computability theory it is more convenient to take the notion of a generalized c.e. set as basic and to derive generalized computable functions as those whose graphs are generalized computably enumerable.

9.5.3 Post's Problem on Incomplete C.E. Sets

Post's most influential achievement during this period was the extraordinarily clear and intuitive paper, "Recursively enumerable sets of positive integers and their decision problems" (1944). Post defined the notion of one set to be *reducible* to another and introduced the term *degree of unsolvability* (1948) for the equivalence class of all sets mutually reducible to one another.

Post's paper (1944) revealed with intuition and great appeal the significance of the computably enumerable sets and the importance of Gödel's incompleteness theorem. Post called Gödel's diagonal set,

$$K = \{e: e \in W_e\}$$

the *complete set* because every c.e. set W_e is computable in K ($W_e \leq_T K$). The set K has the same degree as the halting problem of whether a Turing machine with program P_e halts on a given input x. Moreover, Post felt that the creative property of K revealed the inherent creativeness of the mathematical process. Post posed his famous "Post's problem" of whether there exists a computably enumerable (c.e.) set A such that $\varnothing <_T A <_T K$.

9.5.4 Post Began With Strong Reducibilities

In 1944 researchers did not understand Turing reducibility, even as little as is presented above in section 9.4. Post himself was struggling to understand it, and did not explicitly discuss it until the very end of his paper, and even then only in general terms.

Post's contributions from 1943 to 1954 concerning relative computability are remarkable. First, Post resurrected the concept of oracle machines (1944), which had been buried in Turing's 1939 paper and which other researchers had apparently ignored for five years. Second, Post defined a sequence of strong reducibilities to better understand the concept of a set B being reducible to a set A.

Along with these strong reducibilities, Post defined families of c.e. sets with thin complements, simple, hyper-simple, hyper-hypersimple, in an attempt to find an incomplete set for these reducibilities. These concepts have pervaded the literature and proved useful and interesting, but they did not lead to a solution of Post's problem. Post was able to exhibit incomplete incomputable c.e. sets for several of these stronger reducibilities, but not for Turing reducibility. Post's problem stimulated a great deal of research in the field and had considerable influence.

Slowly Post's understanding deepened of the general case of one set B being reducible (Turing-reducible) to another set A. Post steadily continued gaining a deeper and deeper understanding from 1943 to 1954 until he had brought it to full development. Our modern understanding of relative computability and Turing functionals is due more to Post and his patient and persistent efforts over more than a decade, than it is due to the brief remark by Turing (1939).

When Post wrote his famous paper (1944), Turing's notion of relative computability from an oracle discussed in section 9.4.1 had been mostly ignored. It was only at the end of Post's 1944 paper, in the last section—section 11, "General (Turing) Reducibility"—that Post defined and named for the first time "Turing Reducibility," denoted $B \leq_{\mathrm{T}} A$, and began to discuss it in intuitive terms. Post's four and a half page discussion there is the most revealing introduction to effective reducibility of one set from another. In the same crisp, intuitive style as in the rest of the paper, Post described the manner in which the decision problem for one set S_1 could be reduced to that of a second set S_2. Post wrote it for a c.e. set S_2 in studying Post's problem, but the analysis holds for any set S_2.

9.5.5 Post Explicitly Describes Turing Reducibility

In the 1944 paper (section 11), Post wrote:

Now suppose instead, says Turing [1939] in effect, this situation obtains with the following modification. That at certain times the otherwise machine determined process raises the question is a certain positive integer in a given recursively enumerable set S_2 of positive integers, and that the machine is so constructed that were the correct answer to this question supplied on every occasion that arises, the process would automatically continue to its eventual correct conclusion. We could then say that the machine effectively reduces the decision problem of S_1 to that of S_2. Intuitively, this would correspond to the most general concept of reducibility of S_1 to S_2. For the very concept of the decision problem of S_2 merely involves the answering for an arbitrarily given single positive integer m of the question is m in S_2; and in a finite time but a finite number of such questions can be asked. A corresponding formulation of "Turing reducibility" should then be the same degree of generality for effective reducibility as say general recursive function is for effective calculability.

9.5.6 The Post–Turing Thesis

Post's statement may be restated in succinct modern terms and incorporates the statement implicit in Turing (1939, section 4) in the following extension of Turing's first thesis 9.3 and Post's first thesis 9.10.

Definition 9.11   Post–Turing thesis (Turing 1939, section 4; Post 1944, section 11)   *One set B is effectively reducible to another set A iff B is* Turing reducible *to A by a Turing oracle machine (*$B \leq_{\mathrm{T}} A$*).*

Turing's brief introduction of oracles did not state this as a formal thesis, but it is partly implied by his presentation. Kleene (1952) calls it "Thesis I*" as we shall see. Post makes it explicit and claims that this is the formal equivalent of the intuitive notion of *effectively reducible,* a step as significant as the Church–Turing character-ization of "effectively calculable." If we identify a Turing reduction Φ_e with its graph G_e both informally and formally, then the Post–Turing thesis is equivalent to Post's thesis 9.10 (because G_e is c.e.), which is equivalent to Turing's thesis 9.3.

However, there has been little analysis (along the lines of the extensive analysis of the Church–Turing thesis 9.4 for unrelativized computations) of what constitutes a relative computation of B from A. This is surprising, because the Post–Turing thesis was stated clearly in Post (1944). It is even more surprising because relative comput-ability is used much more often than ordinary computability in the theory of com-putability, applications of computability to other areas such as algebra, analysis, model theory, algorithmic complexity and many more. Also interactive or online computing in the real world is more common than batch processing or offline com-puting, using processes contained entirely inside the machine.

9.6   The Art of Classical Computability

9.6.1   Classical Computability Theory

Classical computability theory is the theory of functions on the integers which are computable by a finite algorithm. This includes the recursive functions of Gödel (1934), and the Turing machines presented in Turing (1936), the λ-definable func-tions of Church and Kleene, and many more. It includes the advances of comput-ability in the 1930s and 1940s by Church, Kleene, and Post, and later developments by other researchers. Turing (1939, section 4) very briefly suggested the concept of an *oracle Turing machine (o-machine)*. Post (1944) developed this into *Turing reduc-ibility (Turing computability)* of a set B from a set A (written $B \leq_{\mathrm{T}} A$) if a Turing machine with A on its oracle tape can compute B. This is a central idea of classical computability theory because it enables us to classify the *information content* of a set, or a formal theory, a model, or an algebraic object.

9.6.2   The Art of Computability

Mathematics is an art as well as a science, and an "art" in two senses. First, "art" means a *skill* or craft which can be acquired and honed by practice. For example, Donald Knuth wrote *The Art of Computer Programming,* a comprehensive mono-graph in several volumes on programming algorithms and their analysis. Second, we develop the art of computability as an *artistic endeavor*, with an appreciation of its mathematical beauty. It is not enough to state a valid theorem with a correct proof. We must see a sense of beauty in how it relates to what came before, what will come after, the definitions, why it is the right theorem, with the right proof, in the right place.

One of the most famous art treasures in the world is Michelangelo's statue of David as a young man before he faces Goliath, displayed in the Accademia Gallery in Florence and carved from pure Carrara marble. There is a long aisle to approach the statue of David. The aisle is flanked with the statues of Michelangelo's unfinished slaves struggling as if to emerge from the block of marble. These figures reveal Michelangelo's work process. There are practically no details, and yet they possess a weight and power beyond their physical proportions. Michelangelo thought of himself, not as carving a statue, but as seeing clearly the figure within the marble and then chipping away the marble to release it. The unfinished slaves are perhaps a more revealing example of this talent than the finished statue of David.

Similarly, it was Alan Turing (1936, 1939) who saw the figure of computability in the marble more clearly than anyone else. Finding a formal definition for effectively calculable functions was the first step, but *demonstrating* that it captured computability was as much an artistic problem as a purely mathematical one. Gödel himself had expressed doubt that it would be possible to do so. What is an effective process and how do we make it precise? The other researchers thought in terms of mathematical formalisms like recursive functions, λ-definable functions, and arithmetization of syntax. It was Turing who saw the computer itself in the marble, a simple intuitive device equipped with only a finite program and using only a finite sequence of strokes at each stage in a finite computation, the vision closest to our modern computer. Even more remarkable, Turing saw how to demonstrate that this mechanical device captured *all* effectively calculable processes. Gödel immediately recognized this achievement in Turing and in no one else.

9.7 The Great Papers of Computability

9.7.1 The Great Books Program

During the 1930s, educators suggested that college students should read the great books of Western culture in the original. At the University of Chicago the principal proponents were President Robert Maynard Hutchins and his colleague Professor Mortimer Adler. The curriculum relied on primary sources as much as possible and a discussion under the supervision of a professor. For decades the Great Books program became a hallmark of a University of Chicago education.

9.7.2 Two Great Papers of Computability

In the first two decades of computability theory, from 1930 to 1950, the primary sources were papers, not books. Most were reprinted in the book by Martin Davis, *The Undecidable: Basic Papers on Undecidable Propositions, Unsolvable Problems, and Computable Functions* (1965). Of course, all of these papers are important, shaped the subject, and should be read by the serious scholar. However, many of these papers are written in a complicated mathematical style which is difficult for a beginner to comprehend. Nevertheless, at least two of these papers are of fundamental importance and are easily accessible to a beginning student. My criteria for selecting these papers are the following.

1. The paper must have introduced and developed a topic of fundamental importance to computability.

2. The topic and its development must be as important today as then.

3. The paper must be written in a clear, informal style, so appealing that any beginning student will enjoy reading it.

There are two papers in computability that meet these criteria.

9.7.3   Turing (1936), Especially Section 9

Turing's 1936 paper is probably the single most important paper in computability. It introduces the Turing machine, the universal machine, and demonstrates the existence of undecidable problems. It is most often used in mathematics and computer science to define computable functions. It is perhaps Turing's best-known and most influential paper.

I am especially recommending section 9, "The extent of the computable numbers," in Turing (1936, 249–254). Here Turing gives a demonstration that the numbers computable by a Turing machine "include all numbers which would naturally be regarded as computable." This is a brilliant demonstration and is necessary for the argument. Without it we do not know that we have diagonalized against *all* potential decidable procedures and therefore we have no undecidable problems. Books on computability rarely give this demonstration even though it is critical, perhaps because of its nonmathematical nature. Every student of computability should read this very short section.

9.7.4   Post (1944), Especially Section 11

Turing (1939) very briefly introduced the notion of an "oracle machine" a Turing machine which could consult an oracle tape (database) but did not develop the idea. In his 1944 paper, "Recursively enumerable sets of positive integers and their decision problems," Emil Post developed two crucial ideas, the structure and information content of computably enumerable (c.e.) sets, and the notion of a set B being *reducible* to another set A.

Turing (1939) never thought of his oracle machine as a device for reducing one set to another. It was simply a local machine interacting with an external database as a laptop might query the Internet. Post was the first to turn the oracle machines into a reducibility of a set B to a set A, written $B \leq_T A$, which Post generously called *Turing reducibility*. Post's entire paper is wonderfully written and easily accessible to a beginner. He begins with simpler reducibilities such as many-one and truth-table and works up to Turing reducibility, which was not understood at the time.

I recommend especially the last section, 11, "General (Turing) reducibility." Post explores informally the idea of a c.e. set S_1 being Turing reducible to another c.e. set S_2. For the next decade Post continued to develop the notions of Turing reducibility and information content. He gave his notes to Kleene before his death in 1954. Kleene revised them and published Kleene–Post (1954), introducing a finite forcing argument as in chapter 6 of Soare (1987) to define Turing incomparable sets each Turing computable in K.

These two notions, computability by a Turing machine in Turing (1936), and reducibility of one set B to another set A in Post (1944), are probably the two most important ideas in computability. The other excellent computability papers in Martin Davis (1965) will be more accessible after a first course in computability.

9.8   Online Computing

The original implementations of computing devices were generally offline devices, such as calculators or batch-processing devices. However, in recent years, the implementations have been increasingly online computing devices that can access or interact with some external database or other device. The Turing o-machine is a better model to study them because the Turing a-machine lacks this online capacity.

Definition 9.12

(i) An online or interactive computing process is one which interacts with its environment, for example a computer communicating with an external database such at the World Wide Web.

(ii) An offline computing process is one which begins with a program and input data, and proceeds internally, not interacting with any external device. This includes a calculator, and batch processing devices where a user handed a deck of punched IBM cards to an operator, who fed them to the computer and produced paper output later.

There are many descriptions in the computing literature about online and interactive processes. In Goldin, Smolka, and Wegner (2006), a chapter by Yuri Gurevich, "Interactive Algorithms 2005," is described,

In this chapter, Gurevich asserts that computer science is largely about algorithms, and broadens the notion of algorithms to include interaction by allowing intra-step interaction of an algorithm with its environment.

About the chapter "A Theory of Interactive Computation," by Jan van Leeuwen and Jiri Wiedermann, the book states,

This chapter asks what a computational theory of interactive, evolving programs should look like. The authors point out that a theory of interactive computation must necessarily lead beyond the classical, finitary models of computation. A simple model of interactive computing is presented consisting of one component and an environment, interacting using single streams of input and output signals.

It appears that the Turing o-machine is a good theoretical model to analyze an interactive process because there is usually a fixed algorithm or procedure at the core, which by Turing's thesis we can identify with a Turing a-machine, and there is a mechanism for the process to communicate with its environment, which when coded into integers may be regarded as a Turing type oracle. Under the Post–Turing thesis 9.11, these real world online or interactive processes can be described by a Turing oracle machine.

In real world computing the oracle may be called a *database* or an environment. A laptop obtaining data from the World Wide Web is a good example. In the real world the database would not be literally infinite but may appear so (like the web) and is usually too large to be conveniently downloaded into the local computer. Sometimes the local computer is called the "client" and the remote device the "server."

9.8.1 Turing Machines and Online Processes

We could continue analyzing to what extent Turing oracle machines can model modern online processes, but let us now examine the reverse direction, that o-machines are online while a-machines are not. The following points appear self-evident.

• Turing oracle machines are online. An o-machine has a fixed program but has the capacity to interact with its environment and receive new data during its computation.

• The original Turing a-machines are not online. A Turing a-machine, even a universal machine, begins with a fixed program and fixed input and proceeds without further outside input until (if ever) it halts.

• A large number and rapidly increasing number of computing processes in the real world are online or interactive. See the authors in Goldin, Smolka, and Wegner (2006) for only a few.

• A large number of books presenting an introduction to computability mention Turing oracle machines and relative computability very late in the book or not at all.

• A large number of books with articles on Turing and the Church–Turing thesis do not mention Turing oracle machines or relative computability at all; for example, Teuscher (2004).

Discussing *only* Turing *a*-machines in modern texts, or *only* the Church–Turing thesis, and not the Post–Turing thesis on oracle computers, is like discussing only batch-processing machines of the 1950s long after the emergence of online computing.

9.8.2 Trial and Error Computing

We expect Turing *a*-machines and *o*-machines to be absolutely correct. However, there are many computing processes in the real world which give a sequence of approximations to the final answer. Turing considered machines which make mistakes. In his talk to the London Mathematical Society on February 20, 1947 (quoted in Hodges 1983, 360–361), Turing said,

I would say that fair play must be given to the machine. Instead of it sometimes giving no answer we could arrange that it gives occasional wrong answers. But the human mathematician would likewise make blunders when trying out new techniques. It is easy for us to regard these blunders as not counting and give him another chance, but the machine would probably be allowed no mercy. In other words if a machine is expected to be infallible, it cannot also be intelligent. There are several theorems which say exactly that. But these theorems say nothing about how much intelligence may be displayed if a machine makes no pretence at infallibility.

Hillary Putnam (1965) described *trial and error* predicates as ones for which there is a computable function which arrives at the correct answer after a finite number of mistakes. In modern terminology this is called a *limit computable* function as described in Soare (in press) or Soare (1987, chapter 3). This is a model for many processes in the real world which allow finitely many mistakes but gradually move closer to the correct answer.

9.8.3 The Limit Lemma

There are several different approaches for computing with finitely many errors.

Definition 9.13
(i) A set A is limit computable if there is a computable sequence $\{A_s\}_{s\in\omega}$ such that for all x,

$$A(x) = \lim_s A_s(x). \tag{9.8}$$

By the limit lemma 9.1 (ii), we call $\{A_s\}_{s\in\omega}$ a Δ_2-*approximation* for A.

*(ii) Given $\{A_s\}_{s\in\omega}$, any function $m(x)$ is a *modulus (of convergence)* if*

$$(\forall x)(\forall s \geq m(x))[\, A\!\restriction\! x = A_s\!\restriction\! x\,]. \tag{9.9}$$

We define the *least (modulus) function*

$$m_A(x) = (\mu s)[\, A \! \upharpoonright x = A_s \! \upharpoonright x \,]. \tag{9.10}$$

This may or may not be a modulus in the sense of (9) for a Δ_2-sequence but is a modulus for a Σ_1^0-sequence.

(iii) If A is c.e. then a computable sequence $\{A_s\}_{s \in \omega}$ is a Σ_1^0-*approximation* to A if $A = \cup_s A_s$ and $A_s \subseteq A_{s+1}$. In this case $m_A(x)$ is a modulus and is called the *least modulus*.

The following three properties are used very often and completely interchangeably without explanation. Some authors introduce the property of limit computable as above, but use the *name* Δ_2^0 for it. It is not correct to *define* a set A to be Δ_2^0 if it has the limit computable property. However, after proving the equivalence of the three properties in the limit lemma 9.1 authors often mention one term (such as A is Δ_2^0 or $A \leq_T \varnothing'$) and then immediately use another property, such as A limit computable, without explanation. Shoenfield (1959) proved the equivalence of (i) and (iii). The equivalence of (ii) follows from Post's Theorem, which asserts the equivalence of (ii) and (iii).

Lemma 9.1   Limit Lemma, Shoenfield, 1959   *The following are equivalent:*

(i) A is limit computable;

(ii) $A \in \Delta_2$;

(iii) $A \leq_T \varnothing'$.

Proof   (i) $\Rightarrow$ (ii). Let $A = \lim_s A_s(x)$ with $\{A_s\}_{s \in \omega}$ computable. Then

$$x \in A \iff (\exists s)(\forall t)[\, t > s \implies A_t(x) = 1 \,]$$
$$x \in \bar{A} \iff (\exists s)(\forall t)[\, t > s \implies A_t(x) = 0 \,]$$

and therefore, $A \in \Sigma_2$ and $\bar{A} \in \Sigma_2$.

(ii) $\Rightarrow$ (iii). Assume there are computable relations R and S such that

$$x \in A \iff (\exists s)(\forall t)R(x,s,t) \qquad \& \qquad x \in \bar{A} \iff (\exists s)(\forall t)S(x,s,t).$$

The predicate $(\forall t)R(x,s,t)$ is Π_1^0 and therefore computable in $\varnothing'$. Hence, the predicate $(\exists s)(\forall t)R(x,s,t)$ is Σ_1 in $\varnothing'$ and therefore c.e. in $\varnothing'$ and likewise $(\exists s)(\forall t)S(x,s,t)$. Therefore, A and $\bar{A}$ are each c.e. in $\varnothing'$. Thus, $A \leq_T \varnothing'$.

(iii) $\Rightarrow$ (i). Fix a computable sequence $\{K_s\}_{s \in \omega}$ with $\cup_s K_s = K \equiv \varnothing'$. Assume $A = \Phi_e^K$. For every x and s define

$$f(x,s) = \begin{cases} \Phi_{e,s}^{K_s}(x) & \textit{if defined;} \\ 0 & \textit{otherwise} \end{cases}$$

For every x the first clause holds for all but finitely many s. Therefore, $A(x) = \lim_s f(x,s)$.

9.8.4 Real World Computing

Now in the real world imagine an example of a computing process with error such as: a robot learning a maze; a financial trader receiving information from around the world updated every second; a meteorologist predicting the weather a week from now given constantly updated weather conditions today. In our idealized model we assume that the individual makes finitely many errors during the process $\{B_t\}_{t \in T}$ for time periods $t \in T$ but eventually gets the correct answer. (In practice, the final answer may not be exactly correct in these examples, but is presumably more accurate than the first approximation B_0. The sequences of improving approximations, even if not exact, are usually useful in financial trading, meteorology, and other approximations in real time.)

9.8.5 Two Models for Computing with Error

The Limit Computable Model with No Oracle

In the limit-computable or approximation model we have a sequence of Turing programs $\{P_t : t \in T\}$ so that P_t computes function g_t at time $t \in T$. There is not necessarily any connection between different programs and we may have to compute all over again with a new program as we pass from time t to $t + 1$.

Suppose the financial trader in Chicago receives data every second $t \in T$ about currency prices in London, Milan, New York, and Tokyo. The configuration at his trading desk may be described using the Limit Lemma by a computable function where g_t is the computable characteristic function of B_t, the configuration of his computation at the end of time t. The computable function g_t gives an algorithm to compute the condition B_t at time t but it gives no relationship between B_t and B_{t+1}. It will not be possible for the trader to write a new program every second. How will the trader write a program to uniformly compute the index g_t for $t \in T$?

The Online Model with an Oracle Machine

By the limit lemma there is a c.e. set A (or even a Δ_2^0 set) and oracle machine Φ_e such that $B = \Phi_e^A$. Now the trader can program the algorithm Φ_e into his laptop once and for all at the start of the trading day. Every second $t \in T$ he receives from New York and abroad the latest quotes A_t which enter directly into his computer by an Internet connection. He does not (and cannot) change the program Φ_e every second.

His algorithm simply receives the "oracle" information A_t from the Internet as it is continually updated, and computes the approximation $B_t(x) = \Phi_e^{A_t}(x)$. His program then executes a trade when the algorithm determines that conditions are favorable. It is difficult to see how this trader could have carried out his business using a batch processing, Turing a-machine model, instead of an online model.

9.9   Three Displacements in Computability Theory

The dictionary defines *displacement* to be the moving of something from its rightful place or position, often when replaced by something else. There are three important issues in computability which have at one time been displaced from their correct or proper positions as evaluated by historical and scientific criteria. These issues are at the very heart of the subject and they define how we think about computability. We now examine these three issues one by one in the next three sections. These items may have been displaced accidentally or without conscious thought or decision, simply acting from the exigencies of the situation at the time, but are not consistent with a careful scientific analysis later.

When computability theory originated in the 1930s, it was a very small field attempting to consolidate its ideas. Furthermore, three of its leaders, Gödel, Turing, and Church, effectively left the field after 1940 and had little direct influence thereafter on its development, although Church supervised the PhD theses of many prominent researchers in the field. After 1940 the field was developed and promulgated primarily by Stephen C. Kleene, with some additional influence by Emil Post as described earlier. In dedicating his book *Degrees of Unsolvability* (1971), Shoenfield recognized Kleene's overwhelming influence:

Dedicated to S. C. Kleene, who made recursive function theory into a theory.

This is entirely accurate, and without Kleene's leadership we would not have the field as we know it today. However, a number of changes took place after 1940, perhaps by accident, that were not consistent with the original development of computability in the 1930s and would not have been approved of by Gödel and Turing.

9.10   Displacement 1: "Recursive" = "Computable"

Starting in 1936, Church and Kleene used the term "recursive" to mean "computable," even though Turing and Gödel later objected. Kleene later introduced the term "recursive function theory" for the subject although Gödel disagreed (see below). This was the first time in history that the term "recursive" which had meant roughly "inductive" acquired the additional meaning "computable" of "calculable." After 1996 the term 'recursive" was again used only to mean "inductive" not "computable" or "calculable." From 1931 to 1934, Church and Kleene had used the λ-definable functions as the formal equivalent of effectively calculable functions, and Church had first proposed his thesis privately to Gödel in that form.

9.10.1 Church Defends His Thesis with "Recursive"

Recall Church's thesis 9.1 (first version, 1934): "A function is effectively calculable if and only if it is λ-definable." When Gödel strongly objected to this thesis, Church turned instead to Gödel's own Herbrand–Gödel general recursive functions as a formalism and proposed in the papers of 1935 and 1936 the well-known form of his thesis, Church's thesis 9.2 (1936a): A function on the positive integers is effectively calculable if and only if it is recursive.

Church and Kleene knew almost immediately, and published by 1936, the proof of the formal equivalence of recursive functions with λ-definable functions. After seeing Gödel's lectures in 1934, Church and Kleene dropped the λ-definable functions and adopted the recursive functions. This was not because of the inadequacy of λ-definable functions in comparison to the recursive functions. Indeed, Church seems to have preferred the λ-definable functions and caused Turing to write his thesis (1939) in that formalism.

Church was very eager for mathematicians to accept his thesis and he knew that the recursive functions were more familiar to a mathematical audience than λ-definable ones. Church and Kleene used the second version of Church's thesis above, phrased in terms of recursive functions, primarily for *public relations* as Kleene (1981a] explained: "I myself, perhaps unduly influenced by rather chilly receptions from audiences around 1933–35 to disquisitions on λ-definability, chose, after general recursiveness had appeared, to put my work in that format." Church and Kleene were simply doing what most scientists do, arrange the work in a framework which will be understandable and appealing to as large a scientific audience as possible. Ironically, this is exactly what caused the change in 1996 from "recursive" back to "computable," because in 1996 the term "computable" was much better understood by a general audience than "recursive." The irony is that the term "computable" was there all along and was preferred by Turing and Gödel.

9.10.2 Church and Kleene Define "Recursive" as "Computable"

By 1936, Kleene and Church had begun thinking of the word "recursive" to mean "computable." Church had seen his first thesis rejected by Gödel and was heavily invested in the acceptance of his 1936 thesis in terms of recursive functions. Without the acceptance of this thesis, Church had no unsolvable problem. Church wrote in

(1936a, 96; in Davis 1965) that a *"recursively enumerable set"* is one which is the range of a recursive function. This is apparently the first appearance of the term "recursively enumerable" in the literature and the first appearance of "recursively" as an adverb meaning "effectively" or "computably."

In the same year Kleene (1936a, 238; in Davis 1965, 238) mentioned a *"recursive enumeration"* and noted that there is no recursive enumeration of Herbrand–Gödel systems of equations that gives only the systems which define the (total) recursive functions. By a "recursive enumeration" Kleene states that he means "a recursive sequence (*i.e.*, the successive values of a recursive function of one variable)." Post (1944), under the influence of Church and Kleene, adopted this terminology of "recursive" and "recursively enumerable" over his own terminology (1943, 1944) of "effectively generated set," "normal set," "generated set." Thereafter, it was firmly established.

9.10.3   Gödel Rejects "Recursive Function Theory"

Neither Turing nor Gödel ever used the word "recursive" to mean "computable." Gödel *never* used the term "recursive function theory" to name the subject; when others did Gödel reacted negatively, as related by Martin Davis.

In a discussion with Gödel at the Institute for Advanced Study in Princeton about 1952–54, Martin Davis casually used the term "recursive function theory" as it was used then. Davis related, "To my surprise, Gödel reacted sharply, saying that the term in question should be used with reference to the kind of work Rosza Péter did."

(See Péter's work on recursions in Péter 1934, 1951.) By 1990, the situation had become very difficult. Most people had access to a personal computer on their desks and the terms of computing were familiar to the general population, but "recursive" was limited to very small number who mainly associated it with a first-year programming course or a definition by induction on mathematics, and almost never with computability. So few people understood the meaning of "recursive" that by 1990 I had to begin my papers with, "Let f be a recursive function (that is, a computable function)," as if I were writing in Chinese and translating back into English.

9.10.4   The Ambiguity in the Term "Recursive"

The traditional meaning of "recursive" as "inductive" led to ambiguity. Kleene often wrote of calculation and algorithms dating back to the Babylonians, the Greeks, and other early civilizations. However, Kleene (1981b, 44) wrote, "I think we can say that recursive function theory was born there ninety-two years ago with Dedekind's Theorem 126 ('Satz der Definition durch Induktion') that functions can be defined by primitive recursion."

Did he mean that recursion and inductive definition began with Dedekind or that computability and algorithms began there? The latter would contradict his several other statements, such as Kleene (1988, 19) where he wrote, "The recognition of algorithms goes back at least to Euclid (c. 330 B.C.)." When one uses a term like "recursive" to also mean "computable" or "algorithmic" as Kleene did, then one is never sure whether a particular instance means "calculable" or "inductive" and our language has become indistinct. Returning "recursive" to its original meaning of "inductive" has made its use much clearer. We do not need another word to mean "computable." We already have one.

9.10.5   Changing "Recursive" Back to "Inductive"

By 1996 the confusion had become intolerable. I wrote an article on "Computability and Recursion" for the *Bulletin of Symbolic Logic* (1996) on the history and scientific reasons for why we should use "computable" and not "recursive" to mean "calculable." "Recursive" should mean "inductive" as it had for Dedekind and Hilbert. At first few were willing to make such a dramatic change, overturning a sixty-year-old tradition of Kleene, and the words "computability theory" and "computably enumerable (c.e.) set" did not come tripping from the lips. However, in a few months more people were convinced by the undeniable logic of the situation. Three years later at the American Mathematical Society conference in Boulder, Colorado, referenced in Soare (2000), most researchers, especially those under forty years old, had adopted the new terminology and conventions. Changing back from "recursive" to "computable" during 1996–1999 has had a number of advantages.

Historical Accuracy

The founders of the two key models of computability, Turing and Gödel, had never used "recursive" to mean computable and indeed had objected when it was so used. The object of everyone was to formally capture the informal concept of "effectively calculable" which Turing machines did to Gödel's satisfaction, while at first Gödel's own model of Herbrand–Gödel recursive functions did not. The object was never to understand the notion of recursions or inductive definitions. In 1935 Church adopted Gödel's recursive functions as a definition of effectively calculable before seeing Turing machines As Kleene relates, Church and Kleene did this as a matter of public relations to relate to a concept mathematicians could understand, not in an attempt to better understand the nature of recursion and inductive definition.

Scientific Accuracy

The words "calculate" and "compute" are very close in the dictionary, the former being a bit more general. The word "recursive" means a procedure characterized by recurrence or repetition from the Latin verb *recurrere*, to run back. The word has nothing to do with "calculate" or "compute." The general public understands the first two words in this context. To the extent that they have any idea about "recursive" they understand it in this context. For example, a first-year programming course speaks of definition by iteration versus definition by recursion.

Name Recognition

Suppose a student is scanning a catalog for a course to take and sees the course title "recursive function theory" versus "computability theory." Which will give him more information about the content of the course? Should a fresh PhD apply for jobs under the general area of his work as the first or second? Should a professor write an abstract for his lecture at another university under the first title or second?

Names do matter. They mattered to Church and Kleene in 1936 when they changed from the term "λ-definable function" to "recursive function" to achieve greater name recognition among mathematicians and to make Church's thesis more convincing before the appearance of Turing. Names matter today as we try to relate our specialty of computability to the world of computers and algorithmic procedures all around us, a world partially created by Turing.

9.11   Displacement 2: Church's vs. Turing's Thesis

9.11.1   Kleene Called it "Thesis I" in 1943

In the 1930s, both Church and Turing thought they were giving definitions of an effectively calculable function, not putting forth a "thesis." These were not even called "theses" at all until Kleene (1943, 60) referred to Church's "definition" as "Thesis I."

9.11.2   Kleene Named It "Church's Thesis" in 1952

Later in his very influential book (1952), it is fascinating to see how Kleene's thinking and terminology progressed from "Thesis I" to "Church's thesis" and not to "Turing's thesis" or the "Church–Turing thesis." Kleene (1952, 300) took up where Kleene (1943) had left off:

This heuristic evidence and other considerations led Church 1936a to propose the following thesis.

Thesis I. Every effectively calculable function (effectively decidable predicate) is general recursive.

This is identical with what we previously called Church's thesis 9.2. Of course, Kleene was aware of other similar "theses" advanced nearly simultaneously, and he continued (1952, 300), "This thesis is also implicit in the conception of a computing machine formulated by Turing 1936–7 and Post 1936."

Next Kleene begins a subtle shift of terminology from "Thesis I" to "Church's thesis." Apparently he did not feel it necessary to include Turing's name when he used the term "Church's thesis." Kleene began a new section, 62, and called it "Church's thesis" instead of "Thesis I" as he had been doing (1952, 317). Kleene wrote, "section 62. Church's thesis. One of the main objectives of this and the next chapter is to present the evidence for Church's thesis (Thesis I) section 60."

9.11.3   Kleene Dropped "Thesis I" for "Church's Thesis"

As Kleene progressed through (1952, section 62, 318–319), he dropped any reference to "Thesis I" and used only "Church's thesis" with no mention of Turing or Post in the thesis. He wrote (1952, 318–319),

Church's thesis, by supplying a precise delimitation of all effectively calculable functions, ...

While we cannot prove Church's thesis, since its role is to delimit precisely an hitherto vaguely conceived totality, we require evidence that it cannot conflict with the intuitive notion which it is supposed to complete; ...

The converse of Church's thesis, *i.e.*, that every general recursive function φ is effectively calculable, we take to be already confirmed by the intuitive notion (cf. section 60).

9.11.4   Evidence for the Computability Thesis

In one of the most familiar parts of the book, Kleene summarized the evidence for "Church's thesis" in section 62 (1952, 319). These arguments have been cited in hundreds of computability books and papers for the last half-century. After some heuristic evidence in (A), Kleene presented perhaps the most powerful evidence, the "(B) Equivalence of diverse formulations", such as the (Herbrand–Gödel) general recursive functions, λ-definable functions, Turing computable functions, and Post's canonical and normal systems (1943, 1946). Ironically, to clinch the evidence for Church's thesis, Kleene began a new part (C) where he appealed to Turing's work and wrote,

(C) Turing's Concept of a Computing Machine
Turing's computable functions [1936–37] are those which can be computed by a machine of a kind which is designed, according to his analysis, to reproduce all sorts of operations which a human computer could perform, working according to preassigned instructions. Turing's notion is thus the result of a direct attempt to formulate mathematically the notion of effective calculability, while other notions arose differently and were afterwards identified with effective calculability. Turing's formulation hence constitutes an independent statement of Church's thesis. (See Church 1937a, 43.)

We see here the amalgamation of different meanings into a single term (just as for "recursive" above). Kleene here was using the term "Church's thesis" to include

Turing's thesis and Turing's justification. Turing's work was to establish the connection between effectively calculable functions and Turing computable functions in Turing's thesis 9.3. As an *intensional* claim it had nothing to do with the recursive functions of Church's thesis 9.2. It was only the equivalence of Turing computable functions first with λ-definable functions and hence with recursive functions which links them *extensionally* but not intensionally.

Remark   *The computability thesis emerges. It is exactly here that Kleene introduces (without explicit mention) another convention and term which has lasted until today. Kleene knows that the various formal definitions all coincide extensionally, and he regards them interchangeably, regardless of their intensional or historical import. From now on when Kleene uses the term "Church's thesis" he means the following "computability thesis." Kleene omits Turing's name from the thesis even though in part (C) above he gave Turing credit as the only one who made a "direct attempt to formulate mathematically the notion of effective calculability."*

Definition 9.14   *The computability thesis. A function on the positive integers is effectively calculable if and only if it is recursive or Turing computable, or defined by any of the other formalisms.*

Note that the computability thesis is essentially the same as what we have called the Church–Turing thesis 9.4. It does not refer to one single man or to one single formalism. The computability thesis, used extensively in the subject, is almost usually listed under the name "Church's thesis," as in the title of the new book by Olszewski and colleagues (2007) with no mention of Turing. Many people today use "Church's thesis" in this way.

9.11.5   Who First Demonstrated the Computability Thesis?

Demonstrating something like the computability thesis requires two steps.

1. A formal mathematical definition for effectively calculable functions. Church (1936a) proposed Gödel's general recursive functions (1934). Turing invented the new formalism of Turing machines because this was closest to his idea of a mechanical process and because it lent itself to proving that any effectively calculable function lay in this class.

2. The second and perhaps more important step is to prove that the informal notion of a person calculating a function can be simulated by the formal model. This step is not a purely mathematical one but it needs to be as convincing and logical as possible. We refer to this step as a "demonstration" rather than a formal "proof."

Although it is not a formal proof, this second step is so crucial that it has been referred to as a "theorem" by Gandy and others. Gandy (1988, 82) observed, "Turing's analysis does much more than provide an argument for 'Turing's thesis,' it proves a theorem." Gandy actually wrote "Church's thesis" not "Turing's thesis" as written here, but surely Gandy meant Turing's thesis, i.e., the computability thesis, at least intensionally, because Turing did not prove anything in (1936) or anywhere else about general recursive functions. Furthermore, as Gandy (1988, 83–84) pointed out, "Turing's analysis makes no reference whatsoever to calculating machines. Turing machines appear as a result, a codification, of his analysis of calculations by humans." Turing's thesis (1936, section 9) stated in definition 9.3 is that every intuitively computable (effectively calculable) function is computable by a Turing machine.

In contrast, Church used the Herbrand–Gödel general recursive functions as his formal model, but even their inventor, Gödel, was not convinced as we have seen in section 9.2 and section 9.3. No modern book uses the Herbrand–Gödel general recursive formalism to define the effectively calculable functions.

A considerably more serious objection is that there was a flaw in Church's demonstration that every effectively calculable function is general recursive. The flaw in Church's argument (1936a, section 7) for his thesis was this. Church began by defining an "effectively calculable" function to be one for which "there exists an algorithm for the calculation of its values." Church analyzed the informal notion of the calculation of a value $f(n) = m$ according to a step-by-step approach (so called by Gandy [1988, 77]) from two points of view, first by an application of an algorithm, and second as the derivation in some formal system, because as he pointed out, Gödel had shown that the steps in his formal system P were primitive recursive. Following Davis (1958, 64) or Shoenfield (1967, 120–121), it is reasonable to suppose that the calculation of f proceeds by writing expressions on a sheet of paper, and that the expressions have been given code numbers, $c_0, c_1, \ldots, c_n$. Define $c_0, c_1, \ldots c_n = p_0^{c_0} \cdot p_1^{c_1} \ldots p_n^{c_n}$. We say that the calculation is *stepwise recursive* if there is a partial recursive function ψ such that $\psi(c_0, c_1, \ldots, c_i) = c_{i+1}$ for all $i, 0 \leq i < n$.

If the basic steps are stepwise recursive, then it follows easily by the Kleene normal form theorem, which Kleene had proved and communicated to Gödel before November 1935 (see Kleene 1987b, 57), that the entire process is μ-recursive. The fatal weakness in Church's argument was the core assumption that the atomic steps were stepwise recursive, something he did not justify. Gandy (1988, 79) and especially Sieg (1994, 80, 87), in their excellent analyses, brought out this weakness in Church's argument. Sieg (80) wrote, "… this core does not provide a convincing analysis: steps taken in a calculus must be of a restricted character and they are assumed, for example by Church, without argument to be recursive." Sieg (78) wrote, "It is precisely here that we encounter the major stumbling block for Church's analysis, and that stumbling block was quite clearly seen by Church," who wrote that without this assumption it is difficult to see how the notion of a system of logic can be given any exact meaning at all. It is exactly this stumbling block which Turing overcame by a totally new approach.

9.11.6   The Computability Thesis and the Calculus

Why all the fuss over names? Why not simply use the term "Church's thesis" invented by Kleene (1952), and let it refer to the "computability thesis?" This is in fact what is widely (and incorrectly) done.

If we had to attach a single name to "the calculus" every time we mentioned it, whose name should it be? Isaac Newton began working on a form of the calculus in 1666 but did not publish it until much later. Gottfried Leibniz began work on the calculus in 1674 and published his account of the differential calculus in 1684 and the integral calculus in 1686. Newton did not publish it until 1687, although most believe he had been working on it before Leibniz began in 1674. There was a great controversy about priority up until Leibniz's death in 1716. The British Royal Society handed down a verdict in 1715 crediting Isaac Newton with the discovery of the calculus, and stating that Leibniz was guilty of plagiarism (although these charges were later proved false). Newton was more established than Leibniz and had vigorous supporters. Newton and his followers campaigned vigorously for his position. The Wiki encyclopedia states,

Despite this ruling of the Royal Society, mathematics throughout the eighteenth century was typified by an elaboration of the differential and integral calculus in which mathematicians generally discarded Newton's fluxional calculus in favor of the new methods presented by Leibniz.

9.11.7   Founders of Computability and the Calculus

There is a parallel between the development of the calculus and the demonstration of the computability thesis.

1. Church and Turing both worked independently on it and came up with different models.

2. Turing began slightly later than Church. Leibnitz began later than Newton. Both Leibniz and Turing worked at a distance and independently of Newton and Church, respectively, unaware of the work by another researcher.

3. Turing's model of Turing machines is overwhelmingly more appealing and popular that Church's model of the (Herbrand–Gödel) general recursive functions, a model which is rarely presented in any books and never used for actual calculations in any courses. The general recursive functions are used only in an historical discussion. (This refers to the Herbrand–Gödel general recursive functions. The Kleene μ-recursive functions have other uses but are not mentioned in the original Church's thesis 9.2.)

4. For the calculus, despite the Royal Society ruling, "mathematicians generally discarded Newton's fluxional calculus in favor of the new methods presented by Leibniz."

5. In computer science, the Turing machines (and other calculating machines like register machines) dominate. The general recursive functions are never seen. Kleene's μ-recursive functions are sometimes used in courses and mistakenly called *recursive functions* but to prove that an effectively calculable function is μ-recursive requires a tedious arithmetization as in Gödel's incompleteness theorem (1931) and is virtually never done.

6. Newton was in the position of power within the Royal Society, which not only affirmed his claim but denied the claim by his rival Leibniz. Church was the senior figure in computability (after Gödel). Church's claim to the computability thesis was affirmed by his former PhD student Stephen Kleene (1952). Kleene occasionally mentioned Turing's thesis and repeatedly used the Turing machine model and Turing's demonstration of its success to demonstrate the computability thesis. However, Kleene deliberately and overwhelmingly established the phrase "Church's thesis" to stand for the "computability thesis," at a time when nobody called it a thesis and when the field was about to rapidly expand in the 1950s and 1960s, and would turn to Kleene for direction as the last representative of the original computability researchers of the 1930s and the most prominent and influential of all computability theorists in the 1950s. The Royal Society was not successful in excluding Leibniz from the calculus, but Kleene was certainly successful in excluding Turing's name from the computability thesis.

Virtually all the papers and books, including Rogers (1967), Soare (1987), and many others followed Kleene's lead. Unlike the calculus, the participants—Church, Turing, and their followers—have given credit to the others. The problem is simply that Kleene has not given Turing credit in his naming of the computability thesis. Kleene could have called it "the computability thesis" analogously with "the calculus." We never refer to "the Newton calculus" or the "Leibniz calculus." Why do we need to give a person's name to the computability thesis? Kleene never denied credit to Turing and in many places, such as his books (1952, 1967), he gives Turing credit for the most intuitive presentation of computability. Kleene just does not include Turing in the name he chose.

Remark *Kleene thought and wrote with tokens, words that are given arbitrary and nonstandard meaning by the author: "recursive" means "computable," "Church's thesis" means the "computability thesis." The arbitrary and sometimes misleading use of words has diminished our communications among ourselves and with other scientific and scholarly colleagues.*

It is ambiguous to use "recursive" with both meanings, inductive and computable, as we have seen. Second, it is simply wrong to use "Church's thesis" to refer to a proposition first demonstrated by Turing and never successfully demonstrated by Church. It would also be wrong to refer to "the Newton calculus" without mentioning Leibniz. Today we refer to "the calculus" without any founder's name. Why not call it simply, "the computability thesis" and not "Church's thesis," or the "Church–Turing thesis?" Which of the three terms is more understandable to an outsider who has never heard about the subject?

9.12 Displacement 3: Turing o-machines

9.12.1 Turing, Post, and Kleene on Relative Computability

In section 9.4 we have seen how Turing (1939, section 4) briefly introduced an oracle machine (o-machine) and in section 9.5 how Post developed relative computability from 1944 up to the influential Kleene–Post (1954) paper. Kleene (1952, 314) took up the theme of relative computability of a function from an oracle set. Analogous to his version of Thesis I considered above, Kleene defined Thesis I* to be the corresponding relative computability thesis which we have called the Post–Turing thesis 9.11. He recommended this thesis but did not give a separate justification. Kleene (1952, 314) wrote, "The evidence for thesis I will also apply to Thesis I*," and on page 319 he continued,

We now summarize the evidence for Church's Thesis (and Thesis I*, end section 61) under three main headings (A)–(C), and one other (D) which may be included under (A).

9.12.2 Relative Computability Unifies Incomputability

The field of computability theory deals mostly with *incomputable,* not computable, objects. The objects considered in degrees of unsolvability, in computable model theory, in differential geometry, as in Csima and Soare (2006) or Soare (2004), all deal with incomputable objects. However, we should not call the subject "incomputability theory" because the underlying theme is the notion of *relative computability* as absolute because of the oracle graph theorem (9.1), and because it relates and unifies the myriad incomputable objects.

9.12.3 The Key Concept of the Subject

The notion of an oracle machine and relative computability is the single most important in the subject.

1. A Turing a-machine can easily be simulated by a Turing o-machine and the latter is scarcely more complicated to explain.

2. Most of the objects considered in computability theory and applications to algebra, model theory, geometry, analysis and other fields are incomputable not computable and relative computability unifies them.

3. Many if not most computing processes in the real world are online or interactive processes, better modeled by an o-machine than an a-machine.

4. A relative computability process Φ_e^A corresponds to a continuous functional on Cantor space analogous to continuous functions in analysis. A function on Cantor space given by an a-machine is merely a constant function.

9.12.4 When to Introduce Relative Computability

In view of the importance of relative computability, and online computing in both theoretical results and real world computing, it is surprising how many computability books introduce oracle machines and Turing functionals so late in the book or not at all. For example, Kleene's book (1952) was the first real book on computability theory and the principal reference for at least fifteen years until Rogers (1967) appeared. Kleene introduced relative computability in Chapter 11 on page 266 by adding the characteristic function of the oracle set A to the Herbrand–Gödel general recursive functions. Rogers (1967) took the Turing machine approach and immediately defined computability using regular Turing machines (a-machines). Rogers quickly became the most readable textbook on computability and remains a popular reference. Rogers introduced relative computability only in chapter 9 (128) using Turing's original definition (1939) of an ordinary Turing machine with the additional capacity to consult an oracle A occasionally during the computation. In another popular introduction, *Computability*, Cutland (1980) introduces relative computability quitely late, on page 167. Boolos and Jeffrey in *Computability and Logic* (1974) do not discuss it at all. The more recent and very extensive books by Odifreddi, *Classical Recursion Theory* Vol. I (1989) and Vol. II (1999) introduce relative computability only on page 175 by adding the characteristic function of oracle set A to the Kleene μ-recursive functions. Lerman (1983) defines relative computability from an oracle by adding the characteristic function of the oracle to the Kleene μ-recursive functions. This occurs on page 11 but Lerman is assuming that the reader has already mastered a first course in computability using a text such as Rogers (1967). Cooper's more recent book (2004a) introduces oracle Turing machines on page 139.

Kleene's second and more introductory book, *Mathematical Logic* (1967, 267), has a brief discussion of reducing one predicate to another and on degrees of unsolvability. The only genuine introduction to computability I found that introduces relative computability immediately is Martin Davis's *Computability and Unsolvability* (1958), which defines it on page 20 of chapter 1 using oracle Turing machines. In

Soare's former book (1987) and new book (in press) Turing *a*-machines come in chapter 1 and Turing *o*-machines at the beginning of chapter 3, after which the book is based on Turing reducibility.

9.13   Evolution of Terminology

9.13.1   The Term "Recursive"

When Dedekind (1888) proved that a definition by recursion uniquely defines a function, he called it "definition by induction." Hilbert (1904) used the term *"rekurrent(e),"* and later (1923) he used *"Rekursion."* The term *"recursive"* was apparently first used in English by Ramsey (1928). (See Gandy [1988], 27, 73.) Skolem (1923) showed that many number-theoretic functions are primitive recursive, and he used *"rekurrierend."*

The concept of *recursion* stems from the verb "recur," "to return to a place or status." The primary mathematical meaning of recursive has always been "defined by induction," as in Scheme V of primitive recursion. Gödel (1931) used the German "rekursiv" to mean what we now call "primitive recursive." After Gödel (1934), "recursive" formally meant "Herbrand–Gödel (general) recursive." The advantage of the Herbrand–Gödel definition of recursive function in Gödel (1934) was that it encompassed recursion on an arbitrary number of arguments and allowed partial functions.

9.13.2   The Term "Computable"

The term "computable" appears as early as 1646 in English usage according to the *Oxford English Dictionary*. Both O.E.D. and *Webster's Third International Dictionary* give the definition of "computable" as roughly synonymous with "calculable," capable of being ascertained or determined by a mathematical process especially of some intricacy. The meaning of "calculate" is somewhat more general including "to figure out," "to design or adapt for a purpose," "to judge to be probable," while "compute" means more "to determine by a mathematical process," or "to determine or calculate by means of a computer."

9.13.3   "Recursive" Acquires the Meaning "Computable"

From 1932 to 1935, Church and Kleene had been studying a class of effectively calculable functions called *λ-definable functions*. By 1934 Kleene had shown that a large class of number theoretic functions were λ-definable. On the strength of this evidence, Church proposed to Gödel around March 1934 (see Davis 1965, 9) that the notion of "effectively calculable" be identified with "λ-definable," a suggestion which Gödel rejected as "thoroughly unsatisfactory."

Following this encounter with Gödel, Church changed the formal definition in Church's thesis from "λ-definable" to "recursive," which was his abbreviation for the Herbrand–Gödel general recursive definition of Gödel (1934). On April 19, 1935, Church presented to the American Mathematical Society his famous proposition published in Church (1936a) and known since Kleene's book (1952) as *Church's thesis*, which asserts that the effectively calculable functions should be identified with the (Herbrand–Gödel) recursive functions. Gödel still refused to accept this identification, even though it was phrased in terms of his own recursive functions.

In 1934 the terms and concepts had been completely clear and distinct. "Effectively calculable" meant the *informal* notion of "specified by a finite algorithm," and "recursive" meant the *formal* notion of "definable by the Herbrand–Gödel equations" and more generally "defined by some kind of induction." That distinction was about to become blurred for the next sixty years, from 1936 to 1996. With the advent of Church (1936a), Kleene (1936a, 1943), and particularly the influential 1952 book by Kleene, "recursive" acquired the additional informal meaning "effectively calculable," and the field came to be known under Kleene as "recursive function theory" or simply "recursion theory" for short, even though Gödel objected that this term should be used only with reference to the work done by Rosza Péter (recursion on several arguments).

By 1936, Kleene and Church had begun thinking of the word "recursive" to mean "computable," or "calculable." Church had seen his first thesis rejected by Gödel and was heavily invested in the acceptance of his 1936 thesis in terms of recursive functions. Without the acceptance of this thesis Church had no unsolvable problem. Church wrote (1936a, 96, reprinted in Davis 1965) that a *"recursively enumerable set"* is one that is the range of a recursive function. This is apparently the first appearance of the term "recursively enumerable" in the literature and the first appearance of "recursively" as an adverb meaning "effectively" or "computably."

In the same year Kleene (1936a, 238; cited in Davis 1965, 238) mentioned a *"recursive enumeration"* and noted that there is no recursive enumeration of Herbrand–Gödel systems of equations which gives only the systems which define the (total) recursive functions. By a "recursive enumeration" Kleene states that he means "a recursive sequence (*i.e.*, the successive values of a recursive function of one variable)." Post (1944), under the influence of Church and Kleene, adopted this terminology of "recursive" and "recursively enumerable" over his own terminology of "effectively generated set," "normal set," "generated set." Thereafter, it became firmly established in the literature.

9.13.4   The Linguistic Assertion of Church's Thesis

The first version of Church's thesis as presented to Gödel privately in 1934 was simply the assertion that the λ-definable functions coincided with the effectively calculable functions. This simply asserted the equality of two classes of functions but not the *identity* of the terms. There was no use of the term "λ" or "λ-definable" to mean "calculable" or "computable."

However, in 1936 both Church and Kleene fervently believed in the validity of Church's thesis (1936a) that the Herbrand–Gödel recursive functions and the effectively calculable functions coincided. Furthermore, Kleene had been disappointed in trying to present to mathematicians his computability results from 1931 to 1934 phrased in the formalism of λ-definable functions. Kleene and Church regarded Gödel's recursive functions as an ideal vehicle to bring mathematicians to a formal definition of effectively calculable functions. They were completely convinced of the thesis and of the appeal and recognition of recursive function, based on mathematical induction that went back at least to Dedekind (1888). Neither Church not Kleene saw anything wrong with going beyond the mere equality of these two classes as expressed in Church's thesis to the use of the term "recursive" to mean "effectively calculable" and to the introduction of new terms such as "recursively enumerable" with a similar meaning. By 1936–1938 both Church and Kleene were using "recursive" in this way.

A hidden consequence of this usage was the *linguistic assertion* of Church's thesis (1936a). If "recursive" now *meant* calculable or computable, then it linguistically established Church's thesis because we have no terms in our language to assert the existence of a function which is effectively calculable but not recursive. We might try to refute Church's first thesis (1934) by exhibiting an effectively calculable function which is not λ-definable. However, it is now a linguistic tautology that we cannot exhibit an effectively calculable function which is not recursive. This was probably not the main motive of Church, but it was a convenient additional feature because Gödel had still not accepted even Church's thesis in (1936a) even when it was formulated with his own recursive function; and without the acceptance of Church's thesis, there are no undecidable problems in mathematics as Church had asserted.

9.13.5   A Second Classical Enlightenment in Italy

Computability advanced rapidly over the next several decades and branched out from computability on the integers to *generalized recursion theory (GRT),* dealing with computability beyond the integers, such as recursion on admissible ordinals, recursion on finite types, and other generalized topics. Computability on the integers (ω-recursion theory) continued to increase in popularity and by 1979 was sometimes called *ordinary recursion theory (ORT)* to distinguish it from GRT.

The International Summer School in Mathematics (C.I.M.E.) met in Bressanone, Italy, high in the Dolomite Alps in a German speaking region near the Austrian border in June, 1979. Gerald Sacks and I were each to give short courses, Gerald's on G.R.T. and mine on ω-recursion theory. On the way to Bressanone, I had stopped for a few days in Florence to see again the masterpieces of the Italian High Renaissance, my favorite period of art, with works by Botticelli, Michelangelo, Leonardo da Vinci, and Raphael, from roughly 1475–1525.

I was still preoccupied with these images as Gerald's course and mine began in Bressanone. As our courses proceeded and Gerald kept using the phrase "ordinary recursion theory" to describe ω-recursion theory, I thought of how inadequate the term "ordinary" is to describe the magnificent work in the 1930s and 1940s by Gödel, Turing, Church, Kleene, and Post. Had anyone ever used the term "ordinary art" to describe the work of Michelangelo and Leonardo? I thought of my colleagues at the University of Chicago, Antoni Zygmund and Alberto Calderone, who worked in "classical analysis," so named to distinguish it from functional analysis. No one called it "ordinary analysis."

From the Florence visit and the memory of several art history courses, I gave a whole lecture on classical art of the Renaissance and *classical* recursion theory, pointing out the similarities in artistic style and parallel elements. The Italians loved to hear about their own art and its relation to computability. My mathematical and art history notes were published as Soare (1981) in the proceedings of the Italian Centro Internazionale Matematico Estivo meeting, but the journal was obscure and few people read that paper. At the Cornell American Mathematical Society meeting in 1982, I presented an expanded version to an audience of several hundred. The mathematical, but not the art history notes, were published as Soare (1985). From these meetings the term *classical recursion theory (CRT)* was born. By the mid-1980s, it had completely replaced the former term *ordinary recursion theory (ORT)* to describe the theory of computable functions on ω. Later, Odifreddi used it for his two-volume book (1989, 1999).

Bressanone represented a kind of second Italian Renaissance, a return to the intuition and esthetic aspects of computability, particularly the beautiful and intuitive papers by Turing (1936) and Post (1944), and the efforts of Lachlan (1970, 1973), and mathematical trees (1975) to reveal the inner beauty and simplicity of the subject. It was no longer enough to have a correct, but incomprehensible proof. The theorems and proofs must be beautiful, motivated, and esthetically appealing.

9.13.6 Ambiguity in the Term "Recursive"

The Kleene–Church assignment of "recursive" to mean "algorithmic" or "calculable" led to ambiguity. On one hand, Kleene identified recursion theory with algorithmic functions, and wrote in Kleene (1988, 190), "The recognition of algorithms goes back at least to Euclid (c. 330 B.C.)."

On the other hand, Kleene (1981b, 44) wrote of Dedekind (1988; in reference to where induction was used to define addition and multiplication), "I think we can say that recursive function theory was born there ninety-two years ago with

Dedekind's Theorem 126 ('Satz der Definition durch Induktion') that functions can be defined by primitive recursion."

Did he mean that recursion and inductive definitions began with Dedekind in 1888 or that computability and algorithms began there? When Kleene used the term "recursive" to also mean "algorithmic," one was never sure whether a particular instance meant "algorithmic" or "inductive." Our language had become indistinct. When a speaker used the word "recursive" in 1990 in front of a general audience, did he mean "defined by induction," "related to fixed points and reflexive program calls," or did he mean "computable?"

"The first rule of good taste in writing is to use words whose meaning will not be misunderstood; and if a reader does not know the meaning of the words, it is infinitely better that he should know he does not know it." (Charles Sanders Peirce, *Ethics of Terminology*, 1906, 131)

9.13.7 Difficulty in Communication

The term "recursive" may have originally been an appropriate term for the subject in 1936 because some mathematicians and scientists understood that term in the sense of "inductive" and because the term "computer" had not yet become known to the general public. By 1990 it was the reverse. Those who had heard the term "recursive" associated it with the second of the elementary programming methods of iteration and recursion (i.e., defined by induction). Very few associated it with the extended Kleene meaning of "defined by a finite procedure" or "calculable." In contrast, Turing had used his Turing machine model to construct a real digital computer during 1940–1945 for cryptanalysis, and John von Neumann used it to design the EDVAC computer architecture where the data and program are stored in the same address space. With the arrival of IBM's Personal Computer (PC) in 1981, the computer was transformed from an arcane object in a special room accessed by a stack of IBM cards in 1960 to a kind of electronic typewriter, capable of all kinds of calculations, compositions, and communication via the Ethernet with other computers.

By 1990 the situation had become very difficult. Many people had access to a personal computer on their desks and the terminology of computing was familiar to the general population, but the term "recursive" was limited to very small number who mainly understood the wrong meaning. They mainly associated it with a first year programming course or a definition by induction on mathematics and almost never with computability. So few people understood the meaning of "recursive" that by 1990 I had to begin my papers with, "Let f be a recursive function (that is, a computable function)," as if I were writing in Chinese and translating back into English.

Furthermore, university students interested in computability failed to recognize the content from the course title "Recursive Function Theory" in the catalog description, and never took the course. Writing letters of recommendation to place graduate students became more difficult because virtually no one on the hiring committee knew what "recursion theory" was.

9.13.8 A Return to the Founders

The founders of the two key definitions of computability, Turing and Gödel, never used the word "recursive" to mean "computable," and objected when it was so used. When others did, Gödel reacted sharply negatively, as related by Martin Davis.

In a discussion with Gödel at the Institute for Advanced Study in Princeton about 1952–54, I [Martin Davis] casually used the term "recursive function theory" as it was used then. "To my surprise, Gödel reacted sharply, saying that the term in question should be used with reference to the kind of work Rosza Péter did."

(See R. Péter's work on recursions in [1934] and [1951].)

The object was never to understand the notion of recursion or inductive definitions. The object was to understand the concept of effectively calculable by a finite procedure.

9.13.9 Making the Change to Computability

By 1995 the confusion had become intolerable. I wrote an article on "Computability and Recursion" for the *Bulletin of Symbolic Logic* (Soare 1996) on the history and scientific reasons for why we should use "computable" and not "recursive" to mean "calculable." "Recursive" should mean "inductive" as it had for Dedekind and Hilbert. At first, few were willing to make such a dramatic change, overturning a sixty year old tradition of Kleene, the most influential leader after 1940. The terms *"computability theory,"* and *"computably enumerable (c.e.) set"* did not come "trippingly on the tongue" (Shakespeare, Hamlet Act 3, Scene 2, 1–4) in 1995 as they do now. However, in a few months more people were convinced by the undeniable logic of the situation. Three years later the A.M.S. conference in Boulder, Colorado had the title, *Computability Theory and Its Applications: Current Trends and Open Problems,* a title that would have been unthinkable a few years earlier. At that meeting, referenced in Soare (2000), most researchers, especially those under forty years old, had adopted the new terminology and conventions. Changing back from "recursive" to "computable" during 1996–1999 has had a number of advantages.

By 1995 Edward Griffor had been invited by Elsevier to edit a volume with the provisional title *Handbook of Recursion Theory,* and he had been soliciting papers from authors in the subject. When he saw my paper on computability and recursion

(Soare 1996), Griffor and Elsevier changed their book title to *Handbook of Computability Theory,* and Griffor asked me to write the first chapter, "The History and Concept of Computability Theory" (Soare 1999a) in addition to the previously scheduled chapter (1999b).

9.14   Epilogue on Computability

Today the term "recursive" means "inductive" as it always has. Few use it to also mean "computable." The change was not merely a change of names but also a change of attitudes. Ironically, by 1990 the subject of recursion theory had been moving ever more inward and away from the general scientific public in spite of the applications mentioned above. Leo Harrington said, "Model Theory is about models, Set Theory is about sets, but Recursion Theory is not about recursion."

The change of names signaled a return to the concepts of Turing and Gödel, with an emphasis on computability, not induction. Books on computability sprang up with a different orientation, such as Cooper (2004) and Enderton (2011). In the last decade Barry Cooper formed the organization *Computability in Europe (CiE),* which meets every summer at a different location and which several hundred people attend. The fields represented in the 2010 meeting included proof theory and computation, computational complexity, computability of the physical, reasoning and computation from Leibniz to Boole, biological computing, web applications and computation. These are diverse fields, but all have the concept of computability in common. The change of terminology has announced to those inside computability and those outside that we are open for communication. I asked Cooper whether he could have achieved such a large and diverse turnout for the CiE meetings under the name "Recursion in Europe." He said no.

9.15   Conclusions

Conclusion 9.1   *For pedagogical reasons, with beginning students it is reasonable to first present Turing a-machines and ordinary computability. However, any introductory computability book should then present as soon as possible Turing oracle machines (o-machines) and relative computability. Parallels should be drawn with offline and online computing in the real world.*

Conclusion 9.2   *We should use "recursive" to mean "defined inductively," not "calculable" or "computable." The subject is fundamentally about the concept of* comput- ability *(not recursion) as those terms and concepts have been understood by Gödel, Turing, and most modern scholars. The subject is* computability theory, *not "recursive function theory" or "recursion theory."*

Church and Kleene (1936) introduced the term "recursive" to mean "computable" primarily for public relations reasons as Kleene (1981) explained (see section 9.2.4), since "recursive functions" were better understood than the Church–Kleene work on λ-calculus. It was also convenient to use the (Herbrand–Gödel) recursive functions in the second statement of Church's thesis (1936) at a time when Gödel found it unsatisfactory. Over the next few decades Kleene reinforced and promulgated this convention, but by the 1990s it had become much more useful for communication and more accurate scientifically and historically to remove the meaning of "computable" from the term "recursive," particularly since Turing and Gödel had both rejected this usage. This change has largely been accomplished since the papers on computability and recursion which appeared in Soare (1996 and 1999). See these papers and the discussion in section 9.10. This emphasis on computability (rather than recursion) and its relation to incomputability has been developed in many recent books and papers such as Cooper (2004).

Conclusion 9.3 *It is much more accurate and informative to refer to the central thesis of the subject as the "Church–Turing thesis," not "Church's thesis" or "Turing's thesis."*

It is misleading to refer to it as "Church's thesis," as many people do, because Church never demonstrated the thesis (at least to the satisfaction of Gödel and modern scholars like Gandy [1988] and Sieg [1994]), but Turing did demonstrate his thesis in a manner convincing to essentially everyone. Church gave a formal model (the Herbrand–Gödel general recursive functions), which was not convincing even to its author, while Turing invented a new model, the Turing *a*-machine, which everyone, including Church and Kleene, agreed was the most convincing of the theses.

Neither Turing nor Gödel thought of this as a thesis. The term "Church's thesis" was started arbitrarily by Kleene alone in 1952. We use the term "the calculus" without the name of either founder, Newton or Leibniz, attached. Why not replace the name in computability by a descriptive and informative term like "computability thesis?" See the discussion in section 9.11.

Conclusion 9.4 *The subject is primarily about incomputable objects, not computable ones, and has been since the 1930s. The single most important concept is that of relative computability to relate incomputable objects.*

More information on Turing, computability, and the material here may be found in these references: Cooper (2004b), Cooper, Löwe, and Sorbi (2007, 2008), Cooper and Odifreddi (2003), Davis (1982, 1988a,b, 2000), Dawson (1997), Epstein and Carnielli (1989), Friedberg (1957), Friedberg and Rogers (1959), Gödel (193?, 1972, 2003), Hilbert (1905, 1926, 1927), Hilbert and Bernays (1934, 1939), Hodges (2004), Kleene (1936a–c, 1944, 1955a–c, 1962a,b, 1963), Kreisel (1970), Löwe and Sorbi

(2008), Muchnik (1956), Post (1947), Shoenfield (1991, 1995), Sieg (1997), Soare (2007, 2009, 2012, 2013, in press), Turing (1947, 1948, 1949, 1950a,b, 1954), Wang (1974, 1981, 1993).

Acknowledgments

This work was partially supported by a grant from the Simons Foundation (No. 204186) to Robert Irving Soare. The grant is in the area of computability theory and applications, funded by the Simons Foundation Program for Mathematics and the Physical Sciences.

References

Church, A. 1935. An unsolvable problem of elementary number theory, preliminary report (abstract), *Bulletin of the American Mathematical Society* 41:332–333.

Church, A. 1936a. An unsolvable problem of elementary number theory. *American Journal of Mathematics* 58:345–363. Reprinted in Davis, *The Undecidable*, 88–107.

Church, A. 1936b. A note on the Entscheidungsproblem. *Journal of Symbolic Logic* 1(1):40–41. Correction 101–102.

Church, A. 1937a. Review of Turing (1936). *Journal of Symbolic Logic* 2:42–43.

Church, A. 1937b. Review of Post (1936). *Journal of Symbolic Logic* 2:43.

Church, A. 1938. The constructive second number class. *Bulletin of the American Mathematical Society* 44:224–32.

Church, A., and S. C. Kleene. 1936. Formal definitions in the theory of ordinal numbers. *Fundamenta Mathematica* 28:11–21.

Cooper, S. B. 2004a. *Computability Theory*. London: Chapman and Hall/CRC Mathematics.

Cooper, S. B. 2004b. The incomparable Alan Turing. Lecture at Manchester University, June, 5, 2004. Published electronically: http://www.bcs.org/server.php?show=ConWebDoc.17130.

Cooper, S. B., B. Löwe, and A. Sorbi, eds. 2007. Computation and Logic in the Real World. Proceedings of the Third Conference on Computability in Europe, Siena, Italy. Lecture notes in computer science, No. 4497. Berlin: Springer-Verlag.

Cooper, S. B., B. Löwe, and A. Sorbi, eds. 2008. *New computational paradigms: Changing conceptions of what is computable*. Berlin: Springer-Verlag.

Cooper, S. B. and P. Odifreddi. 2003. Incomputability in nature. In *Computability and Models: Perspectives East and West*, ed. S. B. Cooper and S. S. Goncharov, 137–160. Dordrecht: Kluwer Academic/Plenum.

Csima, B. F., and R. I. Soare. 2006. Computability results used in differential geometry. *Journal of Symbolic Logic* 71:1394–1410.

Cutland, N. 1980. *Computability: An Introduction to Recursive Function Theory*. Cambridge: Cambridge University Press.

Davis, M. 1958. *Computability and Unsolvability*. New York: McGraw-Hill.

Davis, M., ed. 1965. *The Undecidable: Basic Papers on Undecidable Propositions, Unsolvable Problems and Computable Functions*. New York: Raven Press.

Davis, M. 1982. Why Gödel didn't have Church's thesis. *Information and Control* 54:3–24.

Davis, M. 1988a. Mathematical logic and the origin of modern computers. In *The Universal Turing Machine*, ed. R. Herken, 149–174. Oxford: Oxford University Press.

Davis, M. 1988b. The myth of hypercomputation. In *Alan Turing: Life and Legacy of a Great Thinker*, ed. C. Teuscher, 195–211. Berlin: Springer-Verlag.

Davis, M. 2000. *The Universal Computer: The Road from Leibniz to Turing*. New York: W.W. Norton. (Also published by Norton in 2000 under the title *Engine of Logic*.)

Dawson, J. W. 1997. *Logical Dilemmas: The Life and Work of Kurt Gödel*. Cambridge: A. K. Peters.

Epstein, R. L., and W. A. Carnielli. 1989. *Computability: Computable Functions, Logic, and the Foundations of Mathematics*. Belmont, CA: Wadsworth and Brooks.

Friedberg, R. M. 1957. Two recursively enumerable sets of incomparable degrees of unsolvability. *Proceedings of the National Academy of Sciences of the United States of America* 43:236–38.

Friedberg, R. M., and Rogers, H. 1959. Reducibility and completeness for sets of integers. *Z. Math. Logik Grundlag. Math.* 5:117–25.

Gandy, R. 1980. Church's thesis and principles for mechanisms. In *The Kleene Symposium*, ed. J. Barwise, H. J. Keisler, and K. Kunen, 123–48. Amsterdam: North-Holland.

Gandy, R. 1988. The confluence of ideas in 1936. In *The Universal Turing Machine*, ed. R. Herken, 55–111. Oxford: Oxford University Press.

Gödel, K. 1931. Über formal unentscheidbare Sätze der Principia Mathematica und verwandter Systeme, I. *Monatshefte für Mathematik und Physik* 38:173–78. English translation in Davis, *The Undecidable*, 4–38, and in van Heijenoort, 1967, *From Frege to Gödel: A Source Book in Mathematical Logic, 1879–1931*, 592–616. Cambridge, MA: Harvard University Press.

Gödel, K. 1934. On undecidable propositions of formal mathematical systems. Reprinted in Davis, *The Undecidable*, 39–74.

Gödel, K. 193?. Undecidable Diophantine propositions. In Gödel, *Collected Works III,* 164–75.

Gödel, K. 1946. Remarks before the Princeton bicentennial conference on problems in mathematics. In Davis, *The Undecidable,* 84–88.

Gödel, K. 1951. Some basic theorems on the foundations of mathematics and their implications. In Gödel, *Collected Works III,* 304–323. (This was the Gibbs lecture delivered by Gödel on December 26, 1951, to the American Mathematical Society.)

Gödel, K. 1964. Postscriptum to Gödel 1934. In Davis, *The Undecidable,* 71–73.

Gödel, K. 1972. Some remarks on the undecidability results. In Gödel, *Collected Works II,* 305–06.

Gödel, K. 1986. *Collected Works, Vol. I: Publications 1929–1936*, ed. S. Feferman, J. W. Dawson Jr., S. C. Kleene, G. H. Moore, R. M. Solovay, and J. van Heijenoort. Oxford: Oxford University Press.

Gödel, K. 1990. *Collected Works, Vol. II: Publications 1938–1974*, ed. S. Feferman, J. W. Dawson Jr., S. C. Kleene, G. H. Moore, R. M. Solovay, and J. van Heijenoort. Oxford: Oxford University Press.

Gödel, K. 1995. *Collected Works, Vol. III: Unpublished Essays and Lectures*, ed. S. Feferman, J. W. Dawson Jr., W. Goldfarb, C. Parsons, and R. M. Solovay. Oxford: Oxford University Press.

Gödel, K. 2003. *Collected Works, Vol. V: Correspondence, H–Z*, ed. S. Feferman, J. W. Dawson Jr., W. Goldfarb, C. Parsons, and W. Sieg. Oxford: Clarendon Press.

Goldin, D., S. Smolka, and P. Wegner. 2006. *Interactive Computation: The New Paradigm*. Berlin: Springer-Verlag.

Hilbert, D. 1899. *Grundlagen der Geometrie*. 7th ed. (1930). Leipzig: Teubner-Verlag.

Hilbert, D. 1905. Über die Grundlagen der Logik und der Arithmetik. In *Verhandlungen des dritten Internationalen Mathematiker-Kongresses in Heidelberg vom 8 bis 13 August 1904*, ed. A. Krazer, 174–85. Leipzig: Teubner. English translation in J. van Heijenoort, *From Frege to Gödel*, 129–38.

Hilbert, D. 1926. Über das Unendliche. *Mathematische Annalen* 95:161–90. Translated into English as "On the Infinite," in J. van Heijenoort, *From Frege to Gödel,* 367–92.

Hilbert, D. 1927. Die Grundlagen der Mathematik. Abhandlungen aus dem mathematischen Seminar der Hamburgischen Universität 6, 65–85. Reprinted in van Heijenoort, *From Frege to Gödel,* 464–479.

Hilbert, D., and W. Ackermann. 1928. *Grundzüge der theoretischen Logik*. Berlin: Springer.

Hilbert, D., and P. Bernays. 1934. *Grundlagen der Mathematik I*. Berlin: Springer Verlag.

Hilbert, D., and P. Bernays. 1939. *Grundlagen der Mathematik II*. Berlin: Springer Verlag.

Hodges, A. 1983. *Alan Turing: The Enigma*. New York: Simon and Schuster.

Hodges, A. 2004. Alan Turing: The logical and physical basis of computing. Lecture at Manchester University, June 5, 2004. Published electronically: http://www.bcs.org/ewics.

Kleene, S. C. 1936a. General recursive functions of natural numbers. *Mathematische Annalen* 112:727–42. Reprinted in M. Davis, *The Undecidable*, 236–253.

Kleene, S. C. 1936b. λ-definability and recursiveness. *Duke Mathematical Journal* 2:340–53.

Kleene, S. C. 1936c. A note on recursive functions. *Bulletin of the American Mathematical Society* 42:544–46.

Kleene, S. C. 1938. On notation for ordinal numbers. *Journal of Symbolic Logic* 3:150–5.

Kleene, S. C. 1943. Recursive predicates and quantifiers. *Transactions of the American Mathematical Society* 53:41–73.

Kleene, S. C. 1944. On the forms of the predicates in the theory of constructive ordinals. *American Journal of Mathematics* 66:41–58.

Kleene, S. C. 1952. *Introduction to Metamathematics*. New York: D. Van Nostrand.

Kleene, S. C. 1955a. Arithmetical predicates and function quantifiers. *Transactions of the American Mathematical Society* 79:312–40.

Kleene, S. C. 1955b. On the forms of the predicates in the theory of constructive ordinals (second paper). *American Journal of Mathematics* 77:405–28.

Kleene, S. C. 1955c. Hierarchies of number-theoretical predicates. *Bulletin of the American Mathematical Society* 61:193–213.

Kleene, S. C. 1959. Recursive functionals and quantifiers of finite type I. *Transactions of the American Mathematical Society* 91:1–52.

Kleene, S. C. 1962a. Turing-machine computable functionals of finite types I. In International Congress for Logic, Methodology, and Philosophy of Science 1960, 38–45. Palo Alto, CA: Stanford University Press.

Kleene, S. C. 1962b. Turing-machine computable functionals of finite types II. *Proceedings of the London Mathematical Society* 12(3):245–58.

Kleene, S. C. 1963. Recursive functionals and quantifiers of finite type II. *Transactions of the American Mathematical Society* 108:106–42.

Kleene, S. C. 1981a. Origins of recursive function theory. *Annals of the History of Computing* 3:52–67.

Kleene, S. C. 1981b. The theory of recursive functions, approaching its centennial. *Bulletin of the American Mathematical Society (N.S.)* 5:43–61.

Kleene, S. C. 1981c. Algorithms in various contexts. In *Algorithms in Modern Mathematics and Computer Science*, Proceedings Urgench, Khorezm Region, Uzbek, SSSR, 1979, ed. A.P. Ershov and D. Knuth. Lecture Notes in Computer Science, Vol.122. Berlin: Springer-Verlag.

Kleene, S. C. 1987a. Reflections on Church's thesis. *Notre Dame Journal of Formal Logic* 28:490–98.

Kleene, S. C. 1987b. Gödel's impression on students of logic in the 1930's. In *Gödel Remembered*, ed. P. Weingartner and L. Schmetterer, 49–64. Naples: Bibliopolis.

Kleene, S. C. 1988. Turing's analysis of computability, and major applications of it. In *The Universal Turing Machine*, ed. R. Herken, 17–54. Oxford: Oxford University Press.

Kleene, S. C., and E. L. Post. 1954. The upper semi-lattice of degrees of recursive unsolvability. *Annals of Mathematics* 59:379–407.

Kreisel, G. 1970. Church's thesis: A kind of reducibility axiom for constructive mathematics. In *Intuitionism and Proof Theory*, ed. A. Kino, J. Myhill, and R. E. Vesley, 121–50. Amsterdam: North-Holland.

Lerman, M. 1983. *Degrees of Unsolvability: Local and Global Theory*. Heidelberg: Springer-Verlag.

Löwe, B., and A. Sorbi, eds. 2008. *New Computational Paradigms: Changing Conceptions of What Is Computable*. Heidelberg: Springer-Verlag.

Muchnik, A. A. 1956. On the unsolvability of the problem of reducibility in the theory of algorithms. *Doklady Akademii Nauk SSR* 108:194–97.

Odifreddi, P. 1989. *Classical Recursion Theory*, Vol. 1. Amsterdam: North-Holland.

Odifreddi, P. 1999. *Classical Recursion Theory*, Vol. 2. Amsterdam: North-Holland.

Olszewski, A., J. Wolenski, and R. Janusz, eds. 2007. *Church's Thesis after 70 Years*. Frankfurt: Ontos-Verlag.

Peirce, C. S. 1906. *The Ethics of Terminology*.

Péter, R. 1934. Über den Zussammenhang der verschiedenen Begriffe der rekursiven Funktion. *Mathematische Annalen* 110:612–32.

Péter, R. 1951. *Rekursive Funktionen*. Budapest: Akadémaiai Kiadó (Akademische Verlag). Translated as *Recursive Functions*. New York: Academic Press, 1967.

Post, E. L. 1936. Finite combinatory processes—Formulation I. *Journal of Symbolic Logic* 1:103–05. Reprinted in Davis, *The Undecidable*, 288–291.

Post, E. L. 1941. Absolutely unsolvable problems and relatively undecidable propositions: Account of an anticipation. In Davis, *The Undecidable*, 340–443.

Post, E. L. 1943. Formal reductions of the general combinatorial decision problem. *American Journal of Mathematics* 65:197–215.

Post, E. L. 1944. Recursively enumerable sets of positive integers and their decision problems. *Bulletin of the American Mathematical Society* 50:284–316. Reprinted in Davis, *The Undecidable*, 304–337.

Post, E. L. 1946. Note on a conjecture of Skolem. *Journal of Symbolic Logic* 11:73–74.

Post, E. L. 1947. Recursive unsolvability of a problem of Thue. *Journal of Symbolic Logic* 12:1–11. Reprinted in Davis, *The Undecidable*, 292–303.

Post, E. L. 1948. Degrees of recursive unsolvability: Preliminary report (abstract). *Bulletin of the American Mathematical Society* 54:641–42.

Putnam, H. 1965. Trial and error predicates and the solution to a problem of Mostowski. *Journal of Symbolic Logic* 30:49–57.

Rogers, H. Jr. 1967. *Theory of Recursive Functions and Effective Computability*. New York: McGraw-Hill.

Sacks, G. E. 1990. *Higher Recursion Theory*. Heidelberg: Springer-Verlag.

Shoenfield, J. R. 1967. *Mathematical Logic*. Reading, MA: Addison-Wesley.

Shoenfield, J. R. 1971. *Degrees of Unsolvability*. Amsterdam: North-Holland.

Shoenfield, J. R. 1991. *Recursion Theory*. Lecture notes in logic, Vol. 1. Heidelberg: Springer-Verlag.

Shoenfield, J. R. 1995. The mathematical work of S. C. Kleene. *Bulletin of Symbolic Logic* 1:8–43.

Sieg, W. 1994. Mechanical procedures and mathematical experience. In *Mathematics and Mind*, ed. A. George, 71–117. Oxford: Oxford University Press.

Sieg, W. 1997. Step by recursive step: Church's analysis of effective calculability. *Bulletin of Symbolic Logic* 2:154–180.

Soare, R. I. 1981. Constructions in the recursively enumerable degrees. In *Recursion theory and computational complexity*, ed. G. Lolli. Proceedings of Centro Internazionale Matematico Estivo, June 14–23, 1979, in Bressanone, Italy. Naples: Liguori Editore.

Soare, R. I. 1985. Tree arguments in recursion theory and the $0'''$-priority method. In *Recursion Theory*, A. Nerode and R. A. Shore, ed., 53–106. Proceedings of symposia in pure mathematics, Vol. 42. Providence, RI: American Mathematical Society.

Soare, R. I. 1987. *Recursively Enumerable Sets and Degrees: A Study of Computable Functions and Computably Generated Sets*. Heidelberg: Springer-Verlag.

Soare, R. I. 1996. Computability and recursion. *Bulletin of Symbolic Logic* 2:284–321.

Soare, R. I. 1999a. An overview of the computably enumerable sets. In *Handbook of Computability Theory*, ed. E. Griffor, 199–248. Amsterdam: North-Holland.

Soare, R. I. 1999b. The history and concept of computability. In *Handbook of Computability Theory*, ed. E. Griffor, 3–36. Amsterdam: North-Holland.

Soare, R. I. 2000. Extensions, automorphisms, and definability. In *Computability Theory and its Applications: Current Trends and Open Problems*, ed. P. Cholak, S. Lempp, M. Lerman, and R. Shore, 297–307. Contemporary math, Vol. 257. Providence, RI: American Mathematical Society.

Soare, R. I. 2004. Computability theory and differential geometry. *Bulletin of Symbolic Logic* 10:457–86.

Soare, R. I. 2007. Computability and incomputability. In *Computation and Logic in the Real World*, ed. S. B. Cooper, B. Löwe, and A. Sorbi. Lecture notes in computer science, Vol. 4497. Heidelberg: Springer-Verlag.

Soare, R. I. 2009. Turing functionals and interactive computing. *Annals of Pure and Applied Logic* 160(3):369–99.

Soare, R. I., 2012. Formalism and intuition in computability theory. *Philosophical Transactions of the Royal Society A* 370:3277–3304.

Soare, R. I. 2013. Turing and the Art of Classical Computability. In *Alan Turing: His Work and Impact*, ed. B. Cooper and J. van Leeuwen. Amsterdam: Elsevier.

Soare, R. I. in press. *Computability Theory and Applications: The Art of Classical Computability*. Heidelberg: Springer-Verlag.

Teuscher, C., ed. 2004. *Alan Turing: Life and Legacy of a Great Thinker*. Heidelberg: Springer-Verlag.

Turing, A. M. 1936. On computable numbers, with an application to the *Entscheidungsproblem*. *Proceedings of the London Mathematical Society* 42:230–65. Reprinted in Davis, *The Undecidable*, 115–153.

Turing, A. M. 1937a. A correction. *Proceedings of the London Mathematical Society* 43:544–46.

Turing, A. M. 1937b. Computability and λ-definability. *Journal of Symbolic Logic* 2:153–63.

Turing, A. M. 1939. Systems of logic based on ordinals. *Proceedings of the London Mathematical Society*, 45(2):161–228. Reprinted in Davis, *The Undecidable*, 154–222.

Turing, A. M. 1947. Lecture to the London Mathematical Society on February 20, 1947. In *A. M. Turing's ACE Report of 1946 and Other Papers,* ed. B. E. Carpenter and R. W. Doran,106–124. Cambridge: Cambridge University Press, 1986.

Turing, A. M. 1948. Intelligent Machinery. In *Collected Works of A. M. Turing: Mechanical Intelligence,* ed. D. C. Ince, 107–27. Amsterdam: North-Holland. (Written in September, 1947 and submitted to the National Physical Laboratory in 1948.)

Turing, A. M. 1949. Lecture on June 24, 1949. In An early program proof by Alan Turing, F. L. Morris and C. B. Jones. *Annals of the History of Computing* 6:139–143.

Turing, A. M. 1950a. Computing machinery and intelligence. *Mind* 59:433–60.

Turing, A. M. 1950b. The word problem in semi-groups with cancellation. *Annals of Mathematics* 52:491–505.

Turing, A. M. 1954. Solvable and unsolvable problems. *Science News* 31:7–23.

Wang, H. 1974. *From Mathematics to Philosophy*. London: Routledge & Kegan Paul.

Wang, H. 1981. Some facts about Kurt Gödel. *Journal of Symbolic Logic* 46:653–59.

Wang, H. 1987. *Reflections on Kurt Gödel*. Cambridge, MA: MIT Press.

Wang, H. 1993. On physicalism and algorithmism: Can machines think? *Philosophia Mathematica* 1:97–138.

10 Why Philosophers Should Care about Computational Complexity

Scott Aaronson

The view that machines cannot give rise to surprises is due, I believe, to a fallacy to which philosophers and mathematicians are particularly subject. This is the assumption that as soon as a fact is presented to a mind all consequences of that fact spring into the mind simultaneously with it. It is a very useful assumption under many circumstances, but one too easily forgets that it is false.
—Alan M. Turing (1950)

The theory of computing, created by Alan Turing, Alonzo Church, Kurt Gödel, and others in the 1930s, didn't only change civilization; it also had a lasting impact on philosophy. Indeed, clarifying philosophical issues was the original *point* of their work; the technological payoffs only came later! Today, it would be hard to imagine a serious discussion about (say) the philosophy of mind, the foundations of mathematics, or the prospects of machine intelligence that was uninformed by this revolution in human knowledge three-quarters of a century ago.

However, as computers became widely available starting in the 1960s, computer scientists increasingly came to see computability theory as not asking quite the right questions, since almost *all* the problems we actually want to solve turn out to be computable in Turing's sense; the real question is which problems are *efficiently* or *feasibly* computable. The latter question gave rise to a new field, called computational complexity theory (not to be confused with the "other" complexity theory, which studies complex systems such as cellular automata). Since the 1970s, computational complexity theory has witnessed some spectacular discoveries, which include NP-completeness, public-key cryptography, new types of mathematical proof (such as probabilistic, interactive, and zero-knowledge proofs), and the theoretical foundations of machine learning and quantum computation. To people who work on these topics, the work of Gödel and Turing may look in retrospect like just a warm-up to the "big" questions about computation.

Because of this, I find it surprising that complexity theory has *not* influenced philosophy to anything like the extent computability theory has. The question arises:

why hasn't it? Several possible answers spring to mind: maybe computability theory just had richer philosophical implications. (Though as we'll see, one can make a strong case for exactly the opposite.) Maybe complexity has essentially the *same* philosophical implications as computability, and computability got there first. Maybe outsiders are scared away from learning complexity theory by the "math barrier." Maybe the explanation is social: the world where Gödel, Turing, Ludwig Wittgenstein, and Bertrand Russell participated in the same intellectual conversation vanished with World War II; after that, theoretical computer science came to be driven by technology and lost touch with its philosophical origins. Maybe recent advances in complexity theory simply haven't had enough time to enter philosophical consciousness.

However, I suspect that part of the answer is just *complexity theorists' failure to communicate* what they can add to philosophy's conceptual arsenal. Hence this essay, whose modest goal is to help correct that failure by surveying some aspects of complexity theory that might interest philosophers, as well as several philosophical problems that I think a complexity perspective can clarify.

To forestall misunderstandings, let me add a note of humility before going further. This essay will touch on many problems that philosophers have debated for generations, such as strong artificial intelligence (AI), the problem of induction, the relation between syntax and semantics, and the interpretation of quantum mechanics. *In none of these cases* will I claim that computational complexity theory "dissolves" the philosophical problem—only that it contributes useful perspectives and insights. I'll often explicitly mention philosophical puzzles that I think a complexity analysis either leaves untouched or else introduces itself. But even where I don't do so, one shouldn't presume that I think there are no such puzzles! Indeed, one of my hopes for this essay is that computer scientists, mathematicians, and other technical people who read it will come away with a better appreciation for the subtlety of some of the problems considered in modern analytic philosophy.[1]

10.1 What This Essay *Won't* Cover

I won't try to discuss every *possible* connection between computational complexity and philosophy, or even every connection that's already been made. A small number of philosophers have long invoked computational complexity ideas in their work; indeed, the "philpapers" archive lists thirty-two papers under the heading "computational complexity."[2] The majority of those papers prove theorems about the computational complexities of various logical systems. Of the remaining papers, some use "computational complexity" in a different sense than I do—for example, to encompass computability theory—and some invoke the *concept* of computational complexity, but no particular results from the *field* devoted to it. Perhaps the closest in spirit to this essay are the interesting articles by Cherniak (1984) and Morton (2004). In addition, many writers have made some version of the observations in section 10.4, about computational complexity and the Turing test: see, for example, Block (2002), Parberry (1997), Levesque (2009), and Shieber (2007).

In deciding which connections to include in this essay, I adopted the following ground rules:

1. The connection must involve a "properly philosophical" problem—for example, the justification for induction or the nature of mathematical knowledge—and not just a technical problem in logic or model theory.

2. The connection must draw on *specific insights* from the field of computational complexity theory: not just the *idea* of complexity, or the *fact* that there exist hard problems.

There are many philosophically interesting ideas in modern complexity theory that this essay mentions only briefly or not at all. One example is *pseudorandom generators* (see Goldreich 2010): functions that convert a short random "seed" into a long string of bits that, while not truly random, is so "random-looking" that no efficient algorithm can detect any regularities in it. While pseudorandom generators in this sense are not yet proved to exist,[3] there are many plausible candidates, and the belief that at least some of the candidates work is central to modern cryptography. (Section 10.7.1 will invoke the related concept of pseudorandom *functions*.) A second example is *fully homomorphic encryption*: an extremely exciting new class of methods, the first of which was announced by Gentry (2009), for performing arbitrary computations on encrypted data *without ever decrypting the data*. The output of such a computation will look like meaningless gibberish to the person who computed it, but it can nevertheless be understood (and even recognized as the correct output) by someone who knows the decryption key. What are the implications of pseudorandom generators for the foundations of probability, or of fully homomorphic encryption for debates about the semantic meaning of computations? I very much hope this essay will inspire others to tackle these and similar questions.

Outside of computational complexity, there are at least three other major intersection points between philosophy and modern theoretical computer science. The first one is the *semantics of programming languages*, which has large and obvious connections to the philosophy of language.[4] The second is *distributed systems theory*, which provides both an application area and a rich source of examples for philosophical work on reasoning about knowledge (see Fagin et al. 1995 and Stalnaker 1999). The third is *Kolmogorov complexity* (see Li and Vitányi 2008), which studies the *length* of the shortest computer program that achieves some functionality, disregarding time, memory, and other resources used by the program.[5]

In this essay, I won't discuss *any* of these connections, except in passing (for example, section 10.5 touches on logics of knowledge in the context of the "logical omniscience problem," and section 10.7 touches on Kolmogorov complexity in the context of PAC, or probably approximately correct, learning). In defense of these omissions, let me offer four excuses. First, these other connections fall outside my stated topic. Second, they would make this essay even longer than it already is. Third, I lack requisite background. And fourth, my impression is that philosophers—at least *some* philosophers—are already more aware of these other connections than they are of the computational complexity connections that I want to explain.

10.2 Complexity 101

Computational complexity theory is a huge, sprawling field; naturally this essay will only touch on small parts of it. Readers who want to delve deeper into the subject are urged to consult one of the many outstanding textbooks, such as those of Sipser (2005), Papadimitriou (1994), Moore and Mertens (2011), Goldreich (2008), or Arora and Barak (2009); or survey articles by Wigderson (2007, 2009), Fortnow and Homer (2003), or Stockmeyer (1987).

One might think that, once we know something is *computable*, whether it takes 10 seconds or 20 seconds to compute is obviously the concern of engineers rather than philosophers. But that conclusion would *not* be so obvious, if the question were one of 10 seconds versus $10^{10^{10}}$ seconds! And indeed, in complexity theory, the quantitative gaps we care about are usually so vast that one has to consider them qualitative gaps as well. Think, for example, of the difference between reading a four-hundred-page book and reading *every possible* such book, or between writing down a thousand-digit number and counting to that number.

More precisely, complexity theory asks the question: how do the resources needed to solve a problem scale with some measure n of the problem size: "reasonably" (like n or n^2, say), or "unreasonably" (like 2^n or $n!$)? As an example, two n-digit integers can be multiplied using $\sim n^2$ computational steps (by the grade-school method), or even $\sim n \log n \log \log n$ steps (by more advanced methods [Schönhage and Strassen 1971]). Either method is considered efficient. By contrast, the fastest known method for the reverse operation—*factoring* an n-digit integer into primes— uses $2^{n^{1/3}}$ steps, which is considered inefficient.[6] Famously, this conjectured gap between the inherent difficulties of multiplying and factoring is the basis for most of the cryptography currently used on the Internet.

Theoretical computer scientists generally call an algorithm "efficient" if its running time can be upper-bounded by any polynomial function of n, and "inefficient" if its running time can be lower-bounded by any exponential function of n.[7] These criteria have the great advantage of theoretical convenience. While the exact complexity of a problem might depend on "low-level encoding details," such as whether our Turing machine has one or two memory tapes, or how the inputs are encoded as binary strings, where a problem falls on the polynomial-exponential dichotomy can be shown to be independent of almost all such choices.[8] Equally important are the *closure properties* of polynomial and exponential time: a polynomial-time algorithm that calls a polynomial-time subroutine still yields an overall polynomial-time algorithm, while a polynomial-time algorithm that calls an exponential-time subroutine (or vice versa) yields an exponential-time algorithm. There are also more sophisticated reasons why theoretical computer scientists focus on polynomial time (rather than, say, n^2 time or $n^{\log n}$ time); we'll explore some of those reasons in section 10.5.1.

The polynomial-exponential distinction is open to obvious objections: an algorithm that took 1.00000001^n steps would be much faster in practice than an algorithm that took n^{10000} steps! Furthermore, there are many growth rates that fall between polynomial and exponential, such as $n^{\log n}$ and $2^{2^{\sqrt{\log n}}}$. But empirically, polynomial time *turned out* to correspond to "efficient in practice," and exponential-time to "inefficient in practice," so often that complexity theorists became comfortable making the identification. *Why* the identification works is an interesting question in its own right, one to which we will return in section 10.12.

A priori, insisting that programs terminate after reasonable amounts of time, that they use reasonable amounts of memory, etc., might sound like relatively minor amendments to Turing's notion of computation. In practice, though, these requirements lead to a theory with a completely different character than computability theory. Firstly, complexity has much closer connections with the *sciences*: it lets us pose questions about (for example) evolution, quantum mechanics, statistical physics, economics, or human language acquisition that would be meaningless from a computability standpoint (since *all* the relevant problems are computable). Complexity also differs from computability in the diversity of mathematical *techniques* used: while initially complexity (like computability) drew mostly on mathematical logic, today it draws on probability, number theory, combinatorics, representation theory, Fourier analysis, and nearly every other subject about which yellow books are written. Of course, this contributes not only to complexity theory's depth but also to its perceived inaccessibility.

In this essay, I'll argue that complexity theory has direct relevance to major issues in philosophy, including syntax and semantics, the problem of induction, and the interpretation of quantum mechanics. Or that, at least, whether complexity theory *does or does not* have such relevance is an important question for philosophy! My personal view is that complexity will ultimately prove *more* relevant to philosophy than computability was, precisely because of the rich connections with the sciences mentioned earlier.

10.3   The Relevance of Polynomial Time

Anyone who doubts the importance of the polynomial-exponential distinction need only ponder how many basic intuitions in math, science, and philosophy already implicitly rely on that distinction. In this section I'll give three examples.

10.3.1   The *Entscheidungsproblem* Revisited

The *Entscheidungsproblem* was the dream, enunciated by David Hilbert in the 1920s, of designing a mechanical procedure to determine the truth or falsehood of any well-formed mathematical statement. According to the usual story, Hilbert's dream was irrevocably destroyed by the work of Gödel, Church, and Turing in the 1930s. First, the incompleteness theorem showed that no recursively axiomatizable formal system can encode *all and only* the true mathematical statements. Second, Church's and Turing's results showed that, even if we settle for an incomplete system F, there is *still* no mechanical procedure to sort mathematical statements into the three categories "provable in F," "disprovable in F," and "undecidable in F."

However, there is a catch in the above story, which was first pointed out by Gödel himself in a 1956 letter to John von Neumann that has become famous in theoretical computer science since its rediscovery in the 1980s (see Sipser 1992 for an English translation). Given a formal system F (such as Zermelo-Fraenkel set theory), Gödel wrote, consider the problem of deciding whether a mathematical statement S has a proof in F *with n symbols or fewer*. Unlike Hilbert's original problem, this "truncated *Entscheidungsproblem*" is clearly decidable. For, if nothing else, we could always just program a computer to search through all 2^n possible bit-strings with n symbols, and check whether any of them encodes a valid F-proof of S. The issue is "merely" that this approach takes an astronomical amount of time: if $n = 1000$ (say), then the universe will have degenerated into black holes and radiation long before a computer can check 2^{1000} proofs!

But as Gödel also pointed out, it's far from obvious how to *prove* that there isn't a much better approach: an approach that would avoid brute-force search, and find proofs of size n in time polynomial in n. Furthermore:

If there actually were a machine with [running time] $\sim Kn$ (or even only with $\sim Kn^2$) [for some constant K independent of n], this would have consequences of the greatest magnitude. That is to say, it would clearly indicate that, despite the unsolvability of the *Entscheidungsproblem*, the mental effort of the mathematician in the case of yes-or-no questions could be completely [added in a footnote: apart from the postulation of axioms] replaced by machines. One would indeed have to simply select an *n* so large that, if the machine yields no result, there would then also be no reason to think further about the problem. (Gödel 1956, quoted in Sipser 1992)

If we replace the "~*Kn* or ~*Kn²*" in Gödel's challenge by ~*Kn^c* for an *arbitrary* constant *c*, then we get precisely what computer science now knows as the P versus NP problem. Here P (polynomial time) is, roughly speaking, the class of all computational problems that are solvable by a polynomial-time algorithm. Meanwhile, NP (nondeterministic polynomial time) is the class of computational problems for which a solution can be *recognized* in polynomial time, even though a solution might be very hard to find.[9] (Think, for example, of factoring a large number, or solving a jigsaw or Sudoku puzzle.) Clearly P ⊆ NP, so the question is whether the inclusion is strict. If P = NP, then the ability to *check* the solutions to puzzles efficiently would imply the ability to *find* solutions efficiently. An analogy would be if anyone able to *appreciate* a great symphony could also compose one themselves!

Given the intuitive implausibility of such a scenario, essentially all complexity theorists proceed (reasonably, in my opinion) on the assumption that P ≠ NP, even if they publicly claim open-mindedness about the question. Proving or disproving P ≠ NP is one of the seven-million-dollar Clay Millennium Prize problems[10] (alongside the Riemann hypothesis, the Poincaré conjecture proved in 2002 by Perelman, etc.), which should give some indication of the problem's difficulty.[11]

Now return to the problem of whether a mathematical statement S has a proof with *n* symbols or fewer, in some formal system *F*. A suitable formalization of this problem is easily seen to be in NP. For *finding* a proof might be intractable, but if we're *given* a purported proof, we can certainly check in time polynomial in *n* whether each line of the proof follows by a simple logical manipulation of previous lines. Indeed, this problem turns out to be NP-*complete*, which means that it belongs to an enormous class of NP problems, first identified in the 1970s, that "capture the entire difficulty of NP." A few other examples of NP-complete problems are Sudoku and jigsaw puzzles, the traveling salesperson problem, and the satisfiability problem for propositional formulas.[12] Asking whether P = NP is equivalent to asking whether *any* NP-complete problem can be solved in polynomial time, and is also equivalent to asking whether *all* of them can be.

In modern terms, then, Gödel is saying that if P = NP, then whenever a theorem had a proof of reasonable length, we could *find* that proof in a reasonable amount of time. In such a situation, we might say that "for all practical purposes," Hilbert's dream of mechanizing mathematics had prevailed, despite the undecidability results of Gödel, Church, and Turing. If you accept this, then it seems fair to say that until

P versus NP is solved, the story of Hilbert's *Entscheidungsproblem*—its rise, its fall, and the consequences for philosophy—is not yet over.

10.3.2   Evolvability

Creationists often claim that Darwinian evolution is as vacuous an explanation for complex adaptations as "a tornado assembling a 747 airplane as it passes through a junkyard." Why is this claim false? There are several related ways of answering the question, but to me, one of the most illuminating is the following. In principle, one *could* see a 747 assemble itself in a tornado-prone junkyard—but before that happened, one would need to wait for an expected number of tornadoes that grew *exponentially* with the number of pieces of self-assembling junk. (This is similar to how, in thermodynamics, n gas particles in a box *will* eventually congregate themselves in one corner of the box, but only after $\sim c^n$ time for some constant c.) By contrast, evolutionary processes can often be observed in simulations—and in some cases, even proved theoretically (Rabinovich and Wigderson 1999)—to find interesting solutions to optimization problems after a number of steps that grows only *polynomially* with the number of variables.

Interestingly, in a 1972 letter to Hao Wang (see Wang 1997, 192), Kurt Gödel expressed his own doubts about evolution as follows:

I believe that mechanism in biology is a prejudice of our time which will be disproved. In this case, one disproof, in my opinion, will consist in a mathematical theorem to the effect that the formation within geological time of a human body by the laws of physics (or any other laws of similar nature), starting from a random distribution of the elementary particles and the field, is as unlikely as the separation by chance of the atmosphere into its components.

Personally, I see no reason to accept Gödel's intuition on this subject over the consensus of modern biology! But pay attention to Gödel's characteristically careful phrasing. He does not ask whether evolution can *eventually* form a human body (for he knows that it can, given exponential time); instead, he asks whether it can do so on a "merely" geological timescale. Just as Gödel's letter to von Neumann anticipated the P versus NP problem, so Gödel's letter to Wang might be said to anticipate a recent effort, by the celebrated computer scientist Leslie Valiant, to construct a quantitative "theory of evolvability" (Valiant 2009). Building on Valiant's earlier work in computational learning theory (discussed in section 10.7), evolvability tries to formalize and answer questions about the *speed* of evolution. For example: "what sorts of adaptive behaviors can evolve, with high probability, after only a polynomial number of generations? What sorts of behaviors can be learned in polynomial time, but *not* via evolution?" While there are some interesting early results, it should surprise no one that evolvability is nowhere close to being able to calculate, from first principles, whether four billion years is a "reasonable" or "unreasonable" length of time for the human brain to evolve out of the primordial soup.

As I see it, this difficulty reflects a general point about Gödel's "evolvability" question. Namely, even *supposing* Gödel was right, that the mechanistic worldview of modern biology was "as unlikely as the separation by chance of the atmosphere into its components," computational complexity theory seems hopelessly far from being able to *prove* anything of the kind! In 1972, one could have argued that this merely reflected the subject's newness: no one had thought terribly deeply yet about how to prove *lower bounds* on computation time. But by now, people *have* thought deeply about it, and have identified huge obstacles to proving even such "obvious" and well-defined conjectures as P ≠ NP.[13] (Section 10.4 will make a related point, about the difficulty of proving nontrivial lower bounds on the time or memory needed by a computer program to pass the Turing test.)

10.3.3 Known Integers

My last example of the philosophical relevance of the polynomial-exponential distinction concerns the concept of "knowledge" in mathematics.[14] As of 2011, the "largest known prime number," as reported by GIMPS (the Great Internet Mersenne Prime Search),[15] is $p := 2^{43112609} - 1$. But on reflection, what do we mean by saying that p is "known"? Do we mean that, if we desired, we could literally print out its decimal digits (using about 30,000 pages)? That seems like too restrictive a criterion. For, given a positive integer k together with a proof that $q = 2^k - 1$ was prime, I doubt most mathematicians would hesitate to call q a "known" prime,[16] even if k were so large that printing out its decimal digits (or storing them in a computer memory) were beyond the Earth's capacity. Should we call $2^{2^{1000}}$ an "unknown power of 2," just because it has too many decimal digits to list before the Sun goes cold?

All that should *really* matter, one feels, is that

1. the expression '$2^{43112609} - 1$' picks out a unique positive integer, and

2. that integer has been proven (in this case, via computer, of course) to be prime.

But wait! If those are the criteria, then why can't we immediately beat the largest-known-prime record, like this?

$p' =$ The first prime larger than $2^{43112609} - 1$.

Clearly p' exists, it is unambiguously defined, and it is prime. If we want, we can even write a program that is guaranteed to find p' and output its decimal digits, using a number of steps that can be upper-bounded a priori.[17] Yet our intuition stubbornly insists that $2^{43112609} - 1$ is a "known" prime in a sense that p' is not. Is there any principled basis for such a distinction?

The clearest basis that I can suggest is the following. We know an algorithm that takes as input a positive integer k, and that outputs the decimal digits of $p = 2^k - 1$ *using a number of steps that is polynomial—indeed, linear—in the number of digits of p*. But we do not know any similarly efficient algorithm that provably outputs the first prime larger than $2^k - 1$.[18]

10.3.4 Summary

The point of these examples was to illustrate that, beyond its utility for theoretical computer science, the polynomial-exponential gap is also a fertile territory for philosophy. I think of the polynomial-exponential gap as occupying a "middle ground" between two other sorts of gaps: on the one hand, small quantitative gaps (such as the gap between n steps and $2n$ steps); and on the other hand, the gap between a finite number of steps and an infinite number. The trouble with small quantitative gaps is that they are too sensitive to "mundane" modeling choices and the details of technology. But the gap between finite and infinite has the opposite problem: it is serenely *in*sensitive to distinctions that we actually care about, such as that between finding a solution and verifying it, or between classical and quantum physics.[19] The polynomial-exponential gap avoids both problems.

10.4 Computational Complexity and the Turing Test

Can a computer think? For almost a century, discussions about this question have often conflated two issues. The first is the "metaphysical" issue:

Supposing a computer program passed the Turing test (or as strong a variant of the Turing test as one wishes to define),[20] would we be right to ascribe to it "consciousness," "qualia," "aboutness," "intentionality," "subjectivity," "personhood," or whatever other charmed status we wish to ascribe to other humans and to ourselves?

The second is the "practical" issue:

Could a computer program that passed (a strong version of) the Turing test actually be written? Is there some fundamental reason why it couldn't be?

Of course, it was precisely in an attempt to separate these issues that Turing proposed the Turing test in the first place! But despite his efforts, a familiar feature of anti-AI arguments to this day is that they first assert AI's metaphysical impossibility, and then try to bolster that position with claims about AI's practical difficulties. "Sure," they say, "a computer program might mimic a few minutes of witty banter, but unlike a human being, it would never show fear or anger or jealousy, or compose symphonies, or grow old, or fall in love …"

The obvious follow-up question—and what if a program *did* do all those things?—is often left unasked, or else answered by listing more things that a computer program could self-evidently never do. Because of this, I suspect that many people who *say* they consider AI a metaphysical impossibility, really consider it only a practical impossibility: they simply have not carried the requisite thought experiment far enough to see the difference between the two.[21] Incidentally, this is as clear-cut a case as I know of where people would benefit from studying more philosophy!

Thus, the anti-AI arguments that interest me most have always been the ones that target the practical issue from the outset, by proposing empirical "sword-in-the-stone tests" (in Daniel Dennett's [1995] phrase) that it is claimed humans can pass but computers cannot. The most famous such test is probably the one based on Gödel's incompleteness theorem, as proposed by John Lucas (1961) and elaborated by Roger Penrose in his books *The Emperor's New Mind* (1989) and *Shadows of the Mind* (1996).

Briefly, Lucas and Penrose argued that, according to the incompleteness theorem, one thing that a computer making deductions via fixed formal rules can never do is to "see" the consistency of its own rules. Yet this, they assert, is something that human mathematicians *can* do, via some sort of intuitive perception of Platonic reality. Therefore humans (or at least, human mathematicians!) can never be simulated by machines.

Critics pointed out numerous holes in this argument,[22] to which Penrose responded at length in *Shadows of the Mind*, in my opinion unconvincingly. However, even *before* we analyze some proposed sword-in-the-stone test, it seems to me that there is a much more basic question. Namely, what does one even *mean* in saying one has a task that "humans can perform but computers cannot"?

10.4.1   The Lookup-Table Argument

There is a fundamental difficulty here, which was noticed by others in a slightly different context (Block 2002; Parberry 1997; Levesque 2009; Shieber 2007). Let me first explain the difficulty, and then discuss the difference between my argument and the previous ones.

In practice, people judge each other to be conscious after interacting for a very short time, perhaps as little as a few seconds. This suggests that we can put a finite upper bound—to be generous, let us say 10^{20}—on the number of bits of information that two people A and B would ever realistically exchange, before A had amassed enough evidence to conclude B was conscious.[23] Now imagine a lookup table that stores every possible history H of A and B's conversation, and next to H, the action $f_B(H)$ that B *would* take next given that history. Of course, like Borges' Library of Babel, the lookup table would consist almost entirely of meaningless nonsense, and it would also be much too large to fit inside the observed universe. But all that matters for us is that the lookup table would be *finite*, by the assumption that there is a finite upper bound on the conversation length. This implies that the function f_B is computable (indeed, it can be recognized by a finite automaton!). From these simple considerations, we conclude that if there *is* a fundamental obstacle to computers passing the Turing test, then it is not to be found in computability theory.[24]

In *Shadows of the Mind*, Penrose recognizes this problem, but gives a puzzling and unsatisfying response:

One could equally well envisage computers that contain nothing but lists of totally false mathematical "theorems," or lists containing random jumbles of truths and falsehoods. How are we to tell which computer to trust? The arguments that I am trying to make here do not say that an effective simulation of the output of conscious human activity (here mathematics) is impossible, since purely by chance the computer might "happen" to get it right—even without any understanding whatsoever. But the odds against this are absurdly enormous, and the issues that are being addressed here, namely how one decides *which* mathematical statements are true and which are false, are not even being touched. (1996, 83)

The trouble with this response is that it amounts to a retreat from the sword-in-the-stone test, back to murkier internal criteria. If, in the end, we are going to have to look inside the computer anyway to determine whether it truly "understands" its answers, *then why not dispense with computability theory from the beginning?* For computability theory only addresses whether or not Turing machines *exist* to solve various problems, and we have already seen that that is not the relevant issue.

To my mind, there is *one* direction that Penrose could take from this point to avoid incoherence—though disappointingly, it is not the direction he chooses. Namely, he could point out that, while the lookup table "works," it requires computational resources that grow exponentially with the length of the conversation! This would lead to the following speculation:

(*) *Any* computer program that passed the Turing test would need to be exponentially inefficient in the length of the test—as measured in some resource such as time, memory usage, or the number of bits needed to write the program down. In other words, the astronomical lookup table is essentially the best one can do.[25]

If true, speculation (*) would do what Penrose wants: it would imply that the human brain can't even be *simulated* by computer, within the resource constraints of the observable universe. Furthermore, unlike the earlier computability claim, (*) has the advantage of not being trivially false!

On the other hand, to put it mildly, (*) is not trivially *true* either. For AI proponents, the lack of compelling evidence for (*) is hardly surprising. After all, if you believe that the brain *itself* is basically an efficient,[26] classical Turing machine, then you have a simple explanation for why no one has proved that the brain can't be simulated by such a machine! However, complexity theory also makes it clear that, *even if we supposed (*) held*, there would be little hope of *proving* it in our current state of mathematical knowledge. After all, we can't even prove plausible, well-defined conjectures such as P ≠ NP.

10.4.2 Relation to Previous Work

As mentioned before, I'm far from the first person to ask about the *computational resources* used in passing the Turing test, and whether they scale polynomially or exponentially with the conversation length. While many writers ignore this crucial distinction, Block (2002), Parberry (1997), Levesque (2009), Shieber (2007), and several others all discussed it explicitly. The main difference is that the previous discussions took place in the context of Searle's Chinese Room argument (Searle 1980).

Briefly, Searle proposed a thought experiment—the details don't concern us here—purporting to show that a computer program could pass the Turing test, even though the program manifestly lacked anything that a reasonable person would call "intelligence" or "understanding." (Indeed, Searle argues that *no* physical system can understand anything "purely by virtue of" the computations that it implements.) In response, many critics said that Searle's argument was deeply misleading, because it implicitly encouraged us to imagine a computer program that was *simplistic* in its internal operations—something like the giant lookup table described in section 10.4.1. And while it was true, the critics went on, that a giant lookup table wouldn't "truly understand" its responses, that point is also *irrelevant*. For the giant lookup table is a philosophical fiction anyway: something that can't even fit in the observable universe! If we instead imagine a *compact, efficient* computer program passing the Turing test, then the situation changes drastically. For now, in order to *explain* how the program can be so compact and efficient, we'll need to posit that the program includes representations of abstract concepts, capacities for learning and reasoning, and all sorts of other internal furniture that we would expect to find in a mind.

Personally, I find this response to Searle extremely interesting—since, if correct, it suggests that the distinction between polynomial and exponential complexity has *metaphysical* significance. According to this response, an exponential-sized lookup table that passed the Turing test would not be sentient (or conscious, intelligent, self-aware, etc.), but a polynomially-bounded program with exactly the same input/output behavior *would* be sentient. Furthermore, the latter program would be sentient *because* it was polynomially-bounded.

Yet, as much as that criterion for sentience flatters my complexity-theoretic pride, I find myself reluctant to take a position on such a weighty matter. My point, in section 10.4.1, was a simpler and (hopefully) less controversial one: namely, that if you want to claim that passing the Turing test is *flat-out impossible*, then like it or not, you *must* talk about complexity rather than just computability. In other words, the previous writers (Block 2002; Parberry 1997; Levesque 2009; Shieber 2007) and I are all interested in the computational resources needed to pass a Turing test of length n, but for different reasons. Where others invoked complexity considerations to argue with Searle about the metaphysical question, I'm invoking them to argue with Penrose about the practical question.

10.4.3   Can Humans Solve NP-Complete Problems Efficiently?

In that case, what can we actually *say* about the practical question? Are there any reasons to accept the claim I called (*)—the claim that humans are *not* efficiently simulable by Turing machines? In considering this question, we're immediately led to some speculative possibilities. So for example, *if* it turned out that humans could solve arbitrary instances of NP-complete problems in polynomial time, then that would certainly constitute excellent empirical evidence for (*).[27] However, despite occasional claims to the contrary, I personally see no reason to believe that humans *can* solve NP-complete problems in polynomial time, and excellent reasons to believe the opposite.[28] Recall, for example, that the integer factoring problem is in NP. Thus, if humans could solve NP-complete problems, then presumably we ought to be able to factor enormous numbers as well! But factoring does not exactly seem like the most promising candidate for a sword-in-the-stone test: that is, a task that's easy for humans but hard for computers. As far as anyone knows today, factoring is hard for humans and (classical) computers *alike*, although with a definite advantage on the computers' side!

The basic point can hardly be stressed enough: when complexity theorists talk about "intractable" problems, they generally mean mathematical problems that all our experience leads us to believe are at least as hard for humans as for computers. This suggests that, *even if* humans were not efficiently simulable by Turing machines, the "direction" in which they were hard to simulate would almost certainly be different from the directions usually considered in complexity theory. I see two (hypothetical) ways this could happen.

First, the tasks that humans were uniquely good at—like painting or writing poetry—could be *incomparable* with mathematical tasks like solving NP-complete problems, in the sense that neither was efficiently reducible to the other. This would mean, in particular, that there could be no polynomial-time algorithm even to *recognize* great art or poetry (since if such an algorithm existed, then the task of *composing* great art or poetry would be in NP). Within complexity theory, it's known that there exist pairs of problems that are incomparable in this sense. As one plausible example, no one currently knows how to reduce the simulation of quantum computers to the solution of NP-complete problems *or* vice versa.

Second, humans could have the ability to solve interesting *special cases* of NP-complete problems faster than any Turing machine. So for example, even if computers were better than humans at factoring large numbers or at solving randomly generated Sudoku puzzles, humans might still be better at search problems with "higher-level structure" or "semantics," such as proving Fermat's last theorem or (ironically) designing faster computer algorithms. Indeed, even in limited domains such as puzzle-solving, while computers can examine solutions millions of times faster, humans (for now) are vastly better at noticing *global patterns* or *symmetries* in the puzzle that make a solution either trivial or impossible. As an amusing example, consider the *pigeonhole principle*, which says that $n + 1$ pigeons can't be placed into n holes, with at most one pigeon per hole. It's not hard to construct a propositional Boolean formula φ that encodes the pigeonhole principle for some fixed value of n (say, 1,000). However, if you then feed φ to current Boolean satisfiability algorithms, they'll assiduously set to work trying out possibilities: "let's see, if I put *this* pigeon here, and *that* one there ... darn, it *still* doesn't work!" And they'll continue trying out possibilities for an exponential number of steps, oblivious to the "global" reason why the goal can never be achieved. Indeed, beginning in the 1980s, the field of *proof complexity*—a close cousin of computational complexity—has been able to show that large classes of algorithms *require* exponential time to prove the pigeonhole principle and similar propositional tautologies (see Beame and Pitassi 2001 for a survey).

Still, if we want to build our sword-in-the-stone test on the ability to detect "higher-level patterns" in combinatorial search problems, then the burden is on us to explain what we *mean* by higher-level patterns, and why we think that *no* polynomial-time Turing machine—even much more sophisticated ones than we can imagine today—could ever detect those patterns as well. For an initial attempt to understand NP-complete problems from a cognitive science perspective, see Baum (2004).

10.4.4 Summary

My conclusion is that, if you oppose the possibility of AI in principle, then either

1. you can take the "metaphysical route" (as Searle [1980] does with the Chinese Room), conceding the possibility of a computer program passing every conceivable empirical test for intelligence, but arguing that that isn't enough, or

2. you can conjecture an *astronomical lower bound on the resources* needed either to run such a program or to write it in the first place—but here there is little question of proof for the foreseeable future.

Crucially, because of the lookup-table argument, one option you do *not* have is to assert the flat-out impossibility of a computer program passing the Turing test, with no mention of quantitative complexity bounds.

10.5   The Problem of Logical Omniscience

Giving a formal account of *knowledge* is one of the central concerns in modern analytic philosophy; the literature is too vast even to survey here (though see Fagin et al. 1995 for a computer-science–friendly overview). Typically, formal accounts of knowledge involve conventional "logical" axioms, such as

- If you know P and you know Q, then you also know $P \wedge Q$

supplemented by "modal" axioms having to do with knowledge itself, such as

- If you know P, then you also know that you know P
- If you don't know P, then you know that you don't know P.[29]

While the details differ, what most formal accounts of knowledge have in common is that they treat an agent's knowledge as *closed* under the application of various deduction rules like the ones above. In other words, agents are considered *logically omniscient*: if they know certain facts, then they also know all possible logical consequences of those facts.

Sadly and obviously, no mortal being has ever attained or even approximated this sort of omniscience (recall the Turing quote from the beginning of section 10.1). So for example, I can know the rules of arithmetic without knowing Fermat's last theorem, and I can know the rules of chess without knowing whether White has a forced win. Furthermore, the difficulty is *not* (as sometimes claimed) limited to a few domains, such as mathematics and games. As pointed out by Stalnaker (1999), if we assumed logical omniscience, then we couldn't account for *any* contemplation of facts already known to us—and thus, for the main activity and one of the main subjects of philosophy itself!

We can now loosely state what Hintikka (1962) called the *problem of logical omniscience*:

Can we give some formal account of "knowledge" able to accommodate people learning new things without leaving their armchairs?

Of course, one vacuous "solution" would be to declare that your knowledge is simply a list of all the true sentences[30] that you "know"—and that, if the list happens not to be closed under logical deductions, so be it! But this "solution" is no help at all at explaining *how* or *why* you know things. Can't we do better?

Intuitively, we want to say that your "knowledge" consists of various facts ("grass is green"), together with *some* simple logical consequences of those facts ("grass is not pink"), but not necessarily *all* the consequences, and certainly not all consequences that involve difficult mathematical reasoning. Unfortunately, as soon as we try to formalize this idea, we run into problems.

The most obvious problem is the lack of a sharp boundary between the facts you know right away, and those you "could" know, but only after significant thought. (Recall the discussion of "known primes" from section 10.3.3.) A related problem is the lack of a sharp boundary between the facts you know "only if asked about them," and those you know even if you're *not* asked. Interestingly, these two boundaries seem to cut across each other. For example, while you've probably already encountered the fact that 91 is composite, it might take you some time to remember it; while you've probably *never* encountered the fact that 83190 is composite, once asked you can probably assent to it immediately.

But as discussed by Stalnaker (1999), there's a third problem that seems much more serious than either of the two above. Namely, you might "know" a particular fact if asked about it one way, but not if asked in a different way! To illustrate this, Stalnaker uses an example that we can recognize immediately from the discussion of the P versus NP problem in section 10.3.1. If I asked you whether $43 \times 37 = 1591$, you could probably answer easily (e.g., by using $(40 + 3)\,(40-3) = 40^2 - 3^2$). On the other hand, if I instead asked you what the prime factors[31] of 1591 were, you probably *couldn't* answer so easily.

But the answers to the two questions have the same content, even on a very fine-grained notion of content. Suppose that we fix the threshold of accessibility so that the information that 43 and 37 are the prime factors of 1591 is accessible in response to the second question, but not accessible in response to the first. Do you know what the prime factors of 1591 are or not? ... Our problem is that we are not just trying to say what an agent would know upon being asked certain questions; rather, we are trying to use the facts about an agent's question answering capacities in order to get at what the agent knows, even if the questions are not asked. (Stalnaker 1999, 253)

To add another example: does a typical four-year-old child "know" that addition of reals is commutative? Certainly not if we asked her in those words—and if we tried to *explain* the words, she probably wouldn't understand us. Yet if we showed her a stack of books, and asked her whether she could make the stack higher by shuffling the books, she probably wouldn't make a mistake that involved imagining addition was non-commutative. In that sense, we might say she already "implicitly" knows what her math classes will later make explicit.

In my view, these and other examples strongly suggest that only a small part of what we mean by "knowledge" is knowledge about the truth or falsehood of individual propositions. And crucially, this remains so even if we restrict our attention to "purely verbalizable" knowledge—indeed, *knowledge used for answering factual questions*—and not (say) knowledge of how to ride a bike or swing a golf club, or knowledge of a person or a place.[32] Many everyday uses of the word "know" support this idea:

Do you know calculus?

Do you know Spanish?

Do you know the rules of bridge?

Each of the above questions could be interpreted as asking: *do you possess an internal algorithm, by which you can answer a large (and possibly unbounded) set of questions of some form?* While this is rarely made explicit, the examples of this section and of section 10.3.3 suggest adding the proviso: ... *answer in a reasonable amount of time?*

But suppose we accept that "knowing how" (or "knowing a good algorithm for") is a more fundamental concept than "knowing that." How does that help us *at all* in solving the logical omniscience problem? You might worry that we're right back where we started. After all, if we try to give a formal account of "knowing how," then just like in the case of "knowing that," it will be tempting to write down axioms like the following:

If you know how to compute $f(x)$ and $g(x)$ efficiently, then you also know how to compute $f(x) + g(x)$ efficiently.

Naturally, we'll then want to take the logical closure of those axioms. But then, before we know it, won't we have conjured into our imaginations a computationally omniscient superbeing, who could efficiently compute anything at all?

10.5.1 The Cobham Axioms

Happily, the above worry turns out to be unfounded. We *can* write down reasonable axioms for "knowing how to compute efficiently," and then *go ahead and take the closure of those axioms*, without getting the unwanted consequence of computational omniscience. Explaining this point will involve a digression into an old and fascinating corner of complexity theory—one that probably holds independent interest for philosophers.

As is well known, in the 1930s Church and Kleene proposed definitions of the "computable functions" that turned out to be precisely equivalent to Turing's definition, but that differed from Turing's in making no explicit mention of machines. Rather than analyzing the *process* of computation, the Church-Kleene approach was simply to list *axioms* that the computable functions of natural numbers $f: \mathbb{N} \to \mathbb{N}$ ought to satisfy—for example, "if $f(x)$ and $g(x)$ are both computable, then so is

$f(g(x))$"—and then to define "the" computable functions as the smallest set satisfying those axioms.

In 1965, Alan Cobham asked whether the same could be done for the *efficiently* or *feasibly* computable functions (Cobham 1965). As an answer, he offered axioms that precisely characterize what today we call FP, or function polynomial time (though Cobham called it $\mathcal{L}$). The class FP consists of all functions of natural numbers $f: \mathbb{N} \to \mathbb{N}$ that are computable in polynomial time by a deterministic Turing machine. Note that FP is "morally" the same as the class P (polynomial time) defined in section 10.3.1: they differ only in that P is a class of *decision* problems (or equivalently, functions $f: \mathbb{N} \to \{0, 1\}$), whereas FP is a class of functions with integer range.

What was noteworthy about Cobham's characterization of polynomial time was that it didn't involve *any* explicit mention of either computing devices or bounds on their running time. Let me now list a version of Cobham's axioms, adapted from Arora, Impagliazzo, and Vazirani (1992). Each of the axioms talks about which functions of natural numbers $f: \mathbb{N} \to \mathbb{N}$ are "efficiently computable."

1. Every constant function f is efficiently computable, as is every function which is nonzero only finitely often.

2. *Pairing:* If $f(x)$ and $g(x)$ are efficiently computable, then so is $\langle f(x), g(x) \rangle$, where $\langle , \rangle$ is some standard pairing function for the natural numbers.

3. *Composition:* If $f(x)$ and $g(x)$ are efficiently computable, then so is $f(g(x))$.

4. *Grab bag:* The following functions are all efficiently computable:

· the arithmetic functions $x + y$ and $x \times y$

· $|x| = \lfloor \log_2 x \rfloor + 1$ (the number of bits in x's binary representation)

- the projection functions $\Pi_1(\langle x, y \rangle) = x$ and $\Pi_2(\langle x, y \rangle) = y$

· $bit(\langle x, i \rangle)$ (the ith bit of x's binary representation, or 0 if $i > |x|$)

· $diff(\langle x, i \rangle)$ (the number obtained from x by flipping its ith bit)

· $2^{|x|^2}$ (called the "smash function").

5. *Bounded recursion:* Suppose $f(x)$ is efficiently computable, and $|f(x)| \le |x|$ for all $x \in \mathbb{N}$. Then the function $g(\langle x, k \rangle)$, defined by

$$g(\langle x, k \rangle) = \begin{cases} f(g(\langle x, \lfloor k/2 \rfloor \rangle)) & \text{if } k > 1 \\ x & \text{if } k = 1 \end{cases},$$

is also efficiently computable.

A few comments about the Cobham axioms might be helpful. First, the axiom that "does most of the work" is (5). Intuitively, given any natural number $k \in \mathbb{N}$

that we can generate starting from the original input $x \in \mathbb{N}$, the bounded recursion axiom lets us set up a "computational process" that runs for $\log_2 k$ steps. Second, the role of the "smash function," $2^{|x|^2}$, is to let us map n-bit integers to n^2-bit integers to n^4-bit integers and so on, and thereby (in combination with the bounded recursion axiom) set up computational processes that run for arbitrary *polynomial* numbers of steps. Third, although addition and multiplication are included as "efficiently computable functions," it is crucial that exponentiation is *not* included. Indeed, if x and y are n-bit integers, then x^y might require exponentially many bits just to write down.

The basic result is then the following:

Theorem 10.1   (Cobham 1965; Rose 1984)   *The class* FP, *of functions* $f \colon \mathbb{N} \to \mathbb{N}$ *computable in polynomial time by a deterministic Turing machine, satisfies axioms (1)-(5), and is the smallest class that does so.*

To prove theorem 10.1, one needs to do two things, neither of them difficult: first, show that any function f that can be defined using the Cobham axioms can also be computed in polynomial time; and second, show that the Cobham axioms are enough to simulate any polynomial-time Turing machine.

One drawback of the Cobham axioms is that they seem to "sneak in the concept of polynomial time through the back door"—both through the "smash function," and through the arbitrary-looking condition $|f(x)| \le |x|$ in axiom (5). In the 1990s, however, Leivant (1994) and Bellantoni and Cook (1992) both gave more "elegant" logical characterizations of FP that avoid this problem. So for example, Leivant showed that a function f belongs to FP, if and only if f is computed by a program that can be proved correct in second-order logic with comprehension restricted to positive quantifier-free formulas. Results like these provide further evidence—if any was needed—that polynomial-time computability is an extremely natural notion: a "wide target in conceptual space" that one hits even while aiming in purely logical directions.

Over the past few decades, the idea of defining complexity classes such as P and NP in "logical, machine-free" ways has given rise to an entire field called *descriptive complexity theory*, which has deep connections with finite model theory. While further discussion of descriptive complexity theory would take us too far afield; see the book of Immerman (1998) for the definitive introduction, or Fagin (1993) for a survey.

10.5.2   Omniscience versus Infinity

Returning to our original topic, how exactly do axiomatic theories such as Cobham's (or Church's and Kleene's, for that matter) escape the problem of omniscience? One straightforward answer is that, unlike the set of true sentences in some formal language, which is only *countably* infinite, the set of functions $f: \mathbb{N} \to \mathbb{N}$ is *uncountably* infinite. And therefore, even if we define the "efficiently computable" functions $f: \mathbb{N} \to \mathbb{N}$ by taking a countably-infinite logical closure, we are sure to miss *some* functions f (in fact, almost all of them!).

The observation above suggests a general strategy to tame the logical omniscience problem. Namely, we could refuse to define an agent's "knowledge" in terms of which individual questions she can quickly answer, and insist on speaking instead about which infinite *families* of questions she can quickly answer. In slogan form, we want to "fight omniscience with infinity."

Let's see how, by taking this route, we can give semi-plausible answers to the puzzles about knowledge discussed earlier in this section. First, the reason why you can "know" that $1591 = 43 \times 37$, but at the same time *not* "know" the prime factors of 1591, is that, when we speak about knowing the answers to these questions, we really mean knowing *how* to answer them. And as we saw, there need not be any contradiction in knowing a fast multiplication algorithm but *not* a fast factoring algorithm, even if we model your knowledge about algorithms as deductively closed. To put it another way, by embedding the two questions

Q1 = "Is $1591 = 43 \times 37$?"

Q2 = "What are the prime factors of 1591?"

into *infinite families of related questions*, we can break the symmetry between the knowledge entailed in answering them.

Similarly, we could think of a child as possessing an internal algorithm which, given any statement of the form $x + y = y + x$ (for specific x and y values), immediately outputs *true*, without even examining x and y. However, the child does not yet have the ability to process *quantified* statements, such as "$\forall x, y \in \mathbb{R} \; x + y = y + x$." In that sense, she still lacks the explicit knowledge that addition is commutative.

Although the "cure" for logical omniscience sketched above solves some puzzles, not surprisingly it raises many puzzles of its own. So let me end this section by discussing three major objections to the "infinity cure."

The first objection is that we've simply pushed the problem of logical omniscience somewhere else. For suppose an agent "knows" how to compute every function in some restricted class such as FP. Then how can we ever make sense of the agent *learning a new algorithm?* One natural response is that, even if you have the "latent ability" to compute a function $f \in$ FP, you might not *know* that you have the ability—either because you don't know a suitable algorithm, or because you *do* know an algorithm, but don't know that it's an algorithm for f.

Of course, if we wanted to pursue things to the bottom, we'd next need to tell a story about *knowledge of algorithms*, and how logical omniscience is avoided there. However, I claim that this represents progress! For notice that, even without such a story, we can already explain *some* failures of logical omniscience. For example, the reason why you don't know the factors of a large number might *not* be your ignorance of a fast factoring method, but rather that no such method exists.

The second objection is that, when I advocated focusing on infinite families of questions rather than single questions in isolation, I never specified *which* infinite families. The difficulty is that the same question could be generalized in wildly different ways. As an example, consider the question

Q = "Is 432150 composite?"

Q is an instance of a computational problem that humans find very hard: "given a large integer N, is N composite?" However, Q is *also* an instance of a computational problem that humans find very easy: "given a large integer N *ending in* 0, is N composite?" And indeed, we'd expect a person to know the answer to Q *if* she noticed that 432150 ends in 0, but not otherwise. To me, what this example demonstrates is that, *if* we want to discuss an agent's knowledge in terms of individual questions such as Q, then the relevant issue will be whether there *exists* a generalization G of Q, such that the agent knows a fast algorithm for answering questions of type G, and *also* recognizes that Q is of type G.

The third objection is just the standard one about the relationship between asymptotic complexity and finite statements. For example, if we model an agent's knowledge using the Cobham axioms, then we can indeed explain why the agent doesn't know how to play perfect chess on an $n \times n$ board, for *arbitrary* values of n.[33] But on a standard 8×8 board, playing perfect chess would "merely" require (say) $\sim 10^{60}$ computational steps, which is a constant, and therefore certainly polynomial! So strictly on the basis of the Cobham axioms, what explanation could we possibly offer for why a rational agent, who knew the rules of 8×8 chess, didn't also know how to play it optimally? While this objection might sound devastating, it's important to understand that it's no different from the usual objection leveled against complexity-theoretic arguments, and can be given the usual response. Namely: asymptotic statements are *always* vulnerable to being rendered irrelevant, if the constant factors turned out to be ridiculous. However, experience has shown that, for whatever reasons, that happens rarely enough that one can usually take asymptotic behavior as "having explanatory force until proven otherwise." (Section 10.12 will say more about the explanatory force of asymptotic claims, as a problem requiring philosophical analysis.)

10.5.3   Summary

Because of the difficulties pointed out in section 10.5.2, my own view is that computational complexity theory has not yet come close to "solving" the logical omniscience problem, in the sense of giving a satisfying formal account of knowledge that also avoids making absurd predictions.[34] I have no idea whether such an account is even possible.[35] However, what I've tried to show in this section is that complexity theory provides a well-defined "limiting case" where the logical omniscience problem *is* solvable, about as well as one could hope it to be. The limiting case is where the size of the questions grows without bound, and the solution there is given by the Cobham axioms: "axioms of knowing how" whose logical closure one *can* take without thereby inviting omniscience.

In other words, when we contemplate the omniscience problem, I claim that we're in a situation similar to one often faced in physics—where we might be at a loss to understand some phenomenon (say, gravitational entropy), *except* in limiting cases such as black holes. In epistemology, just like in physics, the limiting cases that we *do* more or less understand offer an obvious starting point for those wishing to tackle the general case.

10.6   Computationalism and Waterfalls

Over the past two decades, a certain argument about computation—which I'll call the *waterfall argument*—has been widely discussed by philosophers of mind.[36] Like Searle's famous Chinese Room argument (Searle 1980), the waterfall argument seeks to show that computations are "inherently syntactic," and can never be "about" anything—and that for this reason, the doctrine of "computationalism" is false.[37] But unlike the Chinese Room, the waterfall argument supplements the bare appeal to intuition by a further claim: namely, that the "meaning" of a computation, to whatever extent it has one, is always *relative to some external observer*.

More concretely, consider a waterfall (though any other physical system with a large enough state space would do as well). Here I do not mean a waterfall that was specially engineered to perform computations, but *really* a naturally occurring waterfall: say, Niagara Falls. Being governed by laws of physics, the waterfall implements some mapping f from a set of possible initial states to a set of possible final states. If we accept that the laws of physics are *reversible*, then f must also be injective. Now suppose we restrict attention to some finite subset S of possible initial states, with $|S| = n$. Then f is just a one-to-one mapping from S to some output set $T = f(S)$ with $|T| = n$. The "crucial observation" is now this: given *any* permutation σ from the set of integers $\{1, \dots, n\}$ to itself, there is some way to label the elements of S and

T by integers in $\{1, \ldots, n\}$, such that we can interpret f as implementing σ. For example, if we let $S = \{s_1, \ldots, s_i\}$ and $f(s_i) = t_i$, then it suffices to label the initial state s_i by i and the final state t_i by $\sigma(i)$. But the permutation σ could have any "semantics" we like: it might represent a program for playing chess, or factoring integers, or simulating a different waterfall. Therefore "mere computation" cannot give rise to semantic meaning. Here is how Searle (1992, 57) expresses the conclusion:

If we are consistent in adopting the Turing test or some other "objective" criterion for intelligent behavior, then the answer to such questions as "Can unintelligent bits of matter produce intelligent behavior?" and even, "How exactly do they do it" are ludicrously obvious. Any thermostat, pocket calculator, or waterfall produces "intelligent behavior," and we know in each case how it works. Certain artifacts are designed to behave as if they were intelligent, and since everything follows laws of nature, then everything will have some description under which it behaves as if it were intelligent. But this sense of "intelligent behavior" is of no psychological relevance at all.

The waterfall argument has been criticized on numerous grounds: see Haugeland (2002), Block (2002), and especially Chalmers (1996) (who parodied the argument by proving that a cake recipe, being merely syntactic, can never give rise to the semantic attribute of crumbliness). To my mind, though, perhaps the easiest way to demolish the waterfall argument is through computational complexity considerations.

Indeed, suppose we actually wanted to use a waterfall to help us calculate chess moves. How would we do that? In complexity terms, what we want is a *reduction* from the chess problem to the waterfall-simulation problem. That is, we want an efficient algorithm that somehow *encodes* a chess position P into an initial state $s_P \in S$ of the waterfall, in such a way that a good move from P can be read out efficiently from the waterfall's corresponding final state, $f(s_P) \in T$.[38] But *what would such an algorithm look like?* We cannot say for sure—certainly not without detailed knowledge about f (i.e., the physics of waterfalls), as well as the means by which the S and T elements are encoded as binary strings. But for *any* reasonable choice, it seems overwhelmingly likely that any reduction algorithm would just *solve the chess problem itself*, without using the waterfall in an essential way at all! A bit more precisely, I conjecture that, given any chess-playing algorithm A that accesses a "waterfall oracle" W, there is an equally good chess-playing algorithm A', with similar time and space requirements, that does *not* access W. If this conjecture holds, then it gives us a perfectly observer-independent way to formalize our intuition that the "semantics" of waterfalls have nothing to do with chess.[39]

10.6.1 "Reductions" That Do All the Work

Interestingly, the issue of "trivial" or "degenerate" reductions also arises *within* complexity theory, so it might be instructive to see how it is handled there. Recall from section 10.3.1 that a problem is NP-*complete* if, loosely speaking, it is "maximally hard among all NP problems" (NP being the class of problems for which solutions can be checked in polynomial time). More formally, we say that L is NP-complete if

1. $L \in$ NP, and

2. given any *other* NP problem L', there exists a polynomial-time algorithm to solve L' using access to an oracle that solves L. (Or more succinctly, $L' \in P^L$, where P^L denotes the complexity class P augmented by an L-oracle.)

The concept of NP-completeness had incredible explanatory power: it showed that *thousands* of seemingly unrelated problems from physics, biology, industrial optimization, mathematical logic, and other fields were all *identical* from the standpoint of polynomial-time computation, and that not one of these problems had an efficient solution unless P = NP. Thus, it was natural for theoretical computer scientists to want to define an analogous concept of P-*completeness*. In other words: among all the problems that *are* solvable in polynomial time, which ones are "maximally hard"?

But how should P-completeness even be defined? To see the difficulty, suppose that, by analogy with NP-completeness, we say that L is P-complete if

1. $L \in P$ and

2. $L' \in P^L$ for every $L' \in P$.

Then it is easy to see that the second condition is vacuous: *every* P problem is P-complete! For in "reducing" L' to L, a polynomial-time algorithm can always just ignore the L-oracle and solve L' by itself, much like our hypothetical chess program that ignored its waterfall oracle. Because of this, condition (2) must be replaced by a stronger condition; one popular choice is

2'. $L' \in \text{LOGSPACE}^L$ for every $L' \in P$.

Here LOGSPACE means, informally, the class of problems solvable by a deterministic Turing machine with a read/write memory consisting of only log n bits, given an input of size n.[40] It's not hard to show that LOGSPACE $\subseteq$ P, and this containment is strongly believed to be strict (though just like with P $\neq$ NP, there is no proof yet). The key point is that, if we want a *non-vacuous* notion of completeness, then the reducing complexity class needs to be *weaker* (either provably or conjecturally) than the class being reduced to. In fact complexity classes even smaller than LOGSPACE almost always suffice in practice.

In my view, there is an important lesson here for debates about computationalism. Suppose we want to claim, for example, that a computation that plays chess is "equivalent" to some other computation that simulates a waterfall. Then our claim is only non-vacuous if it's possible to *exhibit* the equivalence (i.e., give the reductions) within a model of computation that isn't *itself* powerful enough to solve the chess or waterfall problems.

10.7   PAC-Learning and the Problem of Induction

Centuries ago, David Hume (1748) famously pointed out that learning from the past (and, by extension, science) seems logically impossible. For example, if we sample 500 ravens and every one of them is black, why does that give us *any* grounds—even probabilistic grounds—for expecting the 501st raven to be black also? Any modern answer to this question would probably refer to *Occam's razor*, the principle that simpler hypotheses consistent with the data are more likely to be correct. So for example, the hypothesis that all ravens are black is "simpler" than the hypothesis that most ravens are green or purple, and that only the 500 we happened to see were black. Intuitively, it seems Occam's razor *must* be part of the solution to Hume's problem; the difficulty is that such a response leads to questions of its own:

1. What do we mean by "simpler"?

2. *Why* are simple explanations likely to be correct? Or, less ambitiously: what properties must reality have for Occam's razor to "work"?

3. How much data must we collect before we can find a "simple hypothesis" that will probably predict future data? How do we go about finding such a hypothesis?

In my view, the theory of *PAC (probably approximately correct) learning*, initiated by Leslie Valiant (1984), has made large enough advances on all of these questions that it deserves to be studied by anyone interested in induction.[41] In this theory, we consider an idealized "learner," who is presented with points $x_1, \dots, x_m$ drawn randomly from some large set S, together with the "classifications" $f(x_1), \dots, f(x_m)$ of those points. The learner's goal is to infer the function f, well enough to be able to predict $f(x)$ for *most* future points $x \in S$. As an example, the learner might be a bank, S might be a set of people (represented by their credit histories), and $f(x)$ might represent whether or not person x will default on a loan.

For simplicity, we often assume that S is a set of binary strings, and that the function f maps each $x \in S$ to a single bit, $f(x) \in \{0, 1\}$. Both assumptions can be removed without significantly changing the theory. The important assumptions are the following:

1. Each of the sample points $x_1, \ldots, x_m$ is drawn *independently* from some (possibly unknown) "sample distribution" $\mathcal{D}$ over $\mathcal{S}$. Furthermore, the future points x on which the learner will need to predict $f(x)$ are drawn from the same distribution.

2. The function f belongs to a known "hypothesis class" $\mathcal{H}$. This $\mathcal{H}$ represents "the set of possibilities the learner is willing to entertain" (and is typically much smaller than the set of all $2^{|\mathcal{S}|}$ possible functions from $\mathcal{S}$ to $\{0, 1\}$).

Under these assumptions, we have the following central result.

Theorem 10.2 *Consider a finite hypothesis class $\mathcal{H}$, a Boolean function $f : \mathcal{S} \to \{0,1\}$ in $\mathcal{H}$, and a sample distribution $\mathcal{D}$ over $\mathcal{S}$, as well as an error rate $\varepsilon > 0$ and failure probability $\delta > 0$ that the learner is willing to tolerate. Call a hypothesis $h : \mathcal{S} \to \{0,1\}$ "good" if*

$$\Pr_{x \sim \mathcal{D}} [h(x) = f(x)] \geq 1 - \varepsilon.$$

Also, call sample points $x_1, \ldots, x_m$ "reliable" if any hypothesis $h \in \mathcal{H}$ that satisfies $h(x_i) = f(x_i)$ for all $i \in \{1, \ldots, m\}$ is good. Then

$$m = \frac{1}{\varepsilon} \ln \frac{|\mathcal{H}|}{\delta}$$

sample points $x_1, \ldots, x_m$ drawn independently from $\mathcal{D}$ will be reliable with probability at least $1 - \delta$.

Intuitively, theorem 10.2 says that the behavior of f on a small number of randomly chosen points *probably* determines its behavior on *most* of the remaining points. In other words, if, by some unspecified means, the learner manages to find any hypothesis $h \in \mathcal{H}$ that makes correct predictions on all its past data points $x_1, \ldots, x_m$, then provided m is large enough (and as it happens, m doesn't need to be very large), the learner can be statistically confident that h will also make the correct predictions on most future points.

The part of theorem 10.2 that bears the unmistakable imprint of complexity theory is the bound on sample size, $m = \frac{1}{\varepsilon} \ln \frac{|\mathcal{H}|}{\delta}$. This bound has three notable implications. First, even if the class $\mathcal{H}$ contains exponentially many hypotheses (say, 2^n), one can still learn an arbitrary function $f \in \mathcal{H}$ using a *linear* amount of sample data, since m grows only logarithmically with $|\mathcal{H}|$: in other words, like the number of bits needed to *write down* an individual hypothesis. Second, one can make the probability that the hypothesis h will fail to generalize *exponentially small* (say, $\delta = 2^{-n}$), at the cost of increasing the sample size m by only a linear factor. Third, assuming the hypothesis *does* generalize, its error rate ε decreases inversely with m. It is not hard to show that each of these dependencies is tight, so that for example, if we demand either $\varepsilon = 0$ or $\delta = 0$, then no finite m suffices. This is the origin of the name "PAC learning": the most one can hope for is to output a hypothesis that is "probably, approximately" correct.

The proof of theorem 10.2 is easy: consider any hypothesis $h \in \mathcal{H}$ that is *bad*, meaning that

$$\Pr_{x \sim D}\left[h(x) = f(x)\right] < 1 - \varepsilon.$$

Then by the independence assumption,

$$\Pr_{x_1, \dots, x_m \sim D}\left[h(x_1) = f(x_1) \wedge \cdots \wedge h(x_m) = f(x_m)\right] < (1 - \varepsilon)^m.$$

Now, the number of bad hypotheses is no more than the total number of hypotheses, $|\mathcal{H}|$. So by the union bound, the probability that there *exists* a bad hypothesis that agrees with f on all of $x_1, \dots, x_m$ can be at most $|\mathcal{H}| \cdot (1 - \varepsilon)^m$. Therefore $\delta \leq |\mathcal{H}| \cdot (1 - \varepsilon)^m$, and all that remains is to solve for m.

The relevance of theorem 10.2 to Hume's problem of induction is that the theorem describes a nontrivial class of situations where induction is *guaranteed to work* with high probability. Theorem 10.2 also illuminates the role of Occam's razor in induction. In order to learn using a "reasonable" number of sample points m, the hypothesis class $\mathcal{H}$ must have a sufficiently small cardinality. But that is equivalent to saying that every hypothesis $h \in \mathcal{H}$ must have a *succinct description*—since the number of bits needed to specify an arbitrary hypothesis $h \in \mathcal{H}$ is simply $\lceil \log_2 |\mathcal{H}| \rceil$. If the number of bits needed to specify a hypothesis is too large, then $\mathcal{H}$ will always be vulnerable to the problem of *overfitting*: some hypotheses $h \in \mathcal{H}$ surviving contact with the sample data just by chance.

As pointed out to me by Agustin Rayo, there are several possible interpretations of Occam's razor that have nothing to do with descriptive complexity: for example, we might want our hypotheses to be "simple" in terms of their ontological or ideological commitments. However, to whatever extent we interpret Occam's razor as saying that *shorter* or *lower-complexity* hypotheses are preferable, theorem 10.2 comes closer than one might have thought possible to a mathematical justification for why the razor works.

Many philosophers might be familiar with alternative formal approaches to Occam's razor. For example, within a Bayesian framework, one can choose a prior over all possible hypotheses that gives greater weight to "simpler" hypotheses (where simplicity is measured, for example, by the length of the shortest program that computes the predictions). However, while the PAC learning and Bayesian approaches are related, the PAC approach has the advantage of requiring only a *qualitative* decision about which hypotheses one wants to consider, rather than a quantitative prior over hypotheses. Given the hypothesis class $\mathcal{H}$, one can then seek learning methods that work for *any* $f \in \mathcal{H}$. (On the other hand, the PAC approach requires an assumption about the probability distribution over *observations*, while the Bayesian approach does not.)

10.7.1 Drawbacks of the Basic PAC Model

I'd now like to discuss three drawbacks of theorem 10.2, since I think the drawbacks illuminate philosophical aspects of induction as well as the advantages do.

The first drawback is that theorem 10.2 works only for *finite* hypothesis classes. In science, however, hypotheses often involve continuous parameters, of which there is an uncountable infinity. Of course, one could solve this problem by simply discretizing the parameters, but then the number of hypotheses (and therefore the relevance of theorem 10.2) would depend on how fine the discretization was. Fortunately, we can avoid such difficulties by realizing that *the learner only cares about the "differences" between two hypotheses insofar as they lead to different predictions.* This leads to the fundamental notion of *VC-dimension* (after its originators, Vapnik and Chervonenkis [1971]).

Definition 10.1 (VC-dimension) *A hypothesis class $\mathcal{H}$ shatters the sample points $\{x_1, \ldots, x_k\} \subseteq S$ if for all 2^k possible settings of $h(x_1), \ldots, h(x_k)$, there exists a hypothesis $h \in \mathcal{H}$ compatible with those settings. Then $VCdim(\mathcal{H})$, the VC-dimension of $\mathcal{H}$, is the largest k for which there exists a subset $\{x_1, \ldots, x_k\} \subseteq S$ that $\mathcal{H}$ shatters (or if no finite maximum exists, then $VCdim(\mathcal{H}) = \infty$).*

Clearly any finite hypothesis class has finite VC-dimension: indeed, $VCdim(\mathcal{H}) \leq \log_2 |\mathcal{H}|$. However, even an infinite hypothesis class can have finite VC-dimension if it is "sufficiently simple." For example, let $\mathcal{H}$ be the class of all functions $h_{a,b} : \mathbb{R} \to \{0,1\}$ of the form

$$h_{a,b}(x) = \begin{cases} 1 & \text{if } a \leq x \leq b \\ 0 & \text{otherwise.} \end{cases}$$

Then it is easy to check that $VCdim(\mathcal{H}) = 2$.

With the notion of VC-dimension in hand, we can state a powerful (and harder-to-prove!) generalization of theorem 10.2, from Blumer et al. (1989).

Theorem 10.3 *For some universal constant $K > 0$, the bound on m in theorem 10.2 can be replaced by*

$$m = \frac{KVCdim(\mathcal{H})}{\varepsilon} \ln \frac{1}{\delta\varepsilon},$$

with the theorem now holding for any hypothesis class $\mathcal{H}$, finite or infinite.

If $\mathcal{H}$ has infinite VC-dimension, then it is easy to construct a probability distribution $\mathcal{D}$ over sample points such that *no finite number m of samples from $\mathcal{D}$ suffices to PAC-learn a function $f \in \mathcal{H}$*: one really is in the unfortunate situation described by Hume, of having no grounds at all for predicting that the next raven will be black. In some sense, then, theorem 10.3 is telling us that finite VC-dimension is a necessary and sufficient condition for scientific induction to be possible. Once again, theorem 10.3 also has an interpretation in terms of Occam's razor, with the smallness of the VC-dimension now playing the role of simplicity.

The second drawback of theorem 10.2 is that it gives us no clues about how to *find* a hypothesis $h \in \mathcal{H}$ consistent with the sample data. All it says is that, *if* we find such an h, then h will probably be close to the truth. This illustrates that, even in the simple setup envisioned by PAC learning, induction *cannot* be merely a matter of seeing enough data and then "generalizing" from it, because immense computations might be needed to *find* a suitable generalization! Indeed, following the work of Kearns and Valiant (1994), we now know that many natural learning problems— as an example, inferring the rules of a regular or context-free language from random examples of grammatical and ungrammatical sentences—are computationally intractable in an extremely strong sense:

Any polynomial-time algorithm for finding a hypothesis consistent with the data would imply a polynomial-time algorithm for breaking widely used cryptosystems such as RSA![42]

The appearance of *cryptography* in the above statement is far from accidental. In a sense that can be made precise, learning and cryptography are "dual" problems: a learner wants to find patterns in data, while a cryptographer wants to generate data whose patterns are *hard* to find. More concretely, one of the basic primitives in cryptography is called a *pseudorandom function family*. This is a family of efficiently computable Boolean functions $f_s : \{0,1\}^n \rightarrow \{0,1\}$, parameterized by a short random "seed" s, that are *virtually indistinguishable from random functions* by a polynomial-time algorithm. Here, we imagine that the would-be distinguishing algorithm can query the function f_s on various points x, and also that it *knows* the mapping from s to f_s, and so is ignorant only of the seed s itself. There is strong evidence in cryptography that pseudorandom function families exist: indeed, Goldreich, Goldwasser, and Micali (1984) showed how to construct one starting from any pseudorandom *generator* (the latter was mentioned in section 10.1).[43]

Now, given a pseudorandom function family $\{f_s\}$, imagine a PAC-learner whose hypothesis class $\mathcal{H}$ consists of f_s for all possible seeds s. The learner is provided some randomly chosen sample points $x_1, \ldots, x_m \in \{0, 1\}^n$, together with the values of f_s on those points: $f_s(x_1), \ldots, f_s(x_m)$. Given this "training data," the learner's goal is to figure out how to compute f_s for itself—and thereby predict the values of $f_s(x)$ on new points x, points *not* in the training sample. Unfortunately, it's easy to see that *if* the learner could do that, then it would thereby distinguish f_s from a truly random function—and thereby contradict our starting assumption that $\{f_s\}$ was pseudorandom! Our conclusion is that, *if* the basic assumptions of modern cryptography hold (and in particular, if there exist pseudorandom generators), then there must be situations where learning is impossible purely because of computational complexity (and not because of insufficient data).

The third drawback of theorem 10.2 is the assumption that the distribution $\mathcal{D}$ from which the learner is tested is the same as the distribution from which the sample points were drawn. To me, this is the most serious drawback, since it tells us that PAC learning models the "learning" performed by an undergraduate cramming for an exam by solving last year's problems, or an employer using a regression model to identify the characteristics of successful hires, or a cryptanalyst breaking a code from a collection of plaintexts and ciphertexts. It does not, however, model the "learning" of an Einstein or a Szilard, making predictions about phenomena that are different in kind from anything yet observed. As David Deutsch stresses in his recent book *The Beginning of Infinity: Explanations that Transform the World* (2011), the goal of science is not merely to summarize observations, and thereby let us make predictions about similar observations. Rather, the goal is to discover explanations with "reach," meaning the ability to predict what would happen even in novel or hypothetical situations, like the Sun suddenly disappearing or a quantum computer being built. In my view, developing a compelling mathematical model of *explanatory* learning—a model that "is to explanation as the PAC model is to prediction"—is an outstanding open problem.[44]

10.7.2   Computational Complexity, Bleen, and Grue

In 1955, Nelson Goodman proposed what he called the "new riddle of induction," which survives the Occam's razor answer to Hume's original induction problem (see Goodman 1955). In Goodman's riddle, we are asked to consider the hypothesis "All emeralds are green." The question is, why do we favor *that* hypothesis over the following alternative, which is equally compatible with all our evidence of green emeralds?

"All emeralds are green before January 1, 2030, and then blue afterwards."

The obvious answer is that the second hypothesis adds superfluous complications, and is therefore disfavored by Occam's razor. To that, Goodman replies that the definitions of "simple" and "complicated" depend on our language. In particular, suppose we had no words for green or blue, but we did have a word *grue*, meaning "green before January 1, 2030, and blue afterwards," and a word *bleen*, meaning "blue before January 1, 2030, and green afterwards." In that case, we could only express the hypothesis "All emeralds are green" by saying

"All emeralds are grue before January 1, 2030, and then bleen afterwards"

—a manifestly more complicated hypothesis than the simple "All emeralds are grue"!

I confess that, when I contemplate the grue riddle, I can't help but recall the joke about the anti-inductivists, who, when asked why they continue to believe that the future *won't* resemble the past, when that false belief has brought their civilization nothing but poverty and misery, reply, "Because anti-induction has never worked before!" Yes, if we artificially define our primitive concepts "against the grain of the world," then we shouldn't be surprised if the world's actual behavior becomes more cumbersome to describe, or if we make wrong predictions. It would be as if we were using a programming language that had no built-in function for multiplication, but only for $F(x, y) := 17x - y - x^2 + 2xy$. In that case, a normal person's first instinct would be either to switch programming languages, or else to *define* multiplication in terms of F, and forget about F from that point onward![45] Now, there *is* a genuine philosophical problem here: why *do* grue, bleen, and $F(x, y)$ go "against the grain of the world," whereas green, blue, and multiplication go with the grain? But to me, that problem (like Wigner's puzzlement over "the unreasonable effectiveness of mathematics in natural sciences" [Wigner 1960]) is more about the world itself than about human concepts, so we shouldn't expect any purely linguistic analysis to resolve it.

What about computational complexity, then? In my view, while computational complexity doesn't solve the grue riddle, it does contribute a useful insight. Namely, that when we talk about the simplicity or complexity of hypotheses, we should distinguish two issues:

1. The *asymptotic scaling* of the hypothesis size, as the "size" n of our learning problem goes to infinity.

2. The constant-factor overheads.

In terms of the basic PAC model in section 10.7, we can imagine a "hidden parameter" n, which measures the number of bits needed to specify an individual point in the set $S = S_n$. (Other ways to measure the "size" of a learning problem would also work, but this way is particularly convenient.) For convenience, we can identify S_n with the set $\{0, 1\}^n$ of n-bit strings, so that $n = \log_2 |S_n|$. We then need to consider, not just a *single* hypothesis class, but an infinite *family* of hypothesis classes $\mathcal{H} = \{\mathcal{H}_1, \mathcal{H}_2, \mathcal{H}_3, \ldots\}$, one for each positive integer n. Here $\mathcal{H}_n$ consists of hypothesis functions h that map $S_n = \{0,1\}^n$ to $\{0, 1\}$.

Now let L be a *language* for specifying hypotheses in $\mathcal{H}$: in other words, a mapping from (some subset of) binary strings $y \in \{0, 1\}^*$ to $\mathcal{H}$. Also, given a hypothesis $h \in \mathcal{H}$, let

$$\kappa_L(h) := \min\{|y| : L(y) = h\}$$

be the length of the *shortest* description of h in the language L. (Here $|y|$ just means the number of bits in y.) Finally, let

$$\kappa_L(n) := \max\{\kappa_L(h) : h \in \mathcal{H}_n\}$$

be the number of bits needed to specify an *arbitrary* hypothesis in $\mathcal{H}_n$ using the language L. Clearly $\kappa_L(n) \geq \lceil \log_2|\mathcal{H}_n| \rceil$, with equality if and only if L is "optimal" (that is, if it represents each hypothesis $h \in \mathcal{H}_n$ using as few bits as possible). The question that concerns us is how quickly $\kappa_L(n)$ grows as a function of n, for various choices of language L.

What does any of this have to do with the grue riddle? Well, we can think of the details of L (its syntax, vocabulary, etc.) as affecting the "lower-order" behavior of the function $\kappa_L(n)$. So for example, suppose we are unlucky enough that L contains the words *grue* and *bleen*, but not *blue* and *green*. That might increase $\kappa_L(n)$ by a factor of ten or so—since now, every time we want to mention "green" when specifying our hypothesis h, we instead need a wordy circumlocution like "grue before January 1, 2030, and then bleen afterwards," and similarly for blue.[46] However, a crucial lesson of complexity theory is that the "higher-order" behavior of $\kappa_L(n)$—for example, whether it grows polynomially or exponentially with n—is almost completely unaffected by the details of L! The reason is that, if two languages L_1 and L_2 differ only in their "low-level details," then *translating* a hypothesis from L_1 to L_2 or vice versa will increase the description length by no more than a polynomial factor. Indeed, as in our grue example, there is usually a "universal translation constant" c such that $\kappa_{L_1}(h) \leq c\kappa_{L_2}(h)$ or even $\kappa_{L_1}(h) \leq \kappa_{L_2}(h) + c$ for *every* hypothesis $h \in \mathcal{H}$.

The one exception to the above rule is if the languages L_1 and L_2 have different *expressive powers*. For example, maybe L_1 only allows nesting expressions to depth two, while L_2 allows nesting to arbitrary depths; or L_1 only allows propositional connectives, while L_2 also allows first-order quantifiers. In those cases, $\kappa_{L_1}(h)$ could indeed be much greater than $\kappa_{L_2}(h)$ for some hypotheses h, possibly even exponentially greater ($\kappa_{L_1}(h) \approx 2^{\kappa_{L_2}(h)}$). A rough analogy would be this: suppose you hadn't learned what differential equations were, and had no idea how to solve them even approximately or numerically. In that case, Newtonian mechanics might seem just as complicated to you as the Ptolemaic theory with epicycles, if not *more* complicated! For the only way you could make predictions with Newtonian mechanics would be using a huge table of "precomputed" differential equation solutions—and *to you*, that table would seem just as unwieldy and inelegant as a table of epicycles. But notice that in this case, your perception would be the result, not of some arbitrary choice of vocabulary, but of an *objective* gap in your mathematical expressive powers.

To summarize, our choice of vocabulary—for example, whether we take green/ blue or bleen/grue as primitive concepts—could indeed matter if we want to use Occam's razor to predict the future color of emeralds. But I think that complexity theory justifies us in treating grue as a "small-n effect": something that becomes less and less important in the asymptotic limit of more and more complicated learning problems.

10.8 Quantum Computing

Quantum computing is a proposal for using quantum mechanics to solve certain computational problems much faster than we know how to solve them today.[47] To do so, one would need to build a new type of computer, capable of exploiting the quantum effects of superposition and interference. Building such a computer—one large enough to solve interesting problems—remains an enormous challenge for physics and engineering, due to the fragility of quantum states and the need to isolate them from their external environment.

In the meantime, though, theoretical computer scientists have extensively studied what we could and couldn't do with a quantum computer if we had one. For certain problems, remarkable quantum algorithms are known to solve them in polynomial time, even though the best-known classical algorithms require exponential time. Most famously, in 1994 Peter Shor gave a polynomial-time quantum algorithm for factoring integers, and as a byproduct, breaking most of the cryptographic codes used on the Internet today (see Shor 1997). Besides the practical implications, Shor's algorithm also provided a key piece of evidence that switching from classical to quantum computers would enlarge the class of problems solvable in polynomial time. For theoretical computer scientists, this had a profound lesson: if we want to know the limits of efficient computation, we may need to "leave our armchairs" and incorporate actual facts about physics (at a minimum, the truth or falsehood of quantum mechanics!).[48]

Whether or not scalable quantum computers are built anytime soon, my own (biased) view is that quantum computing represents one of the great scientific advances of our time. But here I want to ask a different question: does quantum computing have any implications for *philosophy*—and, specifically, for the interpretation of quantum mechanics?

From one perspective, the answer seems like an obvious "no." Whatever else it is, quantum computing is "merely" an application of quantum mechanics, as that theory has existed in physics textbooks for 80 years. Indeed, *if* you accept that quantum mechanics (as currently understood) is true, then presumably you should also accept the possibility of quantum computers, and make the same predictions about their operation as everyone else. Whether you describe the "reality" behind quantum processes via the many-worlds interpretation, Bohmian mechanics, or some other view (or, following Bohr's Copenhagen interpretation, refuse to discuss the "reality" at all), seems irrelevant.

From a different perspective, though, a scalable quantum computer would *test* quantum mechanics in an extremely novel regime—and for that reason, it could indeed raise new philosophical issues. The "regime" quantum computers would test is characterized not by an energy scale or a temperature, but by computational complexity. One of the most striking facts about quantum mechanics is that, to represent the state of n entangled particles, one needs a vector of size *exponential* in n. For example, to specify the state of a thousand spin-1/2 particles, one needs 2^{1000} complex numbers called "amplitudes," one for every possible outcome of measuring the spins in the {up,down} basis. The quantum state, denoted $|\psi\rangle$, is then a linear combination or "superposition" of the possible outcomes, with each outcome $|x\rangle$ weighted by its amplitude α_x:

$$|\psi\rangle = \sum_{x\in\{up,down\}^{1000}} \alpha_x|x\rangle.$$

Given $|\psi\rangle$, one can calculate the probability p_x that any particular outcome $|x\rangle$ will be observed, via the rule $p_x = |\alpha_x|^2$.[49]

Now, there are only about 10^{80} atoms in the visible universe, which is a much smaller number than 2^{1000}. So assuming quantum mechanics is true, it seems Nature has to invest *staggering* amounts of "computational effort" to keep track of small collections of particles—certainly more than anything classical physics requires![50,51] In the early 1980s, Richard Feynman (1982) and others called attention to this point, noting that it underlay something that had long been apparent in practice: the extraordinary difficulty of simulating quantum mechanics using conventional computers. But Feynman also raised the possibility of turning that difficulty around, by building our computers out of quantum components. Such computers could conceivably solve certain problems faster than conventional computers: if nothing else, then at least the problem of simulating quantum mechanics!

Thus, quantum computing is interesting not just because of its applications, but (even more, in my opinion) because *it is the first technology that would directly "probe" the exponentiality inherent in the quantum description of Nature*. One can make an analogy here to the experiments in the 1980s that first convincingly violated the Bell inequality. Like quantum algorithms today, Bell's refutation of local realism was "merely" a mathematical consequence of quantum mechanics. But that refutation (and the experiments that it inspired) made conceptually important *aspects* of quantum mechanics no longer possible to ignore—and for that reason, it changed the philosophical landscape. It seems overwhelmingly likely to me that quantum computing will do the same.

Indeed, we can extend the analogy further: just as there were "local realist die-hards" who denied that Bell inequality violation would be possible (and tried to explain it away after it was achieved), so today a vocal minority of computer scientists and physicists (including Leonid Levin 2003, Oded Goldreich 2004, and Gerard 't Hooft 1999) denies the possibility of scalable quantum computers, even in principle. While they admit that quantum mechanics has passed every experimental test for a century, these skeptics are *confident* that quantum mechanics will fail in the regime tested by quantum computing—and that whatever new theory replaces it, that theory will allow only classical computing.

As most quantum computing researchers are quick to point out in response, they would be *thrilled* if the attempt to build scalable quantum computers led instead to a revision of quantum mechanics! Such an outcome would probably constitute the largest revolution in physics since the 1920s, and ultimately be much *more* interesting than building a quantum computer. Of course, it is also possible that scalable quantum computing will be given up as too difficult for "mundane" technological reasons, rather than fundamental physics reasons. But that "mundane" possibility is not what skeptics such as Levin, Goldreich, and 't Hooft are talking about.

10.8.1   Quantum Computing and the Many-Worlds Interpretation

But let's return to the original question: suppose the skeptics are wrong, and it *is* possible to build scalable quantum computers. Would that have any relevance to the interpretation of quantum mechanics? The best-known argument that the answer is "yes" was made by David Deutsch, a quantum computing pioneer and staunch defender of the many-worlds interpretation. To be precise, Deutsch thinks that quantum mechanics *straightforwardly* implies the existence of parallel universes, and that it does so independently of quantum computing: on his view, even the double-slit experiment can only be explained in terms of two parallel universes interfering. However, Deutsch also thinks that quantum computing adds emotional punch to the argument. Here is how he put it in his book *The Fabric of Reality* (1997, 217):

Logically, the possibility of complex quantum computations adds nothing to a case [for the many-worlds interpretation] that is already unanswerable. But it does add psychological impact. With Shor's algorithm, the argument has been writ very large. To those who still cling to a single-universe world-view, I issue this challenge: *explain how Shor's algorithm works*. I do not merely mean predict that it will work, which is merely a matter of solving a few uncontroversial equations. I mean provide an explanation. When Shor's algorithm has factorized a number, using 10^{500} or so times the computational resources that can be seen to be present, where was the number factorized? There are only about 10^{80} atoms in the entire visible universe, an utterly minuscule number compared with 10^{500}. So if the visible universe were the extent of physical reality, physical reality would not even remotely contain the resources required to factorize such a large number. Who did factorize it, then? How, and where, was the computation performed?

There is plenty in the above paragraph for an enterprising philosopher to mine. In particular, how *should* a nonbeliever in many-worlds answer Deutsch's challenge? In the rest of this section, I'll focus on two possible responses.

The first response is to deny that, if Shor's algorithm works as predicted, this can only be explained by postulating "vast computational resources." At the most obvious level, complexity theorists have not yet ruled out the possibility of a fast *classical* factoring algorithm.[52] More generally, that quantum computers can solve certain problems superpolynomially faster than classical computers is not a theorem, but a (profound, plausible) *conjecture*.[53,54] If the conjecture failed, then the door would seem open to what we might call "polynomial-time hidden-variable theories": theories that reproduce the predictions of quantum mechanics without invoking any computations outside P.[55] These would be analogous to the *local* hidden variable theories that Einstein and others had hoped for, before Bell ruled such theories out.

A second response to Deutsch's challenge is that, even if we agree that Shor's algorithm demonstrates the reality of vast *computational resources* in Nature, it is not obvious that we should think of those resources as "parallel universes." Why not simply say that there is *one* universe, and that it is quantum-mechanical? Doesn't the parallel-universes language reflect an ironic *parochialism*: a desire to impose a familiar science-fiction image on a mathematical theory that is *stranger* than fiction, that doesn't match *any* of our pre-quantum intuitions (including computational intuitions) particularly well?

One can sharpen the point as follows: *if* one took the parallel-universes explanation of how a quantum computer works too seriously (as many popular writers do!), then it would be natural to make further inferences about quantum computing that are flat-out wrong. For example:

Using only a thousand quantum bits (or qubits), a quantum computer could store 2^{1000} classical bits.

This is true only for a bizarre definition of the word "store"! The fundamental problem is that, when you measure a quantum computer's state, you see only *one* of the possible outcomes; the rest disappear. Indeed, a celebrated result called *Holevo's theorem* says that, using n qubits, there is no way to store more than n classical bits so that the bits can be reliably retrieved later (Holevo 1973). In other words: for at least one natural definition of "information-carrying capacity," qubits have exactly the same capacity as bits.

To take another example:

Unlike a classical computer, which can only factor numbers by trying the divisors one by one, a quantum computer could try all possible divisors in parallel.

If quantum computers can harness vast numbers of parallel worlds, then the above seems like a reasonable guess as to how Shor's algorithm works. But *it's not how it works at all*. Notice that, if Shor's algorithm *did* work that way, then it could be used not only for factoring integers, but also for the much larger task of solving NP-complete problems in polynomial time. (As mentioned in note 12, the factoring problem is strongly believed *not* to be NP-complete.) But contrary to a common misconception, quantum computers are neither known nor believed to be able to solve NP-complete problems efficiently.[56] As usual, the fundamental problem is that measuring reveals just a single random outcome $|x\rangle$. To get around that problem, and ensure that the *right* outcome is observed with high probability, a quantum algorithm needs to generate an *interference pattern*, in which the computational paths leading to a given wrong outcome cancel each other out, while the paths leading to a given right outcome reinforce each other. This is a delicate requirement, and as far as anyone knows, it can only be achieved for a few problems, most of which (like the factoring problem) have special structure arising from algebra or number theory.[57]

A many-worlder might retort: "Sure, I agree that quantum computing involves harnessing the parallel universes in subtle and non-obvious ways, but it's still harnessing parallel universes!" But even here, there's a fascinating irony. Suppose we choose to think of a quantum algorithm in terms of parallel universes. Then, to put it crudely, not only must many universes interfere to give a large final amplitude to the right answer; they must also, by interfering, lose their identities as parallel universes! In other words, to whatever extent a collection of universes is useful for quantum computation, to that extent it is arguable whether we ought to call them "parallel universes" at all (as opposed to parts of one exponentially large, self-interfering, quantum-mechanical blob). Conversely, to whatever extent the universes have unambiguously separate identities, to that extent they're now "decohered" and out of causal contact with each other. Thus we can explain the outputs of any future computations by invoking only one of the universes, and treating the others as unrealized hypotheticals.

To clarify, I don't regard either of the above objections to Deutsch's argument as decisive, and am unsure what I think about the matter. My purpose, in setting out the objections, was simply to illustrate the potential of quantum computing theory to inform debates about the many-worlds interpretation.

10.9   New Computational Notions of Proof

Since the time of Euclid, there have been two main notions of mathematical proof:

1. A "proof" is a verbal explanation that induces a sense of certainty (and ideally, understanding) about the statement to be proved, in any human mathematician willing and able to follow it.

2. A "proof" is a finite sequence of symbols encoding syntactic deductions in some formal system, which start with axioms and end with the statement to be proved.

The tension between these two notions is a recurring theme in the philosophy of mathematics. But theoretical computer science deals regularly with a third notion of proof—one that seems to have received much less philosophical analysis than either of the two above. This notion is the following:

3. A "proof" is any computational process or protocol (real or imagined) that can terminate in a certain way if and only if the statement to be proved is true.

10.9.1   Zero-Knowledge Proofs

As an example of this third notion, consider *zero-knowledge proofs*, introduced by Goldwasser, Micali, and Rackoff (1989). Given two graphs G and H, each with $n \approx 10000$ vertices, suppose that an all-powerful but untrustworthy wizard Merlin wishes to convince a skeptical king Arthur that G and H are *not* isomorphic. Of course, one way Merlin could do this would be to list all $n!$ graphs obtained by permuting the vertices of G, then note that none of these equal H. However, such a proof would clearly exhaust Arthur's patience (indeed, it could not even be written down within the observable universe). Alternatively, Merlin could point Arthur to some *property* of G and H that differentiates them: for example, maybe their adjacency matrices have different eigenvalue spectra. Unfortunately, it is not yet proven that, if G and H are non-isomorphic, there is always a differentiating property that Arthur can verify in time polynomial in n.

But as noticed by Goldreich, Micali, and Wigderson (1991), there is something Merlin can do instead: he can let Arthur *challenge* him. Merlin can say:

Arthur, send me a new graph K, which you obtained *either* by randomly permuting the vertices of G, *or* randomly permuting the vertices of H. Then I guarantee that I will tell you, without fail, whether $K \cong G$ or $K \cong H$.

It is clear that, if G and H are really non-isomorphic, then Merlin can always answer such challenges correctly, by the assumption that he (Merlin) has unlimited computational power. But it is equally clear that, if G and H are isomorphic, then

Merlin must answer some challenges incorrectly, regardless of his computational power—since a random permutation of G is statistically indistinguishable from a random permutation of H.

This protocol has at least four features that merit reflection by anyone interested in the nature of mathematical proof.

First, the protocol is *probabilistic*. Merlin cannot convince Arthur with certainty that G and H are non-isomorphic, since even if they were isomorphic, there's a 1/2 probability that Merlin would get lucky and answer a given challenge correctly (and hence, a $1/2^k$ probability that he would answer k challenges correctly). All Merlin can do is offer to repeat the protocol (say) 100 or 1000 times, and thereby make it less likely that his proof is unsound than that an asteroid will strike Camelot, killing both him and Arthur. Furthermore, even this statistical guarantee is only as secure as Arthur's certainty that his choices during the protocol were "sufficiently random"! In other words, however Arthur generated his "random" challenges for Merlin—by flipping a coin, rolling a die, using a quantum-mechanical random-number source, etc.—we have to assume the method was free from "devious correlations" that would let Merlin cheat.

Second, the protocol is *interactive*. Unlike with proof notions (1) and (2), Arthur is no longer a passive recipient of knowledge, but an active player who challenges the prover. We know from experience that the ability to *interrogate* a seminar speaker—to ask questions that the speaker could not have anticipated, evaluate the responses, and then possibly ask follow-up questions—often speeds up the process of figuring out whether the speaker knows what he or she is talking about. Complexity theory affirms our intuition here, through its discovery of interactive proofs for statements (such as "G and H are not isomorphic") whose shortest known conventional proofs are exponentially longer.

The third interesting feature of the graph non-isomorphism protocol—a feature seldom mentioned—is that its soundness implicitly relies on a *physical* assumption. Namely, if Merlin had the power (whether through magic or through ordinary espionage) to "peer into Arthur's study" and *directly observe* whether Arthur started with G or H, then clearly he could answer every challenge correctly even if $G \cong H$. It follows that the persuasiveness of Merlin's "proof" can only be as strong as Arthur's extramathematical belief that Merlin does *not* have such powers. By now, there are many other examples in complexity theory of "proofs" whose validity rests on assumed limitations of the provers.

As Shieber (2007) points out, all three of the above properties of interactive protocols *also* hold for the Turing test discussed in section 10.4! The Turing test is interactive by definition, it is probabilistic because even a program that printed random gibberish would have *some* nonzero probability of passing the test by chance, and it depends on the physical assumption that the AI program doesn't "cheat" by (for example) secretly consulting a human. For these reasons, Shieber argues that we can see the Turing test *itself* as an early interactive protocol—one that convinces the verifier not of a mathematical theorem, but of the prover's capacity for intelligent verbal behavior.[58]

However, perhaps the most striking feature of the graph non-isomorphism protocol is that it is *zero-knowledge*: a technical term formalizing our intuition that "Arthur learns nothing from the protocol, beyond the truth of the statement being proved."[59] For all Merlin ever tells Arthur is which graph he (Arthur) started with, G or H. But Arthur *already knew* which graph he started with! This means that, not only does Arthur gain no "understanding" of what makes G and H non-isomorphic, he does not even gain the ability to prove to a third party what Merlin proved to him. This is another aspect of computational proofs that has no analog with proof notions (1) or (2).

One might complain that, as interesting as the zero-knowledge property is, so far we've only shown it's achievable for an extremely specialized problem. And indeed, just like with factoring integers, today there is strong evidence that the graph isomorphism problem is *not* NP-complete (Boppana et al. 1987).[60,61] However, in the same paper that gave the graph non-isomorphism protocol, Goldreich, Micali, and Wigderson (1991) also gave a celebrated zero-knowledge protocol (now called the *GMW protocol*) for the NP-complete problems. By the definition of NP-complete (see section 10.3.1), the GMW protocol meant that *every mathematical statement that has a conventional proof (say, in Zermelo-Fraenkel set theory) also has a zero-knowledge proof of comparable size!* As an example application, suppose you've just proved the Riemann hypothesis. You want to convince the experts of your triumph, but are paranoid about them stealing credit for it. In that case, "all" you need to do is

1. rewrite your proof in a formal language,

2. encode the result as the solution to an NP-complete problem, and then

3. like a sixteenth-century court mathematician challenging his competitors to a duel, invite the experts to run the GMW protocol with you over the Internet!

Provided you answer all their challenges correctly, the experts can become *statistically certain* that you possess a proof of the Riemann hypothesis, without learning anything *about* that proof besides an upper bound on its length.

Better yet, unlike the graph non-isomorphism protocol, the GMW protocol does not assume a super-powerful wizard—only an ordinary polynomial-time being who happens to know a proof of the relevant theorem. As a result, today the GMW protocol is much more than a theoretical curiosity: it and its variants have found major applications in Internet cryptography, where clients and servers often need to prove to each other that they are following a protocol correctly without revealing secret information as they do so.

However, there is one important caveat: unlike the graph-nonisomorphism protocol, the GMW protocol relies essentially on a *cryptographic hypothesis*. For here is how the GMW protocol works: you (the prover) first publish thousands of encrypted messages, each one "committing" you to a randomly garbled piece of your claimed proof. You then offer to decrypt a tiny fraction of those messages, as a way for skeptical observers to "spot-check" your proof, while learning nothing about its structure besides the useless fact that, say, the 1729th step is valid (but how could it *not* be valid?). If the skeptics want to increase their confidence that your proof is sound, then you simply run the protocol over and over with them, using a fresh batch of encrypted messages each time. If the skeptics could decrypt all the messages in a single batch, *then* they could piece together your proof—but to do that, they would need to break the underlying cryptographic code.

10.9.2 Other New Notions

Let me mention four other notions of "proof" that complexity theorists have explored in depth over the last twenty years, and that might merit philosophical attention.

• *Multi-prover interactive proofs* (Ben-Or et al. 1988; Babai et al. 1991), in which Arthur exchanges messages with *two* (or more) computationally powerful but untrustworthy wizards. Here, Arthur might become convinced of some mathematical statement, but only under the assumption that the wizards could not communicate with *each other* during the protocol. (The usual analogy is to a police detective who puts two suspects in separate cells, to prevent them from coordinating their answers.) Interestingly, in some multi-prover protocols, even noncommunicating wizards could successfully coordinate their responses to Arthur's challenges (and thereby convince Arthur of a falsehood) through the use of *quantum entanglement* (Cleve et al. 2004). However, other protocols are conjectured to remain sound even against entangled wizards (Kempe et al. 2011).

• *Probabilistically checkable proofs* (Feige et al. 1996; Arora and Safra 1998), which are mathematical proofs encoded in a special error-correcting format, so that one can become confident of their validity by checking only 10 or 20 bits chosen randomly in a correlated way. The *PCP (probabilistically checkable proofs) theorem* (Arora et al. 1998; Dinur 2007), one of the crowning achievements of complexity theory, says that *any* mathematical theorem, in any standard formal system such as Zermelo-Fraenkel set theory, can be converted in polynomial time into a probabilistically checkable format.

- *Quantum proofs* (Watrous 2000; Aaronson and Kuperberg 2007), which are proofs that depend for their validity on the output of a quantum computation—possibly, even a quantum computation that requires a special entangled "proof state" fed to it as input. Because n quantum bits might require ~2^n classical bits to simulate, quantum proofs have the property that it might never be possible to list all the "steps" that went into the proof, within the constraints of the visible universe. For this reason, one's belief in the mathematical statement being proved might depend on one's belief in the correctness of quantum mechanics as a physical theory.

- *Computationally sound proofs and arguments* (Brassard et al. 1988; Micali 2000), which rely for their validity on the assumption that the prover was limited to polynomial-time computations—as well as the mathematical conjecture that crafting a convincing argument for a falsehood would have taken the prover more than polynomial time.

What implications do these new types of proof have for the foundations of mathematics? Do they merely make more dramatic what "should have been obvious all along": that, as David Deutsch argues in *The Beginning of Infinity* (2011), proofs are physical processes taking place in brains or computers, which therefore have no validity independent of our beliefs about physics? Are the issues raised essentially the same as those raised by "conventional" proofs that require extensive computations, like Appel and Haken's proof of the four-color theorem (Appel and Haken 1989)? Or does appealing, in the course of a "mathematical proof," to (say) the validity of quantum mechanics, the randomness of apparently random numbers, or the lack of certain superpowers on the part of the prover represent something qualitatively new? Philosophical analysis is sought.

10.10   Complexity, Space, and Time

What can computational complexity tell us about the nature of space and time? A first answer might be "not much": after all, the definitions of standard complexity classes such as P can be shown to be insensitive to such details as the number of spatial dimensions, and even whether the speed of light is finite or infinite.[62] On the other hand, I think complexity theory does offer insight about the *differences* between space and time.

The class of problems solvable using a polynomial amount of memory (but possibly an exponential amount of time[63]) is called PSPACE, for polynomial space. Examples of PSPACE problems include simulating dynamical systems, deciding whether a regular grammar generates all possible strings, and executing an optimal strategy in two-player games such as Reversi, Connect Four, and Hex.[64] It is not hard to show that PSPACE is at least as powerful as NP:

$P \subseteq NP \subseteq PSPACE \subseteq EXP.$

Here EXP represents the class of problems solvable using an exponential amount of time, and also possibly an exponential amount of memory.[65] Every one of the above containments is believed to be strict, although the only one currently *proved* to be strict is $P \neq EXP$, by an important result of Hartmanis and Stearns (1965) called the time hierarchy theorem.[66,67]

Notice, in particular, that $P \neq NP$ implies $P \neq PSPACE$. So while $P \neq PSPACE$ is not yet proved, it is an extremely secure conjecture by the standards of complexity theory. In slogan form, complexity theorists believe that *space is more powerful than time*.

Now, some people have asked how such a claim could possibly be consistent with modern physics. For didn't Einstein teach us that space and time are merely two aspects of the same structure? One immediate answer is that, even *within* relativity theory, space and time are not interchangeable: space has a positive signature whereas time has a negative signature. In complexity theory, the difference between space and time manifests itself in the straightforward fact that you can *reuse* the same memory cells over and over, but you can't reuse the same moments of time.[68]

Yet, as trivial as that observation sounds, it leads to an interesting thought. Suppose that the laws of physics let us travel *backward* in time. In such a case, it's natural to imagine that time would become a "reusable resource" just like space is—and that, as a result, arbitrary PSPACE computations would fall within our grasp. But is that just an idle speculation, or can we rigorously justify it?

10.10.1 Closed Timelike Curves

Philosophers, like science-fiction fans, have long been interested in the possibility of closed timelike curves (CTCs), which arise in certain solutions to Einstein's field equations of general relativity.[69] On a traditional understanding, the central philosophical problem raised by CTCs is the *grandfather paradox*. This is the situation where you go back in time to kill your own grandfather, therefore you are never born, therefore your grandfather is *not* killed, therefore you *are* born, and so on. Does this contradiction immediately imply that CTCs are impossible?

No, it doesn't: we can only conclude that, *if* CTCs exist, then the laws of physics must somehow prevent grandfather paradoxes from arising. How could they do so? One classic illustration is that "when you go back in time to try and kill your grandfather, the gun jams"—or some other "unlikely" event inevitably occurs to keep the state of the universe consistent. But why should we imagine that such a convenient "out" will always be available, in every physical experiment involving CTCs? Normally, we like to imagine that we have the freedom to design an experiment however we wish, without Nature imposing conditions on the experiment (for example:

"every gun must jam sometimes") whose reasons can only be understood in terms of distant or hypothetical events.

In his paper "Quantum mechanics near closed timelike lines," Deutsch (1991) gave an elegant proposal for eliminating grandfather paradoxes. In particular, he showed that, as long as we assume the laws of physics are quantum-mechanical (or even just classically probabilistic), every experiment involving a CTC admits at least one *fixed point*: that is, a way to satisfy the conditions of the experiment that ensures consistent evolution. Formally, if S is the mapping from quantum states to themselves induced by "going around the CTC once," then a fixed point is any quantum mixed state[70] ρ such that $S(\rho) = \rho$. The existence of such a ρ follows from simple linear-algebraic arguments. As one illustration, the "resolution of the grandfather paradox" is now that you are born with probability 1/2, and *if* you are born, you go back in time to kill your grandfather—from which it follows that you are born with probability 1/2, and so on. Merely by treating states as probabilistic (as, in some sense, they *have* to be in quantum mechanics[71]), we have made the evolution of the universe consistent.

But Deutsch's account of CTCs faces at least three serious difficulties. The first difficulty is that the fixed points might not be *unique*: there could be many mixed states ρ such that $S(\rho) = \rho$, and then the question arises of how Nature chooses one of them. To illustrate, consider the *grandfather anti-paradox*: a bit $b \in \{0, 1\}$ that travels around a CTC without changing. We can consistently assume $b = 0$, or $b = 1$, or any probabilistic mixture of the two—and unlike the usual situation in physics, here there is no possible boundary condition that could resolve the ambiguity.

The second difficulty, pointed out Bennett et al. (2009), is that Deutsch's proposal violates the statistical interpretation of quantum mixed states. So for example, if half of an entangled pair

$$\frac{|0\rangle_A |0\rangle_B + |1\rangle_A |1\rangle_B}{\sqrt{2}}$$

is placed inside the CTC, while the other half remains outside the CTC, then the process of finding a fixed point will "break" the entanglement between the two halves. As a "remedy" for this problem, Bennett et al. (2009) suggest requiring the CTC fixed point ρ to be independent of the entire rest of the universe. To my mind, this remedy is so drastic that it basically amounts to defining CTCs out of existence!

Motivated by these difficulties, Lloyd et al. (2011) recently proposed a completely different account of CTCs, based on *postselected teleportation*. Lloyd et al.'s account avoids both of the problems above—though perhaps not surprisingly, introduces other problems of its own.[72] My own view, for whatever it is worth, is that Lloyd et al. are talking less about "true" CTCs as I would understand the concept, as about postselected quantum-mechanical experiments that *simulate* CTCs in certain interesting respects. If there are any controversies in physics that call out for expert philosophical attention, surely this is one of them.

10.10.2 The Evolutionary Principle

Yet so far, we have not even mentioned what I see as the *main* difficulty with Deutsch's account of CTCs. This is that *finding* a fixed point might require Nature to solve an astronomically hard computational problem! To illustrate, consider a science-fiction scenario wherein you go back in time and dictate Shakespeare's plays to him. Shakespeare thanks you for saving him the effort, publishes verbatim the plays that you dictated, and centuries later the plays come down to you, whereupon you go back in time and dictate them to Shakespeare, etc.

Notice that, in contrast to the grandfather paradox, here there is no logical contradiction: the story as we told it is entirely consistent. But most people find the story "paradoxical" anyway. After all, somehow *Hamlet* gets written, without anyone ever doing the work of writing it! As Deutsch (1991) perceptively observed, if there is a "paradox" here, then it is not one of logic but of *computational complexity*. Specifically, the story violates a commonsense principle that we can loosely articulate as follows:

Knowledge requires a causal process to bring it into existence.

Like many other important principles, this one might not be recognized as a "principle" at all before we contemplate situations that violate it! Deutsch (1991) calls this principle the *evolutionary principle* (EP). Note that some version of the EP was invoked both by William Paley's blind-watchmaker argument, and (ironically) by the arguments of Richard Dawkins (2006) and other atheists against the existence of an intelligent designer.

In my survey article "NP-Complete Problems and Physical Reality" (Aaronson 2005b), I proposed and defended a complexity-theoretic analog of the EP, which I called the NP *hardness assumption*:

There is no physical means to solve NP-complete problems in polynomial time.

The above statement implies $P \neq NP$, but is stronger in that it encompasses probabilistic computing, quantum computing, and *any other computational model* compatible with the laws of physics. See Aaronson (2005b) for a survey of recent results bearing on the NP hardness assumption, analyses of claimed counterexamples to the assumption, and possible implications of the assumption for physics.

10.10.3   Closed Timelike Curve Computation

But can we show more rigorously that closed timelike curves would *violate* the NP hardness assumption? Indeed, let us now show that, in a universe where arbitrary computations could be performed inside a CTC, and where Nature had to find a fixed point for the CTC, we could solve NP-complete problems using only polynomial resources.

We can model any NP-complete problem instance by a function f: $\{0, \dots, 2^n - 1\}$ $\rightarrow \{0, 1\}$, which maps each possible solution x to the bit 1 if x is valid, or to 0 if x is invalid. (Here, for convenience, we identify each n-bit solution string x with the nonnegative integer that x encodes in binary.) Our task, then, is to find an $x \in \{0, \dots, 2^n - 1\}$ such that $f(x) = 1$. We can solve this problem with just a *single* evaluation to f, provided we can run the following computer program C inside a closed timelike curve (Brun 2003; Aaronson 2005b; Aaronson and Watrous 2009):

Given input $x \in \{0, \dots, 2^n - 1\}$:
If $f(x) = 1$, then output x
Otherwise, output $(x + 1) \bmod 2^n$

Assuming there exists at least one x such that $f(x) = 1$, the only *fixed points* of C—that is, the only ways for C's output to equal its input—are for C to input, and output, such a valid solution x, which therefore appears in C's output register "as if by magic." (If there are no valid solutions, then C's fixed points will simply be uniform superpositions or probability distributions over *all* $x \in \{0, \dots, 2^n - 1\}$.)

Extending the above idea, John Watrous and I (following a suggestion by Fortnow) recently showed that a CTC computer in Deutsch's model could solve all problems in PSPACE (see Aaronson and Watrous 2009). (Recall that PSPACE is believed to be even larger than NP.) More surprisingly, we also showed that PSPACE constitutes the *limit* on what can be done with a CTC computer; and that this is true whether the CTC computer is classical or quantum. One consequence of our results is that the "naïve intuition" about CTC computers—that their effect would be to "make space and time equivalent as computational resources"—is ultimately correct, although not for the naïve reasons.[73] A second, amusing consequence is that, once closed timelike curves are available, switching from classical to quantum computers provides no *additional* benefit!

It is important to realize that our algorithms for solving hard problems with CTCs do *not* just boil down to "using huge amounts of time to find the answer, then sending the answer back in time to before the computer started." For even in the exotic scenario of a time travel computer, we still require that all resources used *inside* the CTC (time, memory, etc.) be polynomially-bounded. Thus, the ability to solve hard problems comes solely from *causal consistency*: the requirement that

Nature must find some evolution for the CTC computer that avoids grandfather paradoxes.

In Lloyd et al.'s (2011) alternative account of CTCs based on postselection, hard problems can *also* be solved, though for different reasons. In particular, building on an earlier result of mine (Aaronson 2005c), Lloyd et al. show that the power of their model corresponds to a complexity class called PP (probabilistic polynomial time), which is believed to be strictly smaller than PSPACE but strictly larger than NP. Thus, one might say that Lloyd et al.'s model "improves" the computational situation, but not by much!

So one might wonder: is there any way that the laws of physics could allow CTCs, *without* opening the door to implausible computational powers? There remains at least one interesting possibility, which was communicated to me by the philosopher Tim Maudlin.[74] Maybe the laws of physics have the property that, no matter what computations are performed inside a CTC, Nature always has an "out" that avoids the grandfather paradox, but *also* avoids solving hard computational problems—analogous to "the gun jamming" in the original grandfather paradox. Such an out might involve (for example) an asteroid hitting the CTC computer, or the computer failing for other mysterious reasons. Of course, *any* computer in the physical world has some nonzero probability of failure, but ordinarily we imagine that the failure probability can be made negligibly small. However, in situations where Nature is being "forced" to find a fixed point, maybe "mysterious computer failures" would become the norm rather than the exception.

To summarize, I think that computational complexity theory *changes* the philosophical issues raised by time travel into the past. While discussion traditionally focused on the grandfather paradox, we have seen that there is no shortage of ways for Nature to avoid logical inconsistencies, even in a universe with CTCs. The "real" problem, then, is how to escape the *other* paradoxes that arise in the course of taming the grandfather paradox! Probably foremost among those is the "computational complexity paradox," of NP-complete and even harder problems getting solved as if by magic.

10.11 Economics

In classical economics, agents are modeled as rational, Bayesian agents who take whatever actions will maximize their expected utility $E_{\omega \in \Omega}[U(\omega)]$, given their subjective probabilities $\{p_\omega\}_{\omega \in \Omega}$ over all possible states ω of the world.[75] This, of course, is a caricature that seems almost designed to be attacked, and it *has* been attacked from almost every angle. For example, humans are not even close to rational Bayesian agents, but suffer from well-known cognitive biases, as explored by Kahneman,

Slovic, and Tversky (1982), among others. Furthermore, the classical view seems to leave no room for critiquing people's beliefs (i.e., their prior probabilities) or their utility functions as irrational—yet it is easy to cook up prior probabilities or utility functions that would lead to behavior that almost anyone would consider insane. A third problem is that, in games with several cooperating or competing agents who act simultaneously, classical economics guarantees the existence of at least one *Nash equilibrium* among the agents' strategies. But the usual situation is that there are multiple equilibria, and then there is no general principle to predict which equilibrium will prevail, even though the choice might mean the difference between war and peace.

Computational complexity theory can contribute to debates about the foundations of economics by showing that, even in the idealized situation of rational agents who all have perfect information about the state of the world, it will often be *computationally intractable* for those agents to act in accordance with classical economics. Of course, some version of this observation has been recognized in economics for a long time. There is a large literature on *bounded rationality* (going back to the work of Herbert Simon [1955]), which studies the behavior of economic agents whose decision-making abilities are limited in one way or another.

10.11.1 Bounded Rationality and the Iterated Prisoners' Dilemma

As one example of an insight to emerge from this literature, consider the finite iterated prisoners' dilemma. This is a game where two players meet for some fixed number of rounds N, which is finite and common knowledge between the players. In each round, both players can either "defect" or "cooperate" (not knowing the other player's choice), after which they receive the following payoffs:

	Defect$_2$	Cooperate$_2$
Defect$_1$	1,1	4,0
Cooperate$_1$	0,4	3,3

Both players remember the entire previous history of the interaction.

It is clear that the players will be jointly best off (i.e., will maximize the sum of their payoffs) if they both cooperate. Unfortunately, it is equally clear that, *if the players meet for only one round ($N = 1$), then cooperation is not an *equilibrium*. Regardless of what Player 1 does, Player 2 will do better by defecting than by cooperating, and vice versa.

On the other hand, *if the number of rounds N were unknown or infinite*, then the players could rationally decide to cooperate, similarly to how humans decide to cooperate in real life. That is, Player 1 reasons that if he defects, then Player 2 might retaliate by defecting in future rounds, and Player 2 reasons likewise. Both players conclude that, over the long run, they'll do best *even just for themselves* by cooperating.

The "paradox" is now the following: as soon as the number of rounds N becomes *known*, the above reasoning completely collapses! For clearly, neither player can have anything to lose by defecting *in the very last round*, when the other player no longer has any chance to retaliate. So if both players are rational, then that is exactly what they will do. But if both players *know* that both of them will defect in round N, then neither one has anything to lose by defecting in round $N-1$ *either*. Of course, they can continue inductively like this all the way back to the first round. We therefore get the "prediction" that both players will defect in every round, even though that is neither in the players' own interests, nor what actual humans do in experiments. And all because the number of rounds N was *known*: something that seems intuitively like it shouldn't make any difference!

In 1985, Neyman proposed an ingenious resolution of this paradox (see Neyman 1985). Specifically, he showed that if the two players have *sufficiently small memories*—technically, if they are finite automata with k states, for $2 \leq k < N$—then cooperation becomes an equilibrium once again! The basic intuition is that, if both players lack enough memory to count up to N, and both of them know that, and both know that they both know that, and so on, then the inductive argument in the last paragraph fails, since it assumes intermediate strategies that neither player can implement.

While complexity considerations vanquish *some* of the counterintuitive conclusions of classical economics, equally interesting to me is that they do not vanquish others. As one example, I showed (Aaronson 2005a) that Robert Aumann's celebrated *agreement theorem* (Aumann 1976)—perfect Bayesian agents with common priors can never "agree to disagree"—persists even in the presence of limited communication between the agents.

There are many other interesting results in the bounded rationality literature, too many to do them justice here (but see Rubinstein 1998 for a survey). On the other hand, "bounded rationality" is something of a catch-all phrase, encompassing almost every imaginable deviation from rationality—including human cognitive biases, limits on information-gathering and communication, and the restriction of strategies to a specific form (for example, linear threshold functions). Many of these deviations have little to do with computational complexity per se. So the question remains of whether computational complexity *specifically* can provide new insights about economic behavior.

10.11.2 The Complexity of Equilibria

There are some very recent advances suggesting that the answer is yes. Consider the problem of finding an equilibrium of a two-player game, given the $n \times n$ payoff matrix as input. In the special case of *zero-sum games* (which von Neumann studied in 1928), it has long been known how to solve this problem in an amount of time polynomial in *n*, for example by reduction to linear programming. But in 2006, Daskalakis, Goldberg, and Papadimitriou (see their 2009, and with improvements by Chen and Deng [2006]) proved the spectacular result that, for a *general* (not necessarily zero-sum) two-player game, finding a Nash equilibrium is "PPAD-complete." Here PPAD (polynomial parity argument, directed) is, roughly speaking, the class of *all* search problems for which a solution is guaranteed to exist for the same combinatorial reason that every game has at least one Nash equilibrium. Note that finding a Nash equilibrium *cannot* be NP-complete, for the technical reason that NP is a class of *decision* problems, and the answer to the decision problem "Does this game have a Nash equilibrium?" is always yes. But Daskalakis et al.'s result says (informally) that the search problem of *finding* a Nash problem is "as close to NP-complete as it could possibly be," subject to its decision version being trivial. Similar PPAD-completeness results are now known for other fundamental economic problems, such as finding market-clearing prices in Arrow-Debreu markets (Chen et al. 2009).

Of course, one can debate the economic relevance of these results: for example, how often does the computational hardness that we now know[76] to be inherent in economic equilibrium theorems actually rear its head in practice? But one can similarly debate the economic relevance of the equilibrium theorems themselves! In my opinion, if the theorem that Nash equilibria *exist* is considered relevant to debates about (say) free markets versus government intervention, then the theorem that *finding* those equilibria is PPAD-complete should be considered relevant also.

10.12 Conclusions

The purpose of this essay was to illustrate how philosophy could be enriched by taking computational complexity theory into account, much as it was enriched almost a century ago by taking computability theory into account. In particular, I argued that computational complexity provides new insights into the explanatory content of Darwinism, the nature of mathematical knowledge and proof, computationalism, syntax versus semantics, the problem of logical omniscience, debates surrounding the Turing test and Chinese Room, the problem of induction, the foundations of quantum mechanics, closed timelike curves, and economic rationality.

Indeed, one might say that the "real" question is which philosophical problems *don't* have important computational complexity aspects! My own opinion is that there probably *are* such problems (even within analytic philosophy), and that one good candidate is the problem of what we should take as "bedrock mathematical reality": that is, the set of mathematical statements that are objectively true or false, regardless of whether they can be proved or disproved in a given formal system. To me, if we are not willing to say that a given Turing machine M either accepts, rejects, or runs forever (when started on a blank tape)—and that which one it does is an objective fact, independent of our formal axiomatic theories, the laws of physics, the biology of the human brain, cultural conventions, etc.—then *we have no basis to talk about any of those other things* (axiomatic theories, the laws of physics, and so on). Furthermore, M's resource requirements are irrelevant here: even if M only halts after $2^{2^{10000}}$ steps, its output is as mathematically definite as if it had halted after 10 steps.[77]

Can we say anything *general* about when a computational complexity perspective is helpful in philosophy, and when it isn't? Extrapolating from the examples in this essay, I would say that computational complexity tends to be helpful when we want to know whether a particular fact *does any explanatory work*: sections 3.2, 3.3, 4, 6, and 7 all provided examples of this. Other "philosophical applications" of complexity theory come from the evolutionary principle and the NP hardness assumption discussed in section 10.10.2. *If* we believe that certain problems are computationally intractable, then we may be able to draw interesting conclusions from that belief about economic rationality, quantum mechanics, the possibility of closed timelike curves, and other issues. By contrast, computational complexity tends to be *un*helpful when we only want to know whether a particular fact "determines" another fact, and don't care about the length of the inferential chain.

10.12.1   Criticisms of Complexity Theory

Despite its explanatory reach, complexity theory has been criticized on various grounds. Here are four of the most common criticisms:

1. Complexity theory only makes *asymptotic* statements (statements about how the resources needed to solve problem instances of size n scale as n goes to infinity). But as a matter of logic, asymptotic statements need not have *any implications whatsoever* for the finite values of n (say, 10,000) that humans care actually about, nor can any finite amount of experimental data confirm or refute an asymptotic claim.[78]

2. Many of (what we would like to be) complexity theory's basic principles, such as $P \neq NP$, are currently unproved mathematical conjectures, and will probably remain that way for a long time.

3. Complexity theory focuses on only a limited type of computer—the serial, deterministic Turing machine—and fails to incorporate the "messier" computational phenomena found in nature.

4. Complexity theory studies only the *worst-case* behavior of algorithms, and does not address whether that behavior is representative, or whether it merely reflects a few "pathological" inputs. So for example, even if P ≠ NP, there might still be excellent heuristics to solve *most* instances of NP-complete problems that actually arise in practice; complexity theory tells us nothing about such possibilities one way or the other.

For whatever it's worth, criticisms (3) and (4) have become much less accurate since the 1980s. As discussed in this essay, complexity theory has by now branched out far beyond deterministic Turing machines, to incorporate (for example) quantum mechanics, parallel and distributed computing, and stochastic processes such as Darwinian evolution. Meanwhile, although worst-case complexity remains the best-understood kind, today there is a large body of work—much of it driven by cryptography—that studies the *average-case* hardness of computational problems, for various probability distributions over inputs. And just as almost all complexity theorists believe that P ≠ NP, so almost all subscribe to the stronger belief that there exist *hard-on-average* NP problems—indeed, that belief is one of the underpinnings of modern cryptography. A few problems, such as calculating discrete logarithms, are even known to be *just as hard on random inputs as they are on the hardest possible input* (though whether such "worst-case/average-case equivalence" holds for any NP-complete problem remains a major open question). For these reasons, although speaking about average-case rather than worst-case complexity would complicate some of the arguments in this essay, I don't think it would change the conclusions much.[79] See Bogdanov and Trevisan (2006) for an excellent recent survey of average-case complexity, and Impagliazzo (1995) for an evocative discussion of complexity theory's "possible worlds" (for example, the "world" where NP-complete problems turn out to be hard in the worst case but easy on average).

The broader point is that, even if we admit that criticisms (1)–(4) have merit, that does not give us a license to dismiss complexity-theoretic arguments whenever we dislike them! In science, we only ever deal with imperfect, approximate theories— and if we reject the conclusions of the *best* approximate theory in some area, then the burden is on us to explain why.

To illustrate, suppose you believe that quantum computers will never give a speedup over classical computers for any practical problem. Then as an explanation for your stance, you might assert any of the following:

1. Quantum mechanics is false or incomplete, and an attempt to build a scalable quantum computer would instead lead to falsifying or extending quantum mechanics itself.

2. There exist polynomial-time *classical* algorithms for factoring integers, and for all the other problems that admit polynomial-time quantum algorithms. (In complexity terms, the classes BPP and BQP are equal.)

3. The "constant-factor overheads" involved in building a quantum computer are so large as to negate their asymptotic advantages, for any problem of conceivable human interest.

4. While we don't yet know which of (1)–(3) holds, we can know on some a priori ground that at least one of them has to hold.

The point is that, even if we can't answer every possible shortcoming of a complexity-theoretic analysis, we can still use it to *clarify the choices*: to force people to lay some cards on the table, committing themselves either to a prediction that might be falsified or to a mathematical conjecture that might be disproved. Of course, this is a common feature of *all* scientific theories, not something specific to complexity theory. If complexity theory is unusual here, it is only in the number of "predictions" it juggles that could be confirmed or refuted by mathematical proof (and indeed, *only* by mathematical proof).[80]

10.12.2   Future Directions

Even if the various criticisms of complexity theory don't negate its relevance, it would be great to address those criticisms head-on—and, more generally, to get a clearer understanding of the relationship between complexity theory and the real-world phenomena that it tries to explain. Toward that end, I think the following questions would all benefit from careful philosophical analysis:

• What is the empirical status of asymptotic claims? What sense can we give to an asymptotic statement "making predictions," or being supported or ruled out by a finite number of observations?

• How can we explain the empirical facts on which complexity theory relies: for example, that we rarely see n^{10000} or 1.0000001^n algorithms, or that the computational problems humans care about tend to organize themselves into a relatively small number of equivalence classes?

• Short of proof, how do people form intuitions about the truth or falsehood of mathematical conjectures? What *are* those intuitions, in cases such as P ≠ NP?

• If we think of complexity classes (P, NP, etc.) as collections of problems, then it becomes harder to understand results like those of Baker, Gill, and Solovay (1975), which says that there exists an "oracle" A such that $P^A \neq NP^A$ (and furthermore, this remains true even if P = NP in the "real" world). In philosophical terms, should we think of a complexity class as corresponding to its *definition* rather than its *extension*?

• Do the conceptual conclusions that people sometimes want to draw from conjectures such as $P \neq NP$ or $BPP \neq BQP$—for example, about the nature of mathematical creativity or the interpretation of quantum mechanics—actually depend on those conjectures being true? Are there easier-to-prove statements that would arguably support the same conclusions?

• If $P \neq NP$, then how have humans managed to make such enormous mathematical progress, even in the face of the general intractability of theorem-proving? Is there a "selection effect," by which mathematicians favor problems with special structure that makes them easier to solve than arbitrary problems? If so, then what does this structure consist of?

In short, I see plenty of scope for the converse essay to this one: "Why Computational Complexity Theorists Should Care about Philosophy."

Acknowledgments

This material is based upon work supported by the National Science Foundation under Grant No. 0844626, and is also supported by a DARPA YFA grant, the Sloan Foundation, and a TIBCO Chair.

I am grateful to Oron Shagrir for pushing me to finish this essay, for helpful comments, and for suggesting section 10.7.2; to Alex Byrne for suggesting section 10.6; to Agustin Rayo for suggesting section 10.5; and to David Aaronson, Eric Allender, Seamus Bradley, Alessandro Chiesa, Terrence Cole, Michael Collins, Andy Drucker, Ron Fagin, Michael Forbes, Oded Goldreich, Bob Harper, Gil Kalai, Dana Moshkovitz, Jan Arne Telle, Dylan Thurston, Ronald de Wolf, Avi Wigderson, and Joshua Zelinsky for their feedback.

Notes

1. When I use the word "philosophy" in this essay, I'll *mean* philosophy within the analytic tradition. I don't understand continental or Eastern philosophy well enough to say whether they have any interesting connections with computational complexity theory.

2. See philpapers.org/browse/computational-complexity.

3. The conjecture that pseudorandom generators exist implies the $P \neq NP$ conjecture (about which more later), but might be even stronger: the converse implication is unknown.

4. The *Stanford Encyclopedia of Philosophy* entry on "The Philosophy of Computer Science," plato.stanford.edu/entries/computer-science, devotes most of its space to this connection.

5. A variant, "resource-bounded Kolmogorov complexity," *does* take time and memory into account, and is part of computational complexity theory proper.

6. This method is called the *number field sieve*, and the quoted running time depends on plausible but unproved conjectures in number theory. The best *proven* running time is $2^{\sqrt{n}}$. Both of these represent nontrivial improvements over the naïve method of trying all possible divisors, which takes $\sim 2^n$ steps. See Pomerance (1996) for a good survey of factoring algorithms.

7. In some contexts, "exponential" means c^n for some constant $c > 1$, but in most complexity-theoretic contexts it can also mean c^{n^d} for constants $c > 1$ and $d > 0$.

8. This is not to say that *no* details of the computational model matter: for example, some problems are known to be solvable in polynomial time on a quantum computer, but *not* known to be solvable in polynomial time on a classical computer! But in my view, the fact that the polynomial-exponential distinction can "notice" a modeling choice of this magnitude is a feature of the distinction, not a bug.

9. Contrary to a common misconception, NP does *not* stand for "non-polynomial"! There *are* computational problems that are *known* to require more than polynomial time (see section 10.10), but the NP problems are not among those. Indeed, the classes NP and "non-polynomial" have a nonempty intersection exactly if P ≠ NP.

For detailed definitions of P, NP, and several hundred other complexity classes, see my Complexity Zoo website: www.complexityzoo.com.

10. For more information, see www.claymath.org/millennium/P_vs_NP/

My own view is that P versus NP is manifestly the *most important* of the seven problems! For if P = NP, then by Gödel's argument, there is an excellent chance that we could program our computers to solve the other six problems as well.

11. One might ask: can we *explain* what makes the P ≠ NP problem so hard, rather than just pointing out that many smart people have tried to solve it and failed? After four decades of research, we *do* have partial explanations for the problem's difficulty, in the form of formal "barriers" that rule out large classes of proof techniques. Three barriers identified so far are *relativization*, which rules out diagonalization and other techniques with a "computability" flavor (Baker et al. 1975), *algebrization*, which rules out diagonalization even when combined with the main non-relativizing techniques known today (Aaronson and Wigderson 2009), and *natural proofs*, which shows that many "combinatorial" techniques, if they worked, could be turned around to get faster algorithms to distinguish random from pseudorandom functions (Razborov and Rudich 1997).

12. By contrast, and contrary to a common misconception, there is strong evidence that factoring integers is *not* NP-complete. It is known that if P ≠ NP, then there are NP problems that are neither in P nor NP-complete (Ladner 1975), and factoring is one candidate for such a problem. This point will become relevant when we discuss quantum computing.

13. Admittedly, one might be able to prove that *Darwinian natural selection* would require exponential time to produce some functionality, without thereby proving that *any* algorithm would require exponential time.

14. This section was inspired by a question of A. Rupinski on the website *MathOverflow*. See mathoverflow.net/questions/62925/philosophical-question-related-to-largest-known-primes.

15. www.mersenne.org.

16. Here we implicitly mean: "known" by the entire mathematical community, rather than known by some particular individual when asked about it. Section 10.5 will consider the latter type of knowledge.

17. For example, one could use *Chebyshev's theorem* (also called *Bertrand's postulate*), which says that for all $N > 1$ there exists a prime between N and $2N$.

18. *Cramér's conjecture* states that the spacing between two consecutive n-digit primes never exceeds $\sim n^2$. This conjecture appears staggeringly difficult: even assuming the Riemann hypothesis, it is only known how to deduce the much weaker upper bound $\sim n2^{n/2}$. But interestingly, if Cramér's conjecture is proved, expressions like "the first prime larger than $2^k - 1$" will *then* define "known primes" according to my criterion.

19. In particular, it is easy to check that the set of *computable* functions does not depend on whether we define computability with respect to a classical or a quantum Turing machine, or a deterministic or a nondeterministic one. At most, these choices can change a Turing machine's running time by an exponential factor, which is irrelevant for computability theory.

20. The Turing test, proposed by Turing (1950), is a test where a human judge interacts with either another human or a computer conversation program, by typing messages back and forth. The program "passes" the Test if the judge can't reliably distinguish the program from the human interlocutor.

By a "strong variant" of the Turing test, I mean that besides the usual teletype conversation, one could add additional tests requiring vision, hearing, touch, smell, speaking, handwriting, facial expressions, dancing, playing sports and musical instruments, etc.—even though many perfectly intelligent *humans* would then be unable to pass the tests!

21. One famous exception is John Searle (1992), who has made it clear that, if (say) his best friend turned out to be controlled by a microchip rather than a brain, then he would regard his friend as never having been a person at all.

22. See Dennett (1995) and Chalmers (1996), for example. To summarize:

1. Why should we assume a computer operates within a knowably sound formal system? If we grant a computer the same freedom to make occasional mistakes that we grant humans, then the incompleteness theorem is no longer relevant.

2. Why should we assume that human mathematicians have "direct perception of Platonic reality"? Human mathematicians (such as Frege) have been wrong before about the consistency of formal systems.

3. A computer could, of course, be programmed to output "I believe that formal system F is consistent"— and even to output answers to various follow-up questions about *why* it believes this. So in arguing that such affirmations "wouldn't really count" (because they wouldn't reflect "true understanding"), AI critics such as Lucas and Penrose are forced to retreat from their vision of an empirical "sword-in-the-stone test," and fall back on other, unspecified criteria related to the AI's internal structure. But then *why put the sword in the stone in the first place?*

23. People interacting over the Internet, via email or instant messages, regularly judge each other to be humans rather than spam-bots after exchanging a much smaller number of bits! In any case, cosmological considerations suggest an upper bound of roughly 10^{122} bits in any observable process (Bousso 2000).

24. Some readers might notice a tension here: I explained in section 10.2 that complexity theorists care about the *asymptotic* behavior as the problem size n goes to infinity. So why am I now saying that, for the purposes of the Turing test, we should restrict attention to finite values of n such as 10^{20}? There are two answers to this question. The first is that, in contrast to mathematical problems like the factoring problem or the halting problem, it is unclear whether it even makes *sense* to generalize the Turing test to arbitrary conversation lengths: for the Turing test is defined in terms of human beings, and human conversational capacity is finite. The second answer is that, to whatever extent it *does* make sense to generalize the Turing test to arbitrary conversation lengths n, I *am* interested in whether the asymptotic complexity of passing the test grows polynomially or exponentially with n (as the remainder of the section explains).

25. As Gil Kalai pointed out to me, one could speculate instead that an efficient computer program *exists* to pass the Turing test, but that *finding* such a program would require exponential computational resources. In that situation, the human brain could indeed be simulated efficiently by a computer program, but maybe not by a program that humans could ever *write*!

26. Here, by a Turing machine M being "efficient," we mean that M's running time, memory usage, and program size are modest enough that there is no real problem of principle understanding how M could be simulated by a classical physical system consisting of $\sim 10^{11}$ neurons and $\sim 10^{14}$ synapses. For example, a Turing machine containing a lookup table of size $10^{10^{20}}$ would not be efficient in this sense.

27. And amusingly, if we could solve NP-complete problems, then we'd presumably find it much easier to prove that computers *couldn't* solve them!

28. Indeed, it is not even clear to me that we should think of humans as being able to solve all P problems efficiently, let alone NP-complete problems! Recall that P is the class of problems that *are* solvable in polynomial time by a deterministic Turing machine. Many problems are known to belong to P for quite sophisticated reasons: two examples are testing whether a number is prime (though not factoring it!) and testing whether a graph has a perfect matching (Agrawal, Kayal, and Saxena 2004). In principle, of course, a human could laboriously run the polynomial-time algorithms for such problems using pencil and paper. But is the use of pencil and paper legitimate, where use of a computer would *not* be? What is the computational power of the "unaided" human intellect? Recent work of Drucker (2011), which shows how to use a stock photography collection to increase the "effective memory" available for mental calculations, provides a fascinating empirical perspective on these questions.

29. Not surprisingly, these particular axioms have engendered controversy: they leave no possibility for Rumsfeldian "unknown unknowns," or (a category that he left out) "unknown knowns."

30. If we don't require the sentences to be *true*, then presumably we're talking about *belief* rather than *knowledge*.

31. If you lack the *concept* of a prime factor, then I could simply ask instead for two 2-digit numbers that yield 1591 when multiplied.

32. For "knowing" a person suggests having actually met the person, while "knowing" a place suggests having visited the place. Interestingly, in Hebrew, one uses a completely different verb for "know" in the sense of "being familiar with" (*makir*) than for "know" in the intellectual sense (*yodeya*).

33. For chess on an $n \times n$ board is known to be EXP-complete, and it is also known that P ≠ EXP. See section 10.10, and particularly note 64, for more details.

34. Admittedly, I haven't done justice in this section to the large literature on logical omniscience; readers wishing to delve deeper should see Fagin and Halpern (1987), for example.

35. Compare the pessimism expressed by Paul Graham (2007) about knowledge representation more generally:

In practice formal logic is not much use, because despite some progress in the last 150 years we're still only able to formalize a small percentage of statements. We may never do that much better, for the same reason 1980s-style "knowledge representation" could never have worked; many statements may have no representation more concise than a huge, analog brain state.

36. See Putnam (1998, appendix) and Searle (1992) for two instantiations of the argument (though the formal details of either will not concern us here).

37. "Computationalism" refers to the view that the mind is literally a computer, and that thought is literally a type of computation.

38. Technically, this describes a restricted class of reductions, called *nonadaptive* reductions. An *adaptive* reduction from chess to waterfalls might solve a chess problem by some procedure that involves initializing a waterfall and observing its final state, then using the results of that aquatic computation to initialize a *second* waterfall and observe *its* final state, and so on for some polynomial number of repetitions.

39. The perceptive reader might suspect that we smuggled our conclusion into the assumption that the waterfall states $s_P \in S$ and $f(s_P) \in T$ were encoded as binary strings in a "reasonable" way (and not, for example, in a way that encodes the solution to the chess problem). But a crucial lesson of complexity theory is that, when we discuss "computational problems," we *always* make an implicit commitment about the input and output encodings anyway! So for example, if positive integers were given as input via their prime factorizations, then the factoring problem would be trivial (just apply the identity function). But who cares? If, in mathematically defining the waterfall-simulation problem, we required input and output encodings that entailed solving chess problems, then it would no longer be reasonable to call our problem (solely) a "waterfall-simulation problem" at all.

40. Note that a LOGSPACE machine does not even have enough memory to store its input string! For this reason, we think of the input string as being provided on a special *read-only* tape.

41. See Kearns and Vazirani (1994) for an excellent introduction to PAC learning, and de Wolf (1997) for previous work applying PAC learning to philosophy and linguistics: specifically, to fleshing out Chomsky's "poverty of the stimulus" argument. De Wolf also discusses several formalizations of Occam's razor other than the one based on PAC learning.

42. In the setting of "proper learning"—where the learner needs to output a hypothesis in some specified format—it is even known that many natural PAC learning problems are NP-complete (see Pitt and Valiant 1988, for example). But in the "improper" setting—where the learner can describe its hypothesis using any polynomial-time algorithm—it is only known how to show that PAC learning problems are hard under cryptographic assumptions, and there seem to be inherent reasons for this (see Applebaum, Barak, and Xiao 2008).

43. Furthermore, Håstad et al. (1999) showed how to construct a pseudorandom generator from any *one-way function*: roughly speaking, a function f that is easy to compute but hard to invert even on a random input.

44. This problem is not as hopeless as it might sound! Important progress includes the work of Angluin (1987) on learning finite automata from queries and counterexamples, and that of Angluin et al. (2009) on learning a circuit by injecting values. Both papers study natural learning models that generalize the PAC model by allowing "controlled scientific experiments," whose results confirm or refute a hypothesis and thereby provide guidance about which experiments to do next.

45. Suppose that our programming language provides only multiplication by constants, addition, and the function $F(x, y) := ax^2 + bxy + cy^2 + dx + ey + f$. We can assume without loss of generality that $d = e = f = 0$. Then provided $ax^2 + bxy + cy^2$ factors into two independent linear terms, $px + qy$ and $rx + sy$, we can express the product xy as

$$\frac{F(sx - qy, -rx + py)}{(ps - qr)^2}.$$

46. Though note that, if the language L is expressive enough to allow this, we can simply define green and blue in terms of bleen and grue *once*, then refer back to those definitions whenever needed! In that case, taking bleen and grue (rather than green and blue) to be the primitive concepts would increase $\kappa_L(n)$ by only an *additive* constant, rather than a multiplicative constant.

The above fact is related to a fundamental result from the theory of Kolmogorov complexity (see Li and Vitányi 2008, for example). Namely, if P and Q are any two Turing-universal programming languages, and if $K_P(x)$ and $K_Q(x)$ are the lengths of the shortest programs in P and Q, respectively, that output a given string $x \in \{0, 1\}^*$, then there exists a universal "translation constant" c_{PQ}, such that $|K_P(x) - K_Q(x)| \leq c_{PQ}$ for *every* x. This c_{PQ} is just the number of bits needed to write a P-interpreter for Q-programs or vice versa.

47. The authoritative reference for quantum computing is the book of Nielsen and Chuang (2000). For gentler introductions, try Mermin (2003; 2007) or the survey articles of Aharonov (1998), Fortnow (2003), or Watrous (2008). For a general discussion of polynomial-time computation and the laws of physics (including speculative models beyond quantum computation), see my survey article "NP-Complete Problems and Physical Reality" (Aaronson 2005b).

48. By contrast, if we only want to know what is *computable* in the physical universe, with no efficiency requirement, then it remains entirely consistent with current knowledge that Church and Turing gave the correct answer in the 1930s—and that they did so without incorporating any physics beyond what is "accessible to intuition."

49. This means, in particular, that the amplitudes satisfy the normalization condition $\sum_x |\alpha_x|^2 = 1$.

50. One might object that even in the classical world, if we simply don't *know* the value of (say) an n-bit string, then we *also* describe our ignorance using exponentially many numbers: namely, the *probability* p_x of each possible string $x \in \{0, 1\}^n$! And indeed, there is an extremely close connection between quantum mechanics and classical probability theory; I often describe quantum mechanics as just "probability theory with complex numbers instead of nonnegative reals." However, a crucial difference is that we can always describe a classical string x as "really" having a definite value; the vector of 2^n probabilities p_x is then just a mental representation of our own ignorance. With a quantum state, we do not have the same luxury, because of the phenomenon of *interference* between positive and negative amplitudes.

51. One might also object that, even in classical physics, it takes *infinitely* many bits to record the state of even a single particle, if its position and momentum can be arbitrary real numbers. And indeed, Copeland (2002), Hogarth (1994), Siegelmann (2003), and other writers have speculated that the continuity of physical quantities might actually allow "hypercomputations"—including solving the halting problem in a finite amount of time! From a modern perspective, though, quantum mechanics and quantum gravity strongly suggest that *the "continuity" of measurable quantities such as positions and momenta is a theoretical artifact*. In other words, it ought to suffice for simulation purposes to approximate these quantities to some finite precision, probably related to the Planck scale of 10^{-33} centimeters or 10^{-43} seconds.

But the exponentiality of quantum states is different, for at least two reasons. Firstly, it doesn't lead to computational speedups that are nearly as "unreasonable" as the hypercomputing speedups. Secondly, no one has any idea where the theory in question (quantum mechanics) *could* break down, in a manner consistent with current experiments. In other words, there is no known "killer obstacle" for quantum computing analogous to the Planck scale for hypercomputing. See Aaronson (2004) for further discussion of this point, as well as a proposed complexity-theoretic framework (called "Sure/Shor separators") with which to study such obstacles.

52. Indeed, one *cannot* rule that possibility out, without first proving P ≠ NP! But even if P ≠ NP, a fast classical factoring algorithm might *still* exist, again because factoring is not thought to be NP-complete.

53. A formal version of this conjecture is BPP ≠ BQP, where BPP (bounded-error probabilistic polynomial time) and BQP (bounded-error quantum polynomial time) are the classes of problems efficiently solvable by classical randomized algorithms and quantum algorithms respectively. Bernstein and Vazirani (1997) showed that P ⊆ BPP ⊆ BQP ⊆ PSPACE, where PSPACE is the class of problems solvable by a deterministic Turing machine using a polynomial amount of *memory* (but possibly exponential time). For this reason, any proof of the BPP ≠ BQP conjecture would immediately imply P ≠ PSPACE as well. The latter would be considered almost as great a breakthrough as P ≠ NP.

54. Complicating matters, there *are* quantum algorithms that provably achieve exponential speedups over any classical algorithm: one example is Simon's algorithm (Simon 1994), an important predecessor of Shor's algorithm. However, all such algorithms are formulated in the "black-box model" (see Beals et al. 2001), where the resource to be minimized is the number of queries that an algorithm makes to a hypothetical black box. Because it is relatively easy to analyze, the black-box model is a crucial source of insights about what *might* be true in the conventional Turing machine model. However, it is also known that the black-box model sometimes misleads us about the "real" situation. As a famous example, the complexity classes IP and PSPACE are equal (Shamir 1992), despite the existence of a black box that separates them (see Fortnow 1994 for discussion).

Besides the black-box model, *unconditional* exponential separations between quantum and classical complexities are known in several other restricted models, including communication complexity (Raz 1999).

55. Technically, if the hidden-variable theory involved classical randomness, then it would correspond more closely to the complexity class BPP (bounded-error probabilistic polynomial time). However, today there is strong evidence that P = BPP (see Impagliazzo and Wigderson 1997).

56. There is a remarkable quantum algorithm called *Grover's algorithm* (Grover 1996), which can search any space of 2^N possible solutions in only $\sim 2^{N/2}$ steps. However, Grover's algorithm represents a *quadratic* (square-root) improvement over classical brute-force search, rather than an exponential improvement. And without any further assumptions about the structure of the search space, Grover's algorithm is optimal, as shown by Bennett et al. (1997).

57. Those interested in further details of how Shor's algorithm works, but still not ready for a mathematical exposition, might want to try my popular essay "Shor, I'll do it" (2007).

58. Incidentally, this provides a good example of how notions from computational complexity theory can influence philosophy even just at the level of metaphor, forgetting about the actual results. In this essay, I didn't try to collect such "metaphorical" applications of complexity theory, simply because there were too many of them!

59. Technically, the protocol is "*honest-verifier* zero-knowledge," meaning that Arthur learns nothing from his conversation with Merlin besides the truth of the statement being proved, *assuming* Arthur follows the protocol correctly. If Arthur cheats—for example, by sending a graph K for which he *doesn't* already know an isomorphism either to G or to H—then Merlin's response could indeed tell Arthur something new. However, Goldreich, Micali, and Wigderson (1991) also gave a more sophisticated proof protocol for graph non-isomorphism, which remains zero-knowledge even in the case where Arthur cheats.

60. Indeed, there is not even a consensus belief that graph isomorphism is outside P! The main reason is that, in contrast to factoring integers, graph isomorphism turns out to be extremely easy *in practice*. Indeed, finding non-isomorphic graphs that *can't* be distinguished by simple invariants is itself a hard problem! And in the past, several problems (such as linear programming and primality testing) that were long known to be "efficiently solvable for practical purposes" were eventually shown to be in P in the strict mathematical sense as well.

61. There is also strong evidence that there are short *conventional* proofs for graph non-isomorphism—in other words, that not just graph isomorphism but also graph non-isomorphism will ultimately turn out to be in NP (Klivans and van Melkebeek 2002).

62. More precisely, Turing machines with one-dimensional tapes are polynomially equivalent to Turing machines with k-dimensional tapes for any k, and are also polynomially equivalent to *random-access machines* (which can "jump" to any memory location in unit time, with no locality constraint).

On the other hand, if we care about polynomial differences in speed, and *especially* if we want to study parallel computing models, details about the spatial layout of the computing and memory elements (as well as the speed of communication among the elements) can become vitally important.

63. Why "only" an exponential amount? Because a Turing machine with B bits of memory can run for no more than 2^B time steps. After that, the machine must either halt or else return to a configuration previously visited (thereby entering an infinite loop).

64. Note that, in order to speak about the computational complexity of such games, we first need to generalize them to an $n \times n$ board! But if we do so, then for many natural games, the problem of determining which player has the win from a given position is not only in PSPACE, but PSPACE-*complete* (i.e., it captures the entire difficulty of the class PSPACE). For example, Reisch (1981) showed that this is true for Hex.

What about a suitable generalization of *chess* to an $n \times n$ board? That's also in PSPACE—but as far as anyone knows, only if we impose a polynomial upper bound on the number of moves in a chess game. Without such a restriction, Fraenkel and Lichtenstein (1981) showed that chess is EXP-complete; with such a restriction, Storer (1983) showed that chess is PSPACE-complete.

65. In this context, we call a function $f(n)$ "exponential" if it can be upper-bounded by $2^{p(n)}$, for some polynomial p. Also, note that *more* than exponential memory would be useless here, since a Turing machine that runs for T time steps can visit at most T memory cells.

66. More generally, the time hierarchy theorem shows that, if f and g are any two "sufficiently well-behaved" functions that satisfy $f(n) \ll g(n)$ (for example: $f(n) = n^2$ and $g(n) = n^3$), then *there are computational problems solvable in $g(n)$ time but not in $f(n)$ time*. The proof of this theorem uses diagonalization, and can be thought of as a scaled-down version of Turing's proof of the unsolvability of the halting problem. That is, we argue that, *if* it were always possible to simulate a $g(n)$-time Turing machine by an $f(n)$-time Turing machine, then we could construct a $g(n)$-time machine that "predicted its own output in advance" and then output something else—thereby causing a contradiction.

Using similar arguments, we can show (for example) that there exist computational problems solvable using n^3 bits of memory but not using n^2 bits, and so on in most cases where we want to compare *more versus less of the same computational resource*. In complexity theory, the hard part is comparing two *different* resources: for example, determinism versus nondeterminism (the P=NP problem), time versus space (P=PSPACE), or classical versus quantum computation (BPP=BQP). For in those cases, diagonalization by itself no longer works.

67. The fact that P $\neq$ EXP has an amusing implication: namely, *at least one* of the three inequalities.

1. P $\neq$ NP
2. NP $\neq$ PSPACE
3. PSPACE $\neq$ EXP

must be true, even though proving any one of them to be true *individually* would represent a titanic advance in mathematics!

The above observation is sometimes offered as circumstantial evidence for P $\neq$ NP. Of all our hundreds of unproved beliefs about inequalities between pairs of complexity classes, a large fraction of them *must* be correct, simply to avoid contradicting the hierarchy theorems. So then why not P $\neq$ NP in particular (given that our intuition there is stronger than our intuitions for most of the other inequalities)?

68. See my blog post www.scottaaronson.com/blog/?p=368 for more on this theme.

69. Though it is not known whether those solutions are "physical": for example, whether or not they can survive in a quantum theory of gravity (see Morris et al. 1988 for an example).

70. In quantum mechanics, a *mixed state* can be thought of as a classical probability distribution over quantum states. However, an important twist is that the same mixed state can be represented by *different* probability distributions: for example, an equal mixture of the states $|0\rangle$ and $|1\rangle$ is physically indistinguishable from an equal mixture of $(|0\rangle+|1\rangle)/\sqrt{2}$ and $(|0\rangle-|1\rangle)/\sqrt{2}$. This is why mixed states are represented mathematically using Heisenberg's density matrix formalism.

71. In more detail, Deutsch's proposal works if the state space consists of classical probability distributions $\mathcal{D}$ or quantum mixed states ρ, but *not* if it consists of pure states $|\psi\rangle$. Thus, *if* one believed that only pure states were fundamental in physics, and that probability distributions and mixed states always reflected subjective ignorance, one might reject Deutsch's proposal on that ground.

72. In particular, in Lloyd et al.'s (2011) proposal, the only way to deal with the grandfather paradox is by some variant of "the gun jams": there *are* evolutions with no consistent solution, and it needs to be postulated that the laws of physics are such that they never occur.

73. Specifically, it is *not* true that in a CTC universe, a Turing machine tape head could just travel back and forth in time the same way it travels back and forth in space. If one thinks this way, then one really has in mind a second, "meta-time," while the "original" time has become merely one more dimension of space. To put the point differently: even though a CTC would make time *cyclic*, time would still retain its *directionality*. This is the reason why, if we want to show that CTC computers have the power of PSPACE, we need a nontrivial argument involving causal consistency.

74. This possibility is also discussed at length in Deutsch's paper (1991).

75. Here we assume for simplicity that the set Ω of possible states is countable; otherwise we could of course use a continuous probability measure.

76. Subject, as usual, to widely believed complexity assumptions.

77. The situation is very different for mathematical statements like the continuum hypothesis, which *can't* obviously be phrased as predictions about idealized computational processes (since they're not expressible by first-order or even second-order quantification over the integers). For those statements, it really *is* unclear to me what one means by their truth or falsehood apart from their provability in some formal system.

78. For a beautiful example of a nonasymptotic, "concrete" lower bound on circuit size—illustrating how objection (1) can often be answered with enough hard work—see Stockmeyer and Meyer (2002).

79. On the other hand, it *would* presuppose that we knew how to define reasonable probability distributions over inputs. But as discussed in section 10.4.3, it seems hard to explain what we mean by "structured instances," or "the types of instances that normally arise in practice."

80. One other example that springs to mind, of a scientific theory many of whose "predictions" take the form of mathematical conjectures, is string theory.

References

Aaronson, S. 2004. Multilinear formulas and skepticism of quantum computing. In *Proc. ACM STOC*, 118–27. arXiv:quant-ph/0311039.

Aaronson, S. 2005a. The complexity of agreement. In *Proc. ACM STOC*, 634–43. Electronic Colloquium on Computational Complexity Paper No. TR04–061.

Aaronson, S. 2005b. NP-complete problems and physical reality. *SIGACT News*. arXiv:quant-ph/0502072.

Aaronson, S. 2005c. Quantum computing, postselection, and probabilistic polynomial-time. *Proceedings of the Royal Society of London A* 461(2063):3473–82. arXiv:quant-ph/0412187.

Aaronson, S. 2007. Shor, I'll do it (weblog entry). www.scottaaronson.com/blog/?p=208.

Aaronson, S., and G. Kuperberg. 2007. Quantum versus classical proofs and advice. *Theory of Computing* 3(7):129–157. arXiv:quant-ph/0604056.

Aaronson, S., and J. Watrous. 2009. Closed timelike curves make quantum and classical computing equivalent. *Proceedings of the Royal Society of London A* 465:631–647. arXiv:0808.2669.

Aaronson, S., and A. Wigderson. 2009. Algebrization: A new barrier in complexity theory. *ACM Transactions on Computation Theory* 1(1)411–431.

Agrawal, M., N. Kayal, and N. Saxena. 2004. PRIMES is in P. *Annals of Mathematics* 160:781–793. doi:10.4007/annals.2004.160.781.

Aharonov, D. 1998. Quantum computation: A review. In D. Stauffer, ed., *Annual Review of Computational Physics*, Vol. 4. Singapore: World Scientific. arXiv:quant-ph/9812037.

Angluin, D. 1987. Learning regular sets from queries and counterexamples. *Information and Computation* 75(2):87–106.

Angluin, D., J. Aspnes, J. Chen, and Y. Wu 2009. Learning a circuit by injecting values. *Journal of Computer and System Sciences* 75(1):60–77.

Appel, K., and W. Haken. 1989. *Every Planar Map is Four-colorable*. Providence, RI: American Mathematical Society.

Applebaum, B., B. Barak, and D. Xiao. 2008. On basing lower-bounds for learning on worst-case assumptions. In *Proc. IEEE FOCS*, 211–20.

Arora, S., and B. Barak. 2009. *Computational Complexity: A Modern Approach*. Cambridge: Cambridge University Press.

Arora, S., R. Impagliazzo, and U. Vazirani. 1992. Relativizing versus nonrelativizing techniques: The role of local checkability. Unpublished manuscript.

Arora, S., C. Lund, R. Motwani, M. Sudan, and M. Szegedy. 1998. Proof verification and the hardness of approximation problems. *Journal of the ACM* 45(3):501–555.

Arora, S., and S. Safra. 1998. Probabilistic checking of proofs: A new characterization of NP. *Journal of the ACM* 45(1):70–122.

Aumann, R. J. 1976. Agreeing to disagree. *Annals of Statistics* 4(6):1236–1239.

Babai, L., L. Fortnow, and C. Lund. 1991. Nondeterministic exponential time has two-prover interactive protocols. *Computational Complexity* 1(1):3–40.

Baker, T., J. Gill, and R. Solovay. 1975. Relativizations of the P=?NP question. *SIAM Journal on Computing* 4:431–42.

Baum, E. B. 2004. *What Is Thought?* Cambridge: Bradford Books.

Beals, R., H. Buhrman, R. Cleve, M. Mosca, and R. De Wolf. 2001. Quantum lower bounds by polynomials. *Journal of the Association for Computing Machinery* 48(4):778–797. arXiv:quant-ph/9802049.

Beame, P. and T. Pitassi. 2001. Propositional proof complexity: Past, present, and future. In *Current Trends in Theoretical Computer Science: Entering the 21st Century*, ed. G. Paun, G. Rozenberg, and A. Salomaa, 42–70. Hackensack, NJ: World Scientific Publishing.

Bellantoni, S. and S. A. Cook 1992. A new recursion-theoretic characterization of the polytime functions. *Computational Complexity* 2:97–110.

Ben-Or, M., S. Goldwasser, J. Kilian, and A. Wigderson. 1988. Multi-prover interactive proofs: How to remove the intractability assumptions. In *Proc. ACM STOC*, 113–31.

Bennett, C. H., E. Bernstein, G. Brassard, and U. Vazirani. 1997. Strengths and weaknesses of quantum computing. *SIAM Journal on Computing* 26(5):1510–23. arXiv:quant-ph/9701001.

Bennett, C. H., D. Leung, G. Smith, and J. A. Smolin. 2009. Can closed timelike curves or nonlinear quantum mechanics improve quantum state discrimination or help solve hard problems? *Physical Review Letters* 103(17):170502. arXiv:0908.3023.

Bernstein, E., and U. Vazirani. 1997. Quantum complexity theory. *SIAM Journal on Computing* 26(5):1411–1473.

Block, N. 2002. Searle's arguments against cognitive science. In *Views into the Chinese Room: New Essays on Searle and Artificial Intelligence*, ed. J. Preston and M. Bishop, 70–79. Oxford: Oxford University Press.

Blumer, A., A. Ehrenfeucht, D. Haussler, and M. K. Warmuth. 1989. Learnability and the Vapnik-Chervonenkis dimension. *Journal of the ACM* 36(4):929–965.

Bogdanov, A. and L. Trevisan 2006. Average-case complexity. *Foundations and Trends in Theoretical Computer Science* 2(1):1–106. Electronic Colloquium on Computational Complexity Paper No. TR06-073.

Boppana, R. B., J. Håstad, and S. Zachos. 1987. Does co-NP have short interactive proofs? *Information Processing Letters* 25:127–132.

Bousso, R. 2000. Positive vacuum energy and the N-bound. *Journal of High Energy Physics* 11(38). arXiv:hep-th/0010252.

Brassard, G., D. Chaum, and C. Crépeau. 1988. Minimum disclosure proofs of knowledge. *Journal of Computer and System Sciences* 37(2):156–189.

Brun, T. 2003. Computers with closed timelike curves can solve hard problems. *Foundations of Physics Letters* 16:245–53. arXiv:gr-qc/0209061.

Chalmers, D. J. 1996. *The Conscious Mind: In Search of a Fundamental Theory*. Oxford: Oxford University Press.

Chen, X., D. Dai, Y. Du, and S. H. Teng. 2009. Settling the complexity of Arrow-Debreu equilibria in markets with additively separable utilities. In *Proc. IEEE FOCS*, 273–82.

Chen, X., and X. Deng. 2006. Settling the complexity of two-player Nash equilibrium. In *Proc. IEEE FOCS*, 261–271.

Cherniak, C. 1984. Computational complexity and the universal acceptance of logic. *Journal of Philosophy* 81(12):739–758.

Cleve, R., P. Høyer, B. Toner, and J. Watrous. 2004. Consequences and limits of nonlocal strategies. In *Proc. IEE Conference on Computational Complexity*, 236–249. arXiv:quant-ph/0404076.

Cobham, A. 1965. The intrinsic computational difficulty of functions. In *Proc. Logic, Methodology, and Philosophy of Science II*, ed. Y. Bae-Hillel, 24–30. Amsterdam: North-Holland.

Copeland, J. 2002. Hypercomputation. *Minds and Machines* 12:461–502.

Daskalakis, C., P. W. Goldberg, and C. H. Papadimitriou. 2009. The complexity of computing a Nash equilibrium. *Communications of the ACM* 52(2):89–97.

Dawkins, R. 2006. *The God Delusion*. New York: Houghton Mifflin Harcourt.

Dennett, D. C. 1995. *Darwin's Dangerous Idea: Evolution and the Meanings of Life*. New York: Simon & Schuster.

Deutsch, D. 1991. Quantum mechanics near closed timelike lines. *Physical Review D: Particles and Fields* 44:3197–3217.

Deutsch, D. 1997. *The Fabric of Reality*. London: Penguin.

Deutsch, D. 2011. *The Beginning of Infinity: Explanations that Transform the World*. London: Allen Lane.

Dinur, I. 2007. The PCP theorem by gap amplification. *Journal of the ACM* 54(3):12.

Drucker, A. 2011. Multiplying 10-digit numbers using Flickr: the power of recognition memory. http://people.csail.mit.edu/andyd/rec_method.pdf.

Fagin, R. 1993. Finite model theory: A personal perspective. *Theoretical Computer Science* 116:3–31.

Fagin, R., and J. Y. Halpern. 1987. Belief, awareness, and limited reasoning. *Artificial Intelligence* 34(1):39–76.

Fagin, R., J. Y. Halpern, Y. Moses, and M. Y. Vardi. 1995. *Reasoning about Knowledge*. Cambridge, MA: MIT Press.

Feige, U., S. Goldwasser, L. Lovász, S. Safra, and M. Szegedy. 1996. Interactive proofs and the hardness of approximating cliques. *Journal of the ACM* 43(2):268–292.

Feynman, R. P. 1982. Simulating physics with computers. *International Journal of Theoretical Physics* 21(6–7):467–488.

Fortnow, L. 1994. The role of relativization in complexity theory. *Bulletin of the EATCS* 52:229–244.

Fortnow, L. 2003. One complexity theorist's view of quantum computing. *Theoretical Computer Science* 292(3):597–610.

Fortnow, L. and S. Homer 2003. A short history of computational complexity. *Bulletin of the EATCS* 80:95–133.

Fraenkel, A., and D. Lichtenstein. 1981. Computing a perfect strategy for n x n chess requires time exponential in n. *Journal of Combinatorial Theory A* 31:199–214.

Gentry, C. 2009. Fully homomorphic encryption using ideal lattices. In *Proc. ACM STOC*, 169–178.

Goldreich, O. 2004. On quantum computing. www.wisdom.weizmann.ac.il/~oded/on-qc.html.

Goldreich, O. 2008. *Computational Complexity: A Conceptual Perspective*. Cambridge: Cambridge University Press.

Goldreich, O. 2010. *A Primer on Pseudorandom Generators*. University lecture series, Vol. 55. Providence, RI: American Mathematical Society. www.wisdom.weizmann.ac.il/~oded/PDF/prg10.pdf.

Goldreich, O., S. Goldwasser, and S. Micali. 1984. How to construct random functions. *Journal of the ACM* 33(4):792–807.

Goldreich, O., S. Micali, and A. Wigderson. 1991. Proofs that yield nothing but their validity or all languages in NP have zero-knowledge proof systems. *Journal of the ACM* 38(1):691–729.

Goldwasser, S., S. Micali, and C. Rackoff. 1989. The knowledge complexity of interactive proof systems. *SIAM Journal on Computing* 18(1):186–208.

Goodman, N. 1955. *Fact, Fiction, and Forecast*. Cambridge: Harvard University Press..

Graham, P. 2007. How to do philosophy. www.paulgraham.com/philosophy.html.

Grover, L. K. 1996. A fast quantum mechanical algorithm for database search. In *Proc. ACM STOC*, 212–19. arXiv:quant-ph/9605043.

Hartmanis, J., and R. E. Stearns. 1965. On the computational complexity of algorithms. *Transactions of the American Mathematical Society* 117:285–306.

Håstad, J., R. Impagliazzo, L. A. Levin, and M. Luby. 1999. A pseudorandom generator from any one-way function. *SIAM Journal on Computing* 28(4):1364–1396.

Haugeland, J. 2002. Syntax, semantics, physics. In *Views into the Chinese Room: New Essays on Searle and Artificial Intelligence*, ed. J. Preston and M. Bishop, 379–392. Oxford: Oxford University Press.

Hintikka, J. 1962. *Knowledge and Belief: An Introduction to the Logic of the Two Notions*. Ithaca: Cornell University Press.

Hogarth, M. 1994. Non-Turing computers and non-Turing computability. *Proc. Biennial Meeting of the Philosophy of Science Association,* Vol. 1, 126–138.

Holevo, A. S. 1973. Some estimates of the information transmitted by quantum communication channels. [English translation.] *Problems of Information Transmission* 9:177–183.

Hume, D. 1748. *An Enquiry Concerning Human Understanding*. 18th.eserver.org/hume-enquiry.html.

Immerman, N. 1998. *Descriptive Complexity*. New York: Springer-Verlag.

Impagliazzo, R. 1995. A personal view of average-case complexity. In *Proc. IEEE Conference on Computational Complexity*, 134–147.

Impagliazzo, R., and A. Wigderson. 1997. P=BPP unless E has subexponential circuits: derandomizing the XOR Lemma. In *Proc. ACM STOC*, 220–229.

Kahneman, D., P. Slovic, and A. Tversky. 1982. *Judgment Under Uncertainty: Heuristics and Biases*. Cambridge: Cambridge University Press.

Kearns, M. J., and L. G. Valiant. 1994. Cryptographic limitations on learning Boolean formulae and finite automata. *Journal of the ACM* 41(1):67–95.

Kearns, M. J., and U. V. Vazirani. 1994. *An Introduction to Computational Learning Theory*. Cambridge, MA: MIT Press.

Kempe, J., H. Kobayashi, K. Matsumoto, B. Toner, and T. Vidick. 2011. Entangled games are hard to approximate. *SIAM Journal on Computing* 40(3):848–77. arXiv:0704.2903.

Klivans, A., and D. van Melkebeek. 2002. Graph nonisomorphism has subexponential size proofs unless the polynomial-time hierarchy collapses. *SIAM Journal on Computing* 31:1501–1526.

Ladner, R. E. 1975. On the structure of polynomial time reducibility. *Journal of the ACM* 22:155–171.

Leivant, D. 1994. A foundational delineation of poly-time. *Information and Computation* 110(2): 391–420.

Levesque, H. J. 2009. Is it enough to get the behavior right? In *Proc. IJCAI*, 1439–1444.

Levin, L. A. 2003. The tale of one-way functions. *Problems of Information Transmission* 39(1):92–103. http://www.arxiv.org/abs/cs.CR/0012023.

Li, M., and P. M. B. Vitányi. 2008. *An Introduction to Kolmogorov Complexity and Its Applications*. 3rd ed. New York: Springer-Verlag.

Lloyd, S., L. Maccone, R. Garcia-Patron, V. Giovannetti, and Y. Shikano. 2011. The quantum mechanics of time travel through post-selected teleportation. *Physical Review D: Particles, Fields, Gravitation, and Cosmology* 84: 025007. arXiv:1007.2615.

Lucas, J. R. 1961. Minds, machines, and Gödel. *Philosophy (London, England)* 36:112–127.

Mermin, N. D. 2003. From cbits to qbits: Teaching computer scientists quantum mechanics. *American Journal of Physics* 71(1):23–30. arXiv:quant-ph/0207118.

Mermin, N. D. 2007. *Quantum Computer Science: An Introduction*. Cambridge: Cambridge University Press.

Micali, S. 2000. Computationally sound proofs. *SIAM Journal on Computing* 30(4):1253–1298.

Moore, C., and S. Mertens. 2011. *The Nature of Computation*. Oxford: Oxford University Press.

Morris, M. S., K. S. Thorne, and U. Yurtsever. 1988. Wormholes, time machines, and the weak energy condition. *Physical Review Letters* 61:1446–1449.

Morton, A. 2004. Epistemic virtues, metavirtues, and computational complexity. *Noûs* 38(3):481–502.

Neyman, A. 1985. Bounded complexity justifies cooperation in the finitely repeated prisoners' dilemma. *Economics Letters* 19(3):227–229.

Nielsen, M., and I. Chuang. 2000. *Quantum Computation and Quantum Information*. Cambridge: Cambridge University Press.

Papadimitriou, C. H. 1994. *Computational Complexity*. Reading, MA: Addison-Wesley.

Parberry, I. 1997. Knowledge, understanding, and computational complexity. In *Optimality in Biological and Artificial Networks?* ed. D. S. Levine and W. R. Elsberry, 125–144. Hillsdale, NJ: Lawrence Erlbaum.

Penrose, R. 1989. *The Emperor's New Mind*. Oxford: Oxford University Press.

Penrose, R. 1996. *Shadows of the Mind: A Search for the Missing Science of Consciousness*. Oxford: Oxford University Press.

Pitt, L., and L. Valiant. 1988. Computational limitations on learning from examples. *Journal of the ACM* 35(4):965–84.

Pomerance, C. 1996. A tale of two sieves. *Notices of the American Mathematical Society* 43(12):1473–1485.

Putnam, H. 1988. *Representation and Reality*. Cambridge, MA: MIT Prss.

Rabinovich, Y., and A. Wigderson. 1999. Techniques for bounding the convergence rate of genetic algorithms. *Random Structures and Algorithms* 14(2):111–138.

Raz, R. 1999. Exponential separation of quantum and classical communication complexity. In *Proc. ACM STOC*, 358–67.

Razborov, A. A., and S. Rudich. 1997. Natural proofs. *Journal of Computer and System Sciences* 55(1):24–35.

Reisch, S. 1981. Hex is PSPACE-complete. *Acta Informatica* 15:167–191.

Rose, H. E. 1984. *Subrecursion: Functions and Hierarchies*. Oxford: Clarendon Press.

Rubinstein, A. 1998. *Modeling Bounded Rationality*. Cambridge, MA: MIT Press.

Schönhage, A., and V. Strassen. 1971. Schnelle Multiplikation großer Zahlen. *Computing* 7:281–292.

Searle, J. 1980. Minds, brains, and programs. *Behavioral and Brain Sciences* 3:417–457.

Searle, J. 1992. *The Rediscovery of the Mind*. Cambridge, MA: MIT Press.

Shamir, A. 1992. IP=PSPACE. *Journal of the ACM* 39(4):869–877.

Shieber, S. M. 2007. The Turing test as interactive proof. *Noûs* 41(4):686–713.

Shor, P. W. 1997. Polynomial-time algorithms for prime factorization and discrete logarithms on a quantum computer. *SIAM Journal on Computing* 26(5):1484–509. arXiv:quant-ph/9508027.

Siegelmann, H. T. 2003. Neural and super-Turing computing. *Minds and Machines* 13(1):103–114.

Simon, D. 1994. On the power of quantum computation. In *Proc. IEEE FOCS*, 116–123.

Simon, H. A. 1955. A behavioral model of rational choice. *Quarterly Journal of Economics* 69(1):99–118.

Sipser, M. 1992. The history and status of the P versus NP question. In *Proc. ACM STOC*, 603–618.

Sipser, M. 2005. *Introduction to the Theory of Computation*. 2nd ed., Boston: Thomson Course Technology.

Stalnaker, R. 1999. The problem of logical omniscience, I and II. In *Context and Content: Essays on Intentionality in Speech and Thought*, Oxford Cognitive Science Series, 241–273. Oxford: Oxford University Press.

Stockmeyer, L. J. 1987. Classifying the computational complexity of problems. *Journal of Symbolic Logic* 52(1):1–43.

Stockmeyer, L. J., and A. R. Meyer. 2002. Cosmological lower bound on the circuit complexity of a small problem in logic. *Journal of the ACM* 49(6):753–784.

Storer, J. A. 1983. On the complexity of chess. *Journal of Computer and System Sciences* 27(1):77–100.

't Hooft, G. 1999. Quantum gravity as a dissipative deterministic system. *Classical and Quantum Gravity* 16:3263–79. arXiv:gr-qc/9903084.

Turing, A. M. 1950. Computing machinery and intelligence. *Mind* 59:433–60.

Valiant, L. G. 1984. A theory of the learnable. *Communications of the ACM* 27:1134–42.

Valiant, L. G. 2009. Evolvability. *Journal of the ACM* 56(1): 1–21. Electronic Colloquium on Computational Complexity Paper No. TR06–120.

Vapnik, V., and A. Chervonenkis. 1971. On the uniform convergence of relative frequencies of events to their probabilities. *Theory of Probability and Its Applications* 16(2):264–280.

Wang, H. 1997. *A Logical Journey: From Gödel to Philosophy*. Cambridge, MA: MIT Press.

Watrous, J. 2000. Succinct quantum proofs for properties of finite groups. In *Proc. IEEE FOCS*, 537–546. http://www.arxiv.org/abs/cs.CC/0009002.

Watrous, J. 2009. Quantum computational complexity. In *Encyclopedia of Complexity and Systems Science,* ed. R. A. Meyers, 7174–201. New York: Springer. arXiv:0804.3401.

Wigderson, A. 2007. P, NP and mathematics: A computational complexity perspective. In *Proc. International Congress of Mathematicians 2006* (Madrid), 665–712. Zurich: EMS Publishing House. www.math.ias.edu/~avi/PUBLICATIONS/MYPAPERS/W06/w06.pdf.

Wigderson, A. 2009. Knowledge, creativity and P versus NP. www.math.ias.edu/~avi/PUBLICATIONS/MYPAPERS/AW09/AW09.pdf.

Wigner, E. 1960. The unreasonable effectiveness of mathematics in the natural sciences. *Communications on Pure and Applied Mathematics* 13(1):1–14.

De Wolf, R. 1997. Philosophical applications of computational learning theory: Chomskyan innateness and Occam's razor. Master's thesis, Erasmus University. homepages.cwi.nl/~rdewolf/publ/philosophy/phthesis.pdf.

11 Is Quantum Mechanics Falsifiable? A Computational Perspective on the Foundations of Quantum Mechanics

Dorit Aharonov and Umesh V. Vazirani

Saying that quantum mechanics (QM) is paradoxical is an understatement: Feynman once said, "I think I can safely say that no one understands quantum mechanics" (1964). Quantum mechanics has been a great source of fundamental issues and paradoxes in the philosophy of science, ranging from its statistical nature and stretching of causality to the measurement problem. A totally new kind of philosophical problem arises once we focus on computational aspects of QM.

Indeed, the seeds of this problem go back to the birth of the field of quantum computation, in the demonstration that quantum computers seem to violate the extended Church–Turing thesis. This thesis asserts that any reasonable computational model can be simulated efficiently[1] by the standard model of classical computation, namely, a probabilistic Turing machine. Bernstein and Vazirani (1997) and Simon (1994) showed that quantum computers are capable of exponential speedups over classical models of computing, thus demonstrating the violation of the thesis by quantum computers.[2] That this violation has profound practical consequences became apparent shortly thereafter when Shor (1997) made his seminal discovery of an efficient quantum algorithm for factoring, one that is exponentially faster than any known classical algorithm for this important computational problem. The philosophical implications of this computational view of QM are only just beginning to be understood, and this is the subject of this paper.

At the root of the extravagant computational power of QM is the fact that the state of a quantum system of n spins is a unit vector in a Hilbert space of dimension that scales exponentially in n. This means that 2^n complex numbers are required to describe the state of such a system, as compared to $O(n)$ for a comparable classical system. This number of parameters is larger than the estimated number of particles in the universe, for $n = 500$. This is certainly among the most paradoxical predictions of quantum mechanics. Is this description unnecessarily inefficient? Could there be a different succinct description? This was a question posed by Feynman in his seminal paper (1985), which led to the birth of quantum computation. The theory of quantum computation provides an answer: an exponential description is necessary, as long as we believe that quantum computers provide an exponential speedup over classical computers. A different way to say this is that, as we believe today, the computational complexity exhibited by many-body quantum systems is exponentially more powerful than that of classical systems.

One of the goals of physics research is to test the validity of a theory in various limits—for example, in the limit of high energy, or at the Planck scale, or close to the speed of light. Ideas from quantum computation point at a new regime in which to test quantum mechanics: the limit of high (computational) complexity. The aspects of quantum mechanics that have so far been experimentally verified, to exquisite precision (with certain predictions of quantum electrodynamics verified to within one part in 10^{12}) can all be classified as low-complexity quantum mechanics—many of them rely on little more than single-particle quantum mechanics. The relevant computational complexity measure here is the effective dimension of the Hilbert space in which the state of the system lives, and in those systems, it is very small. Thus a Bose-Einstein condensate, though a macroscopic quantum state, is effectively a two-level quantum system and therefore of low complexity. Moving beyond the practical difficulties in experimentally dealing with large-scale quantum systems, here we ask whether testing QM in the high-complexity limit is even theoretically possible, or whether there are fundamental obstacles that prevent such testing.

At a naive level, the issue is how can an experimentalist test an exponentially more powerful system than his own computational abilities, with the view of testing that it is indeed exponentially more powerful? Slightly more accurately, we ask: how can a classical, computationally restricted experimentalist test the high-complexity aspects of quantum mechanics? The scientific method would suggest setting up an experiment and checking that the outcome is consistent with the prediction of the theory. But if the prediction of the theory requires exponential resources to compute, as we believe is the case for many-body quantum mechanics, is there a way to effectively carry out the procedure laid out in the scientific method in order to test QM? On the face of it, the answer is no, since the predictions of the experiment cannot be computed in a reasonable time (of course the predictions could be efficiently computed using a quantum computer, but the correctness of that result would rely on the exponential scaling of QM, which is what the experiment was trying to test in the first place!). Following this logic, one would deduce that the testing of quantum mechanics in the limit of high complexity is not susceptible to the scientific method.

A more formal way of understanding the issue is in terms of two ways of interpreting the extended Church–Turing thesis. The first interpretation goes back to Alan Turing's conception of a Turing machine as an idealized model for a mathematical calculation (think of the infinite tape as an infinite supply of paper, and the Turing machine control as the mathematician, or for our purposes a mathematical physicist calculating the outcome of an experiment). By this interpretation the

Turing machine—that is, the idealized model of a mathematical calculation—can efficiently simulate any other algorithmic model of computation. This is the interpretation a logician might make. The other interpretation of the extended Church–Turing thesis reads "reasonable model of computation" as "*physically realizable model of computation.*" It argues via the equivalence between Turing machines and cellular automata (which may be regarded as discrete analogs of local differential equations) that Turing machines represent, or capture, the evolution of physical systems in the classical World; they can efficiently simulate any computational model that is reasonable from the point of view of physical implementation. Combining the two interpretations, we get the following: in principle, any scientific theory for the classical World (by the second interpretation) can be formalized as a cellular automaton; this cellular automaton (by the first interpretation) can be efficiently simulated by the mathematical physicist to calculate the outcome of the desired experiment. Thus, by the extended Church–Turing thesis, the outcome of the experiment of any scientific theory can be calculated efficiently by the mathematical physicist. This outcome can then be verified experimentally, following the usual scientific paradigm. The source of the problem explained above is that in a quantum World, we run into a fundamental problem, since the mathematical physicist is still classical, whereas the quantum World that he or she is trying to understand is exponentially more powerful. That is, the two interpretations of the extended Church–Turing thesis diverge exponentially; it no longer holds that the mathematical physicist can calculate efficiently the outcome of quantum experiments. This is the source of the fundamental problem in testing QM in the limit of high complexity.

Vazirani (2007) already observed that Shor's quantum factoring algorithm constitutes a counterexample to the above line of thought, by which the exponential computational complexity of quantum mechanics seems to render it impossible to testing in the usual scientific paradigm. The reason is that Shor's algorithm can be interpreted as a suggestion for a layout of a physical experiment, which tests quantum mechanics in a regime that is believed to be impossible to efficiently simulate by classical computational means. Indeed, a closer examination reveals in what way this experiment lies outside the usual scientific paradigm of "predict the outcome of the experiment and verify that this is the experimental outcome." In the case of quantum factoring, the output of the experiment consists of the prime factors of the input N. The intractability of factoring on a classical computer rules out the possibility of predicting the output of the experiment. Instead, the verification is performed by checking that the product of the prime factors output by the experiment is N. Thus rather than predicting the actual outcome of the experiment, what is predicted is that the outcome passes a test specified by a certain *computational process* (i.e., multiplication of the output numbers results in N). This might seem like a minor difference, between verification and comparing, and in a very special case; however as we shall soon see, it is the tip of the iceberg.

Aharonov, Ben-Or, and Eban (2010) suggested that this view of Shor's algorithm as an experiment verifying quantum mechanics in complex regimes could be greatly generalized by casting it in the framework of interactive proof systems. This is a central concept in computational complexity theory (Goldwasser, Micali, and Rackoff 1985; Babai 1985; and see Arora and Barak 2009). In an interactive proof system, a computationally weak (i.e., of polynomial strength) verifier, Arthur, can interact with a much more powerful (in fact unbounded) but untrusted entity, called the prover, or Merlin. By this interaction he can determine the correctness of an assertion made by Merlin. For this to be possible, Merlin has to be willing to answer a number of cleverly chosen random questions related to the original claim; the questions need to be random so that Merlin cannot prepare in advance, and thus Arthur may catch him if he is trying to cheat by revealing the inconsistencies in his claims. Arthur adaptively generates this sequence of questions based on Merlin's answers, and checks Merlin's answers for consistency. The remarkable property of such protocols is that Arthur can only be convinced of the original claim (with non-negligible probability over the choice of questions) if it is in fact a valid claim. Arthur's confidence in the claim does not depend in any way on his trust in Merlin, but rather in the consistency checks that he is able to perform on Merlin's answers (see Arora and Barak 2009 for some detailed examples of such protocols). In complexity theory, Merlin is a hypothetical being, and the properties of the game between Arthur and Merlin provide deep insights into the nature and complexity of proofs. In the quantum context, Aharonov et al. (2010) suggest to replace the all-powerful prover Merlin by a real entity, namely a quantum system performing quantum evolutions or quantum computations.[3]

Let us understand the implications of such an interactive proof system in the context of a classical experimentalist (who is computationally "weak," namely limited to polynomial computations), who wishes to verify that the outcome of a quantum experiment is consistent with quantum mechanics (which is a computationally powerful system). Let us place the experimentalist in the role of Arthur, and quantum systems (or all of quantum mechanics) in the role of Merlin. Using such protocols of interaction as in interactive proofs, we will derive that although the experimentalist might not be able to verify directly that the outcome of a *single* experiment in isolation is correct (according to the predictions of quantum mechanics), because he would not be able to predict its outcome, he still could set up a sequence of experiments and test that the outcomes of all these experiments jointly satisfied the consistency checks (mandated by the interactive proof system). If they did indeed satisfy them, he could conclude that the outcome of the original experiment was indeed correct according to the predictions of quantum mechanics. Moreover, his confidence in this conclusion would be based only on the success of the consistency tests, which he could perform efficiently. Of course, if the outcomes of the experiments did not pass the consistency tests, then the experimentalist could only conclude that at least one of the experiments failed to meet the predictions of quantum mechanics. The implication would be that something in the sequence of experiments must not fit the theory: either the system was not prepared correctly, or quantum mechanics itself is false.

This kind of an interactive proof between the experimentalist and the quantum system may be thought of as a new kind of experiment, involving a well-designed sequence of interactions (a *protocol*) between the experimentalist and the system. Indeed, this would provide a new paradigm for the scientific method, breaking with the "predict and test" paradigm that goes back several centuries. However, whether such an interactive proof system exists for all of quantum mechanics is currently an open question. Indeed, this is currently one of the most important computational questions about the foundations of quantum mechanics.

Is it plausible that a classical verifier could efficiently check an exponentially more powerful system such as quantum mechanics? The earlier discussion about formulating Shor's algorithm as an interactive experiment provides an example of the possibility of testing QM in complex regimes; note, however, that the factoring problem is special, since it is in the complexity class NP ∩ co–NP, believed not to contain all of quantum computation, and so this does not clearly imply anything for testing quantum mechanics in general. Turning to more general cases, interactive proof systems are known to exist for systems that are more powerful than quantum mechanics, for example, for the class #P of all counting functions.[4] By these interactive proofs, the prover can prove to the weak verifier that he has computed the answer to the #P function correctly, even though such a function is extremely hard for the verifier to compute on his own. However, these interactive proofs are not useful in our context, since the prover in them is all-powerful (or at least as powerful as #P), whereas we need the prover to be no more powerful than QM; how would a restricted prover establish the correctness of a quantum mechanical evolution? The auxiliary random questions generated by Arthur must be solvable efficiently by a quantum system to ensure that the experiments corresponding to the interactive proof are feasible. Hence, this still does not provide an answer to the open question above.

Aharonov et al. (2010) were able to prove an interesting kind of interactive proof system for quantum mechanics, one that partially addresses the above question. In this system, Arthur, the experimentalist, is not purely classical, but can store and manipulate a constant number (3 to be concrete) of qubits, and can exchange qubits with Merlin, who is an arbitrary quantum system. They gave a protocol by which Arthur can verify that an arbitrary quantum experiment (modeled by an arbitrary sequence of quantum gates) has been faithfully carried out by Merlin, by exchanging a sequence of specially chosen quantum messages with Merlin, the quantum system. At all times in this protocol, Arthur holds at most 3 qubits.

One way to understand this protocol is to imagine that a company QWave claims to have experimentally realized a quantum computer, and wishes to convince a potential buyer that the computer is indeed capable of performing an arbitrary quantum computation on up to n qubits. If the potential buyer has the capability of storing and manipulating 3 qubits, and of exchanging qubits with the quantum computer, then by following the protocol of Aharonov et al. (2010), he can verify that the computer faithfully carried out any quantum computation of his choice. Alternatively, assume that an experimentalist trusts that QM describes his system of few qubits to extremely high precision, but does not know that that is true, or to what extent it is true, as the number of particles in the system increases. He can use the above protocol to test this, based on his already established belief that his small systems obey QM to very high precision and a relaxed assumption about the quantum nature of the physical system.[5]

In the following, we flesh out the main ingredients required to make the above line of thought rigorous; and we explain how a computationally weak experimenter (polynomial nearly classical verifier) can test the complex regime of quantum mechanics using interactive experiments.

11.1 Polynomial Time and the Extended Church–Turing Thesis

A fundamental principle in computational complexity theory can be summarized as equating *efficient* and *polynomial time:* computations are considered efficient if they can be carried out in a number of steps that is bounded by a polynomial in the size of the input. Here the size of the input is measured in the number of bits required to specify it. This identification of efficient with polynomial time is to be contrasted with brute force search, which takes exponential time in the size of the input. For example, the satisfiability problem (SAT) asks whether a given propositional formula $f(x_1, \dots, x_n)$ is satisfiable—that is, whether logical values (true and false) can be assigned to its variables in such a way that makes the formula true. There are 2^n such truth assignments, and brute force search over these possibilities is prohibitively expensive—even for $n = 500$, 2^n is larger than estimates for the number of particles in the universe, or the age of the universe in femtoseconds. But is this brute force search necessary? The famous P = NP? question asks whether this problem can be solved in a number of steps bounded by some polynomial in n.

The principle of efficient computation is also closely tied to the extended Church–Turing thesis, which states that any "reasonable" model of computation can be simulated by a (probabilistic) Turing machine with at most polynomial simulation overhead. That is, for any reasonable model of computation there is a polynomial $p(x)$ such that T steps on this model can be simulated in at most $p(T)$ steps on a Turing machine. This means that Turing machines not only capture the notion of effective computability (which is the essence of the original Church–Turing thesis), but they also capture the notion of efficient computation.

As was briefly touched upon at the beginning of this chapter, there are two ways to interpret what it means for a model of computation to be "reasonable." The first may be thought of as modeling a mathematician carrying out a long calculation through a sequence of steps, each of which can be carried out using pencil and paper, and where the recipe for the sequence of steps is finitely specified. The second is to consider a physical model of computation or a digital computer. The computational model must be "reasonable" in the sense that it must be physically realizable in principle. For example, implementing infinite precision arithmetic in a single step would be considered unreasonable, since it does not account for the inevitable noise and inaccuracy in any physical realization. Informally, one may argue that classical physics is described by local differential equations, which taking into account the inevitable noise and lack of infinitely precise control, reduces as a computational model to a cellular automaton. Since cellular automata are polynomially equivalent to Turing machines, the extended Church–Turing thesis may be thought of as providing a constraint on what kinds of functions can be computed efficiently by Nature.

11.2 Interactive Proofs

Let us start with a simple example that is related to a famous problem in mathematics, namely, the graph isomorphism problem. A graph consists of a set of nodes (this set is denoted V) with edges connecting pairs of those nodes (the set of edges is denoted E). In the graph isomorphism problem, we are given two graphs, $G_1 = (V_1, E_1)$ and $G_2 = (V_2, E_2)$, and we wish to test whether the two graphs are isomorphic. That is, is there a bijection $f: V_1 \rightarrow V_2$ on the vertex sets, such that $\{u, v\} \in E_1$ iff $\{f(u), f(v)\} \in E_2$? Edges in G_1 are mapped to edges in G_2 under this bijection and non-edges are mapped to non-edges. There is no efficient algorithm known to solve graph isomorphism in the worst case.

Suppose we had a powerful entity, Merlin, who claimed to be able to solve arbitrary instances of graph isomorphism. How could he convince Arthur about the answer to a particular instance $G_1 = (V_1, E_1)$, $G_2 = (V_2, E_2)$? If the two graphs are isomorphic, then he would simply provide the bijection, and Arthur could efficiently check that this bijection maps edges to edges and non-edges to non-edges. If the number of vertices in each graph were n, then Arthur would need to run over all pairs of nodes to check that edges were mapped to edges and non-edges to non-edges; since the number of pairs is bounded by n^2, his computation is efficient.

Returning to the example, if the two graphs are non-isomorphic, how would Merlin convince Arthur that this was the case? On the face of it, this appears impossible, since Merlin would have to rule out all possible bijections, and there are exponentially many of those as a function of n. This is where the interactive proof comes in. Arthur chooses one of the two graphs at random (according to the flip of a fair coin), and then randomly permutes the vertices and sends the resulting description to Merlin. Merlin is asked to identify which of the two graphs Arthur chose.

The point is that if the two graphs were isomorphic, then there is no way to distinguish a random permutation of one graph from a random permutation of the other (the two distributions are identical). So Merlin can succeed with probability of at most half, or 1/2. On the other hand, if the graphs were not isomorphic, then Merlin, who can solve the graph isomorphism problem, can easily identify which graph was sent to him and answer accordingly. Arthur can of course easily check if Merlin answered correctly. This means that if Merlin tried to convince Arthur of a wrong claim—that the two graphs are not isomorphic, when in fact they are—he would be caught cheating with probability at least half. Repeating this protocol k times independently at random would decrease Merlin's probability of succeeding in convincing Arthur by chance in the case of isomorphic graphs to at most $1/2^k$.

A much more sophisticated protocol works in the case that Merlin claims to be able to solve the problem #SAT (see note 1 for a definition). In this problem, the input is a propositional formula $f(x_1, \ldots, x_n)$ on n Boolean inputs $x_i \in \{0, 1\}$, and the desired output is the number of distinct inputs to f on which it evaluates to 1. In the protocol, Arthur queries Merlin about a number of related propositional formulae $f_1, f_2, \ldots, f_m$ chosen based on f and on some random coins; Arthur accepts only if Merlin's answers satisfy certain consistency checks. The protocol is fairly complicated and will not be discussed here.[6] The important property of this protocol, however, is that if Merlin lies about the answer to the initial problem, then he is forced to keep lying in order to pass the consistency tests, until eventually he lies about a simple enough assertion that even Arthur can independently verify it efficiently.

11.3   Interactive Proofs for Quantum Mechanics

The class of computational problems that can be solved efficiently (in polynomial time) on a quantum computer is denoted by BQP (or bounded error quantum polynomial time). It is well known that BQP $\subseteq$ #P,[7] and so every computational problem that can be solved in polynomial time on a quantum computer can also be solved by a #P solving Merlin. At first sight the interactive proof for #*SAT* described above, which in fact works for any problem in #P, would seem to be exactly the kind of interactive proof system we are seeking for BQP. Unfortunately, the computations that Merlin must perform for this protocol, namely solving #P problems, are (believed to be) too hard to be performed efficiently by a quantum computer. So even though we end up with an interactive proof system for BQP, it is not one in which the prover is a BQP quantum machine. The major open question is whether every problem in BQP has an efficient interactive proof of this type, where the prover is a BQP machine and the verifier is a polynomial time classical machine. If we denote by BPP the class of problems solvable in polynomial time by a probabilistic Turing machine, this translates to the requirement that the verifier is a BPP machine, interacting with a BQP prover.

Definition 11.1 *A problem L is said to have a quantum prover interactive proof (QPIP) if there is an interactive proof system with the following properties:*

- The prover is computationally restricted to BQP .
- The verifier is a (classical) BPP machine.
- For any $x \in L$, P convinces V of the fact that $x \in L$ with probability $\geq 2/3$ after the conversation between them ended (completeness). Otherwise, when $x \notin L$, any prover (even one not following the protocol) fails to convince V with probability higher than $1/3$ (soundness).

Formally, the open question mentioned at the outset of this chapter can be restated to ask whether BQP $\subseteq$ QPIP; that is, whether any problem in BQP has a quantum prover interactive proof system as above; or, alternatively, whether the correctness of the outcome of a polynomial time quantum evolution can be proven to a classical BPP verifier by a BQP prover. Note that the other direction trivially holds: QPIP $\subseteq$ BQP, since any QPIP protocol can be simulated by a *BQP* machine by simulating both prover and verifier, as well as the interaction between them; hence the question can be written as whether BQP = QPIP.

Aharonov et al. (2010) managed to show a somewhat weaker result. To this end, they defined a relaxation of QPIP: the verifier in their definition is a hybrid quantum-classical machine. Its classical part is a BPP machine as above. The quantum part is a register of c qubits (for some constant $c - 3$ would suffice), on which the verifier can perform arbitrary quantum operations, as well as send them to the prover, who can in its turn perform further operations on those qubits and send them back. At any given time, the verifier is not allowed to possess more than c qubits. The interaction between the quantum and classical parts is the usual one: the classical part controls which operations are to be performed on the quantum register, and outcomes of measurements of the quantum register can be used as input to the classical machine. There are two communication channels between the prover and the verifier: the quantum one, in which the constant number of qubits can be sent, and the classical one, in which polynomially many bits can be sent.

Aharonov et al. (2010) proved that with this relaxation of QPIP, which we will denote here by QPIP*, a BQP prover can convince the verifier of any language he can compute:

Theorem 11.1 $BQP \subseteq QPIP*$,
where the other direction, QPIP* $\subseteq$ BQP, is again trivial.

The meaning of this result is that if the verifier trusts that his hybrid classical system with the aid of a constant number of qubits acts according to his quantum mechanical description of it with sufficient confidence, then he can also be convinced with very high confidence of the results of the computation of the most general and complicated quantum computation which takes polynomial time, run on a quantum computer he has no control over.

The mathematical method that was used to prove this result is taken from the realm of cryptography and uses computer science notions such as error correction and authentication; we will attempt to sketch it in the next section.

11.4   How Weak Verifiers Can Test Strong Machines: Proof Idea

As a warm-up to the QPIP* = BQP question, consider the following simple scenario: suppose the verifier wishes to store an n qubit state $|\varphi\rangle$ that she is about to receive, but she has only a constant number of qubits of quantum memory. Fortunately, she can use the services of a quantum memory storage company. The problem is that she does not trust the company. Does the verifier have a way of checking that the storage company eventually returns to her the same state that she sent them? We can think of this problem as the problem of trivial-computation by an untrusted prover: the verifier just wants to verify that the company, here viewed as the prover, did nothing to the state she wants to maintain, or, in other words, that the company applied to it the *identity* computation. The prover wishes to convince the verifier that indeed the state he returns is exactly the state sent by the verifier (regardless of whether this is indeed the case). The challenge is that the verifier cannot measure the state before storing it in the prover's hands, since this will collapse the state; hence the protocol needs to work even if she knows nothing about the state she stores! In fact, when she receives or generates the state, she cannot even hold all its qubits in her laboratory at once.

The idea for solving this problem is in fact quite simple. Let us assume that the verifier generates the unknown quantum state $|\varphi\rangle$ one qubit at a time, and transmits each qubit to the quantum storage company, or the prover, as she generates it. Imagine just for the sake of explanation that $|\varphi\rangle$ is a tensor product state $|\alpha\rangle \otimes |\beta\rangle \otimes$ ..... Before sending the first qubit in the state $|\alpha\rangle$ to the company, the verifier encodes it into the state of, say, two qubits, in the following way. The verifier adds one auxiliary qubit in the known state $|0\rangle$, which will serve as a *check* qubit. The state at the verifier's hands after that is $|\alpha\rangle \otimes |0\rangle$. She then chooses a random unitary U_R uniformly from all the unitaries acting on two qubits, and applies it to her two qubits. She derives the state $U_R(|\alpha\rangle \otimes |0\rangle)$; note that this is a completely random two-qubit state. She sends this state to the company, and then receives the next qubit in the state $|\beta\rangle$, encodes it into another random state by adding an additional auxiliary qubit and applying a random (newly chosen) unitary on $|\beta\rangle \otimes |0\rangle$, sends the resulting state, and so on. By the end of this protocol, the company has received twice as many qubits as the original state.

To retrieve the quantum state from the company, the verifier asks for pairs of qubits back, block by block. On each such block of two qubits, she first applies the inverse of the random unitary, U_R^{-1}, she applied on that block at the time of encoding. She then applies a measurement of *only the check qubit*, and tests that it is indeed in the state $|0\rangle$; she need not measure the first qubit in each block, and this way she does not disturb its state.

Why does this test work with high probability? The point is that the initial state of each block, before applying the random unitary, lives inside a two-dimensional manifold M, described by all states of the form $|\gamma\rangle \otimes |0\rangle$ (for all one-qubit states $|\gamma\rangle$). The random unitary U_R takes the manifold M and maps it onto a random two-dimensional manifold M_R inside the four-dimensional space of the two qubits. Since the company has no information regarding U_R, from its point of view, the resulting manifold M_R is a completely random two-dimensional manifold inside this four-dimensional space. Therefore, if the company tries to alter the state without being caught, or if the company cheated, and in fact, it does not have a reliable quantum memory, the final state of the two qubits will be, with extremely high probability, significantly far away from that manifold, since the company knows nothing about this manifold. When the verifier performs the test of rotating the state of the two qubits back by the inverse unitary (thus rotating the two-dimensional manifold M_R back to the original one M), the state of the auxiliary qubit, which should be $|0\rangle$, will be significantly far away from it; and when the verifier checks that the additional qubit is in the state $|0\rangle$, she will detect that such a change had occurred with high probability.

Notice that in the above explanation we never used our assumption that the initial state is a tensor product state; in fact, everything holds even in the presence of multi-particle entanglement between all different qubits of the original state. This idea thus already contains the seed for the solution we are looking for, because it enables checking the ability to *store* highly complicated states, namely to perform the identity computation on them. This is true even though the verifier herself does not have large enough quantum memory capabilities to even hold the state and, moreover, she doesn't know which state she is trying to store.

This notion of maintaining complicated quantum states by untrusted parties, and the ability to detect whether they were altered, was in fact invented in the context of cryptography and is called a *quantum authentication scheme* (QAS; Barnum et al. 2002). It turns out that the quantum authentication scheme described above is not so useful, since to realize it, we need to efficiently select a random unitary, which involves infinite accuracy issues. Moreover, the security of the above scheme is yet to be proven; technically, this is nontrivial due to the continuous nature of this scheme. Aharonov et al. (2010) describe a slightly more involved QAS whose security is much easier to prove, since it is amenable to a terminology that describes errors in the state as discrete.

To move to the language of discrete errors, recall the notion of Pauli matrices: these are the four 2×2 matrices

$$I = \begin{pmatrix} 1 & 0 \\ 0 & 1 \end{pmatrix}, \sigma_x = \begin{pmatrix} 0 & 1 \\ 1 & 0 \end{pmatrix}, \sigma_y = \begin{pmatrix} 0 & i \\ -i & 0 \end{pmatrix}, \sigma_z = \begin{pmatrix} 1 & 0 \\ 0 & -1 \end{pmatrix} \tag{11.1}$$

acting on one qubit. These four matrices linearly span the continuum of changes that can happen to one qubit. It thus suffices to handle the probability that one of the non-identity operators σ_x, σ_y, σ_z occurs to a qubit to be able to provide bounds on the probability that the state had been altered significantly while in the hands of the company.

We now modify the above-described QAS as follows. The encoding is done essentially as before, by adding one qubit in the state $|0\rangle$ to each qubit in the original state, and applying a random rotation on those two qubits. However, instead of choosing the rotation randomly from all possible unitary operations on two qubits, as in the first QAS, the random unitary U_R is chosen from a finite subgroup of all two-qubit unitaries, called the *Clifford group*. This group is defined to be the group of unitaries C such that when C acts on a Pauli matrix P by conjugation (namely, P is mapped to CPC^{-1}), the resulting matrix is still inside the Pauli group. In other words, the Pauli group is closed to conjugation by matrices from the Clifford group. The reason this property is advantageous is this: imagine that when at the hands of the company, the matrix E is applied to a quantum state ψ, rather than the identity. The effect on the *density matrix* ρ describing the state is that E acts on it by conjugation, so ρ is mapped to $E\rho E^{-1}$. Now, if a random Clifford C is applied to the state before the state is transferred to the hands of the company, and then its reverse is applied when the state is returned, the effective overall action on ρ is $C^{-1}(E(C\rho C^{-1})$ $E^{-1})C = (C^{-1}EC)\rho(C^{-1}E^{-1}C)$. Thus, the effect of first rotating ρ by a Clifford operator (and then rotating back) is that not E was applied, but its conjugation by a random Clifford matrix. Recall that we can span E in terms of Paulies and that the Pauli group is closed to conjugation by matrices from the Clifford group. It turns out that conjugating E by a random Clifford makes E effectively equal to the application of a random Pauli matrix to each qubit independently, and this includes the extra test qubit. At verification stage, such a procedure will go undetected by the verifier's measurements only if the Pauli on the check qubit turns out to be either identity or σ_z, but if it is σ_x or σ_y it will be detected since the measured state will be $|1\rangle$. This happens with probability 0.5.

Hence, it turns out that even though the restriction of the random unitary to the Clifford group seems quite strong (in particular, the Clifford group contains a finite number of elements rather than a continuum!), this choice provides enough randomization to completely randomize the action of the prover, so that any tampering of the state will be detected with high probability.

We therefore have a solution to the simple problem of maintaining a quantum state using an untrusted storage device. It might seem that this problem is far too simple, and almost irrelevant for the more general problem of verifying that a quantum circuit had been applied correctly on the state. In fact, the above idea suffices to solve the entire problem by a simple modification. Imagine now that we have a certain computation, or a specification of a quantum algorithm by a sequence of two-qubit quantum gates, $U_1, \dots, U_T$. We want to make sure that, with high probability, the final state the prover sends us is very close to the correct state, $U_T \cdots U_1 |0^n\rangle$. Given the QAS above, we can achieve this goal as follows. The verifier starts by encoding each qubit in the input state using the Clifford-based QAS above. She then sends these pairs of qubits to the prover one pair at a time. All that the prover needs to do is serve as an untrusted storage device! The verifier is the one to perform the gates one by one, and this is done as follows: to apply the ith gate, the verifier asks the prover to send her the two blocks of two qubits encoding the relevant qubits on which she wants to apply the gate (assuming all gates act on two qubits). Upon receiving those four qubits, she first decodes them, by applying the inverse of the random unitaries to each block (of course she must maintain a classical description of those unitaries in her classical memory so she can carry out these steps). After decoding, she applies the gate U_i on the two decoded qubits, and encodes the two qubits again using two freshly chosen random unitaries; she then sends the two blocks to the prover. This way she had correctly updated the state at the hands of the prover; if the prover does not tamper with it, after time step i he holds an authenticated version of the correct state of the quantum circuit after i gates. Once all gates have been applied this way, the prover (if honest) holds the authenticated version of the final state of the quantum circuit. At this point, the verifier asks the prover to send her all pairs of qubits one by one; once she receives such a pair, she applies the decoding using the inverse of the relevant encoding unitary, and then measures the test qubit in the block to check that it is in the state $|0\rangle$; if all tests pass successfully, she is assured (with constant probability) that the state she had received is correct. Of course, her constant probability can be amplified by repeating the entire process.

The size of the quantum register which the verifier is assumed to possess in this protocol is four qubits, since the length of the encoding of one qubit is two. In fact, three qubits suffice, since it is enough to send one register at a time and wait until the verifier decodes it before sending the second register of two qubits.

11.5   Further Complications: Can the Prover Apply the Gates?

The Clifford-based QAS enables us to prove the main theorem, but there are several problems with this proof. First, it is not fault-tolerant; namely, if the storage devices and the quantum channels between the prover and verifier are faulty and not ideally isolated from the surroundings, then the scheme will quickly fail. Fault tolerance is necessary for the scheme to be applicable in a physically realistic setting. But a more severe criticism can be made against the above scheme: it seems like cheating, as the computation is performed entirely by the verifier! In terms of making progress toward the question of whether QPIP is equivalent to BQP, it is crucial that the prover perform the nontrivial quantum computation, since eventually we want the verifier to be classical. What we want is that the prover apply the quantum gates, *without* learning any information about the encoded qubits that he is applying the gates to; because if he has such information, he can use it to alter the state of the qubits from the correct state, without being caught. Hence, we need some way of encoding the qubits that are delivered to the prover, so that a) he does not know the encoding; and b) he is capable of performing gates on the encoded state nevertheless. Though the above two requirements might seem contradictory, it is possible to achieve both at the same time.

At this point, it is not known how to achieve both goals using the Clifford-based QAS, since it does not seem to have sufficient algebraic structure. Aharonov et al. (2010) achieve this by providing a second QPIP protocol, based on a different QAS, from Ben-Or et al. (2006). We explain this in this section. The result is thus a QPIP in which the verifier does not perform any quantum computation except for the encoding in the beginning; moreover, the interaction with the prover, after those encoded qubits are sent, is completely classical.

The idea of how such a manipulation can be carried over is inspired by the notion of error detection codes from computer science. An error detection code is a mapping of a string of, say, k bits $s \in \{0, 1\}^k$ into a longer string of m bits, $w \in \{0, 1\}^m$. We say this code detects t errors if, whenever t bits or fewer have flipped in w, this fact can be detected. This can be achieved, of course, only if there is sufficient redundancy in the encoding; that is, m is sufficiently larger than k.

Quantum error-detection codes are defined similarly: the encoding is a unitary embedding of the space of quantum states of k qubits into the space of quantum states of m qubits. The notion of bit-flips as errors in the classical case is replaced by non-identity Paulis applied to the qubits. More precisely, in the quantum setting we are faced with quantum errors of the following types: a bit flip, described by the Pauli σ_x (see equation 11.1), a phase flip, described by the Pauli matrix σ_z, and a combination of both, described by σ_y.

One can generalize the notion of quantum error-detecting codes also to qudits, namely to states of higher-dimensional particles, say, each of dimension q; instead of Pauli matrices, one considers their generalizations: σ_x is generalized by the operator $X_q : |x\rangle \mapsto |x + 1 \, mod \, q\rangle$, which we refer to as a generalized bit flip; σ_z is generalized by $Z_q : |x\rangle \mapsto e^{2\pi i x/q} |x\rangle$, which we refer to as a generalized phase flip, and the generalized Pauli group over F_q, applied to one qudit, is the group generated by X_q and Z_q; namely, it consists of the set of combinations of those errors, $X_q^\ell Z_q^n$ for $\ell, n \in \{0, \cdots, q-1\}$.

Why do we discuss error-detection codes in our context? The requirement for error detection resembles the requirements from a QAS in which we need to be able to detect *any* modification induced by the prover to the string of qubits we would like him to maintain. The difference is that the task we are aiming at in the context of QAS is more difficult: in error-detection codes, the goal is to detect any error which tampers with at most t (qu)bits; if more than t (qu)bits have been tampered with, we do not care if this goes undetected. By contrast, in QAS we make no assumption on the number of locations that can be tampered with; we have no control over how the prover can alter the state, and we would like to be able to detect *any* error.

It is not difficult to convince one's self that no error-detection code can achieve this ambitious goal of being able to detect any error. However, if we relax our requirements and allow the detection of errors only with high probability rather than with certainty, this becomes possible! The main idea behind the authentication scheme of Ben-Or et al. (2006) is to use not a fixed error-detection code, but one that is chosen randomly from a large set of possible codes. In this way, *any error* (namely, any combination of non-identity Paulis) is detected by all but a small fraction of codes that can be used, and so, with high probability, any error will be detected.

This randomized encoding resembles the usage of a random unitary in the previous two QAS. The difference is that in the scheme we will now describe, due to the algebraic structure of the codes we use, the prover will be able to apply gates on the states without knowing which of the error-detection codes is being used. We now explain how this is done.

We start with a familiar quantum error-detection code, called the polynomial code (Aharonov and Ben-Or 1997). We operate over the field F_q, for a large prime q. Recall that a polynomial $f = \sum_{i=0}^{d} a_i x^i$ of degree d over this field is determined by its $d + 1$ coefficients a_i. Imagine now we represent this polynomial in terms not of its coefficients, but rather its values at different points of the field, say, $1 \cdots m$. In other words, we encode the polynomial by the string of values $f(j)$ for $j = 1 \cdots m$. If m is larger than $d + 1$, then there is redundancy in this representation and errors can be detected. In fact, if we pick $m = 2d + 1$, then exactly all errors which contain up to d altered locations can be detected. The above scheme gives a classical code (and a very famous one—it is the Reed-Solomon code [Arora and Barak 2009]).

To get a quantum detection code, we need to be able to detect not only classical errors (the generalization of σ_x to quantum systems of dimension q, namely X_q and its powers X_q^ℓ) but also quantum errors, also known as generalized phase flips (the generalizations of σ_z to quantum systems of dimension q, Z_q, and its powers Z_q^n). To achieve this, we consider *superpositions* of all polynomials of degree up to d. We encode each element a in the field F_q by the following state:

$$| S_a \rangle = \sum_{f, deg(f) \leq d, f(0)=a} | f(1), \dots, f(m) \rangle;$$

namely, by the superposition of all strings evaluating a polynomial of degree less than d at m points in the field, where the sum is only over such polynomials whose value at 0 is a. That such a superposition possesses ability to detect classical-like errors of weight up to d, namely errors of type X_q and their powers applied to at most d coordinates, follows from the fact that each string in the superposition possesses it, due to the classical properties of error detection of polynomial codes. The ability to detect d phase flips is less straightforward. It follows from changing the basis and looking at the state after the application of the Fourier transform. Z_q is transformed in this basis to X_q; so being able to correct for generalized bit flips in the new basis translates to correcting phase flips in the original basis. The point is that after applying the Fourier transform, we arrive at the dual of the superposition of all polynomials, which turns out to be also a superposition of those polynomials! Hence, in this basis, too, we can detect bit flips, which means correcting phase flips in the original basis. Since bit flips and phase flips, and their combinations, span the entire unitary group, this means that we are able to detect any error if it did not involve too many locations. This gives us the polynomial quantum code, which can thus be shown to detect errors at up to d locations, namely applications of any combination of the non-identity generalized Paulies on at most d locations.

So far, we have defined only one error-detection code, which we refer to as our *basic* code. We would now like to introduce a randomization process, which would result in a *family* of error-detection codes, such that any error applied by the prover will be detected with high probability.

If we assume that the prover only applies a Pauli operator at each location, then it suffices to randomize the basic code as follows. For each location, a random sign flip ε_i (plus or minus) is chosen independently. $\varepsilon = (\varepsilon_1, \cdots, \varepsilon_m)$ is called the *sign key*. The basic code is modified according to ε by multiplying each location by ε_i, and the result is called the *signed polynomial code*:

$$| S_a |_\varepsilon \rangle = \sum_{f, deg(f) \le d, f(0) = a} | \varepsilon_1 f(1), \ldots, \varepsilon_m f(m) \rangle.$$

It turns out that this randomization suffices to ensure that the verifier detects with high probability any (non-trivial) Pauli group operator applied by the prover on *any number* of locations. This is because in order for it not to be detected, the Pauli applied on top of the sign key has to match the values of a low-degree polynomial, and this happens with small probability.

The above scheme does not suffice, however, to handle a general operator applied by the prover. To this end, Ben-Or et al. (2006) use an additional random key, which they call the *Pauli key*; for each location, the verifier not only picks a random sign, plus or minus, but also a random element of the generalized Pauli group $X_q^{x_i} Z_q^{z_i}$. The Pauli key is denoted $(x, z) = ((x_1, \cdots, x_m), (z_1, \cdots, z_m))$. To encode, the verifier applies the generalized Pauli $X_q^{x_i} Z_q^{z_i}$ on the ith coordinate of the state $|S_a|_\varepsilon\rangle$ encoded by the random signed polynomial code, for all i; this derives the state

$$| S_a |_{\varepsilon, x, z} \rangle = (X_q^{x_1} Z_q^{z_1}) \otimes (X_q^{x_2} Z_q^{z_2}) \otimes \cdots \otimes (X_q^{x_m} Z_q^{z_m}) | S_a |_\varepsilon \rangle.$$

It is technically not too difficult to see that due to symmetry arguments, this randomization by a random Pauli key performed by the verifier makes the general operator that the prover had applied appear effectively as though the prover applied a uniformly chosen random Pauli operator at each location; from there, the argument proceeds as before: it is not difficult to see that applying a random Pauli at each location on a state encoded by a polynomial code (or more generally by a signed polynomial code shifted by some Pauli key) is detected with high probability. This means that this is indeed a QAS which can detect any error with high probability.

It remains to explain how the prover can apply gates on the encoded state even though he does not know the encoding and has no information regarding the Pauli and the sign keys, (x, z) and ε. The idea is that the prover performs the gates assuming that the basic polynomial code was used, namely that ε and (x,z) where trivial. The verifier and prover then need to perform very simple corrections on top of that. Essentially, the verifier needs to update his Pauli and sign keys for each gate the prover applies, where for some gates, the prover needs to measure part of his state and send the classical result to the verifier in order for the verifier to know how to update his keys. We demonstrate the details with two examples of gates, but this maneuver can be done for a universal set of quantum gates.

The first example is very simple. Imagine that the prover is required to apply the gate $X_q : |a\rangle \mapsto |a+1 \bmod q\rangle$, on the encoded state. That is, it is required to take $|S_a|_{\varepsilon,x,z}\rangle \mapsto |S_{a+1}|_{\varepsilon,x,z}\rangle$. This can be achieved if the prover applies the operations $X_q^{\varepsilon_i}$ to the ith coordinate, for all i. To see this, first check the case in which both ε and (x, z) are trivial; indeed, in this case, the state is simply $|S_a\rangle$, and it is easy to check that applying X_q on each coordinate, namely, adding one to every coordinate of the polynomial, translates to adding 1 to the value of the polynomial at 0, namely a. This is the exact operation we wanted. The more general claim, that for general ε applying $X_q^{\varepsilon_i}$ achieves the desired result, is not much more difficult.

However, the prover cannot apply $X_q^{\varepsilon_i}$ on the ith coordinate since he does not know ε_i. So how can the prover apply the gate? Fortunately, the prover need not do anything to apply the gate! Instead, all that needs to be done is that the *verifier* updates his Pauli key by decreasing ε_i from x_i, $x_i \mapsto x_i - \varepsilon_i$; this effectively achieves the same result.

The second example is just slightly more complicated: it is the application of the Fourier transform gate, $F|a\rangle \mapsto \frac{1}{\sqrt{q}} \sum_{b=0}^{q-1} e^{2\pi iab/q} |b\rangle$. Once again, when the keys are trivial, it is easy to check that if the prover applies the gate F on each coordinate in $|S_a\rangle$, the total effect is the desired Fourier transform gate $|S_a\rangle \mapsto \frac{1}{\sqrt{q}} \sum_{b=0}^{q-1} e^{2\pi iab/q} |S_b\rangle$. But we need to correct for the existence of the Pauli and sign keys. First, we observe that the sign key does not change anything in the above argument—that code too is mapped to itself (i.e., it is self-dual) by the coordinate-wise application of the Fourier transform (Ben-Or et al. 2006). As for the correction because of the Pauli key, observe that the conjugation by the Fourier transform maps X_q to Z_q and Z_q to X_q^{-1}, because $Z_q F = F X_q$ and $X^{-1} F = F Z_q$. Hence, the prover can apply the Fourier gate on each coordinate, and the verifier need only correct his Pauli key from (x, z) to $(-z, x)$.

In a very similar way, the prover can perform a universal set of gates without knowing the encoding, namely the sign key or the Pauli key. We proceed just as in the previous scheme: the verifier applies the gates with the help of the prover, as above, one by one, and at the end, the verifier checks for correctness by asking the prover to send him the blocks of encoded qubits, checking that each block lives in the code space of the correct random error-correcting code.

The intriguing fact about this scheme is that the prover can be manipulated to apply the gates without knowing the encoding. This raises hope that similar methods might be applicable even when the verifier is entirely classical, and thus, that a completely classical verifier can be convinced of the correctness of a QM evolution.

Finally, we remark regarding the reasons this scheme enables fault tolerance. First, the fact that the prover can apply gates on his own makes it possible for him to apply gates in parallel on all the qubits he maintains in his memory. In the usual noise model, in which qubits are faulty even when no gates are applied to them (this model is known as "faulty wires"), error correction must be applied constantly on a constant fraction of the qubits (Aharonov and Ben-Or 1996). Since the quantum space of the verifier is limited in our model, the prover must be able to perform those error corrections, and thus must perform many gates in parallel. The proof that this scheme is fault-tolerant relies on standard quantum fault-tolerance proofs (for example, Aharonov and Ben-Or 1997), but some additional care is required since the verifier can only hold a constant number of qubits at a time, while he is the only one who can authenticate qubits.

11.6 Summary

The standard scientific paradigm going back several hundred years—"predict and verify"—is not sufficiently powerful to test quantum mechanics in the high-complexity regime. The exciting possibilities and challenges that this regime poses call for an extension of the scientific paradigm to interactive experiments. Such interactive experiments, inspired by the notion of interactive proofs from computer science, allow testing complex and powerful systems without the need to be able to predict their behavior; the example described here provides a way to do so using a classical verifier with very small-scale quantum capabilities. Whether or not a completely classical verifier can test quantum evolutions is left open.

A number of issues call for further thought. A very difficult question is whether there is a reasonable straw man theory that agrees with current experimental data about QM but *does not* violate the extended Church–Turing thesis. A theory of confirmation based on interactive experiments remains to be developed; important initial steps in this direction were taken in Yaari (2011). Another direction to explore is whether such a theory of interactive experiments might be useful for testing other highly complex systems besides those suggested by QM. It is intriguing to further understand the philosophical foundations of a theory of confirmation in which interaction between a weak verifier and a highly complex physical system can take place.

11.7 Related Work

Initiated independently, and followed by discussions with us, Jonathan Yaari has studied the notion of "interactive proofs with Nature" in his thesis in philosophy of science (Yaari 2011). His thesis provides an initiation of the study of a theory of confirmation based on interactive proofs.

In the context of blind quantum computation, Broadbent, Fitzsimons, and Kashefi (2009) suggest a protocol that provides a possible way of showing that BQP = QPIP* where the verifier needs only a single quantum bit. At this point it is unclear whether the security of this protocol can be rigorously established.

Acknowledgments

U.V. would like to thank Les Valiant, and D.A. would like to thank Oded Goldreich, Madhu Sudan, Guy Rothblum, Gil Kalai, and the late Itamar Pitowsky for stimulating discussions related to the ideas presented here.

Notes

1. By efficient, we mean that the simulation overhead is bounded by some polynomial. That is, t steps on the computational model in question can be simulated in $poly(t)$ steps on a probabilistic Turing machine.

2. These early quantum algorithms were cast in the so-called black-box computational model, which is a restricted model of computation in which such exponential separations can actually be proved; see Nielsen and Chuang (2000).

3. Note that this notion of quantum interactive proofs is very different from another notion of quantum interactive proofs (Watrous 2003), in which Arthur is a quantum polynomial time system and Merlin is a hypothetical all-powerful entity, which is studied in the literature in the context of quantum complexity theory.

4. To define #P, recall, for example, the satisfiability problem, which asks given a propositional formula $f(x_1, \ldots, x_n)$ whether there is a satisfying assignment $a_1, \ldots, a_n$ such that $f(a_1, \ldots, a_n) = 1$. This is a problem in NP; its counting version, denoted #*SAT*, is the question of how many such satisfying assignments there are, out of the 2^n potential solutions.

5. The assumption here is that any physical system involved, including the entire system of the prover, is describable by the general structure of quantum mechanics; that is, it can be assigned a density matrix on a tensor product space. One need not assume, however, that this larger system is coherent, or can be described by pure superpositions, or any other assumption that makes it "fully" quantum; for example, the larger systems could in principle be greatly decohered and even completely classical.

6. It can be found in Arora and Barak (2009); in fact, its discovery was a stepping stone toward one of the most exciting developments in theoretical computer science over the past two decades, namely probabilistically checkable proofs (Arora and Barak 2009).

7. #P is a class of problems which contains the problem #*SAT* defined above, and similar counting problems in which the number of solutions to NP problems should be found.

References

Aharonov, D., and M. Ben-Or. 1996. Polynomial simulations of decohered quantum computers. *Proceedings of the 37th Annual Symposium on Foundations of Computer Science* (*FOCS* 1996).

Aharonov, D. M., and M. Ben-Or. 1997. Fault-tolerant quantum computation with constant error. *Proceedings of the 29th Annual ACM Symposium on Theory of Computing*, 176–88. New York: ACM Press.

Aharonov, D., M. Ben-Or, and E. Eban. 2010. Interactive proofs for quantum computation. *Proceedings of Innovations of Computer Science* (*ICS* 2010), China, 453–69.

Arora, S., and B. Barak. 2009. *Computational Complexity: A Modern Approach*. Cambridge: Cambridge University Press.

Babai, L. 1985. Trading group theory for randomness. *Proceedings of the 17th Annual ACM Symposium on the Theory of Computing*, (*STOC* 1985).

Barnum, H., C. Crépeau, D. Gottesman, A. Smith, and A. Tapp. 2002. Authentication of quantum messages. *Proceedings of the 43rd Symposium on Foundations of Computer Science* (*FOCS* 2002), 449–58.

Ben-Or, M., C. Crépeau, D. Gottesman, A. Hassidim, and A. Smith. 2006. Secure multiparty quantum computation with (only) a strict honest majority. *Proceedings of the 47th Annual IEEE Symposium on Foundations of Computer Science* (*FOCS* 2006), 249–60.

Bernstein, E., and U. Vazirani. 1997. Quantum complexity theory. *SIAM Journal on Computing* 26(5):1411–73.

Broadbent, A., J. Fitzsimons, and E. Kashefi. 2009. Universal blind quantum computation. *Proceedings of the 50th Annual Symposium on Foundations of Computer Science* (*FOCS* 2009), 517–27.

Feynman, R. 1964. Probability and Uncertainty. In *The Character of Physical Law*. Transcript of the Messenger Lectures at Cornell University, November 1964.

Feynman, R. 1985. Quantum mechanical computers. *Optics News* 11(2):11–20.

Goldwasser, S., S. Micali, and C. Rackoff. 1985. The knowledge complexity of interactive proof-systems. *Proceedings of the 17th Annual ACM Symposium on Theory of Computing* (*STOC* 1985), 291–304.

Nielsen, M., and I. Chuang. 2000. *Quantum Computation and Quantum Information*. New York: Cambridge University Press.

Shor, P. W. 1997. Polynomial-time algorithms for prime factorization and discrete logarithms on a quantum computer. *SIAM Journal on Computing* 26(5):1484–1509.

Simon, D. R. 1994. On the power of quantum computation. *Proceedings of the 35th Annual Symposium on Foundations of Computer Science* (*FOCS* 1994), 116–23.

Vazirani, U. 2007. Computational constraints on scientific theories: insights from quantum computing. Paper presented at the Workshop on the Computational World View and the Sciences, California Institute of Technology, Pasadena, CA.

Watrous, J. 2003. PSPACE has constant-round quantum interactive proof systems. *Theoretical Computer Science* 292(3):575–588.

Yaari, J. 2011. *Interactive Proofs as a Theory of Confirmation*. PhD thesis, The Hebrew University of Jerusalem.

About the Authors

Scott Aaronson is associate professor of electrical engineering and computer science at MIT, affiliated with CSAIL, MIT's Computer Science and Artificial Intelligence Laboratory. His research interests center around the limitations of quantum computers, and computational complexity theory more generally. Aaronson is the recipient of the Alan T. Waterman Award of the National Science Foundation, 2012.

Dorit Aharonov is professor of computer science and engineering at The Hebrew University of Jerusalem, Israel. She studies quantum information processes, including quantum algorithms, quantum cryptography, and quantum computational complexity. Her general objective is to better understand fundamental aspects of quantum mechanics, such as entanglement, many-body quantum physics, and the transition from quantum to classical, by using a computational perspective. In 2005 Aharonov was profiled by the journal *Nature* as one of four "young theorists … who are making waves in their chosen fields," and in the following year, she received the Krill Prize for Excellence in Scientific Research.

B. Jack Copeland is professor of philosophy at the University of Canterbury, New Zealand, and director of the Turing Archive for the History of Computing. His books include *Turing: Pioneer of the Information Age* (Oxford University Press), *Alan Turing's Electronic Brain* (Oxford University Press), *The Essential Turing* (Oxford University Press), *Colossus: The Secrets of Bletchley Park's Codebreaking Computers* (Oxford University Press), *Logic and Reality* (Oxford University Press), and *Artificial Intelligence* (Blackwell); and he has published more than 100 articles on the philosophy and history of computing, and on mathematical and philosophical logic. He is a Fellow of the Royal Society of New Zealand.

Martin Davis is a pioneer of computability theory and a renowned mathematical logician. He has been on the faculty of the Courant Institute, New York University, since 1965 and was one of the founding members of the computer science department at NYU. A student of Emil Post and Alonzo Church, Davis is known for his ground-breaking work in automated deduction and for his contributions to the solution of Hilbert's tenth problem, for which he was awarded the Chauvenet and Lester R. Ford Prizes by the Mathematical Association of America and the Leroy P. Steele Prize by the American Mathematical Society. Among his many books are *Computability and Unsolvability* (McGraw-Hill, reprinted Dover), which has been called "one of the few real classics in computer science"; *The Undecidable: Unsolvable Problems and Computable Functions* (Raven, reprinted Dover), and *The Universal Computer: The Road from Leibniz to Turing* (CRC Press).

Solomon Feferman is Patrick Suppes professor of humanities and sciences, emeritus, and professor of mathematics and philosophy, emeritus, at Stanford University; he is a former chair of the department of mathematics at Stanford. Feferman is noted for his many contributions to mathematical logic and the foundations of mathematics. He was awarded the Rolf Schock Prize in Logic and Philosophy in 2003 for his work on the arithmetization of metamathematics, ordinal logics (substantially extending Turing's doctoral work), and predicative analysis. He is a past president of the Association for Symbolic Logic and is a Fellow of the American Academy of Arts and Sciences. Feferman is author of *In the Light of Logic* (Oxford University Press), editor-in-chief of the five-volume *Kurt Gödel: Collected Works* (Oxford University Press), co-author with Anita Burdman Feferman of *Alfred Tarski: Life and Logic* (Cambridge University Press), and co-editor with Jon Barwise of *Model-Theoretic Logics* (Springer-Verlag). In tribute to him is the volume edited by W. Sieg, R. Sommer and C. Talcott, *Reflections on the Foundations of Mathematics: Essays in Honor of Solomon Feferman* (Association for Symbolic Logic).

Saul A. Kripke is distinguished professor of philosophy and computer science at CUNY, Graduate Center, and McCosh Professor of Philosophy Emeritus at Princeton University. While a high school student in Nebraska, he wrote a series of papers that transformed modal and intuitionistic logic and remain canonical works in the field. He has made other significant technical contributions to mathematical logic. During the 60s and 70s, Kripke presented his revolutionary account of reference in lectures that were transcribed and eventually published as his classic *Naming and Necessity* (Blackwell, 1980; first published in 1972 as an article). Another series of lectures was transcribed and published in 1982 as his highly influential *Wittgenstein on Rules and Private Language* (Blackwell). In 2011 he published his first collection of papers, *Philosophical Troubles: Collected Papers, Vol. 1*. In 2001 he won the Schock Prize in Logic and Philosophy. He has received honorary degrees from several institutions and has been a member of the Society of Fellows at Harvard, John Locke Lecturer at Oxford University, the A. D. White Professor-at-Large at Cornell University, professor at Rockefeller University, and visiting professor at several institutions, including the Hebrew University.

Carl J. Posy is professor of philosophy and member of the Center for the Study of Rationality at the Hebrew University of Jerusalem. He is Chairman of the academic committee of the Logic, Language and Cognition Center at the Hebrew University. He is well known for his publications on mathematical intuitionism and constructive mathematics, and his work on the philosophy of mathematics and its history. He is editor of *Kant's Philosophy of Mathematics: Modern Essays* (Kluwer), and his many publications on intuitionism include most recently "Intuitionism and Philosophy" in *The Oxford Handbook of the Philosophy of Mathematics*.

Hilary Putnam is Cogan university professor emeritus of philosophy at Harvard University. He has been a central figure in analytic philosophy since the 1960s, writing extensively on issues in metaphysics and epistemology, philosophy of mathematics, philosophy of physics, philosophy of language, and philosophy of mind. His books include *Renewing Philosophy* (Harvard University Press), *Representation and Reality* (MIT Press), *Reason, Truth and History* (Cambridge University Press), *Pragmatism: An Open Question* (Blackwell), *The Threefold Cord: Mind, Body and World* (Columbia University Press), *Realism with a Human Face* (Harvard University Press), *Words and Life* (Harvard University Press), *The Collapse of the Fact/Value Dichotomy* (Harvard University Press), *Ethics Without Ontology* (Harvard University Press), and *Philosophy in an Age of Science* (Harvard University Press). Putnam is a past president of the American Philosophical Association (Eastern Division), the Philosophy of Science Association, and the Association for Symbolic Logic. He is a fellow of the American Academy of Arts and Sciences, the American Philosophical Society, a Corresponding Fellow of the British Academy and the French Academie des Sciences Politiques et Morales, and holds a number of honorary degrees. In 2010 Putnam received the Prometheus Prize of the American Philosophical Association, and in 2011 he was awarded with the Rolf Schock Prize in Philosophy.

Oron Shagrir is professor of philosophy and former chair of the cognitive science department at the Hebrew University of Jerusalem. He is currently the vice rector of the Hebrew University. His work focuses on the philosophy and history of computing and on the conceptual foundations of cognitive science and computational neuroscience. He has published numerous articles in philosophy and computer science journals, including *Mind, Philosophy of Science, British Journal for the Philosophy of Science, Philosophy and Phenomenological Research, Synthese, Philosophical Studies, Minds and Machines*, and *Theoretical Computer Science*.

Stewart Shapiro is O'Donnell professor of philosophy at Ohio State University and professor of philosophy at St. Andrew's University. His books include *Foundations without Foundationalism: A Case for Second-Order Logic* (Oxford University Press), *Thinking about Mathematics* (Oxford University Press), *Philosophy of Mathematics: Structure and Ontology* (Oxford University Press), and *Vagueness in Context* (Oxford University Press). He is the editor of the recently released *Oxford Handbook of the Philosophy of Mathematics and Logic* and author of many articles on the history and philosophy of mathematics.

Wilfried Sieg is Patrick Suppes professor of philosophy at Carnegie Mellon University and a fellow of the American Academy of Arts and Sciences. He joined Carnegie Mellon's faculty in 1985 as a founding member of the University's philosophy department and served as its Head from 1994 to 2005. He is internationally known for his mathematical work in proof and computation theory, historical work on modern logic and mathematics, and philosophical essays on the nature of mathematics. A collection of essays joining the three aspects of his research was published under the title *Hilbert's Programs and Beyond* (Oxford University Press). As Co-Director of LSEC (Carnegie Mellon's Laboratory of Symbolic and Educational Computing) he has pursued his AProS Project pioneering strategic automated search for natural deduction proofs in logic and elementary set theory; this work is used in interactive, fully web-based logic courses Sieg has developed.

Robert Irving Soare is the Paul Snowden Russell distinguished service professor of mathematics and computer science at the University of Chicago, where he was the founding chairman of the department of computer science. Soare is the author of two books, *Recursively Enumerable Sets and Degrees: A Study of Computable Functions and Computably Enumerable Sets* (Springer), and *Computability Theory and Applications* (Springer). He is also the author of papers in leading journals such as *The Annals of Mathematics*, *The Journal of the American Mathematical Society*, and *The Proceedings of the National Academy of Science, USA*, and of numerous papers on Turing and the concept of computability. Soare has been an invited speaker at the International Congress of Mathematicians and several times at the International Congress of Logic, Methodology, and Philosophy of Science.

Umesh V. Vazirani is the Roger A. Strauch Professor of Electrical Engineering and Computer Science at the University of California, Berkeley, and the director of the Berkeley Quantum Computation Center. He is one of the founders of the field of quantum computing. His 1993 paper with his student Ethan Bernstein on quantum complexity theory gave the first formal evidence that quantum Turing machines violate the extended Church-Turing thesis, and paved the way for Shor's quantum algorithm for factoring integers. In 2005 Vazirani was made a fellow of the Association for Computing Machinery for "contributions to theoretical computer science and quantum computation." He is the author of *An Introduction to Computational Learning Theory* (with Michael Kearns; MIT Press), and *Algorithms* (with Sanjoy Dasgupta and Christos Papadimitriou; McGraw Hill).

Index